The Environmental Protection Agency

THE ENVIRONMENTAL PROTECTION AGENCY

Cleaning Up America's Act

Robert W. Collin

Understanding Our Government

Greenwood Press
Westport, Connecticut • London

Library of Congress Cataloging-in-Publication Data

Collin, Robert W., 1957–
  The Environmental Protection Agency : cleaning up America's act / Robert W. Collin.
   p. cm.—(Understanding our government, ISSN 1556–8512)
  Includes bibliographical references and index.
  ISBN 0–313–33341–6 (alk. paper)
  1. United States. Environmental Protection Agency. 2. Environmental protection—United
States. I. Title. II. Series.
 TD171.C64 2006
  363.7'00973—dc22   2005022203

British Library Cataloguing in Publication Data is available.

Library of Congress Catalog Card Number: 2005022203
ISBN: 0–313–33341–6
ISSN: 1556–8512

First published in 2006

Greenwood Press, 88 Post Road West, Westport, CT 06881
An imprint of Greenwood Publishing Group, Inc.
www.greenwood.com

Printed in the United States of America

The paper used in this book complies with the
Permanent Paper Standard issued by the National
Information Standards Organization (Z39.48–1984).

10 9 8 7 6 5 4 3 2 1

Contents

Series Foreword

Since the founding of our country in 1776, the U.S. government has transformed significantly. Changing societies and events, both domestic and international, have greatly affected the actions and development of our country. The Industrial Revolution, World War II, the civil rights movement, and the more recent "war on terrorism" are just a few of the events that have changed our government and its functions. Depending on the needs of our country at any given time, agencies are developed or terminated, their size and/or budget increased or decreased, or even transferred to another department within the government, in order to meet policy makers' objectives. Whether an independent agency or part of the fifteen executive branch departments overseen by the president and the cabinet, each is given specific responsibilities and all are formed to fulfill an important role for the country and its people.

The Understanding Our Government series was developed to offer an in-depth view of the most powerful, controversial, and misunderstood agencies of the U.S. government and how they have changed American society and, in some cases, the world. Well-known agencies frequently in the media spotlight, such as the Central Intelligence Agency and the National Aeronautics and Space Administration, are included, as well as lesser-known, but important, agencies such as the Bureau of Indian Affairs and the Forest Service. Written by experts on the particular agencies, including former employees or advisory committee members, each volume provides a historical overview of an agency and includes narrative chapters describing such aspects as organization, programs, significant events, controversies, key people, and influence on society, as well as additional topics tailored to the particular agency. Subjects vary greatly among the different titles. Depending on readers' interests or needs, some will be able to find information including the Central Intelligence Agency's role in the Cuban missile crisis, as well as its history of covert operations, while others may be interested in the Environmental Protection Agency's response to environmental disasters such as the *Exxon Valdez* oil spill and the Three Mile Island nuclear accident. Still others may be curious to learn about the Federal Communication Commission's role in communications policy and regulation of the media, and the fine line between censorship and freedom of speech, or the Drug Enforcement Administration's enforcement of drug laws and methods of combating drug trafficking, and how the legalization of certain illegal drugs would affect the agency and the country in general.

Whether readers are students conducting research on a specific agency for a high school or college assignment, or just want to learn more about one or how the government works, our hope is that each will gain further knowledge about the U.S. government and its employees. We want readers to comprehend our nation's significant achievements, yet also understand its failures and how we can learn from them. Over the years, our country has performed great feats, from creating lifesaving drugs to space exploration, but it has also experienced tragedies including environmental catastrophes and terrorist attacks. Readers will learn of how such events shape legislation and public policy, and how they affect everyday life for the citizens of this country. While many agencies have been portrayed in certain ways in newspapers, on television, and in films, such representations have not always been realistic or impartial. As a result, this series attempts to offer fair, objective views of U.S. government agencies, and to allow readers to think about them and form their own opinions.

Steven Vetrano
Greenwood Press

Preface

One of the most significant developments of the twentieth century was the national growth of public concern for the environment. Environmental issues are hard to ignore because they do not lend themselves to political compromises. This concern manifested itself in the creation of the Environmental Protection Agency (EPA) in 1970. Transforming this concern for the environment into effective public policy is the continuing challenge of the EPA. As our knowledge base increases, the EPA's public policies change and adapt. These policies are forged in courts, legislatures, the EPA, and state and local governments. Even as these policies become implemented, we face great uncertainty because of the lack of knowledge about the environment and our interactions with it. Since the formation of the EPA, public concern about the environment has continued to increase. Often the public is not aware of rapidly evolving environmental policies or the EPA's role in them.

This book is for people who want to know their government. The lack of knowledge about the environment and the EPA slows the development of environmental public policy. However, growing and inescapable public concern about accumulating emissions, the distribution of environmental benefits and burdens, and sustainability are driving the public to learn more about the EPA. The EPA offers some of the best environmental information currently available for those who know how to find it. It can often bring its considerable resources to a particular environmental issue.

As Congress continues to consider proposed amendments and reauthorizations of environmental laws, as environmental lawsuits continue to be filed and work their way through the courts, and as our knowledge increases, changes can be expected. The EPA exists in a dynamic policy arena and is itself a very dynamic agency. While no one book can present the last word on the EPA, this book presents the EPA's history and foundations in a way that will increase understanding of the role of the EPA.

I would like to express my gratitude to all those who helped with this book. My research assistant, Robert Ickes, provided timely assistance. I would like to express my appreciation to Willamette University, which provided research support for me through the Willamette College of Law and the Public Policy Research Center. I am also thankful for the support and timely assistance of my editor at Greenwood Press, Steven Vetrano. This book required photographs. Frank Miller from Willamette helped with about ten. One of the leading scholars in the field of environmental justice, Dr. Robert Bullard, gave me access to his personal photograph collection. Brent Merrill, public affairs officer for the Confederated Tribes of the Grande Ronde, editor of *Smoke Signals*, and expert photographer for the Confederated Tribes of the Grand Ronde, became interested in the project and contributed eloquent nature photographs. Sandra Collin provided valuable assistance with the photography. Most of all, I am grateful to my spouse, Robin Morris Collin. From the beginning of this project to the present, she spent innumerable hours giving me unwavering support, valuable insight, and timely editorial feedback.

Acronyms

Some acronyms may have more than one meaning, and are noted.

A

AA: accountable area; adverse action; advices of allowance; assistant administrator; associate administrator; atomic absorption

AANWR: Alaskan Arctic National Wildlife Refuge

A&C: abatement and control

ACBM: asbestos-containing building material

ACE: any credible evidence

ACFM: actual cubic feet per minute

ACM: asbestos-containing material

ACQR: air quality control region

ACWM: asbestos-containing waste material

ADABA: acceptable data base

ADB: applications data base

ADI: acceptable daily intake

ADQ: audits of data quality

ADR: alternative dispute resolution

ADT: average daily traffic

AEA: Atomic Energy Act

AEC: associate enforcement counsels

AEERL: air and energy engineering research laboratory

AEM: acoustic emission monitoring

AH: allowance holders

AHERA: Asbestos Hazard Emergency Response Act

AI: active ingredient

AID: Agency for International Development

AIHC: American Industrial Health Council

AIRMON: Atmospheric Integrated Research Monitoring Network

AL: acceptable level

ALJ: administrative law judge

ALR: action leakage rate

AMBIENS: atmospheric mass balance of industrially emitted and natural sulfur

ANPR: advance notice of proposed rulemaking

ANRHRD: Air, Noise, and Radiation Health Research Division/ORD

APA: Administrative Procedures Act; Acid Precipitation Act

APCD: air pollution control district

APHA: American Public Health Association

APWA: American Public Works Association

AQCR: air quality control region

AQDHS: Air Quality Data Handling System

AQDM: air-quality display model

AR: administrative record

A&R: air and radiation

ARA: assistant regional administrator; associate regional administrator

AS: area source

ASC: area source category

ASHARA: Asbestos in Schools Hazard Abatement Reauthorization Act

ATSDR: Agency for Toxic Substances and Disease Registry

AWT: advanced wastewater treatment

B

BACM: best available control measures

BACT: best available control technology

BADT: best available demonstrated technology

BAF: bioaccumulation factor

BART: best available retrofit technology

BAT: best available technology

BATEA: best available treatment economically achievable

BCT: best control technology

BCPCT: best conventional pollutant control technology

BDAT: best demonstrated achievable technology

BDCT: best demonstrated control technology

BDT: best demonstrated technology

BEJ: best engineering judgment; best expert judgment

BIOPLUME: Model to Predict the Maximum Extent of Existing Plumes

BMP: best management practice(s)

BMR: baseline monitoring report

BOYSNC: beginning of year significant noncompliers

BPJ: best professional judgment

BPT: best practicable technology

BPWTT: best practical wastewater treatment technology

BUN: blood urea nitrogen

C

CA: Citizen Act.

CAA: Clean Air Act; compliance assurance agreement

CAAA: Clean Air Act Amendments

CAER: community awareness and emergency response

CAFE: corporate average fuel economy

CAFO: concentrated animal feedlot; consent agreement/final order

CAG: Carcinogenic Assessment Group

CAS: Center for Automotive Safety; Chemical Abstract Service

CAU: carbon adsorption unit; command arithmetic unit

CB: continuous bubbler

CBA: Chesapeake Bay Agreement; cost/benefit analysis

CBD: central business district

CBEP: community-based environmental project; community-based environmental planning

CBI: compliance biomonitoring inspection; confidential business information

CCEA: conventional combustion environmental assessment

CCHW: Citizens Clearinghouse for Hazardous Wastes

CCID: confidential chemicals identification system

CD: climatological data

CDB: consolidated database

CDBA: central data base administrator

CDBG: community development block grant

CDM: climatological dispersion model; comprehensive data management

CDMQC: Climatological Dispersion Model with Calibration and Source Contribution

CDNS: climatological data national summary

CEI: compliance evaluation inspection

CEM: continuous emission monitoring

CEMS: Continuous Emission Monitoring System

CEQ: Council on Environmental Quality

CERCLA: Comprehensive Environmental Response, Compensation, and Liability Act

CERCLIS: Comprehensive Environmental Response, Compensation, and Liability Information System

CERFA: Community Environmental Response Facilitation Act

CESQG: conditionally exempt small quantity generator

CFC: chlorofluorocarbon

CFM: chlorofluoromethanes

CFR: Code of Federal Regulations

CHIP: chemical hazard information profiles

CI: compression ignition; confidence interval

CKD: cement kiln dust

CLI: consumer labeling initiative

CMB: chemical mass balance

CME: comprehensive monitoring evaluation

CMEL: comprehensive monitoring evaluation log

CMEP: Critical Mass Energy Project

CNG: compressed natural gas

COCO: contractor-owned/contractor-operated

COD: chemical oxygen demand

CPF: carcinogenic potency factor

CQA: construction quality assurance

CSI: CommonSense Initiative; compliance sampling inspection

CSO: combined sewer overflow

CSPA: Council of State Planning Agencies

CWA: Clean Water Act

CZMA: Coastal Zone Management Act

D

DBP: disinfection by-product

DDT: dichlorodiphenyltrichloroethane

DES: diethylstilbesterol

DfE: design for the environment

DMR: discharge monitoring report

DNA: deoxyribonucleic acid

DNAPL: dense nonaqueous phase liquid

DO: dissolved oxygen

DOI: Department of Interior

DOW: Defenders of Wildlife

DPA: Deepwater Ports Act

DRE: destruction and removal efficiency

DS: dichotomous sampler

DSAP: data self-auditing program

DSCF: dry standard cubic feet

DSCM: dry standard cubic meter

DWS: Drinking Water Standard

E

EA: endangerment assessment; enforcement agreement; environmental action; environmental assessment; environmental audit

EAB: Environmental Appeals Board

EAG: Exposure Assessment Group

EAP: environmental action plan

EB: emissions balancing

ECOS: Environmental Council of the States

ECR: enforcement case review

ED: effective dose

EDF: Environmental Defense Fund

EDRS: Enforcement Document Retrieval System

EHC: Environmental Health Committee

EHS: extremely hazardous substance

EI: emissions inventory

EIA: environmental impact assessment; economic impact assessment

EIS: environmental impact statement; Environmental Inventory System

EIS/AS: Emissions Inventory System/area source

EIS/PS: Emissions Inventory System/point source

EL: exposure level

ELI: Environmental Law Institute

ELR: *Environmental Law Reporter*

EMAP: Environmental Mapping and Assessment Program

EnPA: environmental performance agreement

EOP: end of pipe

EPACASR: EPA chemical activities status report

EPCRA: Emergency Planning and Community Right-to-Know Act

EPD: emergency planning district

EQIA: Environmental Quality Improvement Act

ES: enforcement strategy

ESA: Endangered Species Act; environmentally sensitive area

ESH: environmental safety and health

ET: emissions trading

ETP: emissions trading policy

F

FACA: Federal Advisory Committee Act

FACT Act: Food, Agriculture, Conservation, and Trade Act

FE: fugitive emissions

FEPCA: Federal Environmental Pesticide Control Act (amendments to FIFRA)

FERC: Federal Energy Regulatory Commission

FF: federal facility

FFCA: Federal Facility Compliance Act

FFDCA: Federal Food, Drug, and Cosmetic Act

FFFSG: fossil-fuel-fired steam generator

FFIS: Federal Facilities Information System

FHSA: Federal Hazardous Substances Act

FIFRA: Federal Insecticide, Fungicide, and Rodenticide Act

FIP: final implementation plan

FOIA: Freedom of Information Act

FONSI: finding of no significant impact

FP: fine particulate

FPA: Federal Pesticide Act

FPPA: Federal Pollution Prevention Act

FQPA: Food Quality Protection Act

FR: Federal Register or final rulemaking

FRN: Federal Register notice; final rulemaking notice

FS: feasibility study

FSA: Food Security Act

FURS: Federal Underground Injection Control Reporting System

FWCA: Fish and Wildlife Coordination Act

FWPA: Federal Water Pollution Act

G

GCC: Global Climate Convention

GEI: Geographic Enforcement Initiative

GEMI: Global Environmental Management Initiative

GEP: good engineering practice

GIS: Geographic Information Systems

GLWQA: Great Lakes Water Quality Agreement

GMCC: global monitoring for climatic change

GPR: ground-penetrating radar

GPS: groundwater protection strategy

GWM: groundwater monitoring

GWPC: Ground Water Protection Council

GWPS: groundwater protection standard; groundwater protection strategy

H

HAD: health assessment document

HAP: hazardous air pollutant

HAPEMS: Hazardous Air Pollutant Enforcement Management System

HAZMAT: hazardous materials

HCP: hypothermal coal process

HEAL: human exposure assessment location

HEM: human exposure modeling

HEPA: Highly Efficient Particulate Air Filter

HI: hazard index

HMTA: Hazardous Materials Transportation Act

HMTR: Hazardous Materials Transportation Regulations

HOV: high-occupancy vehicle

HRUP: high-risk urban problem

HSDB: hazardous substance database

HSL: hazardous substance list

HSWA: Hazardous and Solid Waste Amendments

HW: hazardous waste

HWDMS: Hazardous Waste Data Management System

HWGTF: Hazardous Waste Groundwater Task Force; hazardous waste ground-water test facility

I

IA: interagency agreement

ICCP: International Climate Change Partnership

ICRE: ignitability, corrosivity, reactivity, extraction

IDLH: immediately dangerous to life and health

IP: inhalable particles

IPM: inhalable particulate matter; integrated pest management

IPP: Implementation Planning Program; independent power producer

IRIS: Integrated Risk Information System

IWC: in-stream waste concentration

IWS: ionizing wet scrubber

J

JOFOC: justification for other than full and open competition

JPA: joint permitting agreement

L

LAA: lead agency attorney

LADD: lifetime average daily dose; lowest acceptable daily dose

LAER: lowest achievable emission rate

LAI: laboratory audit inspection

LC: lethal concentration

LCA: life cycle assessment

LCCA: Lead Contamination Control Act

LCD: local climatological data

LCL: lower control limit

LCM: life cycle management

LCRS: Leachate Collection and Removal System

LD: land disposal

LDCRS: Leachate Detection, Collection, and Removal System

LDIP: Laboratory Data Integrity Program

LDR: land disposal restrictions

LDS: leak detection system

LDT: lowest dose tested

LEL: lowest effect level; lower explosive limit

LEP: Laboratory Evaluation Program

LEPC: local emergency planning committee

LERC: local emergency response committee

LEV: low emissions vehicle

LFG: landfill gas

LFL: lower flammability limit

LLRW: low-level radioactive waste

LMFBR: liquid metal fast breeder reactor

LNG: liquefied natural gas

LQER: lesser quantity emission rates

LQG: large quantity generator

LRTAP: long-range transboundary air pollution

LUIS: Label Use Information System

M

MATC: maximum acceptable toxic concentration

MCL: maximum contaminant level

MCLG: maximum contaminant level goal

MCS: multiple chemical sensitivity

MEI: maximally (or most) exposed individual

MOE: margin of exposure

MOS: margin of safety

MPRSA: Marine Protection, Research, and Sanctuaries Act

MRF: materials recovery facility

MRID: master record identification number

MRL: maximum residue limit (pesticide tolerance)

MSW: municipal solid waste

MTD: maximum tolerated dose

N

NAA: nonattainment area

NAAQS: national ambient air quality standards

NACA: National Agricultural Chemicals Association

NACEPT: National Advisory Council for Environmental Policy and Technology

NAS: National Academy of Sciences

NCEPI: National Center for Environmental Publications and Information

NCMA: National Coastal Monitoring Act

NEPA: National Environmental Policy Act

NEPI: National Environmental Policy Institute

NEPPS: National Environmental Performance Partnership System

NESHAP: national emission standard for hazardous air pollutants

NIEHS: National Institute for Environmental Health Sciences

NETA: National Environmental Training Association

NFRAP: no further remedial action planned

NICT: National Incident Coordination Team

NIOSH: National Institute of Occupational Safety and Health

NOAA: National Oceanographic and Atmospheric Agency

NOAEL: no observable adverse effect level

NOEL: no observable effect level

NOIC: notice of intent to cancel

NOIS: notice of intent to suspend

NORM: naturally occurring radioactive material

NPDES: National Pollutant Discharge Elimination System

NPHAP: National Pesticide Hazard Assessment Program

NPIRS: National Pesticide Information Retrieval System

NRDC: Natural Resources Defense Council

NSDWR: National Secondary Drinking Water Regulations

NSPS: new source performance standards

NSR: new source review

NTI: national toxics inventory

NWPA: Nuclear Waste Policy Act

O

O_3: ozone

OCD: offshore and coastal dispersion

ODP: ozone-depleting potential

ODS: ozone-depleting substance

OECD: Organization for Economic Cooperation and Development

OPA: Oil Pollution Act

OSHA: Occupational Safety and Health Act

P

P_2: pollution prevention

PAI: performance audit inspection (CWA); pure active ingredient compound

PAT: Permit Assistance Team (RCRA)

PCB: polychlorinated biphenyl

PCE: perchloroethylene

PCSD: President's Council on Sustainable Development

PFC: perfluorated carbon

PHSA: Public Health Service Act

PIRG: Public Interest Research Group

PIT: permit improvement team

PM: particulate matter

PMR: proportionate mortality ratio

PMRS: Performance Management and Recognition System

POC: point of compliance

POE: point of exposure

POGO: privately owned/government-operated

POHC: principal organic hazardous constituent

POI: point of interception

POP: persistent organic pollutant

POTW: publicly owned treatment works

POV: privately owned vehicle

PPA: Pollution Prevention Act

PPB: parts per billion

PPE: personal protective equipment

PPIS: pollution prevention incentives for states

PPM: parts per million

PPT: parts per trillion

PPTH: parts per thousand

PRN: pesticide registration notice

PRP: potentially responsible party

PS: point source

PSAM: point source ambient monitoring

PSD: prevention of significant deterioration

PSES: pretreatment standards for existing sources

PSI: pollutant standards index; pounds per square inch; pressure per square inch

PSM: point source monitoring

PSNS: pretreatment standards for new sources

PSU: primary sampling unit

PTE: potential to emit

PUC: Public Utility Commission

PVC: polyvinyl chloride

PWS: public water supply/system

Q

QC: quality control

QCI: quality control index

QUA: qualitative use assessment

R

RA: reasonable alternative; regulatory alternative; remedial action; resource allocation; risk analysis; risk assessment

RACM: reasonably available control measures

RACT: reasonably available control technology

RAD: radiation adsorbed dose (unit of measurement of radiation absorbed by humans)

RAMP: Rural Abandoned Mine Program

RAMS: regional air monitoring system

RBC: red blood cell

RCRA: Resource Conservation and Recovery Act

RCRIS: Resource Conservation and Recovery Information System

RD/RA: remedial design/remedial action

R&D: research and development

RD&D: research, development and demonstration

RDF: refuse-derived fuel

RDNA: recombinant DNA

RDV: reference dose value

REAP: Regional Enforcement Activities Plan

REM/FIT: Remedial/Field Investigation Team

RF: response factor

RFA: Regulatory Flexibility Act

RFB: request for bid

RfC: reference concentration

RFD: reference dose value

RFI: remedial field investigation

RFP: reasonable further programs; request for proposal

RHRS: Revised Hazard Ranking System

RI: remedial investigation

RIA: regulatory impact analysis; regulatory impact assessment

RI/FS: remedial investigation/feasibility study

RIN: regulatory identifier number

RIP: RCRA Implementation Plan

ROC: record of communication

RODS: records of decision system

ROG: reactive organic gas

RP: respirable particulates; responsible party

RPAR: rebuttable presumption against registration

RPM: reactive plume model; remedial project manager

RQ: reportable quantity

RSD: risk-specific dose

RSE: removal site evaluation

RTCM: reasonable transportation control measure

RUP: restricted use pesticide

S

SAB: Science Advisory Board

SAC: suspended and canceled pesticides

SAP: Scientific Advisory Panel

SARA: Superfund Amendments and Reauthorization Act

SC: Sierra Club

SCD/SWDC: soil conservation district/soil and water conservation district

SCFM: standard cubic feet per minute

SCLDF: Sierra Club Legal Defense Fund

SCR: selective catalytic reduction

SCSP: storm and combined sewer program

SDWA: Safe Drinking Water Act

SBS: sick building syndrome

SEA: state enforcement agreement; state/EPA agreement

SEAM: surface, environment, and mining

SEIA: socioeconomic impact analysis

SEIS: supplemental environmental impact statement

SEM: standard error of the means

SEP: standard evaluation procedure; supplementary environmental project

SERC: State Emergency Response Commission

SES: secondary emissions standard

SIC: Standard Industrial Classification

SIMS: secondary ion-mass spectrometry

SIP: State Implementation Plan

SLAMS: state/local air monitoring station

SLN: special local need

SMCL: secondary maximum contaminant level

SMCRA: Surface Mining Control and Reclamation Act

SME: subject matter expert

SMP: state management plan

SMR: standardized mortality ratio

SMSA: Standard Metropolitan Statistical Area

SNAAQS: Secondary National Ambient Air Quality Standards

SNC: significant noncompliers

SNUR: significant new use rule

SO: Sulfur dioxide

SOC: synthetic organic chemical

SOW: scope of work

SPA: Shore Protection Act

SPAR: status of permit application report

SPCC: spill prevention, containment, and countermeasure

SPE: secondary particulate emission

SPS: state permit system

SPSS: Statistical Package for the Social Sciences

SQBE: small quantity burner exemption

SQG: small quantity generator

SRC: solvent-refined coal

SRF: State Revolving Fund

SRM: standard reference method

SRP: special review procedure

SS: settleable solids; Superfund surcharge; suspended solids

SSA: sole source aquifer

SSAC: soil site assimilated capacity

SSEIS: standard support and environmental impact statement; stationary source emissions and inventory system.

SSO: sanitary sewer overflow

STEL: short-term exposure limit

SUP: standard unit of processing

SV: sampling visit or significant violater

SWAP: Source Water Assessment Program

SWC: settlement with conditions

SWDA: Solid Waste Disposal Act

SWPA: source water protection area

T

TAD: technical assistance document

TAG: technical assistance grant

TAP: technical assistance program

TC: target concentration; technical center; toxicity characteristics; toxic concentration

TCDD: dioxin (tetrachlorodibenzo-p-dioxin)

TCDF: tetrachlorodibenzofurans

TCE: trichloroethylene

TCF: total chlorine free

TCLP: total concentrate leachate procedure; toxicity characteristic leachate procedure

TCM: transportation control measure

TCP: transportation control plan

TCRI: toxic chemical release inventory

TD: toxic dose

TDS: total dissolved solids

TEAM: total exposure assessment model

TEL: tetraethyl lead

TIP: Transportation Improvement Program

TIS: Tolerance Index System

TLV: threshold limit value

TLV-STEL: TLV-short-term exposure limit

TLV-TWA: TLV-time-weighted average

TMDL: total maximum daily limit; total maximum daily load

TMRC: theoretical maximum residue contribution

TNCWS: transient noncommunity water system

TNT: trinitrotoluene

TOA: trace organic analysis

TOC: total organic carbon/compound

TP: total particulates

TPC: Testing Priorities Committee

TPY: tons per year

TQM: total quality management

TRI: toxics release inventory

TRIS: Toxic Chemical Release Inventory System

TRO: temporary restraining order

TSCA: Toxic Substances Control Act

TSDF: treatment, storage, and disposal facility

TSP: total suspended particulates

TSS: total suspended (nonfilterable) solids

TTO: total toxic organics

TTY: teletypewriter

TVOC: total volatile organic compounds

TWA: time-weighted average

TWS: transient water system

TZ: treatment zone

U

UAQI: uniform air quality index

UCC: ultraclean coal

UCL: upper control limit

UEL: upper explosive limit

UF: uncertainty factor

UFL: upper flammability limit

ug/m^3: micrograms per cubic meter

UIC: underground injection control

ULEV: ultralow emission vehicle

UMTRCA: Uranium Mill Tailings Radiation Control Act

UNEP: United Nations Environment Program

USC: unified soil classification

USDA: U.S. Department of Agriculture

USDW: underground sources of drinking water

USFS: U.S. Forest Service

UST: underground storage tank

UV: ultraviolet

V

VCM: vinyl chloride monomer

VCP: voluntary cleanup program

VHT: vehicle-hours of travel

VISTTA: visibility impairment from sulfur transformation and transport in the atmosphere

VKT: vehicle kilometers traveled

VMT: vehicle miles traveled

VOC: volatile organic compounds

VP: vapor pressure

VSD: virtually safe dose

VSI: visual site inspection

VSS: volatile suspended solids

W

WAP: waste analysis plan

WCED: World Commission on Environment and Development

WHO: World Health Organization

WHP: wellhead protection program

WHWT: water and hazardous waste team

WLA/TMDL: wasteload allocation/total maximum daily load

WLM: working level months

WMO: World Meteorological Organization

WQIA: Water Quality Improvement Act

WQS: Water Quality Standard

WRDA: Water Resources Development Act

WRI: World Resources Institute

WSRA: Wild and Scenic Rivers Act

WSTB: Water Sciences and Technology Board

WSTP: wastewater sewage treatment plant
WWF: World Wildlife Fund

Z

ZEV: zero emissions vehicle
ZOI: zone of incorporation
ZRL: zero risk level

Introduction

The U.S. Environmental Protection Agency (EPA) is a complex and powerful federal agency. It engages the public in the legislative, judicial, and its own administrative decision-making processes. Its mission is to protect and preserve the environment. This ambitious mission requires a public role in its fulfillment. This book was written to help people understand the EPA as part of their government and to participate in the development of environmental law and policy.

This book provides a historical overview of the EPA since its beginning in 1970. Chapter 1 provides a brief history of the EPA and describes its powers and organizational structure. Because much of the organizational structure of the EPA comes from law, ten laws that are administered by the EPA and that form part of its historic and current organizational structure are described. A brief discussion of the major statutory basis of the EPA presents the EPA's basic legislative mission.

Chapter 2 discusses some notable court cases. Excerpts from and discussion of a sample of these cases convey some of the policy parameters of the EPA in terms of its authority, the contents of the environmental impact statement, hazardous waste, solid waste, and air quality. The EPA is particularly vulnerable to judicial challenges because environmental law allows for citizens suits and, thus, for easier access to federal courts. Lawsuits have determined many basic standards for air quality and have prodded governmental enforcement of environmental laws. Standing to sue and citizen suits are discussed separately.

Chapter 3 examines controversies and issues that have shaped the EPA. Oil drilled and spilled, radiation leaked and disposed of, the cost of pollution control technology, the distribution of environmental benefits and burdens by race and class, and the cleanup of urban areas are some of the major issues that have involved the EPA. These controversies took place in Love Canal, New

York; Alaska (the *Exxon Valdez* oil spill); Three Mile Island, Pennsylvania; Yucca Mountain, Nevada; and Covent, Louisiana. The chronology of events and the role of the EPA in each event are discussed, and the lessons learned as a result of EPA involvement are examined.

Chapter 4 looks at the traditions and culture of the EPA. The policies of 1970–1973 established traditions and helped to form the organizational culture. This period was followed by one of priorities for environmental protection and public health. Cleaning up the environment began in this era. Laws and policy concerning cleanup soon developed. The public is interested in who is responsible for the costs of cleaning up contaminated industrial sites, natural disasters, and pollution. This period also saw the formation of traditions concerning children's health protection and cancer. Science and risk assessment are part of the foundation of the EPA. Topics that reveal how the building blocks of science became tradition and culture at the EPA include the EPA Science Advisory Board, environmental modeling, science and legislation, measurement science, the Relative Risk Reduction Strategies Committee, release of environmental equity reports, and cumulative risks. Another tradition at the EPA is the extensive use of citizen advisory committees, which often include members of the public. The role of federal advisory committees at the EPA, their legal framework, their performance, and how they are used to achieve collaboration are discussed in this chapter. One of the strongest traditions at EPA is the approach to enforcement of environmental laws. The EPA makes extraordinary efforts to help an industry or other polluter comply with the law. This is different from enforcement of criminal law, which focuses on punishment and deterrence. If the offender admits the violation, there is a 75 percent reduction in any fine. Fines are frequently not paid, and only rarely are permits revoked. This situation is often at odds with the public perception that any violation of environmental law will be punished by fines and possible permit revocation. These and other issues related to the public and its involvement with permits conclude Chapter 4.

In Chapter 5 the organization and day-to-day activities of the EPA are described. There are many offices and boards in any federal agency, and the EPA is no exception. Many of the offices that run the internal operations and programs of EPA are discussed here. The offices that are most likely to interact with the public are emphasized. Some offices that are designed to ensure accountability, such as the Office of the Inspector General, are also discussed as they relate to the EPA. EPA headquarters and its relationship with its regions, and the relationship of those regions to the states in each region, form the crux of the intergovernmental relationship that transforms federal environmental law and policy into local action. Part of the action is achieved by permit issuance, renewal, or modification and its subsequent enforcement. Permit issuance and writing is part of the day-to-day activities of the EPA and of many state environmental agencies. The EPA also exerts a strong influence over environmental impact statements. While these are advisory only, they often bring a large amount of information to a particular environmental problem. Part of that information comes from the public, through its participation in environmental decision making. This chapter gives special emphasis to how the public can learn about waste and chemicals listed in the toxics release inventory. This is a special emphasis at EPA, and some states and municipalities have similar legal reporting requirements.

Chapter 6 analyzes policy challenges that the EPA faces in implementing environmental laws. Some of them result from emerging social consensus on a desirable environmental goal, such as sustainability. Federal environmental regulation is complicated by the fact that it must be locally implemented to be effective. Localities tend to control land use. Land use control is a gaping break in the chain of effective intergovernmental relationships linked to environmental decision making. Though state and federal governmental agencies can preempt localities, they seldom do. However, many environmental policies will founder without control of land. U.S. values regarding private property are very strong. One way EPA is seeking to meet this difficult challenge is community-based environmental planning. The pros and cons of this approach are summarized in this chapter.

Another future challenge to the EPA is the issue of environmental justice. The benefits and burdens of industrial and environmental decisions have been disproportionately distributed over time, beginning long before the EPA was formed and the dangers of industrial pollution were known. The distribution of some environmental burdens, such as hazardous waste sites, has been shown to have a racial component. The EPA formed the Office of Environmental Justice and set up a federal advisory committee. It also developed the Federal Interagency Working Group on Environmental Justice. Many low-income communities and communities of color have been on the receiving end of the environmental burdens but not of the environmental benefit. As the population has increased, so has the generation and overall amount of waste. Environmental regulation of and accountability for that waste and waste stream have also increased at all levels of government and society. As landfills become full, there is pressure to back up waste in waste transfer stations, illegally overload or expand current landfill sites, or illegally dump on national lands or reservation lands. This is one example of an environmental set of decisions with disproportionate impacts. Others occur in the areas of environmental law enforcement, environmental policy development, and emissions threshold levels. Modern industrial emissions often mix with past, unregulated industrial emissions. Over time these can accumulate and become evident. Nearby communities often have public health concerns. The difficult challenge for the EPA is to empower all communities to speak for themselves on issues of environmental quality. The National Environmental Justice Advisory Council provided an important national forum for low-income communities and communities of color. This council sponsored important public hearings and wrote reports that served as the foundation for modern EPA policy.

The EPA has many programs involved with sustainability. Sustainability generally refers to not jeopardizing, or irreparably damaging, the resources of the future to meet needs of the present. One of the underlying goals of sustainability is the protection of biodiversity and ecosystems. Sustainability is a global issue, and other countries are actively involved in the development of treaties to assist in sustainable development. Regional environmental vulnerability assessments are one example of some of the EPA's work in this challenging area. This will be difficult for the EPA alone; sustainable practices need to occur at all levels. Not all industries, and certainly not all impacts on the environment, are known or regulated. U.S. urban areas have been ignored until very recently in environmental policy-making circles. One reason they are now included is the heightened social consciousness regarding sustainability, ecosystems, and environmental quality as a whole. Accumulated emissions and risks posed by chemicals, some of which bioaccumulate, increase over time and become noticeable in the most impacted populations. The EPA background on cumulative exposures and risks, the difference between aggregate risk assessment and cumulative risk assessment, and ecosystem approaches at the EPA conclude this chapter.

The leadership of the EPA is important to understanding its development. Six of the most influential EPA administrators are described in their professional, personal, and leadership roles in Chapter 7. All took a very active role in the EPA; some were more public than others. All left their indelible signature on the EPA. They are William Ruckelshaus (1970–1973; 1983–1985), Russell Train (1973–1977), Anne Gorsuch (1981–1983), William Reilly (1989–1993), Carol Browner (1993–2001), and Christine Todd Whitman (2001–2003).

Chapter 8 presents a chronology of key events for the EPA. Between 1970 and 1979 the first steps of a cohesive federal environmental policy were taken with the formation of the EPA. The Ocean Dumping Act, the Clean Air Act, the Federal Environmental Pesticide Control Act, the Safe Drinking Water Act, the Toxic Substances Control Act, the Resource Conservation and Recovery Act, and the Clean Water Act all passed into law during this decade. In implementing these new laws, the EPA observed how much emissions and wastes had built up in the environment. The 1980s was the decade of cleaning up toxic threats to the environment and to public health. Between 1980 and 1989 the EPA began its cleanup policies. It supervised the cleanup of a nuclear power breach at Three Mile Island, Pennsylvania; the Superfund cleanup law was passed; the EPA relocated Times Beach, Missouri, residents because of hazardous chemicals; the Hazardous and Solid Waste Amendments, the Hazardous Chemical Reporting Rule, and the Ocean Dumping Ban Act were passed; and the EPA responded to the *Exxon Valdez* oil spill. In the late 1980s the EPA released toxic inventory data. This information supported the next wave of environmental policy development.

Between 1990 and 1999 the EPA developed pollution prevention policies. The Pollution Prevention Act was passed, setting the stage for a new type of environmental regulation. The EPA restricted land disposal of hazardous wastes, committed to environmental education and to reducing environmental risks to minorities, required full phaseout of CFCs and other ozone depleters, and designated passive smoke as a human carcinogen. In this decade the EPA and New York City ended a long dispute about dumping of sewage sludge. The EPA also implemented the Food Quality Protection Act in 1997. Between 2000 and 2005 pollution policies were developed in the context of national environmental emergencies, judicial decisions, and increasing knowledge of the environment by the public. Many of the new program developments were responses to September 11. The EPA issued a Strategic Plan for Homeland Security eighteen months after the bombing. Another area of program development was the award of brownfield grants to clean up contaminated urban properties.

The Environmental Protection Agency: Cleaning Up America's Act is a research and reference book that is designed to be read by a broad public. Areas of EPA and public interaction are highlighted. The EPA response to a particular issue captures the breadth and depth of the federal government's response to environmentalism. The EPA response is always evolving to meet emerging challenges. Understanding the role of the EPA can help the public become more effectively involved. Many times, community knowledge of environmental conditions and land uses predates accurate environmental records. Baseline environmental data collection and cumulative impact assessment both benefit from more accurate and complete information on human contact with nature.

A Brief History of the Environmental Protection Agency and Its Powers

This chapter provides a thumbnail sketch of the U.S. Environmental Protection Agency (EPA) from its establishment in 1970 until the present. The EPA is a unique, dynamic, and relatively new federal agency. It developed in certain areas very quickly. Other areas of statutory authority were added later, and sometimes revised earlier laws. Much of its authority and organization is defined in legislative and judicial forums. In this chapter we discuss the basic organizational structure, the role of the Council on Environmental Quality (CEQ), some of the fundamental laws implemented by the EPA, and EPA's international engagement. Most of these topics are discussed in greater depth in subsequent chapters.

BASIC ORGANIZATIONAL STRUCTURE

The EPA is the primary federal agency for regulating the national environment. Its creation heralded the beginning of environmental regulation that had long-term impacts. It was created by Executive Order 1110.2 by President Nixon in 1970. From 1969 to 1979, twenty-seven laws designed to protect the environment, as well as hundreds of federal regulations, were passed. The first decade of the EPA also saw improvements in the quality of air, water, and land. The EPA deals with air pollution, water pollution, safe drinking water, hazardous waste disposal, pesticides, radiation, toxic substances, and wildlife. The National Environmental Policy Act (NEPA) of December 6, 1970, cemented the EPA's regulatory control. It was quickly followed by the Resource Recovery Act (Solid Waste) and the Clean Air Act Amendment.

The EPA was created to permit coordinated and effective governmental action in regard to the environment. Through its policies and activities the EPA seeks to abate and control pollution systematically. Its activities include research, monitoring, setting standards and enforcing environmental laws. It also coordinates and supports research and pollution abatement activities with state and local governments, private and public groups, individuals and educational institutions. The EPA cooperates with other federal agencies regarding their impacts on the environment. It is specifically charged with making written public comments on environmental impact statements, especially when the impacts may adversely affect public health or welfare, or environmental quality.

The EPA is an independent agency with the critical obligation to protect and enhance the environment. It has a broad responsibility for research, setting standards, monitoring, and enforcing with regard to air and water pollution, solid waste disposal, radiation, and pesticides. The EPA represents a coordinated approach to each of these problems, guaranteeing that as we deal with one difficulty we do not aggravate others.

The EPA has grown steadily since its formation. The increase in its budget and workforce is displayed in Table 1.1. The EPA grew from a workforce of 4,084 with a budget of $1,003,984,000 in fiscal 1970 to a workforce of 17,850 with a budget of $7,626,537,000 in fiscal 2004. However, this was not steady growth. In twelve of the years, the EPA had budget reductions. Its organizational structure is different from most federal agencies. It was established in the executive branch of the government, and reports directly to the president and conducts its own research. The legislative branch has power over the organizational structure of the EPA, and the courts have set the parameters of its policy by interpreting the statutory basis for its rules and regulations. The EPA has its headquarters in Washington, D.C., and there are ten regional offices.

The EPA regional offices administer the programs and activities on a decentralized basis, and deciding which activities are to be administered by a region is an ongoing concern. Field-based scientific and laboratory facilities implementing national-level programs tend not to be administered on a regional basis. Federal advisory committees of the EPA report directly to headquarters, although the regional offices are often involved. The regional offices work with state environmental agencies through memorandums of understanding, and support many state-level environmental activities that states do not develop. Assistance with permit writing, compliance and enforcement, and the public's right to know are a few of the basic activities supported by the regional offices for the states.

Overlaid onto this structure is an organization based on statutory lines of authority. The person in charge of the EPA is the administrator, and there is a deputy administrator who can act as the administrator if necessary. The Office of the Administrator has four principal officials, called directors. They are the directors of public affairs, legislative liaison, equal opportunity, and international affairs. The director of public affairs handles relations with the media, public and private groups, community groups, and individual citizens. The director of legislative liaison is the principal adviser to the administrator in regard to congressional relations, and her office provides information, assistance,

TABLE 1.1. EPA's Budget and Workforce, 1970–2003

Fiscal Year	Budget	Workforce
FY 1970	$1,003,984,000	4,084
FY 1971	$1,288,784,000	5,744
FY 1972	$2,447,565,000	8,358
FY 1973	$2,377,226,000	9,077
FY 1974	$518,348,000	9,743
FY 1975	$698,835,000	10,438
FY 1976	$771,695,000	9,481
FY 1977	$2,763,745,000	11,315
FY 1978	$5,498,635,000	11,986
FY 1979	$5,402,561,000	12,160
FY 1980	$4,669,415,000	13,078
FY 1981	$3,030,669,000	12,667
FY 1982	$3,676,013,000	11,402
FY 1983	$3,688,688,000	10,832
FY 1984	$4,067,000,000	11,420
FY 1985	$4,353,655,000	12,410
FY 1986	$3,663,841,000	12,892
FY 1987	$5,364,092,000	13,442
FY 1988	$5,027,442,000	14,442
FY 1989	$5,155,125,000	14,370
FY 1990	$5,461,808,000	16,318
FY 1991	$6,094,287,000	16,415
FY 1992	$6,668,853,000	17,010
FY 1993	$6,892,424,000	17,280
FY 1994	$6,658,927,000	17,106
FY 1995	$6,658,227,000	17,663
FY 1996	$6,522,953,000	17,081
FY 1997	$6,799,393,000	17,951
FY 1998	$7,360,946,000	18,283
FY 1999	$7,590,352,000	18,375
FY 2000	$7,562,800,000	18,100
FY 2001	$7,832,212,000	18,000
FY 2002	$8,079,000,000	17,500
FY 2003	$7,616,513,000	17,648
FY 2004	$7,626,537,000	17,850

and advice to Congress. Assistant administrators form the next tier of management. The assistant administrator for equal opportunity is the principal adviser to the administrator on civil rights programs and policies, and her office directs activities required to assure compliance with civil rights laws and with executive orders providing for equal employment opportunities in federally assisted construction contracts. The assistant administrator for international affairs supervises and directs the administration of the Office of

International Affairs, which coordinates services and provides advice on international programs to all parts of the EPA. It is responsible for the exchange of scientific information and personnel.

There are also assistant administrators for planning and management, for standards and enforcement, and for research and monitoring. The assistant administrator for planning and management is responsible for the development and analysis of Agency goals and programs, the estimates of resource needs, and the management of Agency resources. He supervises the development and maintenance of programs for personnel management, audit, organizational analysis, systems development, management information systems, archives, contracts and agreements, grants, facilities management, and libraries. The assistant administrator for standards and enforcement and the general counsel are principal advisers to the administrator concerning the establishment and enforcement of standards of environmental quality. The general counsel is the principal legal adviser and chief law officer of the Agency.

There are two offices under the assistant administrator for standards and enforcement. The Office of Standards and Compliance is responsible for developing Agency-wide systems for establishing guidelines to improve the quality of the environment. It also develops enforcement and compliance measures to implement these guidelines, and reviews the Agency's achievement of in setting and enforcing standards. The second office is the Office of General Counsel. It provides legal opinions and counsel, prepares and reviews proposed legislation, and assists in the formulation and administration of the Agency's policies and programs. The assistant administrator for research and monitoring is the principal science adviser to the administrator. He is responsible for developing research, development, and demonstration programs for the Agency, as well as programs and systems for monitoring the condition of the environment.

There are also commissioners who report to the administrator and whose offices have both expressly and implicitly delegated authority. They are commissioners of water quality, air pollution control, pesticides, radiation, and solid wastes.

The commissioner of water quality is responsible for water pollution control that will enhance and preserve the quality and value of U.S. waters. His office also runs programs to minimize the health effects of contaminants in drinking water and recreational waters.

Safe drinking water is an environmental issue. (Jupiter Images)

The main responsibilities of this office are

- Federal financial assistance to help build municipal waste treatment facilities;
- A water quality management program in cooperation with states, cities, and industry;
- Research, development, and demonstration programs;
- A national water quality monitoring program coordinated with monitoring activities of state and of other federal agencies;
- A technical assistance and support program for public and private agencies and institutions;
- A manpower development and training program;
- Continued federal aid to state water pollution control agencies to assist in carrying out responsibilities for water quality management under the federal Water Pollution Control Act.

A total maximum daily load (TMDL) is a calculation of the maximum amount of a pollutant that a body of water can receive and still meet water quality standards, and a limit of that amount to the pollutant's sources. Water quality standards are set by states, territories, and tribes. They identify the uses for each body of water—for example, drinking water supply, contact recreation (swimming), and aquatic life support (fishing)—and the scientific criteria to support those uses. A TMDL is the sum of the allowable loads of a single pollutant from all contributing sources. The calculation must include a margin of safety to ensure that the water can be used for the purposes the state has designated. The calculation must also account for seasonal variation in water quality and quantity. The Clean Water Act, section 303, establishes the water quality standards and TMDL programs.

Water standards require rapid development, and unlike air quality programs, water quality programs do not have chemically specific standards. Some states allow a process of "mixing" whereby the emissions levels in water are tested after the emissions have mixed with a body of water. The unfortunate consequence of such a policy is that over time the entire body of water gets polluted with runoff and emissions. In Oregon mixing has been allowed, with negative environmental consequences for the 187-mile-long Willamette River that runs north through the state to Portland, the Columbia River, and the Pacific Ocean. Even when there are developed and implemented TMDLs, the results of "mixing" testing are substandard. Water quality and quantity standards present an ongoing challenge to the EPA.

States and territories identify bodies of water not meeting water quality standards; lists of them are provided to the public and EPA every two years. The bodies of water on the lists are priority-ranked based upon severity of the pollution and the uses to be made of the water. States then develop TMDLs for their bodies of water on the list. TMDLs specify the reductions needed to meet water quality standards and allocate those reductions among the pollution sources in the watershed.

The EPA reviews the lists and the TMDLs. If the EPA disapproves them, it must supersede the state. In 1996 the EPA set up a federal advisory committee composed of members with backgrounds ranging from the environmental and agricultural communities to state and local governments. The committee's objective was to recommend ways to improve the effectiveness and efficiency of state, territorial, tribal, and EPA TMDL programs. Its report, issued in July 1998, contains recommendations based on broad agreements reached by the members. Key recommendations include

- Restoring impaired waters must be a high priority;
- Implementing TMDLs is key to program success;
- Communication with the public is critical;
- Stakeholder involvement is key to successful implementation;
- Governments' capacity to do TMDLs must be strengthened;
- An iterative approach to TMDL development and implementation is the best way to make progress in uncertain situations.

The EPA is taking steps to improve the TMDL program by revising the regulations, and the recommendations of the advisory committee are guiding the development of proposed changes. The EPA is also revising the national pollution discharge elimination system (NPDES) and water quality standards regulations. These changes will help achieve reasonable progress in attaining water quality standards.

The EPA is grappling with some thorny issues as it develops the TMDL policy. Many state and local governments are involved, and their actions depend upon what the EPA and other federal agencies do with regard to water policy. Some of the current questions the EPA is considering are the following:

- What types of data and information are needed to identify waters for listing?
- Should waters be listed based on "pollutants" or "pollution"? (Pollutants are residue, chemical wastes, and other materials.)
- What should be the basis for setting priorities for TMDL development?
- What should be the time frame for completing TMDLs?
- Should an implementation plan be required? How should it be developed?
- What additional requirements, if any, should be placed on new or expanding dischargers in impaired bodies of water without TMDLs?

- What actions should the EPA take to ensure expeditious state permit issuance to key pollution sources before and after a TMDL is established?

The commissioner of the Air Pollution Control Office is responsible for the definition, prevention, and control of air pollution. The two primary goals are to find a working definition of air quality that will minimize the dangerous effects of air pollution, and the attainment of a wholesome air environment through the development of technology to control air pollution. The primary air pollution control programs run by this office are

- A federal–state–local regulatory program for stationary-source emissions and air monitoring;
- A national program to regulate motor vehicle emissions;
- Research, demonstration programs, and grants for water quality programs;
- Inspection and testing programs for emission control devices.

The commissioner of the Pesticide Office runs programs that include

- Establishment of tolerance levels for pesticide residues in or on food;
- Registration of pesticide uses;
- Monitoring of pesticide residue levels in foods and in the environment;
- Review of pesticide formulations for efficacy and hazard;
- Research on effects of pesticides on human health, fish and wildlife, and their environments;
- Establishment of guidelines and standards for analytical methods of residue detection.

The commissioner of the Radiation Office is in charge of developing radiation protection guidelines and environmental radiation standards. To this end the Radiation Office monitors levels of background radiation, conducts research and development in radiation protection, and provides technical assistance and training programs.

The commissioner of the Solid Wastes Office is responsible for the regulation of solid waste, and works with state and local governments to do so. His office's responsibilities are the following:

- A research, development, and demonstration program for better methods of solid waste disposal;
- Waste reduction to conserve natural resources;

Recycling decreases waste and helps the environment. (Jupiter Images)

- Recycling;
- Technical and financial assistance to state and local governments and interstate agencies for planning solid waste facilities and programs;
- Providing technical assistance in carrying out solid waste programs.

The assistant administrators and office commissioners report to the Administrator. Office commissioners tend to run programs tied directly to the statutory duties of the EPA and to work more closely with state and local governments.

COUNCIL ON ENVIRONMENTAL QUALITY

The Council on Environmental Quality (CEQ) coordinates federal environmental efforts. It consists of three members appointed by the president, subject to Senate confirmation, who report directly to the president. The CEQ was created under the National Environmental Policy Act (NEPA) of 1970, which also created environmental impact assessment requirements administered by the EPA. The role of the CEQ is primarily advisory. It publishes the *President's Annual Report on Environmental Quality*, which is available in federal depository libraries. The CEQ also establishes regulations regarding NEPA procedures, helps other federal agencies prepare their environmental impact statements, attends meetings of the President's Domestic Policy Council when environmental matters are discussed, resolves environmental conflicts between federal agencies, and works with the World Commission on Environmental Development, a U.N. research agency.

ADMINISTRATIVE LAW JUDGES

The EPA's Office of Administrative Law Judges (OALJ) is an independent office within the Office of the Administrator. The administrative law judges conduct hearings and render decisions in proceedings between the EPA and individuals, businesses, government entities, and other organizations that are or are alleged to be regulated under environmental laws. Administrative law judges preside over enforcement and permit proceedings. Most enforcement actions initiated by the EPA are for the assessment of civil penalties. All litigants are offered the opportunity to resolve enforcement cases through alternative dispute resolution (ADR), with an administrative law judge serving as a neutral third party, prior to assignment of the case for litigation. In essentially every environmental case filed with it, the OALJ offers the parties ADR. The process is initiated only if it is accepted by all parties; the neutral mediator is one of the OALJ's seven judges, all of whom have had mediation training. There is no charge for the mediation.

As stated above, mediation is offered to the parties before the case is assigned to a judge for litigation. After litigation has begun, mediation is still available to the parties, upon their motion, at the discretion of the presiding judge. Mediation is allowed to continue for sixty days and, at the discretion of the neutral third party, may be extended up to an additional sixty days. Thus, if a case is not settled, it can still be concluded through litigation within a reasonable time.

When a case is not settled during mediation, it is handled by one of the office's other judges, who presides over the litigation leading to a decision resolving the case. Confidentiality is strictly observed during and after the mediation process. There is no communication on the substance of the case between the judge who served as mediator and the judge who presides over the litigation; the notes and written records of the mediator are destroyed.

Environmental cases coming before the OALJ involve one or more major environmental statutes. The procedure in most of these cases is governed by the EPA regulations at 40 CFR Part 22. Section 18 of this part was amended in 1999 to facilitate the use of ADR (40 Fed. Reg. 176 and 182 (1999)).

The OALJ's experience with mediation has been favorable. For this reason it has expanded the use of mediation since its inception in 1997, when mediation was offered for only a few selected cases, to offering it for essentially every case.

Federal administrative law judges are certified by the Office of Personnel Management and appointed in accordance with 5 USC3105. They have decisional independence pursuant to Section 557 of the Administrative Procedure Act, 5 USC557, which ensures the fair and impartial resolution of proceedings. Decisions issued by the administrative law judges are subject to review by the Environmental Appeals Board (EAB). The administrative law judge's initial decision, which is a disposition of all of the issues in a proceeding, becomes the final order of the EPA within forty-five days after service upon the parties unless a party appeals to the EAB or the EAB elects to review the initial decision.

ENVIRONMENTAL APPEALS BOARD

The Environmental Appeals Board (EAB) is the final EPA decision maker on administrative appeals under all major environmental statutes that the EPA administers. It is an impartial body independent of the EPA except for the Office of the Administrator. The board typically sits in panels of three judges and makes decisions by majority vote. Currently, nine experienced attorneys serve as its counsel.

The jurisdiction of the EAB is established primarily by regulation. The majority of its cases are appeals from administrative enforcement decisions (mostly civil penalty cases) and from permit decisions. Appeals from administrative enforcement decisions are governed primarily by the Consolidated Rules of Practice (CROP) Governing the Administrative Assessment of Civil Penalties and the Revocation/Termination or Suspension of Permits. Appeals from permit decisions are governed primarily by 40 CFR pt. 124. However, the following permit proceedings are governed by the CROP rather than the part 124 regulations:

1. The revocation or suspension of a permit under section 105(a) or 105(f) of the Marine Protection, Research, and Sanctuaries Act (MPRSA);

2. The termination of an EPA-issued national pollutant discharge elimination system (NPDES) permit under the Clean Water Act;

3. The termination of an EPA-issued permit under the Resource Conservation Recovery Act (RCRA) and the suspension or revocation of authority to operate pursuant to RCRA.

The EAB is also authorized to hear appeals under other statutory and regulatory authorities. In addition to its express regulatory authority, it has delegated authority from the EPA administrator. The EAB considers petitions for reimbursement of costs incurred in complying with cleanup orders issued under the Comprehensive Environmental Response, Compensation, and Liability Act of 1980 (CERCLA). It may also be requested by the administrator, on a specific matter, to "provide advice and consultation; make findings of fact and conclusions of law." Two EAB members constitute a quorum if a three-member panel cannot be convened. If the EAB sits as a panel of two members, and there is a tie vote, the matter is referred to the administrator. The administrator prepares a recommended decision or serves as the final decision maker, as the administrator deems appropriate. Although the federal Rules of Civil Procedure do not apply to EPA administrative proceedings, the EAB looks to them for guidance.

THE LAWS IMPLEMENTED BY THE EPA

The laws that Congress requires the EPA to implement form the basis for its authority and for much of its organizational structure. These laws delegate the authority from Congress to the EPA to promulgate, or create, the rules and regulations necessary to implement these laws. Most of these laws are briefly described here, and also are discussed in later chapters. They are the source of almost all EPA power and authority, and constitute the legal basis for the EPA's programs. In some cases, the EPA carries out its mission through this legislation in cooperation with other governmental agencies. A list of these laws follows.

Environmental Laws Prior to the EPA: 1938–1967

June 25, 1938	Federal Food, Drug, and Cosmetic Act (FFDCA)
July 1, 1944	Safe Drinking Water Act (SDWA)
June 25, 1947	Federal Insecticide, Fungicide, and Rodenticide Act (FIFRA)
June 30, 1948	Federal Water Pollution Control Act (FWPCA)/Clean Water Act (CWA)
July 14, 1955	Air Pollution Control Act/Clean Air Act (CAA)
July 14, 1955	National Emission Standards Act (Motor Vehicle Air Pollution Control Act)
July 12, 1960	Federal Hazardous Substances Act (FHSA)
October 2, 1965	Water Quality Act
October 20, 1965	Solid Waste Disposal Act (SWDA)
October 27, 1965	Shoreline Erosion Protection Act
July 4, 1966	Freedom of Information Act (FOIA)
November 3, 1966	Clean Water Restoration Act
November 21, 1967	Air Quality Act (AQA)

Environmental Laws Since the EPA: 1970–2002

January 1, 1970	National Environmental Policy Act (NEPA)
April 3, 1970	Water Quality Improvement Act (WQIA)
April 3, 1970	Environmental Quality Improvement Act (EQIA)
October 26, 1970	Resource Recovery Act
December 29, 1970	Occupational Safety and Health Act (OSHA; full text)
December 30, 1970	Poison Prevention Packaging Act
January 13, 1971	Lead-based Paint Poisoning Prevention Act
October 21, 1972	Federal Environmental Pesticide Control Act (FEPCA)
October 23, 1972	National Coastal Monitoring Act (NCMA)

October 23, 1972	Marine Protection, Research, and Sanctuaries Act (MPRSA)
October 27, 1972	Coastal Zone Management Act (CZMA)
December 28, 1973	Endangered Species Act (ESA)
March 7, 1974	Water Resources Development Act
March 7, 1974	Shoreline Erosion Control Demonstration Act
July 1, 1974	Safe Drinking Water Act (SDWA)
January 3, 1975	Hazardous Materials Transportation Act (HMTA)
October 11, 1976	Toxic Substances Control Act (TSCA)
October 21, 1976	Resource Conservation and Recovery Act (RCRA)
August 3, 1977	Surface Mining Control and Reclamation Act (SMCRA)
December 27, 1977	Clean Water Act
September 30, 1978	Federal Pesticide Act
November 8, 1978	Uranium Mill Tailings Radiation Control Act (UMTRCA)
June 14, 1980	Asbestos School Hazard Detection and Control Act
June 30, 1980	Acid Precipitation Act (APA/Walter–Logan Act)
October 15, 1980	Used Oil Recycling Act
December 11, 1980	Comprehensive Environmental Response, Compensation, and Liability Act (CERCLA/Superfund Act)
January 7, 1982	Nuclear Waste Policy Act (NWPA)
August 11, 1984	Asbestos in Schools Hazard Abatement Act (ASHAA)
November 8, 1984	Hazardous and Solid Waste Amendments (HSWA)
October 17, 1986	Superfund Amendments and Reauthorization Act (SARA)
October 17, 1986	Emergency Planning and Community Right-to-Know Act (EPCRA)
October 17, 1986	Radon Gas and Indoor Air Quality Research Act
October 22, 1986	Asbestos Hazard Emergency Response Act (AHERA)
February 4, 1987	Water Quality Act
October 31, 1988	Lead Contamination Control Act (LCCA)
November 1, 1988	Medical Waste Tracking Act

November 18, 1988   Ocean Dumping Ban Act

November 18, 1988   Shore Protection Act (SPA)

August 18, 1990   Oil Pollution Act (OPA)

November 5, 1990   Pollution Prevention Act (PPA)

November 5, 1990   Food, Agriculture, Conservation, and Trade Act (FACT Act)

November 16, 1990   National Environmental Education Act

November 28, 1990   Asbestos School Hazard Abatement Reauthorization Act

October 6, 1992   Federal Facility Compliance Act (FFCA)

October 19, 1992   Community Environmental Response Facilitation Act (CERFA)

October 28, 1992   Residential Lead-Based Paint Hazard Reduction Act

March 26, 1996   Land Disposal Program Flexibility Act

August 3, 1996   Food Quality Protection Act (FQPA)

September 30, 1996   Asset Conservation, Lender Liability, and Deposit Insurance Protection Act

January 6, 1999   Chemical Safety Information, Site Security and Fuels Regulatory Relief Act

January 10, 2002   Emergency Supplemental Act

January 11, 2002   Small Business Liability Relief and Brownfields Revitalization Act

June 12, 2002   Public Health Security and Bioterrorism Preparedness and Response Act

Following are summaries of the major provisions of major laws that provide the basis for EPA regulatory authority. It is not possible to go into every statute in depth. Several of the environmental laws are presented in depth in later chapters.

Asbestos Hazard Emergency Response Act (October 22, 1986)

The federal government has enacted several laws and regulations to govern the use of asbestos and to better protect the public from its serious effects. In 1986, the Asbestos Hazard Emergency Response Act (AHERA) was signed into law as Title II of the Toxic Substance Control Act (TSCA). Additionally, the Asbestos in School Hazard Abatement Reauthorization Act (ASHARA), passed in 1990, required accreditation of personnel working with asbestos in schools and public and commercial buildings.

Specifically, the 1986 act outlines a detailed process that ensures the safe management of all asbestos-containing building materials (ACBMs) by a designated person for a local education agency (LEA). Additionally, as mentioned above, the 1990 act required accreditation of personnel working with asbestos. These personnel included inspectors, workers, supervisors, project designers, and management planners (schools only). Although asbestos is hazardous when inhaled, the risk of exposure to airborne fibers is very low. Therefore removal of asbestos from schools is often not the best course of action and may even create a dangerous situation when none previously existed. The EPA requires removal of asbestos to prevent significant public exposure only during demolition or renovation. It does, however, require an in-place, proactive asbestos management program for all LEAs in order to ensure that ACBMs remain in good condition and are undisturbed.

Asbestos is a naturally occurring mineral fiber that may be added to building products to strengthen them and to provide heat insulation and fire resistance. ACBMs include fireproofing material (sprayed on beams), insulation material (on pipes), acoustical or soundproofing material (sprayed on ceilings and walls), and miscellaneous materials such as asphalt, vinyl, and cement that are used to make roofing felts, shingles, siding, wallboard, and floor tiles. Friable asbestos, which can be crumbled or broken by hand pressure, is of the most concern because its fibers can be released into the air more readily and inhaled into the lungs. The presence of asbestos in public buildings such as schools presents the opportunity for inadvertent disturbance and the potential for exposure. Extensive use of a building can lead to frequent repairs that may lead to exposure to fibers if not properly managed. Long-term exposure can increase the amount of fiber that remains in the lung. Fibers embedded in lung tissue over time may cause serious lung diseases including asbestosis and lung cancer.

AHERA requires public and private nonprofit primary and secondary schools to inspect their buildings for ACBMs. The EPA has published regulations that require schools subject to AHERA to do the following:

- Perform an original inspection and periodic reinspections every three years for asbestos-containing material;
- Develop, maintain, and update an asbestos management plan and keep a copy at the school;
- Provide yearly notification to parents, teachers, and employee organizations regarding the availability of the school's asbestos management plan and any asbestos abatement actions taken or planned;
- Designate a contact person to ensure that the responsibilities of the LEA are properly implemented;

- Perform periodic surveillance of known or suspected ACBMs;
- Provide custodial staff with asbestos awareness training.

It is the EPA's goal to provide schools with the technical assistance they need to meet the requirements set forth by Congress. Schools that fail to meet the AHERA requirements are subject to civil enforcement action by the EPA or designated state environmental agency.

Chemical Safety Information, Site Security, and Fuels Regulatory Relief Act (January 6, 1999)

Under Section 112(r) of the Clean Air Act (CAA), by June 21, 1999, certain facilities were required to have in place a risk management program (RMP) and to submit a summary of that program to the EPA. On August 5, 1999, President Clinton signed legislation that removes from coverage by the RMP program any flammable fuel when it is used as fuel or is held for sale as fuel by a retail facility. The legislation also limits access to off-site consequence analysis (OCA) data that are reported in RMPs by covered facilities. The Chemical Safety Information, Site Security, and Fuels Regulatory Relief Act establishes new provisions for reporting and disseminating information under Section 112(r) of the Clean Air Act. The law has two distinct parts that pertain to

- Flammable fuels;
- Public access to OCA (also known as "worst-case scenario") data.

However, flammable fuels used as a feedstock or held for sale as fuel at a wholesale facility are still covered. A retail facility is a facility "at which more than one-half of the income is obtained from direct sales to end users or at which more than one-half of the fuel sold, by volume, is sold through a cylinder exchange program." Despite the removal of flammable fuels from the RMP program, firefighters and other local emergency responders should receive information on the potential off-site effects of accidents involving flammable fuels. The EPA and industry are working with the National Fire Protection Association, a group that develops fire protection codes and standards, to ensure that local responders receive that information. The law does the following:

- Makes OCA data available to federal, state, and local officials, including members of local emergency planning committees, for emergency planning and response purposes;
- Provides for a system for making OCA data available to qualified researchers;
- Prohibits federal, state, and local officials and qualified researchers from publicly releasing OCA data except as authorized by the law;

- Preempts state FOIA laws regarding public access to OCA data unless data are collected under state law;
- Requires that reports be submitted to Congress describing the effectiveness of the RMP regulations in reducing the risk of criminally caused releases, the vulnerability of facilities to criminal and terrorist activity, and the security of transportation of substances listed under CAA Section 112(r).

The new law requires every covered facility to

- Hold a public meeting to share information about the local implications of its RMP, including a summary of the OCA portion of its plan;
- Notify the FBI that it held such a meeting or posted such a notice within one year before, or six months after, August 5, 1999;
- Tell the EPA if it distributes its OCA data to the public without restrictions. The EPA is to maintain a public list of the facilities that have so distributed their OCA data.

Clean Air Act (December 31, 1970)

The Clean Air Act is the comprehensive federal law that regulates emissions into the air from area, stationary, and mobile sources. It authorizes the EPA to establish national ambient air quality standards (NAAQS) to protect public health and the environment.

Children are more severely impacted by events in their environment than adults. (Photograph by Brent Merrill)

The goal of the act was to set and achieve NAAQS in every state by 1975. The setting of maximum pollutant standards was coupled with directing the states to develop state implementation plans (SIPs) applicable to appropriate industrial sources in the state. The act was amended in 1977 primarily to set new goals (dates) for achieving attainment of NAAQS because many areas of the country had failed to meet the deadlines. The 1990 amendments to the Clean Air Act in large part were intended to meet unaddressed or insufficiently addressed problems such as acid rain, ground-level ozone, stratospheric ozone depletion, and air toxins. A few common air pollutants are found all over the United States. They can injure health, harm the environment, and cause property damage.

The EPA calls these pollutants "criteria air pollutants" because it has regulated them by first developing health-based criteria (science-based guidelines) as the basis for setting permissible levels. One set of limits (primary standards) protects health, and another set of limits (secondary standards) is intended to prevent environmental and property damage. A geographic area that meets or does better than

Car and truck emissions can accumulate in cities. The EPA has always made clean air one of its highest priorities. (Jupiter Images)

the primary standard is called an attainment area; areas that don't meet the primary standard are called nonattainment areas. Although the EPA has been regulating criteria air pollutants since the CAA was passed in 1970, many urban areas have been classified as nonattainment for at least one pollutant. It has been estimated that about 90 million Americans live in nonattainment areas.

What we call smog is made up primarily of ground-level ozone. Ozone can be good or bad, depending on where it is located. Ozone in the stratosphere protects human health and the environment, but ground-level ozone is the main harmful ingredient in smog. It is produced by the combination of pollutants from many sources, including smokestacks, cars, paints, and solvents. When a car burns gasoline, releasing exhaust fumes, or a painter paints a house, smog-forming pollutants rise into the sky. Often, wind blows them away from their sources. The smog-forming reactions occur while the pollutants are being blown through the air. This explains why smog is often more severe miles from the source of pollutants than it is at the source.

The smog-forming pollutants literally cook in the sky, and if it's hot and sunny, smog forms more easily. Just as it takes time to bake a cake, it takes time to cook smog—several hours from the time pollutants get into the air until the smog gets really bad. Weather and geography determine where smog goes and how bad it is. When temperature inversions occur (warm air stays near the ground instead of rising) and the air is calm, smog may stay in place for days at a time. As traffic and other sources add more pollutants to the air, the smog gets worse. Vulnerable populations—the elderly, the very young, those with compromised immune systems, asthmatics, and pregnant women—face a dangerous decrease in quality of life and health when smog gets bad. Since smog travels across county and state lines, when a metropolitan area covers two or more states (for instance, the New York metropolitan area includes parts of New

Jersey and Connecticut), their governments and air pollution control agencies must cooperate to solve their problem. Governments on the East Coast from Maine to Washington, D.C., will have to work together in a multistate effort to reduce the area's smog problem.

Here's how the 1990 Clean Air Act reduces pollution from criteria air pollutants, including smog.

First, the EPA and state governors cooperate to identify nonattainment areas for each pollutant. Then the EPA classifies the nonattainment areas according to how badly polluted they are. There are five classes of nonattainment areas for smog, ranging from marginal (relatively easy to clean up quickly) to extreme (will take a lot of work and a long time to clean up).

The 1990 Clean Air Act uses this new classification system to tailor cleanup requirements to the severity of the pollution and set realistic deadlines for reaching cleanup goals. If deadlines are missed, the law allows more time to clean up, but usually a nonattainment area that has missed a cleanup deadline will have to meet the stricter requirements set for more polluted areas. Not only must nonattainment areas meet deadlines, but states with nonattainment areas must show the EPA that they are making reasonable progress toward cleanup before the deadline. States will usually do most of the planning for cleaning up criteria air pollutants, using the permit system to make sure power plants, factories, and other pollution sources meet their cleanup goals.

The comprehensive approach to reducing criteria air pollutants taken by the 1990 act covers many different sources and a variety of cleanup methods. Many of the smog cleanup requirements involve motor vehicles (cars, trucks, buses). Also, as the pollution gets worse, pollution controls are required for smaller sources.

The carbon monoxide and particulate matter cleanup plans are set up like the plan for smog, but only two pollution classes are identified for each (instead of the five for ozone). Getting rid of particulates (soot, dust, and smoke) will require pollution controls on power plants and restrictions on smaller sources such as wood stoves, agricultural burning, and dust from fields and roads.

In 1997 the EPA made some changes to the Clean Air Act. It reviewed the air quality standards for smog and particulates. Based on new scientific evidence, revisions have been made to both standards.

What if a company wants to expand or change a production process or otherwise increase its output of a criteria air pollutant? In such a case, an offset (a reduction of the pollutant by an amount greater than the planned increase) must be obtained somewhere else—from some other stack at the same plant or at another plant owned by the same or some other company in the nonattainment area—so that permit requirements are met and the nonattainment area keeps moving toward attainment. The company must also install tight pollution controls. Since total pollution will continue to decrease, trading offsets among companies is allowed. This is one of the market approaches to cleaning up air pollution in the Clean Air Act.

Volatile organic compounds (VOCs), important smog-forming chemicals, are found in gasoline and many consumer products, from hair spray to charcoal starter fluid to plastic popcorn packaging.

Some air pollutants can cause cancer, birth defects, miscarriages, and other very serious illnesses as well as environmental damage. Air pollutants can kill people swiftly when large quantities are released. The 1984 release of methyl isocyanate at a pesticide-manufacturing plant in Bhopal, India, killed approximately 4,000 people and injured more than 200,000. Such hazardous air pollutants or air toxins, are released from sources throughout the country and from motor vehicles. For example, gasoline contains toxic chemicals. Gases escape from liquid gasoline and form a vapor. When you put gas in your car, you can often see wavy lines in the air at the pump nozzle and you can smell gasoline; that tells you gasoline vapors are in the air. When cars and trucks burn gasoline, air toxins come out of their tailpipes. Vaporization also occurs at large depots where petrochemical products are loaded and off-loaded. The hoses are much larger, and the potential for vapor recovery is greater. Some states have enacted vapor recovery requirements, but they are difficult to enforce. In ports with many depots, the ships are from many different countries and may not be equipped to comply with vapor recovery laws.

Air toxins are also released from small stationary sources such as dry cleaners and auto paint shops, as well as from large stationary sources such as chemical factories and incinerators. The 1990 Clean Air Act deals more strictly with large sources than with small ones.

To reduce air pollution, the EPA must first identify the toxic substances whose release should be reduced. The 1970 Clean Air Act gave the EPA authority to list air toxins for regulation and then to regulate them. The EPA listed and regulated seven chemicals through 1990. The 1990 act includes 189 hazardous air pollutants selected by Congress on the basis of potential health and/or environmental hazard, and it allows the EPA to add new chemicals to the list as necessary.

To regulate hazardous air pollutants, the EPA must identify categories of sources

Vapor recovery systems—from the large systems in the oil depots to the small systems at the gas pump—can prevent the evaporation of gasoline into the air. (Jupiter Images)

that release the 189 chemicals listed by Congress in the 1990 Clean Air Act. They include service stations, electrical repair shops, coal-burning power plants, and chemical plants, and are identified as major (large) or area (small) sources.

Once the categories of sources are listed, the EPA issues regulations. In some cases it may have to specify exactly how to reduce pollutant releases, but wherever possible, companies will have flexibility in choosing how they meet requirements. Pollution sources are to use maximum available control technology (MACT) to reduce pollutant releases. This is a very high level of pollution control. The choice between best available control and most economical control technology depends on the pollution sources. (See Chapter 3.)

The EPA must issue regulations for major sources first, and then for small sources, setting priorities for which small sources to tackle first, based on health and environmental hazards, production volume, and other factors. If a company wishes to increase the amount of air toxins from an operating plant, it may choose to offset the increase so that total pollutant releases from the plant do not increase. Or it may choose to install pollution controls to keep pollutants at the required level.

If a company reduces its releases of a hazardous air pollutant by about 90 percent before the EPA regulates the chemical, it will get extra time to finish cleaning up the remaining 10 percent. This program is expected to result in a speedy reduction of the levels of several important hazardous air pollutants. Under the 1990 Clean Air Act, the EPA is required to study whether and how to reduce hazardous air pollutants from small neighborhood polluters such as auto paint shops and print shops. It also has to look at air pollution after the first round of regulations to see whether the remaining health hazards require further regulatory action.

Cars, trucks, buses, and other mobile sources release large amounts of pollutants such as formaldehyde and benzene. Using cleaner fuels and engines, and making sure that pollution control devices work, should reduce hazardous air pollutants from mobile sources.

The Bhopal tragedy inspired the 1990 Clean Air Act requirement that factories and other businesses develop plans to prevent accidental releases of highly toxic chemicals. It established the Chemical Safety Board to investigate and report on accidental releases of hazardous air pollutants from industrial plants.

Clean Water Act (December 28, 1977) and Federal Water Pollution Control Act Amendments of 1972 (October 18, 1972)

Federal water legislation dates back to the nineteenth century, when Congress enacted the River and Harbor Act (1886), recodified in the Rivers and Harbors Act (1899). Recognizing the threat that dirty water posed to the public health and welfare, Congress passed the federal Water Pollution Control Act (FWPCA) in order to "enhance the quality and value of our water resources and to establish a national policy for the prevention, control and abatement of water pollution." FWPCA and its amendments set out the basic legal authority for federal regulation of water quality. The original act was passed in 1948. Its amendments broadened the federal government's authority in water pollution control. The Water Pollution Control Act Amendments of 1956 strengthened enforcement provisions by providing for an abatement suit at the request of a state pollution control agency. Where health was being endangered, the federal government no longer had to receive the consent of all states involved. The federal role was further expanded under the Water Quality Act (1965), which provided for the setting of water quality standards enforced by state and federal governments and became the basis for interstate water quality standards. The Clean Water Restoration Act (1966) imposed a $100 per day fine on a polluter that failed to submit a required report. The Water Quality Improvement Act (1970) again expanded federal authority, and established a state certification procedure to prevent degradation of water below applicable standards.

Despite the improvements achieved by each amendment to the original act, this legislation was a ragtag mixture. Eleven reorganizations and restructurings of federal agency responsibility compounded the difficulty of effectively implementing the law. To solve these problems, the 1972 amendments to the FWPCA restructured the authority for water pollution control and consolidated authority under the administrator of the EPA.

The objective of the act was to restore and maintain the chemical, physical, and biological integrity of the nation's waters. In order to achieve this objective, the act set two national goals. The first was the elimination of the discharge of all pollutants into the navigable waters of the United States by 1985. The second was an interim level of water quality that provided for the protection of fish, shellfish, and wildlife and of recreation by July 1, 1983. In this framework Congress gave the administrator the legal tools necessary to make progress in water pollution control while continuing to recognize the primary rights and responsibilities of the states to prevent, reduce, and eliminate pollution. The 1972 amendments changed the thrust of enforcement from water quality standards—regulating the amounts of pollutants in a given body of water—to effluent limitations—regulating the amount of pollutants being discharged from particular point sources. Ambient water quality requirements can still dictate the amounts of pollutants permitted to be discharged. The administrator was directed to publish regulations establishing guidelines for effluent limitations by October 18, 1973. These regulations were to identify the most practicable control technology available for various industrial categories. Factors for consideration were the costs and benefits of applying such technology, the age of equipment and facilities involved, and the process employed. Industrial dischargers were to meet these standards by July 1, 1977. Public treatment works were to meet effluent limitations based on secondary treatment by the same date.

In addition, the administrator was to identify the best available technology for preventing and reducing pollution, and was also responsible for identifying technology that would eliminate the discharge of pollutants. In both cases he must take into account the factors enumerated above. Industrial dischargers were obliged to meet these standards by July 1, 1983, the date given for achieving the second national goal designed to protect fish, shellfish, wildlife, and recreation. They must meet zero-discharge requirements if the administrator determined that it would be economically and technologically feasible. By July 1, 1983, public treatment works were to use the most practicable waste treatment technology over the life of the works. New sources of discharge were required to use the best available technology as determined by the administrator and published in the regulations. Zero discharge by 1985 was a goal, not a requirement under the law.

Reflecting the basic state responsibility for water pollution control, the FWPCA required the states to submit to the EPA water quality standards for all interstate and intrastate navigable waters. These state standards were to spell out water use classifications, such as recreation, fish and wildlife propagation, public water supplies, and industrial and agricultural uses. States were then required to set the quality of water required to achieve these uses and to provide detailed plans for maintaining the desired levels of quality. Under this procedure 90 percent of all interstate waters have been classified for either recreation or fish and wildlife propagation. Of the fifty-four jurisdictions covered by the water pollution control program, virtually all have fully approved interstate standards. The EPA has the power to reject state standards that fail to meet the legal requirements. Its rejection of all or part of a state's proposal forces the state to draft an acceptable alternative; failure to revise a proposal will result in the EPA's setting a standard. In the initial review, standards were weighed against their conformity to the old act.

This review and any required revision can include implementation schedules. Future revision of standards, after the initial review, is limited to use classifications and criteria. If the administrator determines that application of the technology required by 1983 will not assure protection of public water supplies, agricultural and industrial uses, and the propagation of a balanced population of shellfish, fish, and wildlife, and allow recreational activities, he may impose such additional controls as are necessary to meet such standards. In addition to setting water quality standards whose effluent limitations will be stringent enough to meet water quality standards, the states are required to establish maximum daily loads of pollutants in the waters that will allow the propagation of fish and wildlife. A similar assessment must be made for thermal discharges.

States are also required to develop a continuing planning process that deals with the changing patterns of water pollution within their boundaries. Beginning in 1975, the states were to submit to Congress and the EPA annual reports with an inventory of all point sources of discharge, an assessment of existing water quality and projected goals, and proposals of programs for nonpoint source control. With increasing urbanization and population growth, nonpoint sources of water pollution increase. Nonpoint sources include runoff from paved lots and filled-in wetlands, agricultural runoff (pesticides, fertilizers, animal waste), and other sources that are not considered "point" sources. They are largely unknown with any degree of specificity, but are thought to be substantial.

The EPA sets effluent standards for both existing point sources and new industrial point sources. It must determine the best available demonstrated control technology and require its installation for at least twenty-seven named categories of sources. If the administrator determines that a zero-discharge standard is practicable, he may set such a standard. As part of his comprehensive authority, the administrator is directed to publish a list of toxic pollutants and effluent limitations for them. Such limitations may constitute an absolute prohibition against discharging. Additionally, the administrator must publish pretreatment standards requiring any industry discharging into a municipal sewage system to pretreat its effluent so that it does not interfere with the operation of the treatment plant or pass through the plant either untreated or without adequate treatment.

The FWPCA was amended in 1970 to ensure that the activities of all federal agencies meet applicable state standards. The law and its recent amendment impose a new requirement on all applicants for a federal license or permit. If a licensed or permitted activity may result in a discharge into navigable waters, a certificate must be obtained from the affected state which assures that the activity will not violate the effluent limitations, guidelines, and other requirements of the 1972 amendments. Through this certification process, harmful pollution can be stopped before it begins. This significant milestone was a departure from the idea of abatement to one of prevention.

Whereas the Rivers and Harbors Act of 1899 had provided for the issuance of permits by the Corps of Engineers, the 1972 amendments to the FWPCA have instituted a new permit program under EPA guidance and assistance that has shifted administration and enforcement to state governments. Under the new law, no discharge is permitted except as authorized by a permit. This new amendment extends to previously exempt municipal discharges, so that all potential pollutants are now covered. Though the EPA issues guidelines for state permit programs, it retains a right to review a state-issued permit affecting another state's water resources. Discharge permits must be consistent with effluent limitations, guidelines, and other requirements of the statute. They must be for periods no longer than five years and may be terminated when there is a violation of a condition of the permit or when changed conditions dictate the need for further reduction of the permitted discharge. Similarly, the EPA may withdraw approval of a state permit program if it determines the state has failed to fulfill the requirements of the act. Permits affecting discharges into ocean waters under this section must be consistent with criteria set by the EPA parallel to the criteria established under the Marine Protection, Research, and Sanctuaries Act of 1972 for ocean dumping permits. By this process, states may not certify discharges that would be potential violations of federal regulations. The Corps of Engineers, the administering agency under the 1899 Act, continues to issue dredge and fill permits under the new law in accordance with criteria comparable to the EPA ocean discharge criteria. An additional permit is required for disposal of sewage sludge in navigable waters.

The EPA has the authority to enforce the provisions of the law through both administrative and judicial channels. When the administrator finds a person to be in violation of a permit condition or other provision of the law, he must notify the polluter, and will either issue an administrative order prohibiting further violation or pursue a judicial remedy. If the administrator finds that violations within a state are widespread due to state inaction, he may so notify the state, and the federal government will assume enforcement responsibilities until the state can satisfy the administrator that it will enforce the law. In order to ensure compliance with the law, the EPA has been given broad inspection and monitoring powers. It has a right of entry to all effluent sources and authority to inspect records, data, and information; monitoring equipment; and effluents. If a state develops similar procedures, the administrator may transfer this authority to the state. The administrator may also bring suit if he finds that a particular pollution source presents an imminent and substantial danger to human health or to individuals' livelihoods, such as the inability to harvest and market shellfish.

The law specifically provides for citizen participation in the judicial enforcement of federal standards. Aggrieved private citizens may seek judicial relief against any polluter for violations of an effluent standard or limitation, or an administrative order issued under an environmental law. Citizens may also institute proceedings against the administrator if he fails to perform an act required of him under the law. Citizen suits have been instrumental in shaping the EPA and are discussed in Chapter 2.

The 1972 amendments give the administrator a broad mandate to establish research programs for the prevention, reduction, and elimination of pollution in navigable waters of the United States. The EPA is directed to establish, in cooperation with all pertinent federal, state, and private parties, comprehensive local and national programs for water pollution control. Specifically the EPA must

- Render technical advice and conduct research;
- Undertake investigations, experiments, training, demonstrations, surveys, and studies;
- Establish advisory commissions to evaluate research progress and proposals;
- Establish a water quality surveillance system to monitor the quality of navigable waters;

- Initiate and promote studies measuring the social and economic costs and benefits of water pollution control activities.

The administrator must also investigate the harmful effects of pollutants on the health and welfare of persons. He must establish field laboratories and research facilities, make a comprehensive study of the pollution of the Great Lakes, and finance pilot treatment works programs. Furthermore, he must investigate pollution resulting from eutrophication, oil spills, pesticides, and thermal discharge.

Since the basic responsibility for cleaning up the nation's waters is retained by state governments, Congress has authorized grants to aid the states' pollution abatement efforts. These provide assistance to states for research and development, manpower training, water quality planning, monitoring, and enforcement. Grants are also available to institutions of higher education for programs designed to bring students into professions that deal with water pollution control. The major thrust of the federal grant effort is directed toward municipalities, for the construction of sewage treatment plants. More than 1,300 local communities have sewer systems that discharge untreated waste. An equal number of communities provide only primary treatment, which removes just 30 percent of some pollutants. The federal share for these projects is 75 percent, with the remainder to be divided between state and local governments and industrial users. Municipalities are also eligible for grants for demonstration projects that utilize new methods for treating sewage,

Sewer and water infrastructure is all around us. Municipal waste treatment in the United States has been supported by EPA efforts. (Photograph © by Frank Miller)

joint systems for handling municipal and industrial waste, and new water purification techniques.

Another area of national concern, oil spills, has produced federal legislation to protect water quality. In 1970 the federal government was given broad authority to clean up oil spills, to make polluters pay the cost of cleanup, and to levy fines and penalties against them. The EPA cooperated with the Coast Guard and other agencies in administering the law and in drafting the national contingency plan for removal of oil spills. The 1972 amendments extended these provisions to the discharge of hazardous substances. An additional approach under the act encourages cooperation between the states by congressional consent to interstate compacts, and the encouragement of uniform state laws relating to the prevention, reduction, and elimination of pollution. These agreements for solving regional problems have been approved by Congress for many years as a kind of middle ground between purely state actions, on the one hand, and exclusive federal solution of regional problems, on the other. The compacts are administered by interstate commissions. Though earlier commissions were limited to studies of regional pollution problems, recently formed commissions have been given authority to issue legally binding pollution abatement orders throughout a multistate region. There have been other innovations. The federal government has entered into several federal–interstate compacts, reflecting the need to protect national interests in those regions. The EPA involves itself by encouraging effective river basin planning, providing expert technical assistance, and supporting manpower training.

The oceans are finite, and there are limits to the amount of sludge, waste, and junk they can safely absorb. The ocean dumping legislation—the Marine Protection, Research, and Sanctuaries Act of 1972, signed into law by President Nixon on October 27, 1972, declares it to be the national policy "to regulate the dumping of all types of materials into ocean waters and to prevent or strictly limit the dumping into ocean waters of any material which would adversely affect human health, welfare or amenities, or the marine environment, ecological systems or economic potentialities." Congress found that the previous law was inadequate and imprecise, and that strict new regulation was required. The new law prohibits the transportation from the United States, for the purpose of dumping into territorial seas or the contiguous zone, any radiological,

Coastal ecosystems are often shared with recreational users. The EPA often divides jurisdiction over these environments with other federal agencies. (Photograph © by Frank Miller)

chemical, or biological warfare agent or any high-level radioactive waste. Additionally, no officer, employee, agent, department, agency, or instrumentality of the federal government shall transport these materials from any location outside the United States for the purpose of dumping into ocean waters. The most sweeping prohibition is that no person may transport any material for the purpose of dumping it into ocean waters without a permit.

The new law provides for two types of permits for activities potentially threatening the ocean environment. One type is issued by the secretary of the army for dumping dredged material. The dumping of this material is subject to the approval of the EPA administrator for compliance with stated criteria, as well as with the designated critical areas established by the EPA. For all other classes of materials—sewage sludge, garbage, chemical wastes, or construction debris—a new permit system has been established under the direct control of the administrator of the EPA. The administrator will issue a permit only after he determines that dumping in a particular instance "will not unreasonably degrade or endanger human health, welfare or amenities, or the marine environment, ecological systems or economic potentialities." In establishing the criteria for future ocean dumping, Congress directed the administrator to consider the following points:

- The need for the proposed dumping;
- The effect of such dumping on human health and welfare, including economic, aesthetic, and recreational values;
- The effect of such dumping on fisheries' resources: plankton, fish, shellfish, wildlife, shorelines, and beaches;
- The effect of such dumping on marine ecosystems, particularly with respect to

   —The transfer, concentration, and dispersion of such material and its by-products through biological, physical, and chemical processes,

   —Potential changes in marine ecosystem diversity, productivity, and stability,

   —Species and community population dynamics;
- The persistence and permanence of the effects of the dumping;
- The effect of dumping particular volumes and concentrations of such materials;
- Appropriate locations and methods of disposal or recycling, including land-based alternatives, and the probable impact of requiring use of such alternative locations or methods upon considerations affecting the public interest;
- The effect on alternative uses of oceans, such as scientific study, fishing, and exploitation of other living and nonliving resources;

• Designation of recommended sites, for which the administrator shall utilize, wherever feasible, locations beyond the edge of the Continental Shelf.

In summary, growing public awareness of and concern for controlling water pollution led to the enactment of the federal Water Pollution Control Act Amendments of 1972. As amended in 1977, this law became commonly known as the Clean Water Act. It established the basic structure for regulating discharges of pollutants into the waters of the United States and gave the EPA the authority to implement pollution control programs, such as setting wastewater standards for industry. The Clean Water Act also continued requirements to set water quality standards for all contaminants in surface waters. The act made it unlawful for any person to discharge any pollutant from a point source into navigable waters, unless a permit was obtained under its provisions. It also funded sewage treatment plants through the construction grants program and recognized the need for planning to address the critical problems posed by nonpoint source pollution.

It is no longer safe to eat fish from many lakes and rivers. The EPA has steadily increased its efforts to bring water pollution under control. (Photograph by Brent Merrill)

Subsequent enactments modified some of the earlier Clean Water Act provisions. Revisions in 1981 streamlined the municipal construction grants process, improving the capabilities of treatment plants built under the program. Changes in 1987 phased out the construction grants program, replacing it with the State Water Pollution Control Revolving Fund (more commonly known as the Clean Water State Revolving Fund). This new funding strategy addressed water quality needs by building on EPA-state partnerships.

Over the years many other laws have changed parts of the Clean Water Act. Title I of the Great Lakes Critical Programs Act (1990), for example, put into place parts of the Great Lakes Water Quality Agreement (1978), signed by the United States and Canada, in which the two nations agreed to reduce certain toxic pollutants in the Great Lakes. That law required the EPA to establish water quality criteria for the Great Lakes, including maximum levels of twenty-nine toxic pollutants that are safe for humans, wildlife, and aquatic life. It also required the EPA to help the states implement the criteria on a specific schedule.

The Office of Water is extensive. As water becomes more of a social concern necessary to meet the challenges of sustainability, the EPA will be even further involved. (See discussion in Chapter 7.)

Comprehensive Environmental Response, Compensation, and Liability Act (December 11, 1980)

This act, known as CERCLA or the Superfund, provides federal monies to clean up uncontrolled or abandoned hazardous-waste sites as well as accidents, spills, and other emergency releases of pollutants and contaminants into the environment. Through the act the EPA is given power to seek out the parties responsible for such releases and assure their cooperation in the cleanup. (See Chapter 3 for an example of how this policy is implemented.)

The EPA cleans up "orphan sites" when responsible parties cannot be identified or located, or when they fail to act. Through various enforcement tools, the EPA obtains cleanup by private parties through orders, consent decrees, and other settlements. It also recovers costs from individuals and companies that are able to pay once a response action has been completed.

The problem of illegal waste practices grows as the amount of waste continues to increase and the amount of landfill space decreases. (Photograph © by Frank Miller)

Endangered Species Act (August 3, 1973)

The Endangered Species Act (ESA) provides a program for the conservation of threatened and endangered plants and animals and their habitats. The U.S. Fish and Wildlife Service (FWS) of the Department of the Interior maintains the list of 632 endangered species (326 are plants) and 190 threatened species (78 are plants). Species include birds, insects, fish, reptiles, mammals, crustaceans, flowers, grasses, and trees. Anyone can petition FWS to include a species on this list. The law prohibits any action, administrative or physical, that results in a "taking" of a listed species or adversely affects its habitat. Any sort of commerce in listed species is prohibited.

The EPA's decision to register a pesticide is based in part on the risk of adverse effects on endangered species and on their habitats. Under other laws the EPA can cancel or restrict the use of certain pesticides if an endangered species will be adversely affected. Under the National Environmental Policy Act environmental impact procedures, if there is an impact on an endangered species, a full environmental impact statement is required.

Federal Insecticide, Fungicide, and Rodenticide Act (October 21, 1972)

The primary focus of this act, known as FIFRA, is federal control of pesticide distribution, sale, and use. The EPA was given authority under FIFRA not only to study the consequences of pesticide usage but also to require users (farmers, utility companies, and others) to register when purchasing pesticides. Through later amendments to the law, users also must be certified as applicators of pesticides. All pesticides used in the United States must be licensed by the EPA. This assures that pesticides will be properly labeled and that if they are used in accordance with directions, they will not cause unreasonable harm to the environment. The original FIFRA was passed in 1947. The October 21, 1972, amendment was also known as the Federal Environmental Pesticide Control Act. Significant amendments related to pesticide re-registration requirements, storage and disposal of suspended/canceled pesticides, indemnity payments, and enforcement issues were passed on October 25, 1988.

Food Quality Protection Act (August 3, 1996)

The Food Quality Protection Act (FQPA) of 1996 amended the Federal Insecticide, Fungicide, and Rodenticide Act (FIFRA) and the Federal Food Drug, and Cosmetic Act (FFDCA). These amendments fundamentally changed the way the EPA regulates pesticides. The requirements included a new safety standard of reasonable certainty of no harm that must be applied to all pesticides used on food crops.

In 1996 Congress unanimously passed landmark pesticide food safety legislation supported by the Clinton administration and a broad coalition of environmental, public health, agricultural, and industry groups. President Clinton signed the bill on August 3, 1996. The EPA regulates pesticides under two major federal statutes. Under FIFRA, the EPA registers pesticides for use in the United States and prescribes labeling and other regulatory requirements to prevent unreasonable adverse effects on health or the environment. Under the FFDCA, the EPA establishes tolerances (maximum legally permissible levels) for pesticide residues in food. Tolerances are enforced by the Department of Health and Human Services/Food and Drug Administration for most foods. The U.S. Department of Agriculture/Food Safety and Inspection Service enforces standards for meat, poultry, and some egg products, as does the U.S. Department of Agriculture/Office of Pest Management Policy. For over two decades, there were efforts to update and to resolve inconsistencies in the two major pesticide statutes, but consensus on necessary reforms remained elusive. The 1996 law represented a major breakthrough, amending both major pesticide laws to establish a more consistent, protective regulatory scheme grounded in sound science. It mandates the following:

- A single, health-based standard for all pesticides in all foods, with special protection for infants and children;
- Expedites approval of safer pesticides;
- Creates incentives for the development and maintenance of effective crop protection tools for American farmers;
- Requires periodic reevaluation of pesticide registrations and tolerances to ensure that the scientific data supporting them are up to date and will remain so;
- Eliminates long-standing problems posed by multiple standards for pesticides in raw and processed foods by means of a single, health-based standard;
- Requires the EPA to consider all nonoccupational sources of exposure, including drinking water, and exposure to other pesticides with a common mechanism of toxicity when setting tolerances.

The new law establishes a strong, health-based safety standard for pesticide residues in all foods through "a reasonable certainty of no harm" as the general safety standard, the same approach used in the 1994 bill. It incorporates language virtually identical to that of the 1994 bill to implement key recommendations of the National Academy of Sciences report *Pesticides in the Diets of Infants and Children* and requires the following:

- An explicit determination that tolerances are safe for children;
- An additional safety factor of up to tenfold, if necessary, to account for uncertainty in data relative to children;

- Consideration of children's special sensitivity and exposure to pesticides. Unlike previous law, which contained an open-ended provision for the consideration of pesticide benefits when setting tolerances, the new law places specific limits on benefits considerations;
- Application only to nonthreshold effects of pesticides (e.g., carcinogenic effects)—benefits cannot be taken into account for reproductive or other threshold effects;
- Review of all existing tolerances within ten years to make sure they meet the requirements of the new health-based safety standard;
- Incorporation of provisions for endocrine testing (screening and testing of chemicals for potential disruption in human endocrine systems), and provision of new authority to require that chemical manufacturers provide data on their products, including data on potential endocrine effects (disruptions in human hormone systems in glands located throughout the body).

The law further limits the level of risk that can be offset by benefits considerations by introducing three "backstops." The first is a limit on the acceptable risk in any one year, which greatly reduces the risks. The second limitation is on the lifetime risk, which allows the EPA to remove tolerances after specific phaseout periods. The third limitation is that benefits cannot be used to override the health-based standard for children.

This law includes enhanced enforcement of pesticide residue standards by allowing the Food and Drug Administration to impose civil penalties for tolerance violations. It also requires distribution of a brochure in grocery stores on the health effects of pesticides, how to avoid risks, and which foods have tolerances for pesticide residues based on benefits considerations. It specifically recognizes a state's right to require warnings or labeling of food that has been treated with pesticides, such as California's Proposition 65. States may not set tolerance levels that differ from national levels unless the state petitions the EPA for an exception based on state-specific situations. National uniformity does not apply to tolerances that include benefits considerations.

Lead Contamination Control Act (November 1, 1988)

The Lead Contamination Control Act of 1988, which amends the Safe Drinking Water Act (SDWA), requires schools to make available to the public, teachers, other school personnel, and parents the results of any testing for lead contamination, and to notify parents, teachers, and employee organizations of the availability of these results. In light of recent studies which reveal that even very low levels of lead in drinking water can have subtle adverse effects on children, the EPA recommends that action be taken to limit exposure or reduce lead in water whenever lead levels exceed 20 ppb.

If test results from all outlets show that the lead levels in a school's drinking water do *not* exceed 20 ppb, the EPA recommends that additional samples be taken in the morning before school opens, and after weekends or vacations. Water that has been sitting in the pipes for a long time may have higher lead levels than during normal use. An alternative to additional testing is to flush the water supply after weekends and vacations. Flushing the water system should be omitted only if further analysis from the first draw of samples taken on Monday morning or after vacations indicates lead levels below 20 ppb.

If test results show lead levels in excess of 20 ppb, then step 2 of the sampling process is started to track down the sources of the lead contamination. In this second step, follow-up samples are taken from outlets that show elevated lead levels and are analyzed. If necessary, additional samples from the plumbing within the building are taken.

Once the sources of contamination are known, appropriate remedial actions can be taken. Ultimately, the choice of sampling in one or two steps is up to the personnel performing the sampling. At small facilities with relatively few sites to be sampled, all of the sampling can be done at once. The number of samples taken depends upon the size of the building, the number of outlets that supply drinking water, and the extent of the contamination. More outlets with elevated lead levels will require correspondingly more follow-up samples to pinpoint the sources of contamination. In general, the larger number of samples will result in the best assessment of the source and extent of the lead in drinking water.

If the results of the initial samples indicate extensive lead contamination of the drinking water, samples from sites not previously tested are taken. It is recommended that any water fountain or tap with lead levels over 20 ppb be taken out of service immediately and kept out of service until the lead levels are below 20 ppb. If the school uses a public water system, it should first notify the supplier, the school board, and state and local governments. Action should be taken to learn what the supplier is doing to reduce lead concentrations in the source water and what corrosion control or other treatment is planned. Working closely with the water supplier may also avoid unnecessary expenditures.

If the school has its own well or other water source, it must take steps to ensure that the provisions of SDWA which apply are carried out. All school staff and the parents or guardians of all students must be notified.

Marine Protection, Research, and Sanctuaries Act (October 23, 1972)

The Marine Protection, Research, and Sanctuaries Act (MPRSA) of 1972 supplements laws already in effect for protection of our water resources. Oil spill prevention and basic water quality standards are dealt with in other legislation and by treaty, and are not affected by the act. With the exception of the Rivers and Harbors Act (Refuse Act of 1899) permits, all permits and licenses authorizing any activity covered by the Marine Protection Act were rendered void by the new law. The MPRSA was amended in 1988 by the Ocean Dumping Ban Act (Ocean Dumping Act). The MPRSA declares that it is the policy of the United States to regulate the dumping of all types of materials into ocean waters and to prevent or strictly limit the dumping into ocean waters of any material that will adversely affect human health, welfare, or amenities, or the marine environment, ecological systems, or economic potentialities. The Ocean Dumping Act makes unlawful the dumping of sludge and industrial waste. Unless authorized by a permit, the MPRSA generally prohibits

1. Transportation of material from the United States for the purpose of ocean dumping;
2. Transportation of material from anywhere for the purpose of ocean dumping by U.S. agencies or U.S.-flag vessels;
3. Dumping of material transported from outside the United States into the U.S. territorial seas.

Under MPRSA, the standard for permit issuance is whether the dumping will "unreasonably degrade or endanger" human health or welfare, or the marine environment. The EPA is charged with developing ocean dumping criteria to be used in evaluating permit applications. It also is responsible for designating recommended sites for ocean dumping. The statute lays out the following factors to be considered by the EPA in developing the permit review criteria:

- Need for dumping;
- Effect of dumping on human health and welfare;
- Effect of dumping on fish, wildlife, shorelines;
- Effect of dumping on marine ecosystems;
- Persistence and permanence of effects;
- Effect of dumping particular volumes and concentrations;
- Effect on alternative uses of oceans (e.g., fishing);
- The need to designate sites beyond the Outer Continental Shelf (OCS) wherever feasible.

Since this is a federal law, states may not independently adopt regulations relating to activities covered by Title I of MPRSA (Section 106). However, states may propose ocean dumping criteria in addition to those of the EPA. If the EPA administrator does not find the new criteria to be inconsistent with the act, the administrator may adopt those criteria and issue regulations to implement them. Only in this way can state-level criteria be brought to bear upon federal actions affected by Title I of MPRSA.

The EPA may issue an order to any person or company that violates the MPRSA. The order may impose a civil penalty plus recovery of any economic benefit of noncompliance, and may also require correction of the violation. Any "person" discharging a pollutant into the ocean must comply with the MPRSA. A "person" is defined as any private person, employee, agent, department, agency, or instrumentality of the federal government, of any state or local unit of government, or of any foreign government. Under Section 105 of the MPRSA, the EPA may assess an administrative civil penalty up to $50,000 against a person who violates the act, its regulations, or an MPRSA permit. There are higher penalties (up to $125,000) for dumping medical waste. Each day of a continuing violation constitutes a separate offense.

National Environmental Education Act (November 16, 1990)

The National Environmental Education Act (NEEA) requires the EPA to provide national leadership to increase environmental literacy. The EPA established the Office of Environmental Education within the Office of Communications, Education, and Media Relations to implement this program. On November 16, 1990, President George H. W. Bush signed the NEEA. The act gave the EPA its first congressional mandate to strengthen and expand environmental education as an integral part of its mission. It mandated various programs and activities, each administered by the EPA's Environmental Education Office.

Environmental education is a learning process that increases people's knowledge and awareness of the environment, develops the necessary skills and expertise to address challenges, that arise, and fosters attitudes, motivations, and commitments to make informed decisions and take responsible action. Unlike most formal education efforts, the most effective environmental education programs have a distinct action component whose purpose is to encourage responsible, enduring decisions and actions that impact the environment. Encouraging action means teaching individuals how to examine a range of possible courses of action to address or resolve an environmental challenge after investigation and evaluation have determined that action is needed. For example, taking action may involve removing lead paint from schools or soil, or creating physical barriers to human exposure once testing has determined that lead contamination is present at levels that adversely impact human health. Environmental education programs that include an action component should not advocate a particular solution to an environmental challenge. Rather, they should provide individuals with the information, critical thinking, and decision-making skills they need to make responsible decisions from a range of options.

National Environmental Policy Act (January 1, 1970)

The National Environmental Policy Act (NEPA; 42USC4321–4347) was one of the first laws to establish the broad national framework for protecting our environment. It both helped establish the EPA's foundational authority and forced a consideration of major environmental impacts. NEPA's basic policy is to ensure that all branches of government give proper consideration to the environment prior to undertaking any major federal action that significantly affects the environment. Many states, the United Nations Educational, Scientific and Cultural Organization, and some tribes have similar versions of environmental impact assessment. NEPA requirements are invoked when airports, buildings, military complexes, highways, parkland purchases, and other federal activities are proposed. Environmental assessments (EAs) and environmental impact statements (EISs), which are assessments of the likelihood of impacts from alternative courses of action, are required from all federal agencies and constitute the most visible NEPA requirement.

NEPA was signed into law on January 1, 1970. It establishes national environmental policy and goals for the protection, maintenance, and enhancement of the environment, and it provides a process for implementation of these goals by the federal agencies. The aspirational goals of NEPA represent the highest ideals of U.S. environmentalism. (See discussion earlier this chapter.) Title I of NEPA contains a declaration of national environmental policy that requires the federal government to use all practicable means to create and maintain conditions under which man and nature can exist in productive harmony. Section 102 requires federal agencies to incorporate environmental considerations in their planning and decision-making through a systematic interdisciplinary approach. Specifically, all federal agencies are to prepare detailed statements assessing the environmental impact of and alternatives to major federal actions significantly affecting the environment. These statements are commonly referred to as environmental impact statements (EISs). Section 102 also requires federal agencies to lend appropriate support to initiatives and programs designed to anticipate and prevent a decline in the quality of the world environment.

Title II of NEPA established the Council on Environmental Quality (CEQ), which oversees NEPA. Its duties and functions are listed in Title II, Section 204, and include gathering information on the conditions and trends in environmental quality; evaluating federal programs in light of the goals established in Title I of the act; developing and promoting national policies to improve environmental quality; and conducting studies, surveys, research, and analyses relating to ecosystems and environmental quality. In 1978 the CEQ promulgated regulations implementing NEPA that are binding on all federal agencies. The regulations address the procedural provisions of NEPA and the administration of the NEPA process, including preparation of EISs. The CEQ has issued guidance on various aspects of the regulations, including the information documents *Forty Most Asked Questions Concerning CEQ's National Environmental Policy Act, Scoping Guidance,* and *Guidance Regarding NEPA Regulations.* Additionally, most federal agencies have promulgated their own regulations and guidance materials that generally follow the CEQ procedures but are tailored for their specific mission and activities.

The NEPA process consists of an evaluation of the environmental effects of a federal undertaking, including its alternatives. There are three levels of analysis, depending on whether an undertaking could significantly affect the environment: categorical exclusion determination; preparation of an environmental assessment/finding of no significant impact; and preparation of an EIS. At the first level, an undertaking may be categorically excluded from a detailed environmental analysis if it meets certain criteria that a federal agency has previously determined as having no significant environmental impact. A number of agencies have developed lists of actions that normally are categorically excluded from environmental evaluation under their NEPA regulations. At the second level of analysis a federal agency prepares a written EA to determine whether a federal undertaking would significantly affect the environment. If it does not, the agency issues a finding of no significant impact, which may address measures that an agency can take to reduce potentially significant impacts. If the EA determines that the environmental consequences of a proposed federal undertaking may be significant, an EIS, a more detailed evaluation of the proposed action and alternatives, is prepared. The public, other federal agencies, and outside parties may provide input for the preparation of an EIS and comment on the draft EIS when it is completed. If a federal agency anticipates that an undertaking may significantly impact the environment, or if a project is environmentally controversial, a federal agency may choose to prepare an EIS without first preparing an EA. After a final EIS is prepared, a federal agency will, at the time of its decision, release a public record of its decision addressing how the findings of the EIS, including consideration of alternatives, were incorporated into the agency's decision-making process.

Generally an EA includes brief discussions of the following: the need for the proposal; alternatives (when there is an unresolved conflict concerning alternative uses of available resources); the environmental impacts of the proposed action and alternatives; and a list of agencies and persons consulted. An EIS should include discussions of the purpose of and need for the action; alternatives; the affected environment; the environmental consequences of the proposed action; lists of preparers, agencies, organizations, and persons to whom the statement is sent; an index; and an appendix. An EIS and a draft EIS are much more extensive than an EA. The draft EIS will include all the environmental alternatives considered by the decision-making agency and is a source of valuable information.

The role of a federal agency in the NEPA process depends on the agency's expertise and relationship to the proposed undertaking. The agency carrying out the federal action is responsible for complying with the requirements of NEPA. In some cases there may be more than one federal agency involved in an undertaking. In this situation, a lead agency is designated to supervise preparation of the EA. Federal agencies, with state, tribal, or local agencies, may act as joint lead agencies. A federal, state, tribal, or local agency having special expertise with respect to an environmental issue or jurisdiction by law may be a cooperating agency in the NEPA process. A cooperating agency has the responsibility to assist the lead agency by participating in the NEPA process at the earliest possible time and by participating in the scoping process, in developing information and preparing EAs as well as portions of the EIS concerning which it has special expertise, and in providing staff support to enhance the lead agency's interdisciplinary capabilities. Federal agencies may refer to the CEQ any interagency disagreements concerning proposed federal actions that might have unsatisfactory environmental effects. The CEQ's role when it accepts a referral is generally to develop findings and recommendations, consistent with the policy goals of Section 101 of NEPA. The referral process consists of certain steps and is carried out within a specified time frame.

The EPA, like other federal agencies, prepares and reviews NEPA documents. However, the EPA has a unique responsibility in the NEPA review process. Under Section 309 of the Clean Air Act, the EPA is required to review and publicly comment on the environmental impacts of major federal actions, including actions that are the subject of EISs. If the EPA determines that the action is environmentally unsatisfactory, it is required by Section 309 to refer the matter to the CEQ. Also, in accordance with a memorandum of agreement between the EPA and the CEQ, the EPA carries out the operational duties associated with the administrative aspects of the EIS filing process. The Office of Federal Activities has been designated the EPA's official recipient of all EISs prepared by federal agencies. The public has an important role in the NEPA process, particularly during scoping, in providing input on what issues should be addressed in an EIS and in commenting on the findings in an agency's NEPA documents. The public can participate in the NEPA process by attending NEPA-related hearings or public meetings and by submitting comments directly to the lead agency. The lead agency must take into consideration all comments on NEPA documents received from the public and other parties during the comment period.

The EPA is legally required to comply with the procedural requirements of NEPA for its research and development activities, facilities construction, wastewater treatment construction grants under Title II of the Clean Water Act (CWA), EPA-issued national pollutant discharge elimination system (NPDES) permits for new pollution sources, and certain projects funded through the EPA's annual appropriations acts. Section 511(c) of the CWA exempts certain EPA actions under the CWA from the requirements of NEPA. Section 7(c) of the Energy Supply and Environmental Coordination Act of 1974 exempts actions under the Clean Air Act from the requirements of NEPA. The EPA is also exempted from the procedural requirements of environmental laws, including NEPA, for CERCLA (Superfund) response actions. Courts have consistently recognized that the EPA procedures or environmental reviews under enabling legislation are functionally equivalent to the NEPA process, and thus are exempt from the procedural requirements in NEPA.

The EPA reviews EISs prepared by other federal agencies and makes those reviews public by publishing summaries of them in the Federal Register. The EPA has also developed a set of criteria for rating draft EISs. The rating system provides a basis upon which the EPA makes recommendations to the lead agency for improving the draft. The EPA's Federal Register–EIS Web site has the full texts of Federal Register documents that deal with all aspects of EISs being prepared by all federal agencies, and is published on a daily basis. The final published decision is called a record of decision. The final EIS is advisory only, and the agency decision maker is not required to choose the least environmentally damaging alternative.

Oil Pollution Act (August 18, 1990)

The Oil Pollution Act (OPA) of 1990, which amended Section 311 of the Clean Water Act, streamlined and strengthened the EPA's ability to prevent and respond to catastrophic oil spills. A trust fund financed by a tax on oil is available to clean up spills when the responsible party is unable or unwilling to do so. The OPA requires oil storage facilities and vessels to submit to the federal government plans detailing how they will respond to large discharges. The EPA has published regulations for aboveground storage facilities, and the Coast Guard has done so for oil tankers. The OPA also requires the development of area contingency plans to prepare and plan for oil spill response on a regional scale.

Pollution Prevention Act (November 5, 1990)

The Pollution Prevention Act (PPA) focuses industry, government, and public attention on reducing the amount of pollution through cost-effective changes in production, operation, and use of raw materials. Opportunities for source reduction are often not realized because of existing regulations, and because the industrial resources required for compliance focus on treatment and disposal. Source reduction is fundamentally different from and more desirable than waste management or pollution control. Pollution prevention also includes practices that increase efficiency in the use of energy, water, or other natural resources, and protect the resource base through conservation. These practices include recycling, source reduction, and sustainable agriculture. The PPA substantially increases the reporting power of the toxics release inventory, as discussed in Chapter 4.

The PPA established a new national policy for environmental protection: "that pollution should be prevented or reduced at the source whenever feasible." This deceptively simple statement heralds a profound change in how the EPA meets its obligations to protect human health and the environment. In the past the EPA emphasized "end of pipe" treatment of waste after it was produced. The PPA moves upstream in the manufacturing process to prevent the waste from being generated in the first place. By now the arguments for this change in emphasis are widely accepted as common sense. Improvements in treatment and disposal techniques have led to dramatic reductions in pollutant loadings, but they have proved costly and have barely kept pace with traditional problems, let alone managing new ones. Perhaps most disturbing is that some of the investments have simply shifted waste from one part of the environment to another.

For example, wastewater treatment plants built to satisfy federal water quality requirements are now among the biggest sources of toxic air emissions at industrial facilities and in some urban areas. With environmental spending by some estimates, approaching 2 percent of gross national product, it has become critical to ensure that our investment is efficient. Pollution prevention is the answer. Reducing waste at the source not only minimizes the cost of treatment and the transfer of pollution, but also can actually strengthen economic competitiveness through more efficient use of raw materials. For example, the 1992 study by the nonprofit organization INFORM, Inc., documented savings of $21.8 million from source reduction activities at fourteen chemical plants. Preventing pollution offers the exciting possibility of reconciling economic growth with environmental protection to enhance the quality of life for ourselves and our children.

Residential Lead-based Paint Hazard Reduction Act (October 28, 1992)

The EPA has been successful in reducing the levels of lead in outdoor air by implementing the national phaseout of lead in motor gasoline and by taking corrective actions at individual stationary sources. Lead still remains a public health concern and continues to threaten children exposed primarily from indoor sources such as paint and dust. There have been significant reductions in the blood lead levels in children since the late 1970s. The reductions can be attributed to removing lead from gasoline and banning lead-soldered food cans. In addition, lead was removed from house paint in 1978.

In 1992 Congress enacted the Residential Lead-Based Paint Hazard Reduction Act, known as Title X of Public Law 102-550, which provides for a comprehensive national approach to dealing with lead-based paint in the nation's homes. The law also calls on the EPA to provide basic information on lead to the American public. Under the 1018 Lead Disclosure Rule, potential home buyers and renters are assured of their right to know about lead hazards before buying or renting a home or apartment. In addition, the EPA is working with states and private industry to ensure that the public is informed of lead-based paint hazards and how to deal with them.

Resource Conservation and Recovery Act (October 21, 1976)

Waste management in the United States was fundamentally changed on October 21, 1976, when Congress passed the Resource Conservation and Recovery Act (RCRA). Hazardous waste disposal is one of the highest priority environmental problems confronting the United States. The Solid Waste Disposal Act is so comprehensive it is generally referred to simply as "RCRA." Congress established RCRA's goals, which are to

- Ensure that wastes are managed in a manner which protects human health and the environment;
- Reduce or eliminate, as expeditiously as possible, the amount of waste generated, including hazardous waste;
- Conserve energy and natural resources through waste recycling and recovery.

RCRA is a significant departure from the end-of-the-pipe pollution control statutes Congress had previously passed. It is intended to be a joint federal and state pollution prevention measure. The federal program provides basic requirements that give consistency to systems that states implement. States implement their own waste management programs so that they can design programs which fit their needs, resources, and economies. RCRA bans open dumping of wastes. It provides a comprehensive national program to encourage source reduction, recycling, and safe disposal of municipal wastes. RCRA mandates strict requirements for treatment, storage, and disposal of hazardous waste to minimize present and future risks. Estimates indicate that approximately 30–35 million tons of hazardous waste are dumped on the ground each year. Many of these substances can blind, cripple, or kill people. They can defoliate plant life, contaminate drinking water supplies, and enter the food chain.

RCRA gives the EPA the authority to control hazardous waste "from cradle to grave." This includes the generation, transportation, treatment, storage, and disposal of hazardous waste. RCRA also sets forth a framework for the management of nonhazardous wastes. The 1986 amendments to RCRA enable the EPA to address environmental problems that could result from underground tanks storing petroleum and other hazardous substances. RCRA focuses only on active and future facilities and does not address abandoned or historical sites. The Federal Hazardous and Solid Waste Amendments are 1984 amendments to RCRA that require phasing out land disposal of hazardous waste. Some of the other mandates of this strict law include increased enforcement authority for the EPA, more stringent hazardous-waste management standards, and a comprehensive underground storage tank program.

Safe Drinking Water Act (December 16, 1974)

The Safe Drinking Water Act (SDWA) was established to protect the quality of drinking water in the United States. It focuses on all waters actually or potentially designated for drinking use, whether from aboveground or underground sources. The act authorizes the EPA to establish standards of purity and requires all owners or operators of public water systems to comply with primary (health-related) standards. State governments, which assume this power from the EPA, also encourage attainment of secondary standards.

The SDWA provides that the states shall have primary enforcement authority with regard to drinking water standards and that the EPA will monitor activities of the states and public water supply systems to the extent necessary to determine if there is an adequate program to enforce the primary standards. Whenever the water delivered by a water supply system is not in compliance with the primary drinking water standards, the supplier of the water must notify its users, appropriate state agencies, and the EPA of the noncompliance and its possible health effects. This provision, coupled with a citizen lawsuit provision, helps make enforcement actions by regulatory agencies less necessary.

The SDWA was originally passed by Congress in 1974 to protect public health by regulating the nation's public drinking water supply. The law was amended in 1986 and 1996, and requires many actions to protect drinking water and its sources: rivers, lakes, reservoirs, springs, and groundwater wells. (SDWA does not regulate private wells that serve fewer than twenty-five individuals.) The SDWA authorizes the EPA to set national health-based standards for drinking water to protect against both naturally occurring and man-made contaminants. The EPA, states, and water systems then work together to ensure that these standards are met. The EPA uses the following steps to set enforceable, health-based drinking water standards.

1. Determine whether a contaminant should be regulated based on peer-reviewed science, including data on how often the contaminant occurs in the environment, how humans are exposed to it, and the health effects of exposure (particularly for vulnerable subpopulations).

2. Set a maximum contaminant level goal (MCLG), the level of a contaminant in drinking water below which there is no known or expected health risk (MCLGs allow for a margin of safety). These goals take into account the risks of exposure for certain sensitive populations, such as infants, the elderly, and persons with compromised immune systems. These goals are not enforceable levels because they do not take available technology into consideration, and therefore are sometimes set at levels that public water systems cannot meet.

3. Propose an enforceable standard in the form of a maximum contaminant level (MCL), the maximum amount of a contaminant allowed in water delivered to a user of any public water system, or a treatment technique (TT), a required procedure or level of technological performance set when there is no reliable method to measure a contaminant at very low levels. MCLs are set as close to MCLGs as feasible, considering available technology and cost. Examples of rules requiring TTs are the Surface Water Treatment Rule (requires disinfection and filtration) and the Lead and Copper Rule (requires optimized corrosion control). Water samples that contain lead or copper exceeding the action level trigger additional treatment or other requirements that a water system must follow. Required testing schedules are part of the enforceable standard.

After determining a proposed MCL or TT that is as close to the MCLG as possible, based on affordable technology, the EPA must complete an economic analysis to determine whether the benefits of that standard justify the costs. If they do not, the EPA may adjust the MCL for a particular class or group of systems to a level that maximizes health risk reduction benefits at a cost that is justified by the benefits. The EPA may not adjust the MCL if the benefits justify the costs to large systems and/or small systems that are unlikely to receive variances.

4. The EPA sets an enforceable MCL or TT. After considering comments on the proposed standard and other relevant information, it makes final an enforceable MCL or TT, including required testing and reporting schedules.

5. States are authorized to grant variances from standards for systems serving up to 3,300 people if the systems cannot afford to comply with a rule (through treatment, an alternative source of water, or other restructuring) and the systems install EPA-approved variance technology. States can grant variances to systems serving 3,301–10,000 people with EPA approval. SDWA does not allow small systems to have variances for microbial contaminants. Under certain circumstances, exemptions from standards may be granted to allow extra time to seek other compliance options or financial assistance. After the exemption period expires, the public water system must be in compliance. The terms of variances and exemptions must ensure no unreasonable risk to public health.

The 1996 amendments to SDWA require that every five years the EPA must establish a list of contaminants that are known or anticipated to occur in public water systems and may require future regulations under SDWA. The list is developed with significant input from the scientific community and other interested parties. After establishing this contaminant candidate list, the EPA identifies contaminants that are priorities for additional research and data gathering. It uses this information to determine whether a regulation is appropriate; this process is repeated for each list every five years. In order to support this decision-making, the EPA has established the National Contaminant Occurrence Database, which stores data on the occurrence of both regulated and unregulated contaminants. The EPA is also required to list and develop regulations for monitoring certain unregulated contaminants. This monitoring data will provide the basis for identifying contaminants that may be placed on future candidate lists and support the EPA administrator's decisions to regulate contaminants in the future.

Adverse health effects from contaminants in drinking water include acute effects that may immediately impact health and chronic effects that may occur if contaminants are ingested at unsafe levels over many years. Drinking water that meets the EPA's health-based standards is generally safe. People who are not healthy as a result of illness, age, or weakened immune systems are more likely to be at risk from certain contaminants in drinking water. Infants and very young children are also more susceptible to some contaminants. Individuals concerned about their particular situations should consult their health care providers. For a list of current drinking water standards, information on potential health effects of specific contaminants, and guidance for persons with severely compromised immune systems, see the EPA Web site at www.epa.gov/safewater/dwhealth.html or call the Safe Drinking Water Hotline at 1-800-426-4791.

Millions of Americans receive high quality drinking water every day from their public water systems (which may be publicly or privately owned). Nonetheless, drinking water safety cannot be taken for granted. There are a number of threats to drinking water: improperly disposed-of chemicals, animal wastes, pesticides, human wastes, wastes injected deep underground, and naturally occurring substances can all contaminate drinking water. Likewise, drinking water that is not properly treated or disinfected, or that travels through an improperly maintained distribution system, may also pose a health risk. Originally the SDWA focused primarily on treatment as the means of providing safe drinking water at the tap. The 1996 amendments greatly enhanced the existing law by recognizing source water protection, operator training, funding for water system improvements, and public information as important for safe drinking water. This approach ensures the quality of drinking water by protecting it from source to tap.

SDWA applies to every public water system in the United States. There are currently more than 160,000 public water systems providing water to almost all Americans at some time in their lives. The responsibility for making sure these systems provide safe drinking water is divided among the EPA, states, tribes, water systems, and the public. SDWA provides a framework in which these parties work together. The EPA sets national standards for drinking water based on sound science to protect against health risks, considering available technology and costs. These national primary drinking water regulations set enforceable maximum levels for particular contaminants in drinking water or require ways to treat water to remove contaminants. Each standard also includes requirements that water systems test for contaminants to make sure standards are achieved. In addition to setting these standards, the EPA provides guidance, assistance, and public information about drinking water; collects drinking water data; and oversees state drinking water programs.

The most direct regulation of water systems is conducted by state programs. States and recognized tribes can apply to the EPA for "primacy," the authority to implement the SDWA within their jurisdictions, if they can show that they will adopt standards at least as stringent as the EPA's and make sure water systems meet these standards. All states and territories except Wyoming and the District of Columbia have received primacy. While no Indian tribe has yet applied for and received primacy, four tribes currently receive "treatment as a state" status, and are eligible for primacy. States, or the EPA acting as a primacy agent, make sure water systems test for contaminants, review plans for water system improvements, conduct on-site inspections and sanitary surveys, provide training and technical assistance, and take action against water systems not meeting standards. To ensure that drinking water is safe, SDWA sets up multiple barriers against pollution, including source water protection, treatment, distribution system integrity, and public information.

Public water systems are responsible for ensuring that contaminants in tap water do not exceed the standards. Water systems treat the water, and must test it frequently for specified contaminants and report the results to states. If a water system is not meeting these standards, it is the system's responsibility to notify its customers. Many water suppliers now are also required to prepare annual reports for their customers. The public is responsible for helping local water suppliers to set priorities, make decisions on funding and system improvements, and establish programs to protect drinking water sources.

States and water suppliers must conduct assessments of water sources to see where they may be vulnerable to contamination. Water systems may voluntarily adopt programs to protect their watershed or wellhead, and states can use legal authorities from other laws to prevent pollution. The SDWA mandates that states have programs to certify water system operators and make sure that new water systems have the technical, financial, and managerial capacity to provide safe drinking water. It also sets a framework for the underground injection control (UIC) program to control the injection of wastes into groundwater. The EPA and states implement the UIC program, which sets standards for safe waste injection practices and bans certain types of injection altogether. All of these programs help prevent the contamination of drinking water.

The EPA provides grants to implement state drinking water programs, and to help each state set up a special fund to assist public water systems in financing the costs of improvements. Small water systems are given special consideration, since they may have a more difficult time paying for improvements because of their smaller customer base. Accordingly, the EPA and states provide them with extra assistance (including training and funding) as well as allowing, on a case-by-case basis, alternative water treatments that are less expensive but still protect public health.

National drinking water standards are legally enforceable, which means that both the EPA and states can take actions against water systems not meeting safety standards. The EPA and states may issue administrative orders, take legal actions, or fine utilities. They also work to increase the understanding of, and compliance with, standards of safe and clean water systems.

The SDWA recognizes that since everyone drinks water, everyone has the right to know what's in it and where it comes from. All water suppliers must notify consumers quickly when there is a serious problem with water quality. Water systems serving the same customers year-round must provide annual reports on the source and quality of their tap water. States and the EPA must prepare annual summary reports of water system compliance with drinking water safety standards and make these reports available to the public.

Superfund Amendments and Reauthorization Act (October 17, 1986)

The Superfund Amendments and Reauthorization Act (SARA) of 1986 reauthorized CERCLA to continue cleanup activities around the country. Several site-specific amendments, clarifications of definitions, and technical requirements were added to the legislation, including additional enforcement authorities. CERCLA, commonly known as the Superfund, was enacted by Congress on December 11, 1980. It created a tax on the chemical and petroleum industries and provided broad federal authority to respond directly to releases or threatened releases of hazardous substances that may endanger public health or the environment. Over five years, $1.6 billion was collected and placed in a trust fund for cleaning up abandoned or uncontrolled hazardous-waste sites. The Superfund is often of the source of great concern and confusion, and is discussed in greater depth in Chapter 4. CERCLA did the following:

- Established prohibitions and requirements concerning closed and abandoned hazardous-waste sites;
- Provided for liability of persons responsible for releases of hazardous waste at these sites;
- Established a trust fund to provide for cleanup when no responsible party could be identified.

The law authorizes two kinds of response actions:

1. Short-term removals where actions may be taken to address releases or threatened releases requiring prompt response;
2. Long-term remedial response actions that permanently and significantly reduce the dangers associated with releases or threats of releases of hazardous substances that are serious, but not immediately

life-threatening. These actions can be conducted only at sites listed on the EPA's National Priorities List (NPL).

CERCLA also enabled the revision of the National Contingency Plan (NCP), which provided the guidelines and procedures needed to respond to releases and threatened releases of hazardous substances, pollutants, or contaminants. The NCP also established the NPL.

SARA amended the Superfund and reflected the EPA's experience in administering that complex during its first six years. It also made several important changes and additions to the program:

- It stressed the importance of permanent remedies and innovative treatment technologies in cleaning up hazardous-waste sites;
- It required Superfund actions to consider the standards and requirements in other state and federal environmental laws and regulations;
- It provided new enforcement authorities and settlement tools;
- It increased state involvement in every phase of the Superfund program;
- It increased the focus on human health problems posed by hazardous-waste sites;
- It encouraged greater citizen participation in making decisions on how sites should be cleaned up;
- It increased the trust fund to $8.5 billion.

SARA also required the EPA to revise the hazard ranking system (HRS) to ensure that it accurately assesses the relative degree of risk to human health and the environment posed by uncontrolled hazardous-waste sites that may be placed on the NPL. The HRS is the principal mechanism the EPA uses to place uncontrolled waste sites on the NPL. It is a numerically based screening system that uses information from initial, limited investigations—the preliminary assessment and the site inspection—to assess the relative potential of sites to pose a threat to human health or the environment. The preliminary assessment and site inspection are used by the EPA to evaluate the potential for a release of hazardous substances from a site.

Emergency Planning and Community Right-to-Know Act (October 17, 1986)

The Emergency Planning and Community Right-to-Know Act (EPCRA) was passed by Congress as part of the SARA and is also referred to as Title III of SARA. The act created a program with two basic goals: to increase public knowledge of and access to information on the presence of toxic chemicals in communities, releases of toxic chemicals into the environment, and waste management activities involving toxic chemicals; and to encourage and support planning for responding to environmental emergencies.

To fulfill these goals, EPCRA created the toxics release inventory (TRI) and the hazardous chemical inventory. This information enables state and local governments and the communities to identify what needs to be done at the local level to better deal with pollution and chemical emergencies. This is an area of great concern in U.S. communities and has facilitated the expansion of public consciousness about the environment. It is discussed in detail in Chapter 4.

The public has the right to information about the amounts, location, and potential effects of hazardous chemicals present in their community. Under the hazardous chemical reporting provision of EPCRA, facilities storing hazardous chemicals in excess of specified amounts must report the chemical type and amount stored to local emergency planning committees (LEPCs) and state emergency response commissions (SERCs). The LEPC and SERC must make the hazardous chemical inventory and accidental release information submitted by local facilities available to the public. EPCRA also created the TRI program, discussed in depth later in this chapter. Under Section 313 of EPCRA, covered facilities are required to submit annual reports to the EPA and to the state on the amounts of toxic chemicals their facility has released into the environment, either routinely or accidentally. The EPA compiles these reports into the TRI database, which informs governments and the public about releases of toxic chemicals into the air, water, and land. The EPA encourages citizens, government entities, and facilities to use these data to establish a chemical profile of their community and to initiate and direct pollution prevention activities and risk reduction analyses. (Pollution prevention avoids the creation of waste, as opposed to pollution control, which concentrates on managing and disposing of waste.)

EPCRA's emergency planning provisions are designed to help the community prepare for and respond to emergencies involving hazardous substances. These functions are carried out by each SERC and by the LEPCs under each SERC's jurisdiction. On tribal lands, the equivalent of the SERC is the Tribal Emergency Response Commission (TERC). These organizations encourage prevention, preparedness, and quick response to chemical emergencies.

Emergency plans help facilities and local and state governments respond to accidents quickly and efficiently. Careful emergency planning can make the difference between disaster and slight inconvenience. These plans outline the procedures a facility and the community should follow in responding to a chemical release. The planning process has a greater impact than the plan itself, encouraging awareness, communication, and coordination of efforts.

EPCRA's emergency planning provisions require facilities to immediately notify SERCs and LEPCs of accidental chemical releases. This notification will activate emergency plans. EPCRA is implemented by two offices within the

EPA. The Chemical Emergency Preparedness and Prevention Office (CEPPO) carries out the emergency planning, emergency response notification, and inventory reporting provisions of the law. The Office of Environmental Information (OEI) implements the toxics release inventory (TRI) aspects.

CEPPO is part of the Office of Solid Waste and Emergency Response. Its mission is to help local and state authorities assemble the necessary information for chemical emergency prevention, preparedness, and response activities.

The division of OEI primarily associated with TRIs is the TRI Program Division, within the Office of Information Analysis and Access. This division oversees the collection of facility release reports and management of the TRI database. It also administers right-to-know components of the program, and provides a toll-free hotline for the public (1-800-424-9346).

A third EPA office is responsible for the enforcement of EPCRA. The Office of Enforcement and Compliance Assistance ensures compliance with U.S. environmental laws while promoting pollution prevention activities to the regulated community.

Toxic Substances Control Act (October 11, 1976)

The Toxic Substances Control Act (TSCA) of 1976 was enacted by Congress to give the EPA the ability to track the 75,000 industrial chemicals currently produced or imported into the United States. The EPA repeatedly screens these chemicals and can require reporting or testing of those that may pose an environmental or human health hazard. The EPA can ban the manufacture and import of chemicals that pose an unreasonable risk. Very few of these chemicals are actually tested for threats to public health. The TSCA is discussed in detail in Chapter 5.

The EPA has mechanisms in place to track the thousands of new chemicals with either unknown or dangerous characteristics that industry develops each year. It can then control these chemicals as necessary to protect human health and the environment. TSCA supplements other federal statutes, including the Clean Air Act and the toxic release inventory under EPCRA.

Following a fatal chemical-release accident in Bhopal, India, the Emergency Planning and Community Right-to-Know Act (EPCRA) provisions were enacted to promote emergency planning, to minimize the effects of an accident such as occurred at Bhopal, and to provide the public with information on releases of toxic chemicals in their communities.

INTERNATIONAL EPA ENGAGEMENT

In 1970 of the Office of International Affairs (OIA) was created within the office of the administrator. In 1989 its head was elevated to an assistant administrator to provide both focus and visibility to the EPA's growing international mandate. The history of OIA reflects the EPA's expanded commitment to international environmental programs in connection with the U.S.–Mexico border area, the North America Free Trade Agreement, trade and the environment, and the effects of persistent organic pollutants. It has evolved from a coordinating and advisory office to one that manages international operations. OIA, with the rest of the EPA, works with other countries on international environmental issues such as climate change, protection of marine environments, lead phaseout, and international transport of hazardous waste. Among other functions, OIA

- Manages the EPA's programs with Mexico, Canada, and other countries;
- Provides leadership, analysis, and coordination of the EPA's positions on such major international issues as marine pollution and the environment and trade, and coordinates with international policy bodies, including the North American Commission for Environmental Cooperation and the World Trade Organization;
- Develops and implements international technical assistance;
- Designs innovative programs for global environmental challenges such as transboundary pollution and marine pollution;
- Provides essential support services, including management of the EPA's international travel and visitors programs.

OIA is directed by an assistant administrator nominated by the president and confirmed by the Senate. The assistant administrator is assisted by a deputy assistant administrator and five office directors. The five OIA offices are

1. The Office of International Environmental Policy, which promotes effective international environmental and trade policies and agreements that reduce significant risk to human health and ecosystems from climate change, toxic chemicals, and other hazards of international concern;
2. The Office of Technology Cooperation and Assistance, which develops and implements a broad range of international technical assistance, training, information management, and capacity-building programs in priority countries and regions, including programs for climate-changing toxic chemicals;
3. The Office of Western Hemisphere and Bilateral Affairs, which provides environmental and country-specific expertise in support of the EPA's bilateral capacity-building, technical assistance, and policy programs for priority countries and regions;

4. The Office of Management Operations, which manages the international travel and visitors programs as well as OIA's grants, contracts, interagency cooperative agreements, budget and finances, human resources, information systems, and administrative operations;

5. The Office of Children's Health Protection, which participates in the World Health Organization's Task Force for the Protection of Children's Environmental Health, is involved in the task force's current and proposed activities, including developing a manual on children's environmental health, preparing plans of action for countries, providing advice on specific threats, preparing and disseminating training materials, and promoting research on emerging issues.

As the EPA faces the challenges of sustainability, ecosystem approaches, and cumulative impacts, it will expand its international presence.

This chapter has described the EPA's organizational structure, workforce, offices, and statutory structure. The laws Congress requires the EPA to implement are the basis for its authority and structure. The newness of the EPA and the laws that it implements, creates dynamic policy challenges and opportunities. States, Congress, courts, and communities have grappled with environmental issues. Congress has passed laws for the EPA to implement. As the EPA has exerted its newfound authority, it has often been challenged in the courts. As U.S. society has become more engaged in environmental issues, so has the EPA. Because many of the laws implemented by the EPA allow citizens to sue in court, many of the policy parameters are confronted and refined in courts of law. We examine some notable cases and conflict resolution approaches in the next chapter.

$$\star\ \text{\textbf{2}}\ \star$$

Notable Cases Affecting the EPA

The role of the courts in shaping the EPA has been powerful. Since the EPA is a new agency with strong, encompassing regulatory authority, it is the function of the courts to determine its policy parameters. The judicial resolution of some of the conflicts faced by the EPA have shed some light on these foundational policy choices. The power of the EPA to require consideration of environmental impacts, to protect endangered species, and to protect land, air, and water from pollution is directly related to its mission. The small sample of cases that follows, represents areas of foundational policy choices reinforced and shaped by the courts. Most areas of new environmental policy are challenged in the courts. Many of these cases are dismissed, summarily judged, not reported, or settled. It is not always easy to get into court. Several procedures must be followed and requirements must first be met.

JUDICIAL STANDING REQUIREMENTS

The role of the courts is dependent on access to them. Generally, a party must have "standing" to access the courts, which usually requires an injury in fact within the zone of interests protected by law. The court generally needs to be able to develop some type of remedy for the alleged wrong. The constitutional basis for judicial authority comes from Article III of the U.S. Constitution. State courts and federal courts both have jurisdictional limitations. Issues of standing, in addition to the time, energy, and cost of a lawsuit, often limit access to the courts.

The legal requirements of judicial standing are fourfold:

1. The challenged action will cause plaintiff some actual or threatened injury in fact;

2. The injury is fairly traceable to the challenged action;

3. The injury is redressable by judicial action;

4. The injury is to an interest arguably within the scope of interests protected by the statute alleged to be violated or by the Constitution.

The first three are requirements of Article III of the U.S. Constitution. The fourth is jurisprudential (judge-made) and can be changed by Congress. Congressional power is the origin of the power to bring citizen suits. Organizations have standing to sue if the members themselves would have standing to sue and the interests the organization seeks to protect are germane to its purposes.

The U.S. Supreme Court has considered the standing issue in at least seven environmental cases. The first case was *Sierra Club v. Morton*. The Sierra Club challenged a plan by Disney Enterprises to build a $35 million resort in the Mineral King Valley in the Sierra Nevada Mountains.

The Sierra Club, a nonprofit environmental advocacy group, challenged the project on the grounds that approval of the plan by the U.S. Forest Service had violated federal environmental laws. The Sierra Club did not base its claim on the harm to its individual members but invoked its status as an environmental advocacy group. In 1972 the Supreme Court held this was not enough proof of injury in fact, and denied the Sierra Club standing to sue. In 1990, in *Lujan v. National Wildlife Federation*, the Supreme Court further restricted standing. This case involved a Bureau of Land Management (BLM) review of past executive orders protecting many public lands from resource development. In 1976 Congress required the BLM to review withdrawal of public lands from resource protection in eleven western states and decide whether to open these lands up to mining, logging, and ranching. The National Wildlife Federation alleged that the BLM would definitely open these lands up to mining. The Supreme Court held the federation lacked standing because it had suffered no injury in fact. Even though members had affidavits claiming that they lived in the vicinity, the Court concluded that actual presence was required. Further, the Court stated that even if members were actually present in the vicinity, plaintiffs could challenge only those

Courts have a strong role in deciding EPA policy and practices. (Jupiter Images)

aspects of the program which personally affected them and their actual usage of the land. Last, in 2000, in *Friends of the Earth v. Laidlaw Environmental Services Inc.*, the Supreme Court found standing in a Clean Water Act case where the plaintiff lived in the area but did not use the river because of the pollution. Friends of the Earth filed a citizen suit under the Clean Water Act against Laidlaw Environmental Services, a company that had violated the limits of its mercury permit many times.

Land uses with large environmental impacts, such as golf courses, can often face court battles. (Photograph by Brent Merrill)

Standing ultimately determines who can use the power of the courts. Causes of action for violations of environmental laws are relatively new. As the number and size of environmental conflicts and concerns have increased, the dispute resolution function of the EPA has expanded. In addition, because plaintiffs are required to seek satisfaction through administrative agencies before going to court—called exhaustion of administrative remedies—more cases are being handled in EPA's Dispute Resolution Office. (See discussion in Chapter 5.)

Once a case is in court, many judges seek to settle a lawsuit rather than consume judicial resources. The judicial process can take years if appeals are made. Even if a plaintiff wins a substantial judgment, it may be reduced on appeal. The tremendous difficulties of judicial access make citizen suit provisions of many environmental statutes seem privileged.

REVIEW OF ADMINISTRATIVE DECISIONS

Courts are sought as decision-making forums because they are so powerful. This is especially true in reviews of administrative agency decisions. Courts can say what the law is and can review any administrative decision on both substantive and procedural grounds. Courts decide who can sue the EPA. This in itself can control many of the policy decisions facing the EPA. Courts can decide the point in the Agency decision-making process at which to intervene. This can have a dramatic effect on EPA functions. Courts also decide on the scale of issues before them. They like narrow issues and generally try to avoid political ones. How much a court examines an agency decision is also important. Many courts will defer to agency expertise on complicated issues. For example, the EPA often presents complicated issues of science. Thus the degree of judicial scrutiny of a particular decision, from strict to very little, is very important to the EPA mission. The role of science in the courts generally, and the role of science in defending EPA decision-making in particular, is given great judicial deference. Therefore it is notable when a court case proceeds all the way to a reported decision.

As a relatively new federal agency facing many large-scale environmental issues, problems, and controversies, the EPA is constantly developing new policies. It is often in court and its organizational structure is set up for it to be in court. Unlike most other federal agencies, many of the laws that EPA administers have provisions for citizen lawsuits. These allow private citizens to sue polluters and other environmental offenders on behalf of the EPA. Many of these private citizens are represented by the legal defense funds of such environmental organizations as the Sierra Club, the Natural Resources Defense Council, and the Environmental Defense Fund.

CITIZEN SUITS

In 1970 Congress gave citizens the authority to file federal lawsuits as "private attorneys general" to enforce the Clean Air Act, intending to fill the vast void left by inadequate enforcement by federal and state regulators and to ensure compliance and deter illegal activity. Now, more than a dozen federal environmental statutes, numerous state laws, and many foreign laws allow for such "environmental citizen suits." In 2002 alone, environmental and conservation groups, states, landowners, developers, and companies collectively provided advance notice of intent to bring federal environmental citizen suits nearly 200 times. Citizen suit provisions allow plaintiffs to have a different requirement for "standing," as discussed earlier in this chapter.

Citizen suits provide a vehicle by which individuals or environmental organizations can contribute to the protection of the environment by suing polluters, typically industrial or government operations that discharge illegal quantities of obnoxious substances into water, emit excess air pollutants, or violate federal and state laws pertaining to the handling of solid and hazardous waste. Generally, before such a lawsuit can be initiated, a notice of intent to file the lawsuit must be provided to the facility believed to be violating federal environmental requirements, to the state in which the facility is located, and to the EPA. Those wishing to bring a citizen suit must do so on their own or through an attorney they hire. Anyone desiring to pursue a citizen suit should refer to the specific citizen suit provisions contained in the particular law believed to be violated and the regulations issued to implement that law.

The use of citizen suits in environmental litigation, especially as applied to private party litigation, presents a number of challenges and considerations that must be carefully weighed. Citizen suit provisions within environmental statutes typically state that "any person" may bring an action against "any person" for the violation of a permit, standard, regulation, condition requirement, prohibition, or order, or for any condition that may present an imminent and substantial danger to the environment. These suits may name any governmental agency, including the EPA, as defendant for its failure to perform a nondiscretionary duty. Citizen suits that seek redress of technical permit violations without attendant damage claims are typically the province of public interest groups and governmental authorities. Except in unusual circumstances such violations are not profitably pursued by private parties. A significant litigation advantage of the citizen suit provisions is the availability of a federal forum, which can be especially weighty in locales where a jury may favor the defendant because it is a local employer or where a jury will be drawn from a historically conservative pool.

The primary consideration in citizen suits is counsel's understanding and analysis of the facts. Counsel must be satisfied that the technical merits of the case can be clearly established. Citizen suit provisions usually require official notice from the prospective plaintiff to the defendant of the latter's failure to comply with permit requirements or other environmental standards. Once the notice has been sent, the filing of suit must be delayed for a statutorily pre-scribed time period. Notification has been held to be mandatory, and failure to comply is a bar to a citizen suit. Generally, plaintiffs prefer to be as vague as possible in most matters, so as to allow maximum flexibility. Within the context of the notice requirement, plaintiffs are required to be specific con-cerning the conduct that has led to the violation of statutory or regulatory provisions or permit conditions. Defendants have argued that by failing to note precisely how a violation occurred, the notice is insufficient to allow claims based on those violations to proceed in the court. A notice should include enough information to permit its recipient to identify the specific standard, limitation, or order that has allegedly been violated, the activity alleged to be in violation, the person or persons responsible for the alleged violation, the location of the alleged violation, the date or dates of such violation, and the full name and address of the person giving notice. The purpose of the notice requirement is to give the violator the opportunity to bring itself into compliance and thus render the citizen suit unnecessary. The notice must be sent to the violator, the state in which the violation occurred, and the administrator of the EPA by registered mail, return receipt requested. The plaintiff should state in the complaint that notice has been given and attach proof that it was. Assuming that all the above standing and pleading requirements are met, and that the plaintiff has exhausted administrative remedies at the EPA, the case quickly enters the court system.

Citizen suits are one method of harnessing the energy and commitment of citizens to achieve public environmental protection goals because they au-thorize citizens to enforce environmental laws and regulations. Since 1790 U.S. citizens have been able, in limited cases, to sue to enforce rights granted by statute to the population as a whole. These citizen suits have been used to enforce federal regulations in areas ranging from antitrust to consumer protection. Many state legislatures view these suits as a cost-saving measure because they theoretically reduce demand on the state attorney general's office to prosecute environmental violations and crimes.

Although the concept of a citizen suit is not new, the statutes permitting citizen enforcement of environmental laws and regulations are unique. In most other areas where citizen suits are permitted, a personal economic interest, such as an interest in correcting unfair competition or preventing fraud, must coincide with the claimed public rights. In citizen suits brought under environmental protection statutes, however, there is no such personal economic stake in the outcome. The environmental statutes truly provide citizens with the authority to represent the interests of the public. Environmental citizen suits in their strongest form might even be characterized as permitting citizens to sue on behalf of the environment itself. Few other nations have extended such rights to their citizens.

The Clean Air Act (CAA), enacted in 1970, was the first federal environmental statute of the modern era with a citizen suit provision. The provision's underlying structure is the basis for citizen suit clauses in almost every other major piece of federal environmental legislation. Today citizens can bring suit against private parties and governments for violations of certain sections of statutes regulating air, water, toxic waste, endangered species, mining, noise, the outer Continental Shelf, and more. Under many statutes the remedies available to the citizen are equivalent to those granted to the federal agency charged with administering the statute.

The basic citizen suit provision permits any "person" (an individual, organization, or corporation) to sue any other "person" (including the United States) who is violating the requirements of the given act. As discussed above, before filing suit, a citizen must notify state and federal agencies as well as the alleged violator that a lawsuit is pending. This notice provision is important, because the threat of a citizen suit often prompts the violator to halt its violations, or at least to negotiate with the potential plaintiff. As long as the violation continues and the state or federal government is not pursuing a "diligent enforcement" court action against the alleged violator, a lawsuit may be filed. Once the suit is filed, the EPA has no power to dismiss it and may affect the outcome only by intervening in the case.

If the citizen prevails, the court may order the defendant to stop the violating activities. In certain circumstances the court costs and attorney fees associated with bringing the action may be awarded to the plaintiff. Some statutes allow the plaintiff to ask the court to impose civil penalties upon the violator that are payable to the U.S. Treasury. As some of the cases below illustrate, citizen suits can force the EPA to enact environmental policy.

JUDICIAL INTERVENTION

The EPA is involved with a great deal of law in its interpretation of statutes, promulgation of rules and regulations, running of the Agency, regulatory enforcement, and lawsuit defense. It is an agency designed to handle political and legal demands. The following cases are a sample of the many cases with EPA involvement.

EPA Authority

The EPA's authority was challenged almost as soon as it was formed. It is an umbrella agency that has power over other federal and state agencies in unprecedented ways. It administers nine major federal environmental statutes: the Clean Air Act; the Clean Water Act; the Comprehensive Environmental Response, Compensation, and Liability Act (Superfund); the Marine Protection, Research, and Sanctuaries Act; the Resource Conservation and Recovery Act; the Federal Insecticide, Fungicide, and Rodenticide Act; the Toxic Substances Control Act; the Noise Control Act; and the Safe Drinking Water Act. The EPA helps administer four other environmental statutes. It reports directly to the president, and has its own lawyers and its own information. The EPA is required to follow the Administrative Procedure Act, the National Environmental Policy Act (NEPA), and the U.S. Constitution. It can operate only within the scope of legislatively delegated authority.

The EPA does not have a general charter. The executive order creating it moved existing executive branch functions from other federal agencies with a specific mandate or policy statement. Thus the EPA is required to implement the environmental statutes without a comprehensive strategy, but statute by statute. Each statute has specific goals in regard to environmental quality. The mission of the EPA is to develop research, rules, and regulations to meet these goals within the limits of each particular statute. It is also the overall mission of the EPA to enforce rules and regulations, as well as to seek methods of achieving compliance with them. Because it has such a strong and unique basis for authority, the EPA's authority is often challenged in court. The challenges come from citizen suits, industry, state governments, and other federal agencies. The first challenge to EPA's authority came from the site where the EPA first exerted it—other federal agencies. The question arose as to how much authority the EPA had to compel another federal agency to comply with NEPA.

NEPA expands the substantive authority of every federal agency to include protection of environmental values. Federal agencies have been forced by courts using NEPA and EIS requirements to consider environmental impacts when any federal action is considered. The federal government owns over 25 percent of the nation's land. NEPA has an extensive reach over these lands; it applies to the preparation of resource management plans and forest plans; and to the leasing of land for grazing, oil and gas exploration and development, and timber harvesting in national forests. NEPA also extends to federal regulatory activities, such as permitting and licensing regulations. NEPA also reaches federal infrastructure by generally covering the constructions of roads, airports, dams, bridges, sewage treatment plants, and some pipelines.

In 1978 the EPA promulgated official NEPA regulations after President Jimmy Carter required it to do so by Executive Order 11991. From 1970 until then NEPA had been a vaguely worded statute relied on by the courts to create a type of "common law." The 1978 regulations mainly codified this common law, and clarified and underscored judicially interpreted responsibilities of federal agencies. EPA-issued rules and regulations have the power of law and are often subjected to judicial review in the courts. The EPA also issues guidance, technical manuals, and fact sheets that do not have the force of law. NEPA is still generally enforced in the courts. The federal agencies decide for themselves how to comply with it. If they fail to fully comply with NEPA, then aggrieved private parties, nonprofit groups, or others can proceed to federal court after exhausting administrative remedies. Once a NEPA case is in court, judges have great power. They determine fact and applicable laws, and also must consider whether the government has met its obligation to consider the environmental impact of its actions. This is often done by examining the record.

Contents of Environmental Impact Statement

Once the authority of the EPA is firmly established, the next foundational policy choice made in the courts involves the contents of the environmental impact statement (EIS).

The EPA's responsibility for rating and filing federal EISs is derived from Section 309 of the Clean Air Act. Federal EISs are filed with the EPA, which is responsible for publishing a notice of availability in the Federal Register. The EPA reviews and provides written comments on the EISs of other federal agencies. It rates draft EISs (explained below) on the basis of environmental effects of the proposed action and on the adequacy of the document. The EPA also specifies the criteria used for its ratings, procedures for follow-up actions for the lead agency, and procedures for the distribution of comments. Besides giving low ratings, the EPA can deny a permit or recommend that another agency under its purview not issue a permit.

The basic process of a NEPA-based environmental impact assessment begins with an environmental assessment of a proposed action or activity with major federal and/or state involvement. The purpose of this assessment is to determine if there could be significant impacts on the environment. If there are none, then a finding of no significant impact (FONSI) is issued. If there are some significant impacts, a notice of intent (NOI) is issued. After the NOI, a scoping process takes place and the lead agency examines significant impacts and major issues, and gives notice to interested parties. Stakeholders and interested parties may propose draft alternatives, which are weighed against the "no action" alternative in terms of environmental impacts. Different alternatives may mitigate environmental impacts. The draft EIS is issued for public comment, and is generally available in the Federal Register. This can be a lengthy document with complicated scientific data. The Agency decision maker, then selects the alternative, and publishes the final EIS in the Federal Register. This is called the record of decision (ROD). The ROD is generally required before a court will review a case involving an administrative agency. The decision maker is not required to choose the least environmentally harmful alternative and also considers the economic impact of the proposed action. The public generally does not receive notice until a FONSI or NOI is issued.

NEPA does not require an agency to assess every impact or effect of its proposed action, but only the impacts or effects on the physical environment. The terms "environmental effect" and "environmental impact" in NEPA require an agency to evaluate the environmental impact of its proposals under certain circumstances, and includes a requirement of a reasonably close causal relationship between a change in the physical environment and the effect at issue. Although cumulative environmental impacts are what require a comprehensive impact statement, determination of the extent and effect of such factors, particularly identification of the geographic area within which they may occur, is a task assigned to the special competencies of the appropriate agencies. (See discussion in Chapter 7.)

The *Calvert Cliffs Coordinating Committee, Inc. v. U.S. Atomic Energy Commission* case was the first thorough judicial interpretation of NEPA. The case involved the Atomic Energy Commission (AEC) and those who protested AEC rules that limited its duty to consider environmental impacts in the licensing of nuclear power plants. The AEC asserted that its rules complied with NEPA. When a Maryland-based public interest group, the Calvert Cliffs Coordinating Committee, tried to stop the licensing of a nuclear power plant on Chesapeake Bay, it claimed that environmental issues were not properly considered when the AEC promulgated these rules. In requiring the AEC to comply with NEPA, the court held that agencies must consider environmental impacts to the fullest extent possible. It laid the foundation for all current EPA authority under NEPA. The most important part of this decision was its distinction between the substantive and procedural aspects of NEPA, between the amounts of discretion afforded an agency in carrying out these two obligations, and between the different standards of judicial review of each type of agency action. Judge Skelly Wright held that agency duties under NEPA are judicially enforceable. He also held that Section 102 of NEPA imposed inflexible procedural duties on all agencies to fully consider all environmental impacts. Agencies do not have the discretion to avoid responsibilities under NEPA as enforced by the EPA. This court holding solidified the foundation of authority for the EPA, and was followed in later cases.

While *Calvert Cliffs Coordinating Committee, Inc. v. U.S. Atomic Energy Commission* is a notable case because of the mandate of a process of environmental impact assessment, the decision did not mandate that the agency decision maker choose the least environmentally harmful alternative. In *Strycker's*

Environmental issues are very political in the federal courts. (Jupiter Images)

Bay Neighborhood Council, Inc. v. Karlen, the Supreme Court held that NEPA does not impose judicially enforceable substantive requirements. This is an important parameter of authority for the EPA.

Congress envisioned that federal agencies would use NEPA as a planning tool to integrate environmental, social, and economic concerns directly into projects and programs. However, the first twenty years of NEPA application have focused on decisions related to site-specific construction, development, or resource extraction projects. NEPA is virtually ignored in formulating specific policies and often is skirted in developing programs, usually because agencies believe that NEPA cannot be applied within the time available or without a detailed proposal. Instead, agencies tend to examine project-level environmental effects in microscopic detail. The reluctance to apply NEPA analysis to programs and policies reflects the concern that microscopic detail will be expected if NEPA is applied even when such depth of analysis is not possible that early in the proposal development stage. Recent analysis of NEPA in courts indicates that the political affiliation of the judge has a large impact on his acceptance of NEPA requirements.

Hazardous Waste

Solid waste can be deemed "hazardous" if it is toxic, ignitable, corrosive, or reactive or if it appears on the EPA list of hazardous wastes. The EPA established four classifications of hazardous waste: acutely hazardous chemical products, nonacutely hazardous chemical products, and two lists of wastes that exhibit characteristics of hazard (one of the two lists includes wastes that have all of the following characteristics, and the other includes wastes that have only one of the characteristics)—toxicity, ignitability, corrosivity, and reactivity.

Our society creates large amounts of waste, some of it hazardous. Many generators of hazardous waste seek to avoid that label by mixing such waste with other material. To stop this practice, the EPA adopted the "mixture" rule and the "derived from" rule. A mixture of a hazardous waste with other solid waste is also hazardous waste. The "derived from" rule states that any solid waste generated from the treatment, storage, or disposal of a hazardous waste is also hazardous waste. This expanded definition of hazardous waste brought judicial challenges to the EPA.

It is now recognized that the potential for a landfill to pollute the environment is likely to remain for many decades after the disposal of refuse has ceased. To surrender a site license, a landfill operator must be able to demonstrate to the EPA that the condition of the land is such that it is unlikely to pollute the environment or harm human health.

One of the main pathways by which a landfill might pollute the environment is the contamination of the surrounding land and groundwater by leachate leaking through the base and/or sides. To prevent such leakage, the EPA often stipulates that the leachate level within a landfill must be maintained at or below a certain depth. Modern sites and new landfill cells are constructed with effective provisions for leachate control that may include geotextile liners and basal drainage layers. Traditional methods of leachate control at older sites generally rely upon retrofitted vertical wells, but their impact is often limited.

In *Chemical Waste Management, Inc. v. EPA*, the EPA's treatment standards for leachate were challenged. Leachate is created when rainwater percolates through wastes stored in a landfill. Leachate derived from hazardous waste is also hazardous waste under EPA rules. The court upheld the EPA rule. Ultimately, hazardous waste is better treated when it is well contained. Allowing hazardous material to leach into the ecosystem creates greater environmental damage and higher cleanup costs.

EPA regulation of hazardous materials and wastes will continue to be contested in courts. There is little social agreement as to what to do with these wastes. Some can be made less hazardous, some become less hazardous with time, and some may become more hazardous with time. Public knowledge about these materials has increased as communities along transit routes for hazardous materials and waste become involved with this issue. Communities located near places where hazardous materials and wastes accumulate have begun to voice concern about public health threats.

Solid Waste

Solid waste is defined by the Resource Conservation and Recovery Act (RCRA) as any garbage, refuse, sludge, or "other discarded material, including solid, liquid, semisolid, or contained gaseous material"—excluding solid or dissolved materials in domestic sewage, irrigation return flows, or industrial discharges from point sources. The legal exclusions leave large quantities of hazardous materials unregulated by RCRA.

An important policy parameter for the EPA is how recycled materials are covered under RCRA. In *American Mining Congress v. EPA*, the court held that RCRA did not cover spent industrial materials that are recycled and reused in an ongoing manufacturing or industrial process.

The court reasoned that these materials have not yet become part of the waste disposal problem but are destined for beneficial reuse or recycling in a

Massive urban infrastructure has large a impact on the environment. It is very difficult for courts to handle modern, complicated environmental problems. (Photograph © by Frank Miller)

continuous process by the generating industry. Later decisions modified this decision in favor of the EPA by holding that only materials meant for immediate reuse in another phase of the industry's ongoing production process are not discarded. Industrial materials that are part of waste treatment systems are discarded and covered by RCRA.

Air Quality

The first federal regulation of air pollution was based on the Air Pollution Act of 1955, which was designed to support research on air pollution under the former Department of Health, Education and Welfare (HEW). The actual regulation of air pollution remained with the states. The Clean Air Act of 1963 gave HEW limited jurisdiction over interstate air pollution issues. The Air Quality Act of 1967 authorized the first full federal regulatory air pollution policy. However, these federal programs remained in the states' control. The Clean Air Act of 1970 came into law at the same time the EPA was formed. It gave the EPA the authority to develop and administer plans for achieving compliance with ambient air quality standards in states without adequate plans. In 1977 this act was amended to allow for the prevention of significant deterioration of clean air areas, and for more stringent standards for non-attainment areas that remain out of compliance with ambient air quality standards. The 1990 amendments substantially changed how air pollution is regulated. Compliance with ambient air quality standards is still a primary focus, but the increase in the number of regulated facilities puts an additional focus on new and existing point sources for air pollution. Air pollution control is an area the EPA considers central to it mission. It invests significant resources in air programs and receives challenges to its authority to regulate air pollution.

In one of the early court cases the Natural Resources Defense Council (NRDC) sued the EPA to include lead standards in issuing air permits (*NRDC v. Train*). The NRDC sued under a citizen suit provision in the 1970 Clean Air Act to require the EPA to place lead on the list of air pollutants. The EPA was resisting doing so because it stated that listing a pollutant was a discretionary, not a mandatory, act. The court held that once specific statutory conditions were met, it was mandatory that the EPA list lead as an air pollutant. Judicial construction of the underlying statutes of the EPA can both mandate that the EPA actually develop new policy and constrain its authority.

Smoke emits chemicals into the air. (Jupiter Images)

The focus of *Alaska v. EPA* centers on the Teck Cominco Alaska, Inc. (Cominco) zinc concentrate mine that operates in northwestern Alaska. The mine is the region's largest private employer and is considered to be a "major emitting facility" under the Clean Air Act. Pursuant to Section 160, enacted as part of 1977 amendments to the act, emissions from any source shall not interfere with a state plan to prevent the significant deterioration of air quality. (These amendments are known as the Prevention of Significant Deterioration of Air Quality requirements, or PSD.) The purposes of the PSD requirements include "to protect public health and welfare from any actual or potential adverse effect which in the Administrator's judgment may reasonably be anticipate[d] to occur from air pollution," to preserve air quality in national parks and wilderness areas, to ensure that economic growth is balanced with the preservation of existing clean air resources, and "to assume that any decision to permit increased air pollution . . . is made only after careful evaluation of all the consequences of such a decision."

Section 165 of the act sets out preconstruction requirements for major emitting facilities and states that no such facility may be constructed or operated unless a PSD permit prescribing emission limitations has been issued for the facility. Furthermore, any major emitting facility must have the best available control technology (BACT), defined as "an emission limitation based on the maximum degree of reduction of each pollutant subject to regulation . . . emitted from or which results from any major emitting facility, which the permitting authority . . . taking into account energy, environmental, and economic impacts and other costs, determines is achievable for such facility." Under the CAA, a limited class of sources must obtain advance EPA approval for the BACT prescribed in the permit. (See discussion of BACTs in Chapter 3.)

Northwestern Alaska, the location of the Cominco mine, is classified as an attainment area for nitrogen dioxide. The PSD requirements therefore apply to emissions of that pollutant in the region. In 1988, the Alaska Department of Environmental Conservation (ADEC) issued Cominco a permit to operate the mine under the act, authorizing Comnico to use five diesel generators. It issued a second permit to Cominco in 1994 that allowed the addition of a sixth generator. In 1996 Cominco initiated a state-funded project to expand zinc production by 40 percent, which would increase nitrogen oxide emissions by more than forty tons per year. Cominco applied to the ADEC for a PSD permit to allow increased electricity generation. On March 3, 1999, the ADEC preliminarily proposed as BACT a technology known as selective catalytic reduction (SCR), which reduces nitrogen oxide emissions by 90 percent. In response, Cominco added a seventh generator and proposed, as BACT, an alternative technology known as Low NOx, which reduces nitrogen oxides by only 30 percent.

On May 4, 1999, the ADEC issued a first draft PSD permit for the construction of the Cominco addition, naming Low NOx as BACT. While the ADEC initially focused on SCR as BACT, finding it to be "technologically, environmentally, and economically feasible," the ADEC ultimately endorsed the alternative suggested by Cominco. During the public comment period, the ADEC heard concerns from the U.S. National Park Service (NPS), which objected to the use of Low NOx as BACT for the facility. The EPA then wrote to the ADEC on July 29, 1999, questioning its approval of Low NOx as BACT, since the ADEC had already found SCR to be economically and technologically feasible. After receiving EPA comments, the ADEC issued a second draft permit on September 1, 1999, again finding Low NOx to be BACT. However, in this second draft permit the ADEC abandoned its assessment that SCR was "technically and economically feasible" and instead found that SCR imposed "a disproportionate cost" on the mine. The EPA protested the second permit—particularly the ADEC's justification of rejecting SCR for reasons of cost-effectiveness, which the EPA stated were "not supported by the record and were clearly erroneous." The EPA suggested a revision of the permit to include analysis of the specific economic impacts of using SCR on the Cominco mine, which Cominco declined, partially on the basis of confidentiality concerns.

The ADEC issued its final PSD permit and technical analysis on December 10, 1999, approving Low NOx as BACT for the mine and neglecting to include the economic analysis suggested by the EPA. The ADEC justified its decision by stating that SCR would have an "adverse effect on the mine's 'unique and continuing impact on the economic diversity of the region' and on the venture's 'world competitiveness,'" without specifying how disclosing the financial aspects of SCR would harm this competitiveness. That same day the EPA invoked its authority under Sections 113(a)(5) and 167 of the act, prohibiting the ADEC from issuing a PSD permit to Cominco unless the ADEC explained why SCR wasn't BACT for the facility. On February 8, 2000, the EPA issued a second order pursuant to Sections 113(a)(5) and 167, prohibiting Cominco from beginning construction or modification activities at the mine. A third order issued on March 7, 2000, and superseding the February 8 order "generally prohibited Cominco from acting on the ADEC's December 10 permit but allowed limited summer construction."

On July 30, 2002, the Ninth Circuit Court of Appeals held that the EPA had authority to issue the stop orders and had properly exercised its discretion in doing so. The Ninth Circuit further stated that the EPA had properly exercised its discretion "because (1) Cominco failed to 'demonstrate that SCR was economically infeasible,' and (2) the 'ADEC failed to provide a reasoned justification for its elimination of SCR as a control option.'" The Supreme Court granted certiorari to resolve the scope of the EPA's authority under Sections 113(a)(5) and 167.

In its analysis of the EPA's review authority under Sections 113(a)(5) and 167, the Supreme Court noted that "EPA reads the Act's definition of BACT, together with the CAA's explicit listing of BACT as a 'preconstruction re-quirement,' to mandate not simply a BACT designation, but a determination of BACT faithful to the statute's definition." The Court then held that the EPA "rationally construed the Act's text and that the EPA's construction warrants our respect and approbation." In its reasoning the EPA argued that absent national guidelines governing prevention of significant deterioration of air quality, two things may happen: (1) a state with clean air resources will lose industry to more permissive states, and (2) industry will play states against one another, moving to the state that adopts the most permissive pollution controls. This is known as a race to the bottom, meaning that states with the least environmental control will attract more industry. The Court noted that the CAA statutory construction advanced by the EPA reflected many inter-pretive guides issued by the EPA, and stated that "we 'normally accord par-ticular deference to an agency interpretation of "longstanding" duration.'"

The ADEC argued that the statutory definition of BACT "unambiguously assigns 'the permitting authority' alone determination of the control tech-nology qualifying as 'best available.'" In response, the Court acknowledged that while state agencies would be in the best position to make case-by-case BACT determinations, this does not allow them to make "unreasonable determinations." The Court further stated that the "EPA claims no prerogative to designate the correct BACT; the Agency asserts only the authority to guard against unreasonable designations." To be sure, the EPA acknowledged in its brief "the need to accord appropriate deference" to states' designations and disclaimed any intention to "second guess" state decisions. The Court concluded that "EPA's limited but vital role in enforcing BACT is consistent with a scheme that 'places primary responsibilities and authority with the states, backed by the Federal Government.'"

The controversy between the best and the most economical pollution control technology is muddied when there are permit violations. Some argue that the permits themselves allow for too much in terms of emissions and too little in terms of reporting, monitoring, and enforcement. Industry argues that the basis for permits is flawed because many regulations and practices assume full-out constant production in their emission calculation. As concern rises over cumulative emissions, this false assumption of full-out production is again problematical. (See discussion of cumulative impacts in Chapter 7.) The controversy between the best and the most economical pollution control technology policies is ongoing at state and federal levels of environmental policy.

The relationship between states and the EPA under the CAA is what some call "cooperative federalism." Under the CAA the federal air quality standards are established, but the states have some discretion in determining how those federal standards are met. It is unclear, under the Clean Air Act, how much flexibility the states have to determine what BACT is for a particular facility, assuming that more than one determination complies with federal standards. In determining BACT, the EPA recommends using a "top-down methodology." This methodology requires the applicant for a permit to first examine the most stringent alternative for BACT, which is then established as BACT unless the applicant demonstrates, and the permitting authority in its informed judgment agrees, that technical considerations, or energy, environmental, or economic impacts, justify a conclusion that the most stringent technology is not "achievable" in that case. If the most stringent technology is eliminated in this fashion, then the next most stringent alternative is considered, and so on.

Environmental litigation is very complex, and there are many cases. Often environmental jurisprudence is uneven. This particular case aided in the environmental policy-making context because it helped the EPA respond quickly to legal concerns around controversial legal issues that often surround complex environmental problems regarding air quality and federal–state intergovernmental relations.

INTERGOVERNMENTAL COMMUNICATIONS AND CONFLICT RESOLUTION

In some ways Congress always intervenes in the EPA when it passes laws for the EPA to implement and when it passes the budget for the EPA in any given year. In some years the EPA is caught in the cross fire of intense political controversy that is played out in the congressional budgetary process. In both cases, intergovernmental communication is used to help resolve conflict. Intergovernmental communication from the EPA also helps states meet their regulatory obligations.

The Office of Congressional and Intergovernmental Relations (OCIR) is EPA's principal point of contact for Congress, states, and local governments. It serves as liaison with these constituencies on the Agency's major programs (e.g., air/pesticides, water, and waste) as well as on intergovernmental issues. (See discussion in Chapter 5.)

WHEN THE EPA IS FURLOUGHED

When an employee is furloughed, he or she does not work and does not get paid. Generally, only nonessential employees are furloughed. State and local governments furlough employees occasionally. When EPA is caught in a budget crisis thanks to Congress, it faces the possibility of a shutdown—closing for normal business and furloughing employees. Only Congress may authorize appropriations, and if has not done so, agencies have no money, cannot operate, and therefore close down.

At the beginning of the fiscal year, usually October, a continuing resolution (CR) is passed. It may be extended for months if short-term CRs are passed as stopgaps, since the end of each CR can result in a shutdown if there is neither a new CR nor an annual appropriations act. Congress moves slowly, as it is supposed to do. Although there may be action to pass one or more CRs or appropriations bills, there may not be enough time to do so before the end of September. In addition to the intractability of the issues directly related to the budget, such as spending and tax cuts, there are distractions that may lead to hearings and legislation. Any or all of these factors can lead to a failure to enact a CR by September 30, and that failure will lead to an automatic shutdown. Thus there can be goodwill, no overt intention to close the government, and much movement to avoid a shutdown, but it may still come about.

What happens when employees are furloughed? Generally, nonessential employees do not work and do not get paid—a severe disruption in their cash flow. And the ability of the EPA to meet its missions and ongoing contractual, project-based obligations is impaired. The EPA is often the federal agency most impacted by furloughs. One three-week government furlough gave journalists the opportunity to examine a barely functioning EPA and some resulting environmental impacts.

Government employees are not the only ones idled during a shutdown. Private sector companies and state agencies with federal government contracts, funding, and other links struggle with the ripple effects from the shutdown.

On July 14, 2000, Sen. Pete Domenici (R-N.M.) released a General Accounting Office (GAO) report, *Radiation Standards: Scientific Basis Inconclusive, and EPA and NRC Disagreement Continues*, which concluded that without congressional intervention, the EPA and the Nuclear Regulatory Commission (NRC) "may not resolve their differences" over radiation protection standards that would govern the proposed Yucca Mountain repository for used nuclear fuel. The following is a statement by Joe F. Colvin, the Nuclear Energy Institute's president and chief executive officer, commenting on the GAO findings.

> It is clear from the General Accounting Office report that the Nuclear Regulatory Commission and the EPA have been and continue to be at loggerheads over the development of radiation protection standards for the proposed repository at Yucca Mountain. This regulatory stalemate is not serving the public interest, and the industry renews its call for Congress to resolve it by establishing a science-based radiation protection standard consistent with international levels.

(See discussion of Yucca Mountain in Chapter 3.)

The nuclear energy industry was heartened that the GAO had identified and articulated this problem so clearly. The absence of a science-based radiation standard would only bring further troubles for a nuclear waste repository program already years behind schedule. The GAO report provided valuable insights on the challenges that can be confronted safely, cost-effectively, and in a timely manner only by resolution of this problem.

Furloughs affected other important, ongoing EPA missions. Work at Superfund sites was at a standstill because Congress and President Clinton could not agree on a budget. Congress had proposed slashing the EPA's budget by 25 percent, but the president vetoed the measure. Meanwhile, during the impasse, funding for the agency was stopped and the Superfund program basically was shut down. Just hours before another shutdown, Congress and the president agreed to a CR, now known as the Balanced Budget Down Payment Act, to keep all government agencies open until at least March 15, 2001.

The EPA was funded through March 15 at the levels contained in the EPA appropriations bill vetoed by the president, approximately $5.71 billion. This was an increase over the other CRs. Even at this level, EPA Administrator Carol Browner said that layoffs and furloughs would be necessary. From the closing of national parks to the halting of Superfund cleanups, impacts of the furlough were reported in newspapers across the country.

> Environmental clean-up workers will cease their efforts at 18 sites across the Southeast until the budget dilemma is resolved.... Work will continue at five other sites, including the LCP Chemicals site in Brunswick, one of the most polluted sites in the nation, until the public health threat diminishes.
>
> Air, water and soil inspections that help ensure compliance with environmental regulations also have been halted. States that depend

on the EPA for money to help pay for tests and inspections are feeling the pinch. (*Atlanta Constitution*)

In addition to the furloughed EPA staff, hundreds of workers for 10 prime contractors who receive tens of millions of dollars a year for regional EPA projects have been idled, many without pay....

The cleanup of New Bedford Harbor, where PCB levels are thousands of times higher than legal safety levels....

The construction of an alternative water supply for 240 residents who live within a mile of the Davis Liquid hazardous waste site in Smithfield, R.I.... (*Boston Globe*)

Every day, 240 calls to the Drinking Water Contamination Hot Line now go unanswered. The EPA's efforts to prevent cryptosporidium from contaminating city water supplies—something that proved a deadly threat in the City of Milwaukee—have been badly delayed. EPA enforcement efforts have completely stopped. (*Washington Post*, quoting President Clinton)

In some cases, the closing of national parks has begun to spill over into the tourist industry. About 100 fishing guides in the Florida Keys have been hit hard by the shutdown of the Everglades National Park, at the tip of the state.

"I personally have lost about $4,000 in bookings," said Hank Brown, an Islamorada, Fla., fishing guide. (*Los Angeles Times*)

A private company that laid off 280,000 workers would save big bucks. But the furlough of federal employees actually raised the budget deficit—by as much as $2 billion. Some of the hidden costs of the stalemate....

Extra costs (security and equipment maintenance) associated with closing down and reopening projects such as Superfund cleanups run by private companies. Interest payments by states borrowing money to continue services like federal unemployment. Cost: roughly $100 million. (*Newsweek*)

Workers were sent home this month from hundreds of Superfund sites because the EPA ran out of money to pay contractors and agency employees to supervise them. Administration officials said that cleanup operations were unlikely to resume soon at more than half of the idled sites because of the budget impasse. (*New York Times*)

The EPA is temporarily abandoning 16 of 19 hazardous waste sites in Colorado....

The Colorado sites to be abandoned include the Summitville mine near Del Norte in southwestern Colorado where EPA engineers have been trying to stop the acid drainage that has been flowing into nearby streams and killing fish.

The EPA said work may continue at some of the 16 sites targeted for closure because cleanups are being funded by private industry. (*Rocky Mountain News*)

EPA contractors across the country received "stop work" orders yesterday, the first wave of several that could jeopardize the jobs of up to 10,000 Superfund workers.

In Houston, Peter Arrowsmith, president of NUS, a Superfund contractor, said his company had started laying off employees and would soon have 125 employees, 15 percent of his workforce, sent home without pay.

Michael Tilchin, director of Superfund programs at CH2M Hill Ltd., said "hundreds of employees" would be furloughed. His company is helping clean up an old manufacturing plant in Hellertown, Pa., where hazardous wastes have contaminated the groundwater. (*Washington Post*)

Although CRs prevented furloughs, the EPA as a whole was not given its full funding. As a result, some of the work supposed to be done by EPA contractors was left undone, because the contractors could not be paid. The delay in finalizing a federal budget had tremendous impact throughout the country, and Superfund cleanups were not immune. The EPA was particularly hard hit by the lack of funding, and most EPA employees were furloughed at least once during the budget negotiations. Even when the furlough ended, EPA employees faced uncertain employment prospects.

Clearly, the EPA has encountered controversy in both the courts and Congress. Many of these controversies are intrinsic to environmental policy-making and are representative of conflicts about the environment that occur in society. Our social attitudes and opinions about the environment change as our knowledge base expands to make more information accessible to more people. As human populations increase, as wastes increase and accumulate, so does environmental conflict. Many of these conflicts have a court case and congressional action associated with them. In most of the controversies and issues in the next chapter, the EPA role was a developing one, balancing dynamic priorities of public health, environmental protection, and the economy.

☆ **3** ☆

Controversies and Issues

The EPA's role in the important environmental issues of the time set the tone for the development of new environmental laws and policies. Many of these issues sparked controversies that continue today. Many of these controversies involve intractable environmental problems of hazardous wastes, nuclear energy, and the distribution of the costs and benefits of environmental protection. With accumulating industrial emissions and increased knowledge among both the scientific community and the public at large, these environmental controversies will dominate environmental policy-making for years to come. They involve activities that have the potential for large-scale environmental impact and often threaten the public health, safety, and welfare. They also often involve new policies that require changes in human behavior, and they have shaped the EPA.

LOVE CANAL AND THE HOOKER CHEMICAL COMPANY

One resounding controversy for the EPA and everyone involved was the issue of danger from contamination in communities. In many of these instances the contamination began long before the EPA existed. Citizens demand full access to information in these instances. When EPA Administrator Anne Gorsuch balked at turning over EPA Superfund files under a congressionally issued subpoena (see discussion in Chapter 7), Congress responded with subpoenas and contempt citations to EPA employee Rita Lavelle. Assaults on the Superfund were so impassioned that Lavelle, director of that program, was jailed for lying to Congress about corruption in her Agency division. Distrust and emotions run high in these controversies, which can occur in any community. The scientific basis for determining threats to public health is given strict scrutiny by the affected community.

The tension between public health protection activities (or their lack) and contaminated communities continues to be a persistent problem for the EPA and related agencies. As wastes continue to accumulate at existing waste sites, their effects on the environment and communities tend to be more pernicious. A historic controversy in this area that set the stage for many subsequent EPA cleanup programs and policies was Love Canal.

Love Canal began in 1892 when William T. Love tried to dig a canal to connect the upper and lower parts of the Niagara River in New York State. The canal was never completed, and in 1920–1953 it was used as a dump for hazardous wastes. From 1947 to 1952, Hooker Chemicals and Plastic took over the fifteen-acre site, and by 1952 had buried thousands of tons of toxic chemicals there. In 1953 the canal area was filled in with dirt. In 1953 Hooker sold the canal for $1 to the Board of Education of the city of Niagara Falls, New York, and wrote into the deed a disclaimer of responsibility for future damages due to the presence of buried chemicals. The board subsequently built a school there and sold off the balance of the land, on which residences were built. Many schools in the United States are built on sites where the land is inexpensive but near residential areas. These sites are often old dumps or landfills where the ground has not settled enough for industrial and commercial development.

On October 3, 1976, the *Niagara Gazette* reported that materials from a chemical landfill between 97th and 99th Streets had been seeping into basements of homes in the area. There were also reports of illness and injuries to human, animal and plant life. Some of the women in the blue-collar community reported miscarriages. The first response of the state environmental agency to this latter concern was that these women had had abortions and wanted to keep that quiet because of religious repercussions. There was great concern and division in the community. Some wanted action taken to solve the health issues. Others wanted to keep reports of the problem quiet so they could sell their homes. If news of the contamination got out, they would not be able to sell their property. This is fact happened, trapping the residents in their homes. Many in the community were employed by industrial manufacturers in the area and feared that if they spoke out, they would lose their jobs. Love Canal was assisted by a community organizer named Lois Gibbs, a self-described housewife who founded the Citizens Clearinghouse for Hazardous Chemicals.

On November 2, 1976, the *Niagara Gazette* reported that chemical analyses of residues near the old Love Canal dump site indicated the presence of fifteen organic chemicals, including three toxic chlorinated hydrocarbons. On November 4, the *Gazette* reported that toxic chemicals seeping into cellars of homes were being carried through city storm sewers and improperly discharged into the Niagara River. As with many other environmental issues, it was not until the health threats of toxicity began to reach the broader community and permeate the ecosystem that they got the attention of local government and the state.

State and EPA officials began to investigate the dumping of the hazardous wastes in the old canal bed. In September 1977, Representative John J. La-Falce (D-Tonawanda) and the EPA began looking into problems at Love Canal. Love Canal was declared a health hazard. In May 1978, the EPA concluded from air sampling in basements of homes at Love Canal that toxic vapors were a serious health threat. The state health department released a plan for medical studies of residents. In June 1978, New York State continued studies and did some house-to-house air, water, and soil sampling and collecting of blood samples for analysis. The following month, Governor Hugh Carey signed legislation granting additional emergency powers to the state health commissioner to deal with Love Canal problems and appropriated $500,000 for long-range health studies.

On August 2, 1978, acting under these new powers, the state health commissioner declared a state of emergency at the Love Canal and ordered the closing of the 99th Street School and evacuation of pregnant women and children under age two. Five days later, President Jimmy Carter approved emergency financial aid for the area so New York State could start buying the homes of the 236 families eventually relocated, at a cost of $10 million. Over this period of time most residents who could afford to move out did so. Some of the residents died. On November 10, 1978, 200 tons of dioxin, a lethal chemical, was reported to be buried in the canal. Residents' fears heightened. On November 22, over 200 chemical compounds were identified as being buried in the canal. On December 8, reports of findings of dioxin and other chemicals and the state's refusal to relocate another fifty-four families on the outskirts of the contaminated area brought vehement protests from the residents. They considered themselves trapped in a prison of toxicity by an unresponsive government. One protest led to the arrest of seven Love Canal home owners. The charges were later dropped.

On January 23, 1979, Dr. Beverly Paigen, a cancer researcher at Roswell Park Memorial Institute in Buffalo, urged evacuation of more families in light if her study revealing a high rate of birth defects and miscarriages among Love Canal families. On February 8, New York State announced it would pay temporary relocation costs for about thirty families with either pregnant women or children under age two who lived between 97th and 103rd Streets after documenting existence of birth deformities and pregnancy-related problems outside the first ring of the Love Canal.

On March 21, Congress began hearings into Love Canal problems. At these hearings residents and others argued that the state underestimated the scope of health problems and failed to respond in an efficient and timely manner. On April 11, Representative Albert Gore (D-Tenn.) charged that Love Canal could have been avoided if Hooker Chemicals and Plastic had paid attention to danger signals. He cited an internal Hooker memorandum, dated June 18, 1958, which described three or four children burned by materials at the Love Canal.

On April 14, 1979, reports circulated that dioxin levels at Love Canal were 100 times higher than previously stated, and that this deadly contaminant was also found at Bloody Run Creek, near Niagara University. Ten days later the EPA approved $4 million for remedial work at the Love Canal. The city of Niagara Falls received $1 million in Federal Disaster Assistance Administration funds to help pay debts incurred at the Love Canal.

On May 4, 1979, New York State found traces of highly toxic chemicals around the 93rd Street School and ordered more tests to determine the extent of contamination. The Carter administration revealed plans for a $1.63 billion Superfund for hazardous-waste cleanups across the country. On July 12, the EPA announced creation of a special task force to aid in identification and cleanup of toxic-waste sites, including thirty-six on the Niagara Frontier (western New York State). On August 30, the city of Niagara Falls Board of Education closed the 93rd Street School pending the outcome of further studies of chemical contaminants. Students were transferred to other schools throughout the city. On September 4, over 200 Love Canal residents took up residence at Stella Niagara Education Park after being moved out of hotels and motels in the area. They had left the canal area after complaining of noxious odors from the remedial work. Reports from the workers doing the remedial work are hard to find.

On September 26, the first Love Canal lawsuits, naming Hooker and three public agencies, were filed. On October 3, the New York State Supreme Court rejected a $2.5 billion lawsuit filed on behalf of 900 Love Canal residents. Because the standard for causality in science could neither prove nor disprove that the toxic chemicals caused any of the damage, the residents did not meet the legal burden of proof. On October 14, a U.S. House of Representatives subcommittee recommended relocation of another 140 families after reviewing research by Dr. Paigen that showed chemicals from the Love Canal were migrating. By October 31, over 800 lawsuits totaling $11 billion had been filed naming Hooker, the city, the county, and the board of education as defendants. In November, a federal report indicated that the odds of Love Canal residents contracting cancer were as high as 1 in 10.

On November 6, remedial work on the canal was considered complete, and the state said that 110 temporarily relocated families could return home. On December 20, the Justice Department initiated a $124 million lawsuit against Hooker in connection with chemicals buried at four sites in the city of Niagara Falls. Three months later the EPA announced it had found four chemicals suspected of causing cancer in air samplings at Love Canal. When chemicals are buried and then dug up, they often volatilize into the air. Chemicals also can move through the ground into water and into the air. This affects surrounding, often wealthier, communities that have political and economic power. In April 1980, New York State filed a $635 million lawsuit against Occidental Petroleum and two of its subsidiaries—Hooker Chemical and Hooker Chemicals and Plastics, claiming they were responsible for the Love Canal disaster.

On May 17, 1980, the EPA announced that chromosome damage had been found in eleven of thirty-six Love Canal residents who had been tested. This damage was beyond the worst fears of residents, whose claims of cancer and other health concerns had been dismissed by scientists and government officials for years. Scientists still cannot prove that the chemicals caused this damage because the sample size of thirty-six is too small to support statistical analysis. They can argue that simple correlation of two events does imply causality. (See the discussion in Chapter 4.) On May 19, the remaining residents demanded immediate evacuation of another 710 families. Well organized by now through the heroic efforts of Lois Gibbs, angry residents detained two EPA officials for about six hours at the Love Canal Homeowners' Association offices. They urged the declaration of a national emergency. On May 21, President Carter declared Love Canal a national emergency, paving the way for relocation of the 710 families.

In summary, the seventy-acre Love Canal site encompassed a hazardous-waste landfill where chemical waste products were disposed of from 1942 to 1952. In 1953 the original sixteen-acre hazardous-waste landfill was covered, and a school and more than 200 homes were built nearby. Residents reported odors and residues as early as the 1960s, and studies in the 1970s showed that numerous toxic chemicals were migrating from the landfill and contaminating nearby waterways. In 1978, Governor Hugh Carey ordered the purchase of homes surrounding the canal. In 1978 and 1980, President Jimmy Carter declared two separate environmental emergencies and, as a result, approximately 950 families were evacuated from a ten-block area surrounding the canal. The emergency declaration area included neighborhoods adjacent to the site covering 350 acres. In 1980, the Comprehensive Environmental Response, Compensation, and Liability Act (CERCA), also known as Superfund, which addresses abandoned hazardous waste sites, was passed largely due to the problems at Love Canal. (See discussion in Chapters 1 and 4.) Between 1977 and 1980, New York State and the federal government spent about $45 million at the site: $30 million for relocation of residents and health testing, $11 million for environmental studies, and $4 million for a demonstration grant (under the Resource Conservation and Recovery Act) to build a leachate collection and treatment system.

Once there was little doubt that Love Canal needed to be cleaned up, the question remained of how to clean it up. A study completed in 1982 recommended construction of a slurry wall and cap to contain groundwater in the site as the long-term solution. In July 1982, the EPA signed a $6,995,000 cooperative agreement with New York for construction of a slurry wall and cap, four feasibility studies, and a long-term monitoring study to determine seasonal variations in groundwater levels and leaching. In September 1982, $892,800 was added to demolish the school, install a synthetic membrane over a temporary clay cap, and erect a fence.

In 1985, New York State Department of Environmental Conservation installed the forty-acre cap and improved the leachate collection and treatment system, including the construction of a new leachate treatment facility. In May 1985, in a record of decision (ROD), the EPA implemented a remedy for the sewers and the creeks that included

- Hydraulically cleaning the sewers;
- Removal and disposal of the contaminated sediments;
- Inspecting the sewers for defects that could allow contaminants to migrate;
- Limiting access to, and dredging and hydraulically cleaning, the African American Creek culverts;
- Removing and storing contaminated sediments from Black and Bergholtz creeks.

The state cleaned 62,000 linear feet of storm and sanitary sewers in 1986, and an additional 6,000 feet were cleaned in 1987. In 1989, approximately 14,000 cubic yards of sediments were dredged from Black and Bergholtz creeks. Clean riprap was placed in the creek beds, and the banks were replanted with grass. Prior to final disposal, the sewer and creek sediments and other wastes (33,500 cubic yards) were stored at Occidental Chemical Company's (OCC) Niagara Falls RCRA-permitted facilities. In October 1987 the EPA selected a means to destroy and dispose of the dioxin-contaminated sediments from the sewers and creeks:

- Construction of an on-site facility to dewater and contain the sediments;
- Construction of a separate facility to treat the dewatered contaminants through high temperature thermal destruction;
- Thermal treatment of the residuals stored at the site from the leachate treatment facility and other associated Love Canal waste materials;
- On-site disposal of any nonhazardous residuals from the thermal treatment or incineration process.

In 1989, OCC, the United States, and New York State entered into a partial consent decree to address some of the required remedial actions: the processing, bagging, and storage of the creek sediments, as well as other Love Canal wastes including the sewer sediments. Also in 1989, the EPA published an explanation of significant differences (ESD), which provided for these sediments and other remedial wastes to be thermally treated at OCC's facilities rather than at the site. In November 1996, a second ESD addressed a further modification of the 1987 ROD to include off-site, EPA-approved thermal treatment and/or land disposal of the stored Love Canal waste materials. In December 1998, a third ESD announced a 10 ppb treatability variance for dioxin in the stored Love Canal waste materials. The sewer and creek sediments and other waste materials were subsequently shipped off-site for final disposal, and this historic remedial action was deemed complete in March 2000.

OCC is responsible for the continued operation and maintenance of the leachate treatment facility and groundwater monitoring. The site is monitored on a continual basis through numerous wells installed throughout the area. The yearly monitoring results show that the site containment and leachate collection and treatment facility are operating as designed. Numerous cleanup activities, including landfill containment, leachate collection and treatment, and the removal and ultimate disposal of the contaminated sewer and creek sediments and other wastes, have been completed at the site. These completed actions have eliminated the significant contamination exposure pathways at the site. The site was deemed "construction complete" on September 29, 1999.

On September 30, 2004 the EPA finalized its decision to remove the Love Canal site from the Superfund National Priorities List (NPL). (See NPL discussion in Chapter 1.) All cleanup work at the site was completed, and follow-up monitoring conducted since 1989 (and continuing today) confirmed that the cleanup goals had been reached. Through a series of plans, the EPA and the New York State Department of Environmental Conservation contained and secured the wastes already disposed of in the canal so that they were no longer leaking into surrounding soils and groundwater, and also revitalized properties in the neighborhood surrounding the canal.

Today the area known as Love Canal is considered a revitalized community. Forty acres are covered by a synthetic liner and clay cap, and surrounded by a barrier drainage system. Contamination from the site is also controlled by a leachate collection and treatment facility. Neighborhoods to the west and north of the canal have been revitalized; more than 200 formerly boarded-up homes have been renovated and sold to new owners, and 10 new apartment buildings have been constructed. The area east of the canal has been sold for light industrial and commercial redevelopment. The Love Canal site will continue to be monitored and will remain eligible for cleanup work in the event that a change in site conditions should warrant such an action.

This time line reveals extensive resident, science, state, local, judicial, and EPA involvement in the Love Canal controversy. The controversy illustrates some of the public health issues that confront the EPA, especially with regard to cleanup and relocation. Love Canal reshaped how the EPA approached cleanup, public involvement, and cities. Where the waste from a cleanup goes is the basis of the controversy in Warren County, North Carolina, discussed later in this chapter.

The current governmental response to these controversies is more focused agency involvement. In these instances one particular non-EPA agency is often involved, and many of its recommendations are directed to the EPA.

The mission of the Agency for Toxic Substances and Disease Registry (ATSDR), an agency of the Department of Health and Human Services, is to serve the public by using the best science, taking responsive public health actions, and providing trustworthy health information to prevent harmful exposures and diseases related to toxic substances. ATSDR is directed by congressional mandate to perform specific functions concerning the effect on public health of hazardous substances in the environment. These functions include public health assessments of waste sites, health consultations concerning specific hazardous substances, health surveillance and registries, response to emergencies resulting from releases of hazardous substances, applied research in support of public health assessments, information development and dissemination, and education and training concerning hazardous substances.

As the lead public health agency responsible for implementing the health-related provisions of Superfund, ATSDR is charged with assessing health hazards at specific hazardous-waste sites, helping to prevent or reduce exposure and the illnesses that result, and increasing knowledge and understanding of the health effects that may result from exposure to hazardous substances. Its mission, as revised in the strategic plan for 2002–2007, is to serve the public by using the best science, taking responsive public health actions, and providing trusted health information to prevent harmful exposures and diseases related to toxic substances. The mission is supported by the following Agency goals:

Goal 1. Evaluate human health risks from toxic sites and take action in a timely and responsive manner.

Goal 2. Ascertain the relationship between exposure to toxic substances and disease.

Goal 3. Develop and provide reliable, understandable information for affected communities, tribes, and stakeholders.

Goal 4. Build and enhance effective partnerships.

Goal 5. Foster a quality work environment at ATSDR.

To achieve the mission and goals, ATSDR works with the Centers for Disease Control and Prevention (CDC) and a host of partner organizations. Together, these organizations work to serve the following:

- Communities—those directly affected by exposure to toxic substances in the environment;
- Health care providers—those who diagnose and treat exposure in communities;
- Tribal, state, and local governments—entities working to build the capacity to address environmental public health issues;

- Industry—chemical manufacturers and other businesses impacted by the release of toxic substances;
- National organizations—groups that take part in the environmental public health mission;
- The EPA and other federal agencies—other groups that seek to treat and prevent toxic exposure;
- Congress—as representatives of communities.

In order for ATSDR to carry out its statutory responsibilities, it has a joint office of the director with the National Center for Environmental Health (NCEH). The Office of the Director contains eight functional units. In addition, there are three offices and five program-specific divisions to support and implement program areas:

1. Public health assessments
2. Toxicological profiles
3. Emergency response
4. Exposure and disease registries
5. Health effects research
6. Health education
7. Literature inventory/dissemination
8. Special initiatives in environmental health.

Since 1986, ATSDR has been required by law to conduct a public health assessment at each of the sites on the EPA national priorities list. (See discussion in Chapter 1.) The aim of these evaluations is to find out if people are being exposed to hazardous substances and, if so, whether that exposure is harmful and should be stopped or reduced. If appropriate, ATSDR also conducts public health assessments when petitioned by concerned individuals. Public health assessments are carried out by environmental and health scientists from ATSDR and from the states with which it has cooperative agreements.

The first concern is exposure. ATSDR scientists review environmental data to see how much contamination is at a site, where it is, and how people might come into contact with it. Generally ATSDR does not collect its own environmental sampling data but reviews information provided by the EPA, other government agencies, businesses, and the public. When there is not enough environmental information available, the report will indicate what further sampling data are needed. If the review of the environmental data shows that people have or could come into contact with hazardous substances, ATSDR scientists evaluate whether there will be any harmful effects from these exposures. The report focuses on the health impact on the community as a whole, rather than on individual risks. Again, ATSDR generally uses existing scientific information, which can include the results of medical, toxicological, and epidemiological studies and the data collected in disease registries.

The science of environmental health is still developing, and sometimes scientific information on the health effects of certain substances is not available. When this is the case, the report will suggest what further research studies are needed. The report presents conclusions about the level of health threat posed by a site and recommends ways to stop or reduce exposure in its public health action plan. ATSDR is primarily an advisory agency, so usually these reports identify what actions are appropriate to be undertaken by the EPA, other responsible parties, or the research or education division of ATSDR. If there is an urgent health threat, ATSDR can issue a public health advisory warning people of the danger. It can also authorize health education or pilot studies of health effects, full-scale epidemiological studies, disease registries, surveillance studies, or research on specific hazardous substances. Had this process been in place during the Love Canal crisis, much time and money would have been saved. It is also possible that the health of the residents of Love Canal would have been protected, and that the years of emotional confrontation at all levels of government could have been avoided.

The health assessment is an interactive process. ATSDR solicits and evaluates information from numerous city, state, and federal agencies; the

Former industrial sites often present expensive and controversial cleanup problems. (Photograph © by Frank Miller)

companies responsible for cleaning up the site; and the community. It then shares its conclusions with them. Agencies are asked to respond to an early version of the report to make sure that the data they have provided are accurate and current. When informed of ATSDR's conclusions and recommendations, the agencies may begin to act on them before the final release of the report. ATSDR also needs to learn what people in the area know about the site and what concerns they may have about its impact on their health. Consequently, throughout the evaluation process ATSDR gathers information and comments from the people who live or work near a site, including residents of the area, civic leaders, health professionals, and community groups. To ensure that the report responds to the community's health concerns, an early version is distributed to the public for comments. All the comments are responded to in the final version of the report.

The environmental controversies around Love Canal shaped all who were involved with it. This controversy resulted in the eventual cleanup of the site and revitalization of the community, stronger cleanup legislation, and the development of another agency's public health focus on environmental issues. Our urban landscapes are littered with thousands of contaminated sites that need to be cleaned up.

The toxic chemicals in these sites follow the paths of nature in water, air, and land to other communities. The EPA needed to develop a way to handle these environmental issues, and Love Canal gave them a lesson. Cleanup of contaminated communities remains controversial, but there is a better awareness of how to engage this particular environmental problem.

EXXON VALDEZ: OIL SPILLED

Oil spills have the power to mobilize a nation. The oil spill off the California coast at San Clemente helped to create an image that showed why the EPA was needed. There are many spills of all sorts at ports and drilling operations around the world. Oil has devastating effects on wildlife. If it is not contained, it will reach all parts of the tidal ecosystem and may bioaccumulate up the food chain to affect people. In 1989 more than 11 million gallons of crude oil spilled from the *Exxon Valdez* into Prince William Sound off Alaska. This spill

The *Exxon Valdez* oil spill may have irreparably damaged ecosystems. Joe Bridgman, information officer for the Alaska Department of Environmental Conservation, discovered subsurface oil from a seemingly clean beach at Meares Point, Perry Island, Prince William Sound. (Photo courtesy of the Exxon Valdez Oil Spill Trustee Council)

83

contributed to the deaths of more than 250,000 seabirds, 2,800 sea otters, 300 harbor seals, 250 bald eagles, and nearly two dozen whales, and continues to affect wildlife populations today. Indigenous people who subsist on wildlife are suffering health problems as these chemical bioaccumulate up the food chain.

On March 24, 1989, shortly after midnight, the oil tanker *Exxon Valdez* struck Bligh Reef in Prince William Sound, Alaska, spilling more than 11 million gallons of crude oil. The spill was the largest in U.S. history and tested the abilities of local, national, and industrial organizations to prepare for, and respond to, a disaster of such magnitude. Many factors complicated the cleanup efforts following the spill. The size of the spill and its remote location, accessible only by helicopter and boat, made government and industry efforts difficult and tested existing plans for dealing with such an event. The spill posed threats to the delicate food chain that supports Prince William Sound's commercial fishing industry. Also in danger were 10 million migratory shorebirds and waterfowl, hundreds of sea otters, and dozens of other species, such as harbor porpoises and sea lions, and several varieties of whales. Since the incident occurred in open navigable waters, the U.S. Coast Guard's on-scene coordinator had authority over all activities related to the cleanup effort.

His first action was to immediately close the port of Valdez to all traffic. A U.S. Coast Guard investigator and a representative from the Alaska Department of Environmental Conservation visited the scene of the incident to assess the damage. By noon on Friday, March 25, the Alaska Regional Response Team had been brought together by teleconference, and the National Response Team was activated soon thereafter.

Alyeska, the association that represents seven oil companies which operate in Valdez, including Exxon, first assumed responsibility for the cleanup in accordance with the area's contingency planning. Alyeska opened an emergency communications center in Valdez shortly after the spill was reported and set up a second operations center in Anchorage. The Coast Guard quickly expanded its presence on the scene, and personnel from other federal agencies also arrived to help. EPA specialists in the use of experimental bioremediation technologies assisted in the spill cleanup, and the National Oceanic and Atmospheric Administration (NOAA) provided weather forecasts for Prince William Sound that allowed the cleanup team to adapt its methods to changing weather conditions. Specialists from the Hubbs Marine Institute in San Diego, California, set up a facility to clean oil from otters, and the International Bird Research Center of Berkeley, California, established a center to clean and rehabilitate oil-covered waterfowl.

Three methods were tried in the effort to clean up the spill: burning, mechanical cleanup, and chemical dispersants. A trial burn was conducted during the early stages of the spill. A fire-resistant boom was placed on tow lines, and each end of the boom was attached to a ship. The two ships with the boom between them moved slowly throughout the main portion of the slick until the boom was full of oil. The two ships then towed the boom away from the slick and the oil was ignited. The fire did not endanger the main slick or the *Exxon Valdez* because of the distance separating them. Because of unfavorable weather, no additional burning was attempted. Shortly afterward, the spill mechanical cleanup was started, using booms and skimmers. (Skimmers had not been readily available during the first twenty-four hours following the spill.) Thick oil and heavy kelp tended to clog the equipment. Repairs to damaged skimmers were time-consuming. Transferring oil from temporary storage vessels into more permanent containers was difficult because of the oil's weight and thickness. Continued bad weather slowed the recovery efforts, and tides dispersed the oil throughout the sound.

In addition, a trial application of dispersants was performed. The use of dispersants was controversial. Alyeska had less than 4,000 gallons of dispersant available at its terminal in Valdez, and no application equipment or aircraft. A private company applied dispersants on March 24 with a helicopter and dispersant bucket. Because there was not enough wave action to mix the dispersants with the oil in the water, the Coast Guard representatives at the site concluded that the dispersants were not working, and so their use was discontinued. Efforts to save sensitive areas were begun early in the cleanup. Sensitive environments were identified, defined according to degree of cleanup, and then ranked for cleanup according to priority. Seal pupping locations and fish hatcheries were given the highest importance, and for these areas special cleaning techniques were approved. Despite the identification of sensitive areas and the rapid start-up of shoreline cleaning, wildlife rescue was slow. Adequate resources for this task did not reach the accident scene quickly enough. Through direct contact with oil or because of a loss of food resources, many birds and mammals died.

In the aftermath of the *Exxon Valdez* incident, Congress passed the Oil Pollution Act of 1990, which required the Coast Guard to strengthen its regulations on oil tankers and their owners and operators. Today, tanker hulls provide better protection against spills resulting from a similar accident, and communications between vessel captains and vessel traffic centers have improved to make for safer sailing.

NOAA's Hazardous Materials Response Division has monitored *Exxon Valdez* spill impacts and recovery processes on intertidal shorelines in Prince William Sound since 1990. Their studies and conclusions do not include birds, mammals, or fish.

Exxon Valdez oil persists in certain environments, especially in areas sheltered from weathering processes, such as in the subsurface of certain gravel shorelines and in some soft substrates containing peat. Experts continue to grapple with the concept of ecological recovery in terms of how to define and measure it. A commonly used definition, the "return to conditions as they were before the spill," is neither practical nor ecologically realistic for changeable intertidal systems. It is considered too expensive, and not enough is known about the ecology of the area. Specific measurable components that denote recovery of particular aspects of the ecosystem are discussed below.

Parallelism, a statistical test that measures whether numbers of plants and animals at oiled sites change over time in a manner similar to those at unoiled sites, provides an analytical and ecologically realistic measure of recovery. Recovery based on parallelism between oiled and unoiled intertidal populations occurred for most of the studied species by 1992–1993. Continuing differences between oiled and unoiled sites that suggest incomplete recovery (as of 1998) include species differences in faunal populations, different sand grain sizes and structures, and lower populations at oiled sites. Some or all of these differences could be a result of natural variability, but continued monitoring will help elucidate whether oiling and subsequent hot water washing played a role. Current evidence implies that oiled and hot-water-washed sites initially suffered more severe declines in population than oiled and not-washed sites. However, organisms from both types of oiled sites showed parallelism with unoiled populations on a similar time frame (by 1992–1993). Chemical contamination by polyaromatic hydrocarbons in tissues of mussels and clams was significantly elevated over background levels (all study sites combined) through 1992 for mussels and 1996 for clams. Environmental exposure, sediment size, and initial oil concentrations affected oil weathering processes. By 1997, residual oil found in patches in sediments at a few locations ranged from moderately to extremely weathered, with oil from deep subsurface reservoirs under gravel beaches the least weathered.

The initial governmental response to this controversy was studied. The very large spill size, the remote location, and the character of the oil tested spill preparedness and response capabilities. Government and industry plans, individually and collectively, proved to be wholly insufficient to control an oil spill of the magnitude of the *Exxon Valdez* incident. Initial industry efforts to get equipment on scene were unreasonably slow, and once it was deployed, the equipment could not cope with the spill. Moreover, the various contingency plans did not refer to each other or establish a workable response command hierarchy. This resulted in confusion and delayed the cleanup, which allowed the oil to spread.

A report prepared by the National Response Team was requested by President George H. W. Bush and undertaken by Secretary of Transportation Samuel K. Skinner and EPA Administrator William K. Reilly. The report addressed the preparedness for, the response to, and early lessons learned from the *Exxon Valdez* incident. The president also asked Secretary Skinner to coordinate the efforts of all federal agencies involved in the cleanup, and Administrator Reilly to coordinate the long-term recovery of the affected areas of the Alaskan environment. These efforts are still ongoing. The report addressed a number of important environmental, energy, economic, and health implications of the incident.

The lack of preparedness for oil spills in Prince William Sound and the inadequate response actions mandated improvements in the way the nation plans for and reacts to oil spills of national significance. Prevention is the first line of defense. Avoidance of accidents remains the best way to assure the quality and health of the environment. Preparedness must be strengthened. Exxon was not prepared for a spill of this magnitude—nor were Alyeska, the state of Alaska, and the federal government. It is clear that the planning for and response to the *Exxon Valdez* incident were unequal to the task. Contingency planning in the future needs to incorporate realistic worst-case scenarios and to include adequate equipment and personnel to handle major spills. Adequate training in the techniques and limitations of oil spill removal is critical to the success of contingency planning. Organizational responsibilities must be clear, and personnel must be knowledgeable about their roles. Realistic exercises that fully test the response system must be undertaken regularly. Under the leadership of the Coast Guard, the National Response Team is conducting a study of the adequacy of oil spill contingency plans throughout the country.

Response capabilities must be enhanced to reduce environmental risk. Oil spills—even small ones—are difficult to clean up. Oil recovery rates are low. Both public and private research is needed to improve cleanup technology. Research should focus on mechanical, chemical, and biological means of combating oil spills. Decision-making processes for determining what technology to use should be streamlined, and strategies for the protection of natural resources need to be rethought. Oil is a resource that is inherently dangerous to use and transport. There is no fail-safe prevention, preparedness, or response system. Technology and planning can reduce the chance of accidents and mitigate their effects, but may not stop them from happening. The *Exxon Valdez* incident has highlighted many problems associated with liability and compensation when an oil spill occurs. Comprehensive U.S. oil spill liability and compensation legislation is necessary, as soon as possible, to address these concerns. The petrochemical industry is a highly protected and highly polluting industry that exerts substantial political power in state legislatures and in Congress.

Studies of the long-term environmental and health effects must be undertaken expeditiously and carefully. Broad-gauge and carefully structured environmental recovery efforts, including damage assessments, are critical to assure the eventual full restoration of Prince William Sound and other affected areas.

The EPA is attempting to help Exxon use bioremediation techniques. As part of a cooperative agreement with Exxon on the bioremediation project in Prince William Sound, the EPA agreed to provide information that would help Exxon decide whether to use nutrients as a technique to clean up oil-contaminated shorelines in Alaska in 1989. All data to make a definitive recommendation on the efficacy of bioremediation were not available then. However, given the data then available, the significant potential positive benefits, the perceived absence of adverse ecological effects, and the limited time remaining in the 1989 summer season in Alaska, the EPA supported an

Exxon proposal for nutrient addition on oil contaminated shorelines. The EPA recommended nutrient types, pretreatment application rates, and monitoring for the cleanup of the spill.

The potential for algal blooms from nutrient addition and direct toxicity to marine biota from the oleophilic fertilizer (during or after application) is greatest in protected, poorly flushed embayments, particularly if large portions of the shoreline are treated. When such embayments are considered for bioremediation, the mixing characteristics of nutrients should be established prior to their application. If the information shows adequate flushing and dilution of the fertilizers (complete and rapid transport of the fertilizers off the beaches into receiving waters) under the worst-case situation, then large-scale application of nutrients in these types of embayments is appropriate. If the sufficiency of flushing and dilution is questionable for controlling algal blooms and toxicity, ecological monitoring should be carried out along with the fertilizer application. If monitoring results demonstrate any adverse environmental effect, the application of the fertilizer should be terminated immediately.

It is likely that Prince William Sound will be contaminated with oil for years to come. The effects of tides, the value of indigenous people's knowledge, bioremediation techniques, and the resource needs for such an effort were some of the lessons learned from this disaster. Such an event will be repeated. Accidents will happen in the transportation of and drilling for oil, and in the transport of hazardous materials and wastes, by sea, train, truck, or air. The substantial political power of the petrochemical industries will continue to be pitted against the undeniable and irreversible environmental effects their actions have on people and their environments. This is the focus of the next controversy.

OIL DRILLING IN THE ARCTIC NATIONAL WILDLIFE REFUGE: OIL DRILLED?

Alaska's Arctic National Wildlife Refuge is the crown jewel of America's refuge system. Located in the state's remote northeast corner, this 19.6-million-acre wildlife sanctuary is a natural wonder: a sweeping expanse of tundra with marshes and lagoons, with rivers dramatically situated between the foothills of the Brooks Range and the wide, icy waters of the Beaufort Sea. The oil companies have wanted to drill for oil in the biological heart of the refuge, its coastal plain that is an area critical to the survival of many birds and mammals. About 160 bird species, including species that visit the lower forty-eight states, find breeding, nesting, or resting places on the coastal plain. The plain is the most important onshore denning area in the United States for polar bears. It is the principal calving ground of the 130,000-strong migratory Porcupine caribou herd, the second largest caribou herd in the United States and a key source of food, clothing, and medicine for the Gwich'in Indians, one of the world's few remaining subsistence cultures.

Grizzly bears, wolverines, wolves, arctic foxes, whales, and other species also thrive in the region. The 1980 law that created the Arctic National Wildlife Refuge also closed 1.5 million acres of the coastal plain to gas and oil exploration unless specifically authorized by Congress. More than 90 percent of the coastal lands west of the Arctic National Wildlife Refuge have already been opened to drilling, with many documented negative effects on wildlife and habitat.

Despite claims by the big oil companies that they can drill, and have drilled, responsibly on Alaska's North Slope, spills are commonplace. At the Prudhoe Bay oil field, just sixty miles west of the refuge, reportable spills of oil products and hazardous substances happen frequently, and are compounded by the noise and air pollution industrialization brings. Shortly after drilling started in this area, the central arctic caribou herd shifted its calving grounds away from development, resulting in the use of less favorable habitats. Oil contamination from leaks in the trans-Alaska pipeline during transfer to tankers and from tanker accidents occurs frequently (most notably in 1989, when more than 10 million gallons of crude oil spilled from the Exxon Valdez into Prince William Sound). Biologists are also concerned about the long-term environmental effects of the millions of gallons of waste from oil and gas operations that is disposed of in open pits, injected into the subsurface, frozen into the permafrost, and discharged directly into the air and water. Drilling in the Arctic National Wildlife Refuge could be particularly disastrous for wildlife because the area targeted includes some of the refuge's most critical and sensitive habitat.

Biologists project that the birthrate of the Porcupine caribou may fall by 40 percent if drilling is allowed. They also believe seismic exploration could disturb denning adult polar bears and cause them to abandon their cubs. Even small spills would be disastrous for seals and other marine mammals found along the refuge coastline because oil and chemicals from spills tend to accumulate within their air holes. Some indigenous people rely on these marine animals for food. The liver of seals is particularly prized, but the liver is an organ where pollutants accumulate. And disturbances of any duration could have impacts on populations of snow geese, trumpeter swans, arctic terns, and the other migratory birds that visit the refuge to feed and breed.

Developing an oil-producing operation is a lengthy and expensive process, and is feasible only when oil prices are high. The OPEC nations control the price of oil and would quickly cut the amount they supply to offset any influx of oil from new sources. For years, whenever the political climate has been favorable, drilling advocates have pushed for legislation to open the refuge. Now they find the political climate favorable, partly because of national security concerns. There is concern that the speculative amount of oil that could be had from the coastal plain in Alaska would not necessarily decrease our dependence on foreign oil, would do little to strengthen our national security, and would not produce cost savings for consumers.

Proponents of drilling in the Arctic Refuge claim that large amounts of oil are underneath its fragile coastal plain. They often quote amounts of "technically recoverable oil" that might lie there. This is the amount of oil that could be recovered without any regard to cost, a figure that does not take into account the actual cost of bringing the oil to domestic markets. When economic factors are considered, the mean amount of economically recoverable oil drops to just 3.2 billion barrels. The cost of drilling in the Arctic Refuge is so high that the U.S. Geological Service says that if the price of oil fell to $16 a barrel, there would actually be little, if any, economically recoverable oil in the coastal plain. These cost–benefit analyses do not consider intangible impacts of leaks, spills, fugitive emissions, cumulative emissions, transportation impacts on other goods and services, and aesthetic values on the environment.

What is the value of 3.2 billion barrels of oil? In the U.S. context, on a daily basis the current consumption is about 19.5 million barrels of oil, an annual total of about 7 billion barrels each year. Given this rate of consumption, if Arctic oil were our nation's only source, it would fuel America's demand for less than six months. The United States sits on only 2 percent of the world's total crude oil reserves and currently produces 9 percent of the world's total oil supply (2.1 billion barrels a year in 1999). Our consumption of oil grossly exceeds what is produced domestically or is capable of being produced in the future. With only 5 percent of the world's population, the United States consumes 26 percent of the world's oil. Even if all the economically recoverable oil from the Arctic Refuge (3.2 billion barrels) were combined with the amount the United States produces annually from all other domestic sources (2.1 billion barrels), it still would not meet one year's demand for oil. At its peak of production, Arctic Refuge oil could supply perhaps 1 percent of U.S. energy needs.

Regardless of whether oil from the coastal plain would reduce our dependence on foreign oil, total independence from foreign oil would still not affect the price paid for oil. OPEC nations control over 75 percent of the world's oil reserves and produce 42 percent of the oil currently consumed throughout the world. OPEC meets several times a year to agree on production levels. This collusion of oil powers sets the worldwide price for all oil based on simple supply and demand principles. OPEC members have the majority of the supply and the United States has the majority of demand. Thus the United States, because of its minimal oil reserves and small contribution to the world market, cannot affect the world price of oil through domestic production alone.

Even if drilling our way to energy independence were the answer, Americans who are concerned about reducing prices at the gas pump would be disappointed. The oil and gas industry itself estimates that oil from the Arctic Refuge would not be available for at least seven to ten years, due to the complicated nature of leasing, exploration, and infrastructure construction.

If demand for oil were to come into line with domestic supplies, other ways to curb demand would still have to be found. One of the single biggest changes would be to go farther on a gallon of gas. Other ways to curb demand are important. Conservation measures and new technology should be explored. Fully two-thirds of America's demand for oil is generated by transportation (cars, SUVs, heavy trucks, jets, etc.). Therefore, the biggest single step we can take to reduce our dependence on oil is to make cars and trucks more fuel efficient.

On March 16, 2005, the U.S. Senate voted to take the first step toward drilling for oil in the Arctic National Wildlife Refuge as part of the Federal Budget Resolution. A bipartisan group of senators attempted to safeguard this national treasure and the native people and wildlife that depend on it, but fifty-one senators voted against an amendment to strip Arctic drilling revenues from the Budget Resolution. The Bush administration and its allies in Congress advanced their plan for Arctic Refuge drilling through the complicated budget process by slipping in an assumption of $2.4 billion in revenues to the federal treasury from leasing and development of the Arctic Refuge. These numbers are considered speculative by some. Given that oil leases on the North Slope of Alaska have historically sold for about $50 an acre, the budget figure voted on by Congress is inflated to at least eighty times that average. Even after the vote on the amendment, the Senate must still pass the budget resolution before it goes to a conference committee. There the committee must iron out differences between the two spending plans; the House plan does not assume Arctic Refuge drilling revenues. The conference report is then subject to a straight up or down vote in both the House and the Senate. The next step is the Budget Reconciliation Bill; Congress must pass the actual legislation to authorize opening the Arctic Refuge to drilling. When the budget was brought to the floor, recently, Senators Maria Cantwell (D-Wa.), Olympia Snowe (R-Me.), and John Kerry (D-Mass.) offered an amendment to strip Arctic drilling revenues from the bill; it lost by a vote of 51–49.

On August 10, 2005, over twenty House Republicans, including three committee chairmen, asked the Speaker of the House not to use a budget procedure to approve oil drilling in the Arctic National Wildlife Refuge. Under congressional rules, drilling could be authorized if the Resource Committee decides to rely on an expected $2–4 billion from potential oil lease sales in the Arctic Refuge to meet budget targets. The House has approved drilling in the refuge, but the Senate has filibustered against it. If the budget reconciliation document passes the House and is signed by the president, it is not subject to filibuster.

As the United States faces significant energy issues in the future, the EPA will encounter increased pressure to open up federal lands, even national parks, for resource development. The EPA may yet have a role in the way this controversy unfolds through its environmental impact review under NEPA. The opening up of a wildlife refuge for oil drilling is uncharted territory for all involved.

THREE MILE ISLAND: RADIATION LEAKED

Another area of controversy is nuclear energy and how to get rid of radioactive wastes. There is no social consensus on how to dispose of this waste, which can be dangerous for tens of thousands of years. However, the possibility of a runaway nuclear breakdown or meltdown has always been present. The involvement of the EPA in this issue is extensive.

Nuclear power is often more politically acceptable when oil prices are high. Currently there is a proposal from the Bush administration to build more nuclear power plants and to streamline that process by reducing the ability to consider objections to environmental impacts. In the 1970s the Washington Public Power Supply System (WPPSS) was going to build five nuclear power plants. At that time there was an OPEC oil embargo against the United States and gas was even rationed for a short time. The Sierra Club sued WPPSS based upon the need for an environmental impact assessment for each plant. The court delays caused significant construction cost overruns. Most of the plants were never built, and the ones that were built, were not operationalized. An enormous amount of litigation in five states in the Pacific Northwest followed, resulting in an enormous default. More than $43 billion of bonds sold for this project were defaulted on.

People are very concerned about the human and environmental consequences of a runaway nuclear reaction. The power unleashed by such a reaction can be enormous. These fears were realized and explored in the Three Mile Island episode.

Beginning on March 28, 1979, a series of mechanical, electrical, and human failures led to a severe meltdown of the reactor core at the Three Mile Island (TMI) nuclear power plant. A meltdown is the most dangerous type of nuclear power accident. At Three Mile Island there was a "loss of coolant" accident—cooling water that surrounds the core and keeps it cool was lost. The temperature of the core rose so high that the materials melted. In the worst case a meltdown breaches the containment building, resulting in a massive release of radiation. Fortunately, this did not occur during the TMI accident. (If the reactor at Chernobyl had had a containment building, the severity of the accident would have been greatly reduced.) Some radioactive gases did

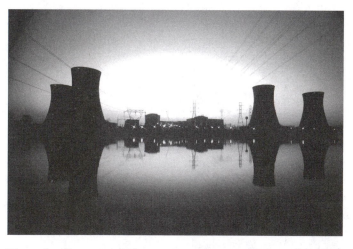

Thermal pollution is another aspect of the environmental impact of nuclear power. Nuclear power reactors need to be near water to keep reactor temperatures down. (Jupiter Images)

escape to the atmosphere at Three Mile Island. The estimated average dose to area residents was about 1 millirem, roughly one-sixth the exposure from a full set of chest X rays, and about 1 percent of the natural radioactive background dose for the area. The maximum dose to a person at the site boundary would have been less than 100 millirem.

On March 28, the EPA arrived and immediately stationed experts with radiation monitoring equipment around the power plant to assess the potential for radiation exposure to people living in the vicinity. The EPA remained in the area for eight years, maintaining a field office monitoring the air. It transferred this activity to the Commonwealth of Pennsylvania in 1989.

The accident began about 4:00 A.M. on March 28, 1979, when the plant experienced a failure in the secondary, nonnuclear section of the plant. The main feedwater pumps stopped running due to either a mechanical or an electrical failure, which prevented the steam generators from removing heat. First the turbine, then the reactor, automatically shut down. The pressure in the primary system (the nuclear portion of the plant) immediately, began to increase. In order to prevent that pressure from becoming excessive, the pilot-operated relief valve (a valve located at the top of the pressurizer) opened. The valve should have closed when the pressure decreased by a certain amount, but it did not. Signals available to the operator failed to show that the valve was still open. As a result, cooling water poured out of the stuck-open valve and caused the core of the reactor to overheat. As coolant flowed from the core through the pressurizer, the instruments available to reactor operators provided confusing information. There was no instrument that showed the level of coolant in the core. Instead, the operators judged the level of water in the core by the level in the pressurizer, and since it was high, they assumed that the core was properly covered with coolant. In addition, there was no clear signal that the pilot-operated relief valve was open. As a result, as alarms rang and warning lights flashed, the operators did not realize that the plant was experiencing a loss-of-coolant accident. They took a series of actions that made conditions worse by reducing the flow of coolant through the core.

Because adequate cooling was not available, the nuclear fuel overheated to the point at which the zirconium cladding (the long metal tubes that hold the nuclear fuel pellets) ruptured, and the fuel pellets began to melt. It was later found that about half of the core melted during the early stages of the accident. Although the TMI-2 plant suffered a severe core meltdown, the most dangerous kind of nuclear power accident, it did not produce the worst-case consequences that reactor experts had long feared. In a worst-case accident, the melting of nuclear fuel would lead to a breach of the walls of the containment building and release massive quantities of radiation to the environment. This did not occur at Three Mile Island.

The accident caught federal and state authorities unprepared. They were concerned about the small releases of radioactive gases that were measured off-site by the late morning of March 28, and even more concerned about the potential threat that the reactor posed to the surrounding population. They did not know that the core had melted, but they immediately took steps to try to gain control of the reactor and ensure adequate cooling of the core. The regional office of the Nuclear Regulatory Commission (NRC) in King of Prussia, Pennsylvania, was notified at 7:45 A.M. on March 28. Within fifteen minutes, NRC headquarters in Washington, D.C., was alerted, and the NRC Operations Center in Bethesda, Maryland, was activated. The regional office promptly dispatched the first team of inspectors to the site, and other agencies, such as the Department of Energy and the EPA, also mobilized their response teams. Helicopters hired by TMI's owner, General Public Utilities Nuclear, and the Department of Energy were sampling radioactivity in the atmosphere above the plant by midday. A team from the Brookhaven National Laboratory was also sent to assist in radiation monitoring. At 9:15 A.M. the White House was notified, and at 11:00 A.M. all nonessential personnel were ordered off the plant's premises.

By the evening of March 28, the core appeared to be adequately cooled and the reactor appeared to be stable. But new concerns arose by the morning of Friday, March 30. A significant release of radiation from the plant's auxiliary building, done to relieve pressure on the primary system and avoid curtailing the flow of coolant to the core, caused a great deal of confusion and consternation. In an atmosphere of growing uncertainty about the condition of the plant, the governor of Pennsylvania, Richard L. Thornburgh, consulted with the NRC about evacuating the population near the plant. Eventually he and NRC Chairman Joseph Hendrie agreed that it would be prudent for those people most vulnerable to radiation to evacuate the area. Thornburgh announced that he was advising pregnant women and pre-school-age children within five miles of the plant to leave the area.

Within a short time the presence of a large hydrogen bubble in the dome of the pressure vessel, the container that holds the reactor core, stirred new worries. The concern was that the bubble might burn or even explode, and rupture the pressure vessel. In that event the core would fall into the containment building and perhaps cause a breach of containment. The hydrogen bubble was a source of intense scrutiny and great anxiety, among both government authorities and the general population, throughout the day on Saturday, March 31. The crisis ended when experts determined on Sunday, April 1, that the bubble could not burn or explode because of the absence of oxygen in the pressure vessel. Further, by that time the utility had succeeded in greatly reducing the size of the bubble.

Detailed studies of the radiological consequences of the accident have been conducted by the NRC, the EPA, the Department of Health, Education and Welfare (now Health and Human Services), the Department of Energy, and the Commonwealth of Pennsylvania. Several independent studies have also been conducted. Estimates are that the average dose to about 2 million people in the area was only about 1 millirem. To put this into context, exposure from a full set of chest X rays is about 6 millirem. Compared with the natural radioactive background dose of about 100–125 millirem per year for the area, the collective dose to the community from the accident was very small (although this does not measure accumulated impacts or consider any dose response differences in the exposed population). The maximum dose to a person at the site boundary would have been less than 100 millirem. In the months following the accident, although questions were raised about possible adverse effects from radiation on human, animal, and plant life in the TMI area, none could be directly correlated to the accident. Thousands of samples of air, water, milk, vegetation, soil, and foodstuffs were collected by groups monitoring the area. Very low levels of radionuclides could be attributed to releases from the accident. However, comprehensive investigations and assessments by several respected organizations have concluded that in spite of serious damage to the reactor, most of the radiation was contained and that the actual release had negligible effects on the physical health of individuals or the environment. These organizations did not investigate cumulative impacts or vulnerable populations.

The accident was caused by a combination of personnel error, design deficiencies, and component failures. It permanently changed both the nuclear industry and the NRC. Public fear and distrust increased, the NRC's regulations and oversight became broader and more robust, and management of the plants was scrutinized more carefully. The problems identified through careful analysis of the events during those days have led to permanent and sweeping changes in how the NRC regulates its licensees—which, in turn, has reduced the risk to public health and safety.

Here are some of the major changes that have occurred since the accident:

- Upgrading and strengthening of plant design and equipment requirements—including fire protection, piping systems, auxiliary feedwater systems, containment building isolation, reliability of individual components (pressure relief valves and electrical circuit breakers), and the ability of plants to shut down automatically;

- Identifying human performance as a critical part of plant safety, revamping operator training and staffing requirements, improving instrumentation and controls for operating the plant, and establishing fitness-for-duty programs for plant workers to guard against alcohol or drug abuse;

- Improved instruction to avoid the confusing signals that plagued operations during the accident;

- Enhancement of emergency preparedness to include immediate NRC notification requirements for plant events and an NRC operations center that is now staffed twenty-four hours a day. Drills and response plans are now tested by licensees several times a year, and state and local agencies participate in drills with the Federal Emergency Management Agency and NRC;

- Establishment of a program to integrate NRC observations, findings, and conclusions about licensee performance and management effectiveness into a periodic, public report;

- Regular analysis of plant performance by senior NRC managers who identify plants needing additional regulatory attention;

- Expansion of the NRC's resident inspector program—first authorized in 1977—whereby at least two inspectors live nearby and work exclusively at each plant in the United States to provide daily surveillance of licensee adherence to NRC regulations;

- Expansion of performance-oriented as well as safety-oriented inspections, and the use of risk assessment to identify vulnerabilities of any plant to severe accidents;

- Strengthening and reorganization of enforcement as a separate office within the NRC;

- The establishment of the Institute of Nuclear Power Operations, the industry's own policing group, and formation of what is now the Nuclear Energy Institute to provide a unified industry approach to generic nuclear regulatory issues, and to interaction with NRC and other government agencies;

- The installation of additional equipment by licensees to mitigate accident conditions and monitor radiation levels and plant status;

- Use of major initiatives by licensees in early identification of important safety-related problems, and in collecting and assessing relevant data, so lessons of experience can be shared and quickly acted upon;

- Expansion of the NRC's international activities to share enhanced knowledge of nuclear safety with other countries in a number of important technical areas.

Today, the TMI-2 reactor is permanently shut down and defueled, with the reactor coolant system drained, the radioactive water decontaminated and evaporated, radioactive waste shipped off-site to an appropriate disposal site, reactor fuel and core debris shipped off-site to a Department of Energy facility, and the remainder of the site being monitored. The owner says it will keep the facility in long-term, monitored storage until the operating license for the TMI-1 plant expires.

The controversies and issues that surround nuclear power will persist as coal and oil reserves become depleted and more countries turn to nuclear energy for power. The safety of nuclear power plants was raised again after the terrorist attacks on the United States on September 11, 2002. Another set of issues and controversies centers on the disposal of nuclear waste, which is generated without regard to how safe the plant actually is.

DISPOSAL OF NUCLEAR WASTE AT YUCCA MOUNTAIN: RADIATION DISPOSED?

The controversy around a threatened nuclear meltdown is different from the controversy around radioactive waste. Much like oil spills and oil exploration, a nuclear explosion is reactive and the disposal of radioactive wastes is planned.

Yucca Mountain is the Department of Energy's potential geological repository designed to store and dispose of spent nuclear fuel and high-level radioactive waste. If it is approved, the site would be the nation's first geological repository for disposal of this type of radioactive waste. The site is located in Nye County, Nevada, about 100 miles northwest of Las Vegas. It is federally owned land on the western edge of the Department of Energy's Nevada Test Site. The repository would be approximately 1,000 feet below the top of the mountain and 1,000 feet above the groundwater.

To understand some of the environmental policy issues surrounding the Yucca Mountain waste repository proposal, it is necessary to understand the regulatory context of nuclear power in the United States. Much of the nuclear waste disposal policy was developed prior to the existence of the EPA.

The Atomic Energy Commission (AEC) was essentially self-regulating. In 1946 the Atomic Energy Act established a federal monopoly over the use, control, and ownership of nuclear technology. In 1955 the AEC asked the National Academy of Sciences (NAS) to study methods for disposing of radioactive wastes from nuclear weapons production in the United States. The AEC was disbanded in 1974, and some of its functions eventually became the responsibility of the Department of Energy (DOE), the Nuclear Regulatory Commission, and the EPA. In 1957 an NAS report to the AEC recommended that transuranic and high-level radioactive wastes be buried in geological formations and that the feasibility of using salt beds or salt domes as a disposal medium be investigated. In 1964 Congress amended the Atomic Energy Act to allow private ownership of nuclear materials (i.e., fuel) but maintained certain controls over its possession and use in the interest of public health and safety—including the obligation for disposal. In 1970 the AEC tentatively selected a nuclear waste repository site in salt deposits near Lyons, Kansas. Two years later the federal government withdrew that site from consideration because of concerns that drilling for underground transportation facilities in the vicinity might have compromised the salt deposits' geological integrity.

In 1974, the Energy Reorganization Act specifically charged the Energy Research and Development Agency (forerunner of the DOE) with the responsibility to construct and operate a facility for disposal of civilian high-level nuclear waste. In 1981, after extensively evaluating numerous alternatives, the DOE issued a record of decision opting for geological disposal of such waste. (There is also an increasing amount of low-level radioactive waste generated by the military.) In 1982 the Nuclear Waste Policy Act (NWPA) directed the DOE to begin disposing of spent nuclear fuel in a geological repository by January 31, 1998, and prescribed a process for selecting a disposal site. In 1983 the DOE selected nine sites in six states for study as potential sites for a first repository. In accordance with the NWPA, the DOE identified sites in seventeen eastern states as potential locations for a second repository. In 1986 the secretary of energy nominated five of the nine sites for further consideration, and President Reagan approved three sites (Hanford, Washington; Deaf Smith County, Texas; and Yucca Mountain, Nevada) for further study.

In 1987 the NWPA was amended to direct the DOE to study only Yucca Mountain as a potential repository. In 1992 the Energy Policy Act was enacted, requiring the EPA to develop site-specific public health and safety standards for Yucca Mountain. Although the EPA had been involved in some of the issues of radiation regulation, this was one of the most direct congressional mandates.

In 1997 the Energy and Water Development Appropriations Act directed that by September 30, 1998, the secretary of energy must provide a Yucca Mountain viability assessment (VA) to the president and Congress. In 1998 the federal government defaulted on its obligation to begin removing spent nuclear fuel from reactor sites by January 31, 1998. The DOE issued its viability assessment of Yucca Mountain, drawing upon two decades of scientific research to conclude that a geological repository capable of protecting public health and safety for thousands of years can be designed and built at Yucca Mountain. The VA also published DOE's schedule for moving forward with such a repository. In 1999 the NRC and the EPA proposed regulations for the licensing of Yucca Mountain, should it be selected. The DOE issued its draft environmental impact statement for Yucca Mountain, which concluded that the proposed project would have essentially no adverse impact on public health and safety. This meant that for 10,000 years radiation levels would be well below EPA and NRC proposed limits, and less than 1 percent of natural background radiation in the vicinity of Yucca Mountain.

In 2001, the DOE released its science and engineering report for Yucca Mountain, which provided updated scientific results, described an enhanced design, and opened the public comment period preceding a site recommendation decision. In 2001, the DOE released its preliminary site suitability report, which compared its scientific results with site selection criteria and concluded that the proposed repository would be capable of meeting the EPA's stringent radiation protection standard. This report ended the DOE's twenty-year, $7 billion scientific site characterization program. In 2002, the DOE made its final site recommendation on Yucca Mountain. Should the DOE recommend the site, the president would decide whether to go forward.

Should Nevada object to the president's decision, Congress would also have to approve the site for the project to move forward. The DOE is scheduled to apply to the NRC for a license to construct and operate a repository at Yucca Mountain.

The NRC would be expected to issue a license for construction of a repository at Yucca Mountain in 2007 if regulatory requirements for public health and safety protection are satisfied. The DOE would be expected to complete construction of a repository, and the NRC to license its operation if regulatory requirements for public health and safety protection are satisfied, by 2010. Between 2060 and 2300, the DOE would be expected to apply to the NRC for a license to close the repository. If all requirements for assuring public health and safety for thousands of years into the future are met, the NRC would issue a license allowing the repository to be closed. This would be the final decision on geological disposal of nuclear waste at Yucca Mountain.

In summary, in 1982 Congress established a national policy to solve the problem of nuclear waste disposal, the Nuclear Waste Policy Act. The DOE is responsible for finding a site, building a facility, and operating the repository. It studied nine locations for ten years and then narrowed the final choices down to three: Hanford, Washington; Deaf Smith County, Texas; and Yucca Mountain, Nevada. In 1987, Wes Barnes, director of the Yucca Mountain Project (an offshoot of the DOE) decided that the desolate mountain ridge in southwestern Nevada will be the final resting place. More than 100 U.S. commercial nuclear reactors plan to deposit the worst of their nuclear waste deep into the mountain. It is to be stored permanently, and the project says it will be guaranteed for 10,000 years. The project proposes that the containers be surrounded by impermeable layers of volcanic rock to guarantee safety.

In 2000, the DOE reported that there was about 40,000 tons of spent nuclear fuel in the United States. The fuel rods are now placed in cooling ponds near the plants. Most pools are full or nearly full. Since time was running out, Yucca Mountain was the only site left. A huge boring machine is digging a tunnel twenty-five feet wide into the mountain. Two miles of tunnel have already been excavated, and three more miles remain to be completed. The facility is planned to receive waste by 2010. The Nevada state government opposed to putting the depository in Yucca Mountain. Many people who disagree with the project say the site can safely hold the waste for only 100 years. The DOE stresses that if there are any problems with the project, it will recommend against storing nuclear waste in the mountain.

There are some very important concerns that a group of scientists and technicians is researching. Some of the hydrologic engineers who openly protested selection of the site lost their jobs. One of their concerns is the history of volcanic activity in the area and fear of an eruption. Another is earthquakes, which are a possibility because there is a fault line not far away. The main concern is more elementary: whether water will leak into the depository. The containers will eventually begin to decompose. The surrounding rock now will protect the environment on the surface, and it is hoped that it will do so for thousands of years. The movement of water is believed to be the only way that radionuclides can pass this natural barrier. The temperature of the stored waste is about 1500°F. If liquid water seeps into the stored nuclear waste, it will become steam, increasing the pressure under the mountain. This could push the radioactive steam up through some of the fault lines that exist on the mountain.

The people of Nevada have many different views about the project. Some feel that the federal government will push the project through whether or not it is proved to last safely for 10,000 years and whether or not the site is suitable. People want to feel that the area will be safe for succeeding generations to live in. Any type of leak would be traumatic for the environment. Others feel that if Americans are going to benefit from the use of nuclear power, they should have to pay the price. Some are looking forward to the new jobs that will be available at Yucca Mountain. Most people feel that storing nuclear waste safely for thousands of years is "crazy."

The Shoshone Indians have ancestral lands that lie within the Nevada Test Site. They are fearful of the project and state that the treaty they signed in 1863 did not give full control of their tribal lands to the United States. The Shoshone claim that decades of aboveground nuclear testing have caused cancer and other sicknesses among their people. The EPA responded to tribal issues concerning Yucca Mountain in the following manner.

Public comment indicated that the EPA should consult with Indian tribes about their traditional and customary uses of lands in the Yucca Mountain area, and the risk characteristics should consider such tribal uses. The EPA's response was that although the EPA had indicated there are no Indian reservations located within the Yucca Mountain area or its immediate vicinity, the Paiute and Shoshone tribes use the area for traditional and customary purposes, including traditional gathering of food. It is the tribes' contention that these traditional and customary uses need to be researched in cooperation with the tribes and incorporated into the formula upon which the draft standards are based. There may be traditional and customary uses of natural springs, wildlife, and vegetation that would significantly impact the risk calculations. For example, if a tribe uses sweat lodges, they are exposed to much higher rates of radiation. The Spokane tribe of Washington State developed a sweat lodge model of risk exposure when it halted the use of low-level radioactive material as fill for the Midnite Mine. Some tribes eat dirt from certain areas as a valuable source of minerals. Some tribes believe that use of a word or image will bring that word or image to them. If the risk of cancer is discussed with the tribe, its members may not feel comfortable, and will fail to establish a presence in the discussion. Some tribes mined uranium and suffered from the exposure to it. Some sites are sacred to indigenous people in the area, and they do not wish to disclose the location of these sites because it could lead to theft of cultural artifacts and erosion of the religious significance of the site.

Tribes felt that the EPA's radiation experts were not sufficiently knowledgeable about the traditional and customary tribal uses of the area's resources to incorporate them properly into the formula upon which the draft standards for public safety are based. Thus, the proposed standards may not be based upon accurate assumptions. Certain tribes contend that their lifestyle, including the types of plants and animals they consume, does not provide as much shielding and protection, and has different exposure pathways than the models used by the DOE in its off-site radiation exposure studies, thus leading to increased risk. Tribes feel that they need to be consulted directly. The EPA has responded that it has a duty to consult with those tribes whose aboriginal homelands will be potentially impacted by the proposed Yucca Mountain repository when developing its risk assessment model and identifying potential exposure pathways.

Many potentially affected tribes have submitted comments to the EPA, and some have passed resolutions in response to the proposed rule. These activities have provided the EPA with valuable information regarding the tribes' perspectives on the proposed radiation protection standard for Yucca Mountain. The EPA has considered these comments in preparing the final rule.

After considering the description of tribal land uses in the area of Yucca Mountain, the EPA has concluded that the rural–residential risk management plan fully protects tribal members and the resources they use for four reasons. First, the tribal use of natural springs apparently occurs in the vicinity of Ash Meadows. The EPA is not aware of any other downward gradient from Yucca Mountain where water discharges in natural springs, with the possible exception of springs in Death Valley. Second, these natural springs are likely fed by the carbonate aquifer that is beneath the alluvial aquifer now being used by the town of Amargosa Valley (including at Lathrop Wells), and is likely to be used in the future.

The question of whether the carbonate aquifer would be contaminated by releases from the Yucca Mountain disposal system has not been resolved by the DOE. Third, the available data indicate that although it is likely that the alluvial aquifer would be contaminated by releases from the Yucca Mountain repository, flow is generally upward from the carbonate aquifer into the overlying aquifers, suggesting that there is no potential for radionuclides to move downward into the carbonate system. Fourth, if downward movement were to occur, radionuclide concentrations would be significantly diluted in the larger carbonate flow system. As a result, springs fed from the carbonate aquifer would have lower contamination levels than would wells at Lathrop Wells, which tap aquifers closer to and more directly affected by the source of potential contamination. Thus, tribal users of natural springs fed by the carbonate aquifer would experience lower contamination levels than users of the alluvial aquifer at Lathrop Wells. The EPA's hydrological assumptions are based on current water flows, that could change drastically if an earthquake occurs in the area.

The EPA's standards address all environmental pathways: air, groundwater, food, and soil. The standards protect the residents closest to the repository up to 15 millirem per year, a risk no greater than 3 chances in 10,000 of contracting a fatal cancer. This level is within the EPA's acceptable risk range for environmental pollutants. It does not measure accumulated impacts or the actual vulnerability of the affected population. The residents closest to the repository who are in the path of any potential releases are at Lathrop Wells, Nevada, which is about twelve miles from the site. The EPA's final standards require calculation of doses at a distance no greater than about 10.8 miles from the repository. The potential risk for those at greater distances would be even less. The EPA's only regulatory authority for Yucca Mountain comes from the Energy Policy Act of 1992, which directs the EPA to set radiation protection standards for Yucca Mountain.

This controversy shows no sign of abating. Very few communities will accept a land use that exposes its residents to 3 chances in 10,000 of getting cancer. This waste must move along the roads and railroads of the United States. Some cities have begun to limit the roads over which such hazardous wastes can be transported. The wastes are as dangerous in transit as they are in storage, where they now stay awaiting a resting place.

The projected date that Yucca Mountain will accept radioactive wastes is 2010. The state of Nevada did not allow renewal of the water rights to this facility, forcing contractors to truck in water. The standard of radiation emission for ten thousand to one million years in the future is an issue that remains unresolved. On August 9, 2005, the EPA proposed a limit of 350 millirems per year for that period. Until Yucca Mountain opens, many U.S. nuclear power plants will store waste on-site in steel barrels. This system is known as "dry cast storage" and is itself controversial. It is possible that a temporary storage facility will open at Yucca Mountain for dry cask storage.

BEST AVAILABLE CONTROL TECHNOLOGY VS. MOST ECONOMICAL POLLUTION CONTROL TECHNOLOGY

Not all the controversies at the EPA are public battles involving courts and legislatures. Some are difficult questions about the best environmental policy approach even when all the facts are known and accepted as true. This is the case with the EPA rules and regulations about pollution control technology requirements for industry. (See discussion in Chapter 2.) When the best available pollution control technology is very expensive, how much can the EPA require of industry? How much can the EPA allow a state to regulate pollution control technology? It is essentially a question of who pays for pollution control. What if the most economical pollution control technology does an incomplete job?

Prior to 1977 the Clean Air Act did not regulate the quality of air in regions of the United States that met or exceeded national ambient air quality standards (NAAQS) any differently than regions in which the air was particularly dirty. Although Section 101(b)(1) of the 1970 Amendments to the Clean Air Act stated that the preeminent purpose of the act was "to protect and enhance the quality of the Nation's air resources so as to promote the public health and welfare," the EPA did not implement regulations designed to protect "against significant deterioration of the existing clean air areas" until 1974. The initial regulations required that the states ensure the maintenance of air quality in clean areas even though these areas did not violate any federal pollution emissions standards.

In the 1977 Amendments to the Clean Air Act, Congress explicitly created a new framework "for maintaining air quality in those regions which are in compliance with the national standards." Known as "prevention of significant deterioration" (PSD), these statutory provisions require that any new or modified "major emitting facility" in an attainment area apply for a preconstruction permit showing that emissions from the source "will not cause, or contribute to, air pollution in excess of . . . maximum allowable increase or maximum allowable concentration for any pollutant." Under the PSD program, stationary sources must demonstrate that "the proposed facility is subject to the best available control technology for each pollutant subject to regulation . . . emitted from . . . such facility." The best available control technology determination for any new or modified stationary source is made on a case-by-case basis by the state permitting authority, "taking into account energy, environmental, and economic impacts and other costs."

From 1977 through the early 1990s, the EPA rarely filed enforcement actions for alleged failures to obtain applicable new source review (NSR) permits and approvals. In the early 1990s economic data suggested that production had greatly increased in various regulated industrial sectors. The EPA's records showed that many sources in these sectors had invested substantial capital to expand production capacity, but had not updated pollution controls. Consequently, in 1992 the EPA began to target specific industries suspected of NSR violations. It started with the wood products, pulp and paper, and petroleum refining industries. Soon thereafter, the EPA launched an aggressive and controversial enforcement campaign against the electric utility industry. In 1996 the EPA requested and analyzed business records, primarily of power plants in the Midwest and Southeast, pursuant to Section 114 of the CAA. Data regarding past modifications prompted the Department of Justice (DOJ) to file eight enforcement actions against electric utilities between 1999 and 2000. Each lawsuit alleged that the defendant had made a major modification without the necessary NSR permits and approvals. In many instances, the source expanded capacity, extended the life of the plant, or redesigned existing emissions units without obtaining a permit. Many defendants disputed the EPA's claims, refused to correct alleged violations, or insisted that the project cited, qualified for exceptions.

The EPA's enforcement actions brought the NSR controversy to the forefront of public debate. New York State Attorney General Eliot Spitzer filed citizen suits against seventeen U.S. power plants for failure to comply with the NSR program. The northeastern states were concerned that air pollution upwind from them was destroying their environment through acid rain. The Adirondack Mountains of upstate New York were particularly hard hit, with many lakes dying and some species becoming endangered.

The court consolidated the lawsuits with the federal enforcement actions. Other states, mostly those downwind of major power plants, intervened in the action. Additionally, citizen groups and coalitions, such as the Sierra Club, the Natural Resource Defense Council, and the Clean Air Task Force, either moved to intervene or initiated their own actions. Before the proceedings progressed to trial, one defendant, Tampa Electric Company, entered into a consent decree with the DOJ.

In both the Clean Air Act generally and the PSD program specifically, Congress granted the EPA an extensive oversight function to ensure that states acted in compliance with the terms of the statute. According to the terms of the PSD permit program, the EPA is authorized to "take such measures, including issuance of an order... as necessary to prevent the construction or modification of a major emitting facility which does not conform to the [PSD permit] requirements."

The Supreme Court clarified and expanded the scope of the EPA's PSD oversight and enforcement authority in *Alaska Department of Environmental Conservation v. EPA*. It ruled on two additional cases interpreting the Clean Air Act and denied review to a significant third case addressing a controversial section of the statute. In the first of these cases to be decided, *Alaska Department of Environmental Conservation v. EPA*, both the Court and the states were divided in their support of the ruling. By a 5–4 vote, the Court held that the EPA may overrule state environmental regulators when the latter have unreasonably arrived at a "best available control technology" to combat industry-produced air pollution.

The Red Dog zinc mine in northwest Alaska is the world's largest zinc mine and the region's largest private employer. When Teck Cominco Alaska (Cominco), the operator of the mine, decided in 1996 to expand production, it sought the required permit from the state under the Clean Air Act's PSD program. This program is designed, in part, to maintain clean air in parts of the country that already have clean air, as that region of Alaska does. Under the PSD, any pollution-emitting facility wishing to modify its operations in such a way as to exceed a prescribed amount of pollution must equip its new facility with the best available control technology (BACT), defined by the Clean Air Act as "an emission limitation based on the maximum degree of [pollutant] reduction... which the permitting authority... taking into account energy, environmental, and economic impacts and other costs, determines is achievable for [the] facility." Alaska is the permitting authority in this case, operating through the Alaska Department of Environmental Conservation (ADEC). The EPA found Alaska's BACT determination to be unreasonable and arbitrary because the ADEC ruled out what it had previously judged to be the most effective pollution control without providing evidence of its impact on the mine's profitability. After the EPA prohibited issuance of a permit, the ADEC challenged the EPA's authority to issue such an order, asserting that the Clean Air Act granted it—ADEC—and not the EPA, the final word. On appeal, the Ninth Circuit disagreed with the ADEC, as did the Supreme Court, which found explicit language in the Clean Air Act granting oversight to the EPA when a local agency's BACT determination is not "faithful to the statute's definition." The Court approved the EPA argument that Congress's goal in instituting the PSD program—to maintain the quality of clean-air regions—would not be met if the EPA did not maintain a surveillance role regarding BACT determinations.

There are databases containing case-specific information on the "best available" air pollution technologies that have been required to reduce the emission of air pollutants from stationary sources (e.g., power plants, steel mills, chemical plants). This formation has been provided by state and local permitting agencies. The RACT/BACT/LAER Clearinghouse (http://cfpubl_epa.gov/rblc/htm/b102.cfm) also contains a database that summarizes the EPA emission limits required in new source performance standards, national emission standards for hazardous air pollutants, and maximum achievable control technology. Air Quality Management District published its first BACT guidelines in May 1983, and a major revision in October 1988. It is often a matter of pride for environmental plant managers to be the model for the best available pollution control technology. The pollution control industry grows every year, is recessionproof, and brings in investment from other countries.

California's approach spans some of the policy differences between the best and the most economical pollution control technologies. On October 20, 2000, the governing board of California's air quality management districts approved revisions to the NSR regulations that (1) maintained the federal lowest achievable emission rate requirement for major polluting facilities and (2) established a minor source BACT (MSBACT) for nonmajor polluting facilities that will consider cost before making MSBACT more stringent. California has broken out the lowest achievable emission rate, and has included minor sources, though it is debatable whether the state has in fact lowered emission to the lowest rate.

The question of the cost of pollution control and prevention is filled with controversy. Often the cleanest approach is the expensive approach, especially if it requires new technology. The standards themselves fluctuate in response to changing environmental conditions, such as new sources of emissions and new pollution control technologies. Even the basis for current standards may change if cumulative emissions and impacts begin to be considered in EPA policy-making venues. The question of who pays how much for which level of environmental cleanliness is a policy controversy that is constantly tinkered with at the federal, state, and local levels.

ENVIRONMENTAL JUSTICE: WARREN COUNTY AND THE SHINTECH CONTROVERSIES

Love Canal presented a controversy involving a contaminated community facing an environmental threat from chemicals, mainly dioxin. Yucca Mountain presents the controversy of where to store nuclear wastes. Warren County presents the controversy of siting hazardous wastes in a predominantly African American community. The Shintech controversy presents the issue of concentrating industrial land uses and sites in an African American community.

Environmental justice refers to the effects and processes related to the distribution of environmental burdens and benefits. Environmental justice is not a subsection of environmentalism. Certain marginalized populations in U.S. society have been on the receiving end of environmental burdens while other groups have been on the receiving end of environmental benefits. When environmental history brings out uncomfortable racism in our past, policies of equal environmental protection and sustainability will require a remedy of those wrongs. Environmental regulation through the EPA is relatively new. Early programs of environmental protection did not reach all industrial emissions, and still do not reach all emissions. Today U.S. urban areas are sinks of accumulating industrial, commercial, and residential emissions, and will require extensive cleanup to equalize environmental protection and to lay the groundwork for sustainability.

On January 12, 2004, after waiting more than two decades, an environmental justice victory finally came to the residents of predominately African American Warren County, North Carolina. Since 1982, county residents had lived with the legacy of a 142-acre toxic-waste dump. Detoxification work began on the dump in June 2001, and the last cleanup work was scheduled to end in December 2003. State and federal sources spent $18 million to detoxify or neutralize contaminated soil stored at the Warren County PCB (polychlorinated biphenyl) landfill. A private contractor hired by the state dug up and burned 81,500 tons of oil-laced soil in a kiln whose temperature reached more than 800°F to remove the PCBs. The soil was put back in a football field size pit, re-covered to form a mound, graded, and seeded with grass.

The landfill had been constructed to contain 40,000 cubic yards (60,000 tons) of highly PCB-contaminated soil scraped up from more than 210 miles of road shoulders in North Carolina. The PCBs came from the Raleigh-based Ward Transfer Company. A Jamestown, New York, trucking operation owned by Robert J. Burns obtained PCB-laced oil from the Ward Transfer Company for resale. Faced with economic loss as a result of the EPA ban on resale of the toxic oil in 1979, the waste hauler illegally dumped it along 217 miles of North Carolina roadways. He was probably not unique in this practice. Waste transit and terminal routes often went from the Northeast to the Southeast. Between June 1978 and August 1978, over 30,000 gallons of waste oil contaminated with PCBs were illegally discharged along roadsides in fourteen North Carolina counties. The PCBs resulted in the EPA designating the roadsides as a Superfund site in order to protect public health. The controversial landfill was owned by the North Carolina Department of Environment and Natural Resources and was located about sixty miles northeast of Raleigh, off North Carolina SR 1604 and U.S. Highway 401. The toxic-waste dump was forced on the tiny community of Afton, more than 84 percent of whose population was African American in 1982. The home ownership rate in Afton among African Americans was about 66 percent, compared with the national rate of about 44 percent. This quiet, stable community reacted strongly to what it perceived as a toxic assault.

When North Carolina Governor James B. Hunt decided to bury the contaminated soil in Afton, Warren County residents organized themselves into a group that was later joined by national civil rights leaders, church leaders, African American elected officials, environmental activists, labor leaders, and youth. The state began hauling more than 6,000 truckloads of the PCB-contaminated soil to the landfill in mid-September 1982. Two weeks later, more than 414 protesters had been arrested. In the end, over 500 protesters were arrested. This was one of the first times people had been arrested for protesting the location of a hazardous-waste site. Although the protests did not stop the trucks, the marches, demonstrations, and jailings focused the national media spotlight on Warren County. The protests prompted the Congressional Black Caucus to request the General Accounting Office (GAO) to investigate hazardous-waste landfill siting and the racial composition of the host communities. The 1983 GAO study reported that African Americans made up a majority in three of the four communities with hazardous waste landfills in EPA Region IV (eight Southern states), that at least 26 percent of the population in all four communities had incomes below the poverty level, and that most of this population was African American.

North Carolina state officials had surveyed ninety-three sites in thirteen counties before settling on Warren County. The landfill was permitted by the EPA under the Toxic Substances Control Act. The Warren County PCB landfill site was not the most scientifically suitable one because the water table there is very shallow, only five to ten feet below the surface, and the residents of the community get all of their drinking water from local wells. Warren County residents pleaded for a more permanent solution rather than a cheap "quick fix" that would eventually end up with the PCBs leaking into the groundwater and wells. State and federal officials nevertheless chose a landfill, the least expensive alternative.

By 1993 the landfill was failing, and for a decade community leaders pressed the state to decontaminate the site. Residents of Warren County were searching for guarantees that the government was not creating a future Superfund site which would threaten nearby residents. North Carolina state officials and EPA officials could give no guarantees; there is no such thing as hazardous-waste landfill that is 100 percent guaranteed not to leak... eventually. Many people of color have long held the belief, with ample cause, that some residents "have the wrong complexion for protection."

In reality, all landfills inevitably leak, and the Warren County PCB landfill was no exception. The question was not if the facility would leak, but when it would leak, PCBs into the environment. The landfill was technically designed to be a "dry-tomb" landfill, but it was capped with a million gallons of water in it. Even after its detoxification, some Warren County residents are still questioning the completeness of the cleanup, especially the presence of contamination that may have migrated beyond the 3-acre landfill site and into the 137-acre buffer zone that surrounds it and the nearby creek and outlet basin. PCBs are persistent, bioaccumulative, and toxic pollutants. That is, they are highly toxic, long-lasting substances that can build up in the food chain to levels that are harmful to humans and the ecosystem. PCBs are not something most Americans would want as a next-door neighbor. They are probable human carcinogens, have developmental effects such as low birth weight, and disrupt hormone function.

Warren County is located in eastern North Carolina. The twenty-nine counties in that area are noticeably different from the rest of North Carolina. According to the 2000 census, whites comprised 62 percent of the population in eastern North Carolina (versus 72 percent statewide). African Americans were concentrated in the northeastern and central parts of the region. Warren County was one of six counties in the region where African Americans comprised a majority of the population in 2000: Bertie (62.3 percent), Hertford (59.6 percent), Northhampton (59.4 percent), Edgecombe (57.5 percent), Warren (54.5 percent), and Halifax (52.6 percent). Eastern North Carolina was also significantly poorer than the rest of the state. In 1999, per capita income in North Carolina was $26,463; in the eastern region it was only $18,550.

Warren County is African American, poor, rural, and politically disenfranchised. It had a population of 16,232 in 1980. African Americans comprised 63.7 percent of the county population and 24.2 percent of the state population in 1980. The county continues to be economically worse off than the state as a whole on all major social indicators. Per capita income for Warren County residents was $6,984 in 1982 (versus $9,283 for the state). Warren County residents earned about 75 percent of the state per capita income. The county ranked 92nd out of 100 counties in median family income in 1980.

The Shintech case was a test of whether the EPA will protect people of color and low-income communities in accordance with President Clinton's

St. James Citizens for Jobs and the Environment and Allies holds a press conference in opposition to Shintech, Convent, Louisiana, 1997. (Environmental Justice Resource Center, Clarke Atlanta University, Atlanta, Georgia)

Executive Order 12898 on environmental justice, which states that federal agencies must identify and address the disproportionate effects of environmental hazards on minority and low-income communities. Four years before Shintech announced its plans to build a PVC plant in Convent, the Louisiana State Advisory Committee to the U.S. Commission on Civil Rights issued a report on environmental racism in Louisiana. It stated that existing hazardous-waste and chemical facilities disproportionately impacted African American communities along the industrial corridor between Baton Rouge and New Orleans. This corridor is known as Cancer Alley because of the high rates of many types of cancer there.

In 1996 Shintech announced its plans to build a PVC plant in Convent. At a public hearing regarding the proposed air permit for Shintech held on December 9, 1996, 300 citizens showed up to voice their opposition. In response to such strong opposition, Region VI of the EPA recommended that the Louisiana Department of Environmental Quality (DEQ) address environmental justice concerns before making a final decision regarding the issuance of the air permit. Regardless of overwhelming public concern, on May 23, 1997, the DEQ granted Shintech its Title V air permit. That February, Shintech had been issued its land use permit. The only remaining permit necessary for operation was the water permit. In the summer of 1998 the EPA was scheduled to issue a final decision on the Shintech case. However, that June the EPA's final decision was delayed because it had asked its Science Advisory Board (SAB) to review its techniques for determining disproportionate "burden." The EPA assessed disproportionate burden using data from the 1990 census and estimates of industry-reported air emissions. The SAB decision was expected in October 1998. After more than two years of struggle, Shintech announced on September 17, 1998, that it would not build a PVC plant in Convent, Louisiana.

Unequal distributions of environmental benefits and burdens in the past, present, and future will continue to be a controversial issue for the EPA. As the EPA and state regulatory agencies began implementation and enforcement of environmental rules and laws, those seeking to avoid their coverage and reach placed industrial uses and waste disposal/transfer facilities in the path of least resistance. These can be communities of color, low-income communities, or sites that already have similar uses. Over time these practices have placed increased stress on the environment and the communities. As the EPA embarked on its cleanup policies, it uncovered large disparities between disenfranchised communities and well-organized communities in terms of cleanup needs. In the early 1990s, under Administrator William Reilly, the EPA discovered that the best predictor of where an uncontrolled hazardous waste is, was not the air, land, or water conditions. It was the race of the population. The greater the proportion of people of color, the greater the chance that an

Rev. Dr. Benjamin F. Chavis Jr. campaigns for environmental justice. (Photograph by Gene Young)

uncontrolled hazardous-waste site existed nearby—to 99.9 percent of certainty (or 1 chance in 10,000 chance of being random). Because it is the EPA's mission to protect the environment, Reilly needed to use scarce tax dollars as efficiently as possible. If he was to succeed in his environmental mission, he had to engage the discussion of racism.

Both waste-disposal siting and industry-siting practices have replicated environmental disproportionality in terms of race and income all across the United States since the beginning of the twentieth century. Current and future environmental policy makers will need to uncover uncomfortable patterns of racism to fully eradicate the environmental effects of these practices.

The EPA has exercised a strong leadership role in environmental justice under both Republican and Democratic presidential administrations. (See discussions in Chapter 6 and Chapter 8.) After formation of the Office of Environmental Justice President Clinton issued an executive order on environmental justice (Executive Order 12898; see Appendix 1).

This executive order (EO) is still hotly contested at the EPA. The Office of the Inspector General (OIG) performed a thorough program analysis of the EPA and the Office of Environmental Justice (OEJ) to determine whether the EO was implemented. The OIG process is a long, thorough process that requires

President Clinton signing Executive Order 12898.

a formal response and programmatic changes from the EPA. It determined that the EPA had not implemented this order. The current position of the EPA is that it will protect all communities equally *and* will not implement the recommendations of the OIG report. The head of the OEJ, Barry Hill, has accused the OIG of racism. The EPA has not made required appointments to the National Environmental Justice Advisory Council (NEJAC) or arranged for its required meetings. There is concern that the Bush administration and EPA Administrator Stephen L. Johnson will eliminate the OEJ and NEJAC. There is great concern among Congressional Black Caucus members, and they are considering submitting new legislation in 2005 to institutionalize OEJ at the EPA.

As wastes have accumulated and as society has become more aware of their presence, the EPA has become more involved. Wastes, especially dangerous wastes, are always controversial. Preventing concentration of hazardous and industrial land uses in politically disenfranchised communities ultimately protects the environment for everyone. This is especially true if social goals of ecosystem sustainability are in place. The next step in addressing this controversy is determining how to adaptively clean up and reuse formerly contaminated land. Cities are where most people of color reside and where the most pollution and waste sites exist.

CITIES, THE EPA, BROWNFIELDS, PORTFIELDS, AND GRAYFIELDS

The U.S. environmental movement did not include urban issues until recently. Cities were often the port of entry for immigrants and migrants, explicitly marginalized groups. They also formed at multimodal transportation hubs, such as a river port and a railroad depot. In the centuries before EPA regulation, U.S. cities accumulated large amounts of waste. When these communities become contaminated, the EPA has a role to play.

The EPA application of environmental policy in urban areas is relatively new. Urban areas are much more complex than parks, forests, or other areas with low population. The EPA was formed at approximately the same time as many state environmental agencies. Many U.S. urban areas had at least a century of unrestrained industrialization, with no environmental regulation and no land use control whatsoever. Environmental movements focused on unpopulated areas, and did not

Cities such as Chicago are where most people of color live and where most pollution accumulates. (Photograph by Brent Merrill)

consider public health as a primary focus, instead emphasizing conservation and preservation of nature and biodiversity. They relied on citizen lawsuits. (See discussion in Chapter 2.) This adversarial winner-take-all approach did not include cities or people of color. One of the first cases involving NEPA alleged that African American people were themselves pollution requiring an environmental impact statement. Cities were the dynamic melting pots of new immigrants, and the destination of three waves of African Americans migrating north after the Civil War. These groups faced substantial discrimination in housing, employment, education, and municipal services. As industry and technology rapidly expanded in the city, so did these populations. As waste from industries increased and accumulated over time in the cities, so did the exposure to these wastes faced by immigrants, African Americans, and low-income people generally. These populations have faced tremendous displacement pressure when urban renewal policies increase gentrification, but African Americans and other people of color encounter additional difficult challenges in obtaining new housing within the same community (or elsewhere) after displacement. For example, when these populations are displaced, they often face paying a disproportionately high percentage of income for housing as well the loss of important and intangible community culture.

About 80 percent of the U.S. population lives in metropolitan areas. They face a number of pressing environmental problems, including exposure to toxic chemicals from Superfund sites, landfills, incinerators, leaded paint and gasoline, brownfields, industrial release, and pesticide use. In this context, EPA Regions 1 and 3 have identified "urban livability" as a strategic priority. Focusing on the upper mid-Atlantic to the Northeast, their mission is twofold: (1) to promote a better understanding of physical, chemical, and biological processes for detecting, assessing, and managing risks associated with the use and disposal of hazardous substances in urban environments; and (2) to disseminate the results of the research and provide technical expertise to various stakeholders, including community groups, municipal officials, the EPA, state and local regulators, and industry.

As urban areas grow and age, the current patterns of development and redevelopment can cause environmental degradation. Air quality is degraded through increased mobile, area, and point source emissions. Water quality is degraded through increased runoff volume, decreased infiltration, poor runoff quality, and increased discharge from point sources. Farmland and open spaces are converted to industrial, commercial, and residential use, often leaving abandoned, contaminated brownfields in the urban core.

The manner in which development or redevelopment takes place can significantly increase or decrease these impacts. The nation is still in the early stages of urban environmentalism, a complex subject with intricate and important histories. The potential for truly unintended consequences of nascent EPA revitalization policies for people, for places, and for policy is great. Hazardous wastes are accumulating every day, combining with a century of

Some residential sites of pollution are so toxic that demolition of the structure is the only way to clean them up. The demolished material is treated as hazardous waste. (Photograph © by Frank Miller)

relatively unchecked industrial waste that continues to pollute land, air, and water on a bioregional basis. The wastes in our ecosystem respect no man-made boundary, and any consequences of urban environmental intervention, through policy or otherwise, unintended or intended, affect us all.

Current environmental goals of sustainability will not be possible without inclusion of cities. For this reason, thorough and rigorous examination of any and all unintended consequences of emerging urban cleanup policies is necessary. Such examinations will be costly, time-consuming, and controversial. Mistakes will be made, lawsuits filed, legislation introduced, and protests occur. The EPA is moving very slowly in this direction through its new brownfields policies.

Brownfields are real properties the expansion, redevelopment, or reuse of which may be complicated by the presence or potential presence of a hazardous substance, pollutant, or contaminant. Cleaning up and reinvesting in these properties takes development pressures off undeveloped, open land, and both improves and protects the environment. Since its inception in 1995, the EPA's Brownfields Program has grown into a results-oriented program that has changed the way contaminated property is perceived, addressed, and managed. It is designed to empower states, communities, and other stakeholders in economic redevelopment to work together in a timely manner to prevent, assess, safely clean up, and sustainably reuse brownfields. It is estimated that there are more than 450,000 brownfields in the United States. Cleaning up and reinvesting in these properties increases local tax bases, facilitates job growth, utilizes existing infrastructure, takes development pressures off undeveloped, open land, and both improves and protects the environment. Initially, the EPA provided small amounts of seed money to local governments that launched hundreds of two-year brownfield pilot projects. Through passage of the Small Business Liability Relief and Brownfields Revitalization Act in 2002, some small, effective EPA polices passed into law. The Brownfields Law expanded the EPA's assistance by providing new tools for the public and private sectors to promote sustainable brownfields cleanup and reuse.

Grants continue to serve as the foundation of the EPA's Brownfields Program by supporting revitalization efforts through funding environmental assessment, cleanup, and job-training activities. Brownfields assessment grants provide funding for brownfield inventories, planning, environmental assessments, and community outreach. Brownfields Revolving Loan Fund grants capitalize loans that are used to clean up brownfields. Brownfields job-training grants provide environmental training for residents of affected communities. Brownfields cleanup grants provide direct funding for cleanup activities at certain properties with planned green space, recreational, or other nonprofit uses. The EPA's investment in the Brownfields Program has leveraged more than $6.5 billion in brownfields cleanup and redevelopment funding from the private and public sectors, and has created approximately 25,000 new jobs. The Brownfields Program continues to look to the future by increasing the types of properties it addresses, forming new partnerships, and undertaking new initiatives to help revitalize communities across the nation.

The Portfields Initiative, a federal government interagency effort, is led by the National Oceanic and Atmospheric Administration (NOAA). It is aimed at working with port communities in revitalizing waterfront areas, improving marine transportation (such as barges), and restoring and protecting coastal resources. Three port cities will receive federal support in the cleanup and reuse of contaminated properties: New Bedford, Massachusetts; Tampa, Florida; and Bellingham, Washington. Each was selected for its strong commitment to redevelopment, its particular needs, and the quality of its proposal to work with eight different federal agencies. The EPA will assess the needs of the cities and provide technical support in the cleanup of any brownfields sites.

The period since 1995 has seen the rise of "big box" stores, the consolidation and turnover of many retail chains, and a continuous push to provide commercial space that is larger, more diverse, and more amenity-rich. While all this activity may have benefited consumers, it has left a large number of vacant, obsolete malls and shopping centers in its wake. These properties, known as grayfields, are not usually considered assets to their communities.

But as we approach buildout of developable land, they provide important redevelopment opportunities.

Grayfields are typically located on major commercial corridors that offer excellent visibility and access. They often include large tracts of land under single ownership, thus eliminating the need to assemble many small parcels. These sites are ideal for large redevelopment projects, such as multifamily residential communities, updated commercial centers, and mixed-use developments. In appropriate areas, they also have the potential to be converted into office or low-impact industrial space that can accommodate primary employers. Although grayfields are typically less difficult to redevelop than brownfields, they present their own set of challenges. Demolition of large commercial buildings is expensive, and the sites are often covered with large areas of pavement that must be removed. Regulatory and financial incentives can help offset these costs, particularly for properties that are in less-than-ideal locations or are otherwise difficult to market.

The emerging controversies around cities facing the EPA are cleanup and revitalization of neighborhoods. Levels of cleanup are currently being debated in rules promulgated by the EPA. It is generally less expensive to clean up land to industrial standards, and more expensive to clean it up to residential standards. The level of cleanliness of the land determines how adaptive its reuse can be. Limited adaptive reuse tends to keep property values low, which in turn lowers the tax base, which in turn determines the level of municipal services available for the community.

Another controversial issue is how much inquiry a prospective purchaser of land needs to make in order to remain an innocent purchaser (thus avoiding some liability for cleanup of any contamination). The Small Business Liability Relief and Revitalization Act (the Brownfields Law) clarifies Comprehensive Environmental Response, Compensation, and Liability (CERCLA) liability provisions for certain landowners and potential property owners. It provides liability protections for certain property owners if they comply with certain provisions, including conducting all appropriate inquiries into present and past uses of the property and the potential presence of environmental contamination on the property. The Brownfields Law amends CERCLA to include an interim standard for conducting all appropriate inquiries, and requires the EPA to promulgate regulations that establish federal standards and practices for conducting all appropriate inquiries. The standards and practices are relevant to

- The innocent landowner defense against CERCLA liability;
- The contiguous property exemption from CERCLA liability;
- The bona fide prospective purchaser exemption to CERCLA liability;
- The brownfields site characterization and assessment grant programs.

The EPA developed the proposed rule by setting federal standards for all appropriate inquiries under a negotiated rulemaking process. Negotiated rulemaking brings together representatives of various interest groups and a federal agency to establish the text of a proposed rule. The EPA decided to use this process after a convening of affected stakeholders.

Standards and Practices for All Appropriate Inquiries was signed by the EPA Administrator and published in the Federal Register on August 26, 2004. It would establish specific regulatory requirements for conducting all appropriate inquiries into the previous ownership, uses, and environmental conditions of a property for the purposes of qualifying for certain landowner liability protections under CERCLA. Currently, the EPA is reviewing the comments received in response to the proposed rule and considering the issues raised by commentators. After considering all issues raised by public comments, it will respond to the comments and develop a final rulemaking policy.

These developing rules and regulations will find expression in controversies regarding urban cleanup. At some point, issues such as how much due diligence is required to know how polluted a site is will be moot because of the accumulation of emissions and wastes over time. Everyone will know that the site is polluted. However, the actual standards of cleanliness and safety will continue to be controversial. In areas of the industrialized Northeast, banks now require prospective property owners to obtain an environmental assessment as a condition of obtaining a mortgage for the purchase of a property. Banks and lending institutions do not want to be held liable for cleaning up pollution. Developers of contaminated sites can now get environmental insurance to help prevent the costs of liability for cleanup from stopping the project. With wastes increasing as fast as our knowledge about them and with large financial institutions entering the forum of urban environmentalism, it is likely that this particular controversy will grow.

Many communities are able to resist polluting land uses without having to provide scientific proof that the emissions would harm them. Other communities, especially in areas with a concentration of commercial and industrial uses, feel that science is used against them. Generally, the longer one waits to clean up accumulating industrial pollution, the more it migrates through the ecosystem. This can increase the actual cost of a cleanup as well as the threat to the community. To the extent that scientific standards are used to determine toxicity and the degree and type of hazard, they can influence the cost of any cleanup. The actual standards for cleanup are still developing. (See discussion of how to do a cleanup in Chapter 4.)

Urban environmentalism is a sign of maturation in environmental public policy. It confronts all the flash points of race, environmental justice, wastes, land use control and private property, and accumulated impacts. The dangerous chemicals in a waste site can synergize, and almost always migrate through the ecosystem to other communities. The EPA will not be able to meet future

It often is difficult to see the effects of ecological degradation until species become extinct. (Photograph by Brent Merrill)

challenges of sustainability, community-based environmental protection, and ecosystem approaches without this confrontation.

All the controversies discussed above are symbolic of large societal power struggles to engage pernicious environmental issues. None of the cases is unique. All of them represent other cases that exist across the United States. These cases are dynamic, and the issues they represent are controversial. Unlike other areas of federal policy, such as housing, transportation, and education, the environment can be politically compromised only so long before the underlying controversies must be addressed. The EPA cannot avoid them. Some of these controversial issues will require new terminology. For example, the case study method of environmental analysis may have to give way to a "place study" method of analysis. The case study method is premised on the idea that results from one case can be generalized to others. This is of great assistance when developing national policy, but may not reflect the true state of the environment in application. No one place or culture is the same as another. All environmental policies are tested in the real world of local implementation. If an ecosystem in one place is different from that in another place, then implementation of a particular environmental policy in the second place may fail. The place study method of analysis was developed by the National Environmental Justice Advisory Council to incorporate issues of ecology and of the culture of the people in that place. It was recommended for application to brownfields programs. (The author was a member of the team making this recommendation.)

All these controversies engage most of the future challenges to the EPA. The future challenges of community-based environmental protection, sustainability, ecosystem approaches, and cumulative impacts strongly resonate with controversial concepts of environmental justice, pollution control technologies, and urban environmentalism. (See discussion in Chapter 6.) This situation will require changes in the tradition and culture of the EPA.

☆ 4 ☆

Traditions and Culture
of the EPA

BEGINNING POLICIES: 1970–1973

The creation of the EPA in 1970 brought a number of federal programs concerned with various aspects of the environment under the control of a single regulatory agency. In the same year Congress passed the Clean Air Act, which directed the EPA to set national air quality standards. In these early years many traditions and cultures were formed at the EPA. The task was to create a functioning federal administrative agency out of fifteen agencies and parts of agencies from throughout the federal government, two of which, in the case of pesticides, had conflicting missions. The initial structure reflected the gross nature of the pollution problems as they were then perceived. Air and water programs were under one assistant administrator. The assistant administrator for categorical Programs had responsibility for almost everything else: pesticides, radiation, and solid waste.

The first and most important mission was to establish the credibility of the EPA, so as to ensure that the public and the regulated community realized that the government was serious about its charge to protect the environment. One way to do that was through enforcement. Shortly after its creation, the EPA filed lawsuits against the cities of Detroit, Cleveland, and Atlanta for polluting their rivers with sewage. Similar actions against industry followed. These actions resulted in demonstrable improvement of water quality in these cities and extensive progress in alleviating industrial pollution. Equally important was the goal of educating and working with the public. Establishment of the EPA was a response to many expressions of concern by the public about the quality of the environment. It rapidly became clear that the EPA would be able to carry out its mission only if the public understood both these problems and the EPA's mandate to address them.

The second immediate challenge was to create awareness of and support for the EPA. A large-scale public affairs program was undertaken at headquarters and in the regional offices. Every senior EPA official had a heavy schedule of speaking engagements to rally understanding of and support for the EPA. Against this backdrop of aggressive enforcement and education, the regulatory efforts of the EPA began to play out. The EPA was already starting to wrestle with congressionally imposed deadlines as it began to implement the requirements of the Clean Air Act of 1970. It was required to set criteria for national ambient air quality standards 120 days after the Clean Air Act passed and 150 days after the EPA began operation. What was so striking about that process was the paucity of sophisticated scientific data upon which the EPA made sound regulatory judgments. In addition, there was lack of economic analysis of the impacts of such standards and regulations.

The EPA, in the early days, spent much of its time creatively interpreting the statutes it had to administer. Prior to the passage of the Clean Water Act in 1972, it began implementing a discharge permit program under the 1899 Rivers and Harbors Act. That effort led to such logic as defining hot water discharges from power plants as refuse. One of the highlights of the EPA's early water pollution control efforts was the signing of the Great Lakes Water Quality Agreement in 1972. This historic agreement with Canada, driven by a mutual international decision to save a world treasure, has, over its lifetime, resulted in substantial improvement in the water quality of the Great Lakes. In 1971, the EPA's response to the dumping of wastes was to initiate Operation 5000, a program to close 5,000 open dumps and replace them with, or convert them to, sanitary landfills—requiring a six-inch soil cover at the end of each day.

In the mid-1970s, the EPA began to assume its massive regulatory stance. The Clean Water Act and the reauthorization of the Federal Insecticide, Fungicide, and Rodenticide Act in 1972, the passage of the Resource Conservation and Recovery Act in 1976, and the reauthorization of the Clean Air Act in 1977 set in motion the regulatory machinery in operation today. What defined the EPA in its earliest days was less the need to set a regulatory agenda than a need to convey a sense of mission and purpose to the public, the states, and the regulated community. The EPA set out to create a federal environmental presence, to set a uniform level of expectation that would end "forum shopping" among the states by industry, and to ensure that people knew the EPA would enforce environmental regulations. These goals set the stage for the more sophisticated regulatory posture the EPA assumes today.

For the first twenty years, the EPA was basically reactive. As environmental problems were identified, the public conveyed its concern to Congress, and Congress passed laws to try to solve the problems within some, often well-defined, time frame. The EPA then implemented the laws using the resources—budget and staff—allocated by Congress. Consequently, it has seen its missions largely as managing the reduction of pollution in general, and, pollution that is defined in the laws that it administers, in particular. The EPA's internal programmatic structure mirrors the environmental legislation that it is required to implement. Moreover, the tools the EPA traditionally has used to reduce pollution have been limited to the emission controls it could force polluters to apply through regulatory action. This reactive mode has limited the efficiency and effectiveness of the EPA's environmental protection efforts. Because of its tendency to react to environmental problems defined in specific environmental laws, the EPA has made little effort to compare the relative seriousness of different problems. Moreover, it has done very little to anticipate environmental problems or to take preemptive actions that reduce the likelihood of the occurrence of an environmental problem.

Because most of the EPA's program offices have been responsible for implementing specific laws, they have tended to view environmental problems separately. Each program office has been concerned primarily with the problems it has been mandated to remediate, and questions of relative seriousness or urgency generally have remained unasked. Consequently, there has been little correlation between the resources dedicated to different environmental problems and the relative risks posed by those problems.

DYNAMIC PRIORITIES: ENVIRONMENTAL PROTECTION, PUBLIC HEALTH, AND THE ECONOMY

The predominant climate from which the EPA's predecessor programs arose was decades-old public health traditions. The Public Health Service had a tradition of not intervening in any problem unless invited by state officials, a situation that did little to foster strong enforcement. The preventive, pragmatic, disease-specific nature of public health traditions was simply not interventionist enough to lead the fight for restoration of the environment.

The relationship between public health and environmental law and policy was first about controlling pollution and other toxic substances. Water pollution, air pollution, and other environmental toxins can have significant, deleterious effects on the public's health. The EPA policy makers tried to devise methods and strategies to lessen the public health risks posed by these polluting substances, and this effort has grown with increased emphasis on accumulating emissions and impacts. (See discussion of cumulative impacts in Chapter 6.) Although pollution control might be the most obvious and important intersection between environmental policy and public health, legal and policy decisions regarding the management and preservation of the nation's natural resources also potentially affect the public's health significantly. Preserving plant and animal species, allocating water resources, and managing the nation's public lands, to name just a few examples, potentially bear on matters of public health and safety. For instance, some plant species have the potential to be turned into helpful and perhaps lifesaving pharmaceuticals.

The EPA has registered those plants as pesticides that are genetically altered to contain pesticide as part of their makeup. (Jupiter Images)

Forest fires pose significant human health risks in addition to harming the environment. Risky activities on the public lands can imperil both participants and bystanders. And prohibiting extractive activities such as mining or oil drilling on the public lands may result in lost jobs, in turn causing negative health effects on those who become unemployed.

The EPA was a hybrid formed from all these many and frequently conflicting patterns. The young EPA was confronted with a tremendously difficult regulatory mission. How should ecological goals be balanced with those related to public health and the common law rights of the individual? How should scientific findings be interpreted? What are the limits of science in environmental policy-making? What is causality and what is correlation, over time? How are gradations of uncertainty communicated to lawmakers, reporters, regulated industries, and citizens? How can the EPA control dangerous land uses in the face of a strong private property tradition in the United States? The regulatory challenge was so great that the EPA quickly became, and today remains, involved in many of the most controversial issues in the federal government. (See discussion in Chapter 3.) Yet the EPA has made important progress in cleaning up the U.S. air and water. The persistent organochlorine pesticides of the mid-1980s, such as DDT, have been largely eliminated, and fair to good progress is being made in dealing with abandoned hazardous-waste sites. The challenges of the future involve extremely important but less visible problems of environmental justice, cross-media pollution, stratospheric ozone depletion, and protection of air and water supplies against accumulating types of toxic substances. Public opinion polls indicate that the people are firmly committed to the fulfillment of the EPA's public health and environmental goals. Controversy continues over the appropriate direction, application, and scale of the EPA's future regulatory mission. The EPA's laws are still reauthorized and amended one at a time. This prevents some newer approaches to environmental policy-making that concern sustainability, cumulative impacts, cross-media pollution, and ecological thinking. (See discussion in Chapter 6.)

The EPA's legally assigned missions always seem bigger than its resources. As Congress works to resolve the problem of the deficit in any given year, EPA managers have to make sure they and their coworkers learn new ways to improve their effectiveness as regulators. The policy of cleaning up the environment is simple on its face, but difficult to develop. Most of the policy starts as legislation that empowers the EPA to promulgate rules and regulations to enact the law. The steadfast commitment to clean up, a tradition in most forms of environmentalism, is also present at the EPA, but as a federal agency the EPA is interpreted through the structure of law in the agency's creation and in its implementation. The following discussion concerns how the law of cleanup evolved at the EPA. It demonstrates the tension between dynamic priorities of public health and environmental protection, and illustrates how much the role of law affects the traditions and culture of a federal agency such as the EPA. One particular controversy associated with early EPA responses to cleanup was Love Canal. (See discussion in Chapter 3.)

The Ethos of Cleaning Up the Environment

The law of cleanup emerged in the 1980s. Complicated policy frontiers were met head-on. The problems of cleanup are some of the most controversial. Insistent questions concerning standards for cleanliness, relocation of people, site remediation, mitigation remedies and their enforcement, citizen monitoring, and human and ecological health risks have to be answered. Many of these questions remain, and involve more and more people. (See discussion of the toxics release inventory in Chapter 5.) The following discussion details the EPA response, with an emphasis on its processes, policies, and procedures.

The EPA involvement in cleanup issues was substantially increased with the passage of several important laws. The Superfund Amendments and Reauthorization Act of 1986 reauthorized the Comprehensive Environmental Response, Compensation, and Liability Act (CERCLA) to continue cleanup activities around the country. Several site-specific amendments, definition clarifications, and technical requirements were appended to the legislation, including additional enforcement authority. CERCLA, commonly known as Superfund, had been enacted by Congress on December 11, 1980. This law created a tax on the chemical and petroleum industries and provided broad federal authority to respond directly to releases or threatened releases of hazardous substances that might endanger public health or the environment. Over five years, $1.6 billion was collected and was placed in a trust fund for cleaning up abandoned or uncontrolled hazardous-waste sites. CERCLA

- Established prohibitions and requirements concerning closed and abandoned hazardous-waste sites;
- Provided for liability of persons responsible for releases of hazardous waste at these sites;
- Established a trust fund to provide for cleanup when no responsible party could be identified.

The law authorized two kinds of response actions: (1) short-term removals, where actions were taken to address releases or threatened releases requiring prompt response; (2) long-term remedial responses that permanently and significantly reduced the dangers associated with releases or threats of releases of hazardous substances that were serious, but not immediately life-threatening. These actions can be conducted only at sites on the EPA's national priorities list.

CERCLA also enabled the revision of the National Contingency Plan (NCP). The NCP provided the guidelines and procedures for responding to releases and threatened releases of hazardous substances, pollutants, or contaminants. It also established the NPL.

The Superfund Amendments and Reauthorization Act (SARA) amended CERCLA on October 17, 1986. It reflected the EPA's experience in administering the complex Superfund program during its first six years and made several important changes and additions to the program. SARA

- Stressed the importance of permanent remedies and innovative treatment technologies in cleaning up hazardous-waste sites;
- Required Superfund actions to consider the standards and requirements found in other state and federal environmental laws and regulations;
- Provided new enforcement authorities and settlement tools;
- Increased state involvement in every phase of the Superfund program;
- Increased the focus on human health problems posed by hazardous-waste sites;
- Encouraged greater citizen participation in decisions on how sites should be cleaned up;
- Increased the size of the trust fund to $8.5 billion.

SARA also required the EPA to revise the hazard ranking system (HRS) to ensure that it accurately assessed the relative degree of risk to human health and the environment posed by uncontrolled hazardous-waste sites that may be placed on the NPL. The HRS is the principal mechanism the EPA uses to place uncontrolled waste sites on the NPL. It is a numerically based screening system that uses information from initial, limited investigations—the preliminary assessment and the site inspection—to assess the relative potential of sites to pose a threat to human health or the environment. They are used to evaluate the potential for a release of hazardous substances from a site.

The preliminary assessment (PA) is a limited-scope investigation performed on every CERCLIS site. It collects readily available information about a site and its surrounding area, and is designed to distinguish, based on limited data, between sites that pose little or no threat to human health and the environment and sites that may pose a threat and thus require further investigation. The PA also identifies sites requiring assessment for possible emergency response actions. If the PA results in a recommendation for further investigation, a site inspection (SI) is performed. The EPA publication *Guidance for Performing Preliminary Assessments Under CERCLA* (PB92-963303, EPA 9345.0-01A, September 1991) provides more information on conducting PAs.

An SI identifies sites that enter the NPL site listing process and provides the data needed for HRS scoring and documentation. SI investigators typically collect environmental and waste samples to determine what hazardous substances are present at a site. They determine if these substances are being released to the environment and assess if they have reached nearby targets. The SI can be conducted in one stage or two. The first stage, or focused SI, tests hypotheses developed during the PA and can yield information sufficient to prepare an HRS scoring package. If further information is necessary to document an HRS score, an expanded SI is conducted. The EPA publication *Guidance for Performing Site Inspections Under CERCLA: Interim Final* (PB92-963375, EPA 9345.1-05, September 1992) provides more information on conducting SIs.

Information collected during the PA and SI is used to calculate an HRS score. Sites with an HRS score of 28.50 or greater are eligible for listing on the NPL and require the preparation of an HRS scoring package. HRS scores do not determine the priority in funding EPA remedial response actions because the information collected to develop the scores is not sufficient to determine either the extent of contamination or the appropriate response for a particular site. The sites with the highest scores do not necessarily come to the EPA's attention first—this would require stopping work at sites where response actions were already under way. The EPA relies on more detailed studies in the remedial investigation/feasibility study that typically follows listing. The HRS uses a structured analysis approach to scoring sites that assigns numerical values to factors relating to risk on the basis of conditions at the site. The factors are grouped into three categories:

1. Likelihood that a site has released or has the potential to release hazardous substances into the environment;
2. Characteristics of the waste (e.g., toxicity and waste quantity);
3. People or sensitive environments (targets) affected by the release.

In addition, four pathways can be scored under the HRS:

1. Groundwater migration (drinking water);
2. Surface water migration (drinking water, human food chain, sensitive environments);
3. Soil exposure (resident population, nearby population, sensitive environments);
4. Air migration (population, sensitive environments).

After scores are calculated for one or more pathways, they are combined using a root-mean-square equation to determine the overall site score. The electronic scoring systems Superscreen and Quickscore can be used to do the scoring calculations. HRS Superscreen is a decision support model created by the Office of Superfund Remediation and Technology Innovation of the EPA to assist site assessment investigations and HRS scoring and documentation. It provides electronic mechanisms for accurate, efficient, and convenient scoring and documenting sites according to the rules of the HRS. HRS Superscreen allows one to enter and evaluate site-specific information including sampling data, waste quantities, physical parameters, and target data, as well as to enter descriptive narrative text and reference citations to document entered data and select specific HRS factor values.

HRS Superscreen is designed to do the following:

- Improve the computerized HRS scoring of sites;
- Provide a user-friendly, Windows-based environment for documenting site scores;
- Integrate the Superfund chemical data matrix to provide substance characteristics;
- Minimize mathematical scoring errors;
- Facilitate SI reporting and decision-making;
- Generate a draft HRS documentation record, EPA's NPL characteristics data collection form, and data entry reports for further editing in a word processor.

The data and resulting scores rely on understanding of and adherence to the rules of the HRS. Use of Superscreen does not guarantee that an HRS package which is submitted for NPL consideration is either qualified or compliant with the guidance and rules of the HRS. It does not produce a final HRS package; the information generated by the program still needs to be reviewed and edited by a person familiar with the HRS. All HRS packages and HRS scores are subject to EPA headquarters inspection and qualification.

HRS Quickscore also was created by the Office of Superfund Remediation and Technology Innovation of the EPA to assist in scoring sites using HRS. It is an electronic set of HRS score sheets that executes real-time site score calculations. It was designed to assist in developing a conceptual site model for Superfund site assessments and is intended for use by individuals who plan and implement preliminary assessments, site inspections, and other data collection efforts according to the HRS rules, as well as for individuals who write and review HRS documentation records.

HRS Quickscore's key functions include the following:

- Quick HRS pathway and site score calculations;
- HRS score sheet preparation and printing;
- Easy identification of HRS data gaps in the conceptual site model;
- Back-of-the-envelope (accessible and interactive) tracking of data gaps, notes, refinements, and adjustments in scenario testing;
- Scratch-pad capabilities to make notes as you work.

The data and resulting scores rely on the user's understanding of and adherence to the rules of the HRS. Use of Quickscore does not guarantee that a document is either qualified or compliant with the guidance and rules of the HRS. All HRS packages and HRS scores are subject to EPA inspection and qualification.

If all pathway scores are low, the site score is low. However, the site score can be relatively high even if only one pathway score is high. This is an important requirement for HRS scoring, because some extremely dangerous sites pose threats through only one pathway.

After a site is listed on the NPL, a remedial investigation/feasibility study (RI/FS) is performed at the site. The remedial investigation serves as the mechanism for collecting data to characterize site conditions, determine the nature of the waste, assess risk to human health and the environment, and conduct treatability testing to evaluate the potential performance and cost of the treatment technologies being considered.

The FS is the mechanism for the development, screening, and detailed evaluation of alternative remedial actions. It and the RI are conducted concurrently—data collected in the RI influence the development of remedial alternatives in the FS, which in turn affects the data needs and scope of treatability studies and additional field investigations. This phased approach encourages the continual scoping of the site characterization effort, which minimizes the collection of unnecessary data and maximizes data quality.

Scoping is the initial planning phase of the RI/FS process. Many of the planning steps begun here are continued and refined in later phases of the RI/FS. Scoping typically begins with the collection of existing site data, including data from previous investigations, such as the preliminary assessment and site inspection. On the basis of this information, site management planning is undertaken to do the following:

- Preliminarily identify boundaries of the study area;
- Identify likely remedial action objectives and whether interim actions may be necessary or appropriate;
- Establish whether the site may best be remedied as one or several separate operable units.

Once an overall management strategy is agreed upon, the RI/FS for a specific project or the site as a whole is planned. Typical scoping activities include

- Initiating the identification and discussion of potential applicable or relevant and appropriate requirements with the support of the EPA, and determining the types of decisions to be made and identifying the data needed to support these decisions;
- Assembling a technical advisory committee to assist in activities, serve as a review board for important deliverables (written work products), and monitor progress during the study;
- Preparing the work plan, sampling and analysis plan, health and safety plan, and community relations plan.

Field sampling and laboratory analyses are initiated during the site characterization phase of the RI/FS. A preliminary site characterization summary is prepared to provide the EPA with information on the site early in the process, before preparation of the full RI report. This summary is useful in determining the feasibility of potential technologies and in assisting both the lead and the support agencies with the initial identification of applicable or relevant and appropriate requirements. The summary can also be sent to the Agency for Toxic Substances and Disease Registry (ATSDR) to assist the EPA in performing health assessments. (See discussion of ATSDR in Chapter 3.) A baseline risk assessment is developed to identify the existing or potential risks that may be posed to human health and the environment by the site. Because this assessment identifies the primary health and environmental threats at the site, it provides valuable input to the development and evaluation of alternatives during the feasibility study.

The development of alternatives phase of the RI/FS process usually begins during scoping, when likely response scenarios may first be identified. The development of alternatives requires the following:

- Identifying remedial action objectives;
- Identifying potential treatment, resource recovery, and containment technologies that will satisfy these objectives;
- Screening the technologies on the basis of their effectiveness, implementability, and cost;
- Assembling technologies and their associated containment or disposal requirements into alternatives for the contaminated media at the site or for the operable unit.

Alternatives can be developed to address the contaminated medium, a specific area of the site, or the entire site. Once potential alternatives have been developed, it may be necessary to screen out certain options to reduce the number of alternatives that will be analyzed. The screening process is usually done on a general basis and with limited resources because the information necessary to fully evaluate the alternatives may not be complete at this point in the process.

Treatability investigations are the next-to-last phase of the RI/FS process. They are conducted primarily to

- Provide sufficient data to allow treatment alternatives to be fully developed and evaluated during the detailed analysis phase and to support the remedial design or remedial action of selected alternatives;
- Reduce cost and performance uncertainties for treatment alternatives to acceptable levels so that a remedy can be selected;
- Enable a detailed analysis.

Potentially Responsible Parties

All work is done under the control of potentially responsible parties (PRPs), who are responsible for the long-term performance of the remedy. The PRPs are former or current owners of the property, shippers of the material to be cleaned up, creators of the chemical, and those who stored toxic chemicals on the property. They pay for the cleanup to the extent that they can be found, and have assets. They are jointly and severably liable. That is, the EPA can sue any one of them for the cost of the cleanup, regardless of the degree of liability. PRPs then can sue each other to the degree to which they are liable. This results in much litigation and negotiation, which is why it is important for citizens to know the EPA cleanup process. The process can become muddled as PRPs negotiate liability, and attempt to avoid liability and reduce cleanup costs. Some companies file for bankruptcy to avoid liability. Cleanup liability is an enormous issue in brownfields policies. (See discussion in Chapter 3.) One large unanswered question is municipal liability for a cleanup. If a municipality forecloses on an abandoned contaminated site for failure to pay property taxes, it is then the owner and liable for cleanup. This happened in Milwaukee, Wisconsin. If the owner of a contaminated site gives it to a non-profit organization, the new owner is liable for cleanup. This happened to a church in Oakland, California. If the municipality does not foreclose on the contaminated site, it loses the revenue from taxes it could otherwise receive, and it has a contaminated property in its midst.

The PRP provides the input necessary to effect site remediation whether it is done with in-house resources or through the use of hired contractors. It assigns the work to the remedial design professional (RDP), the remedial assistance contractor (RAC), and the independent quality assurance team (IQAT).

The primary function of the RDP is to provide the PRP with a set of plans and specifications for the proposed remediation that meets the requirements, is within budget, and is on schedule. Major tasks for which the RDP may be responsible include collecting, evaluating, and interpreting data required for the design (providing a complete engineered design of the remedial assistance); identifying and obtaining easements, permits, and approvals necessary for the RDP/RAC; updating plan and specification changes during construction.

In addition to the above responsibilities, the RDP will usually be required to provide a resident engineer to act as the PRP's agent on the site during construction. This person is one of the most critical in establishing and maintaining construction quality. Typically the resident engineer is required to

- Serve as the PRP's and RDP's liaison with the contractor;
- Maintain job records, review submittal schedules, and log shop drawings and samples;
- Review work, disapprove defective work, and verify that test and start-up procedures are accomplished;
- Prepare progress reports, make recommendations concerning inspections and tests, and draft change orders;
- Conduct the prefinal and final inspection of completed work;
- Prepare a project closeout report.

The contractor's primary responsibility is to meet the quality standards specified by the design and accepted trade practices. The contractor is responsible to the PRP for implementing and maintaining the program. The following is a list of responsibilities that generally apply to RACs on most jobs:

- Obtain all necessary construction permits and approvals;
- Construct the project according to the plans and specifications;
- Provide progress schedules and other required submittals;
- Maintain "record drawings" at the site, properly noting all changes made during construction;
- Be responsible for project safety;
- Implement and maintain a construction quality control (QC) program;
- Cooperate fully with inspection authorities.

The IQAT members are from testing and inspection organizations, independent of the contractor, who are responsible for examining and testing materials, procedures, and equipment during the construction. Since the PRP is responsible for the remediation, the IQAT is hired by the PRP. Typical functions of the IQAT are the following:

- Direct and perform tests for quality assurance inspection activities;
- Verify that the construction QC plan is implemented;

- Perform independent on-site inspections of the work to assess compliance with project standards;
- Verify that equipment and testing procedures meet the test requirements;
- Report the results of all inspections to the PRP and EPA.

When engaging an oversight official capable of providing support in all technical aspects of remedial design and remedial assistance, it is important to know the person's duties. The oversight official has some form of contractual relationship with the EPA. In addition to reviewing PRP submittals and reports, he makes on-site observations of the work in progress to monitor the PRP's quality assurance program. The oversight official does not have authority to authorize any deviation from the contract documents or assume any of the responsibilities of the contractor. The recommended options available for oversight support include the alternative remedial contract strategy (ARCS); which in the U.S. Army Corps Detailed Analysis is the last phase of the RI/FS process. Once sufficient data are available, alternatives are evaluated in detail with respect to nine criteria that the EPA has developed to address the statutory requirements and preferences of CERCLA: (1) overall protection of human health and the environment; (2) compliance with applicable or relevant and appropriate requirements; (3) long-term effectiveness and permanence; (4) reduction of toxicity, mobility, or volume; (5) short-term effectiveness; (6) implementability; (7) cost; (8) state acceptance; and (9) community acceptance.

The alternatives are analyzed individually against each criterion and then compared against each other to determine their respective strengths and weaknesses and to identify the key trade-offs that must be balanced for the site. The results of the detailed analysis are summarized so that an appropriate remedy consistent with CERCLA can be selected.

The EPA response to the public outcry and congressional requirement for cleanup of dangerous places was so strong that cleanup became a tradition and part of EPA's culture. It is a continuing challenge. Fortunately, sophisticated computer hardware and software are making it easier for federal regulators to stay abreast of huge volumes of data. Even so, there can be no technological substitute for solid strategic planning as the EPA faces both foreseeable and unforeseeable challenges. One area of increased emphasis has been children and their environment. Children represent a vulnerable population from a public health perspective and challenge scientific risk models.

Children's Health Protection

Children are a major concern of the public, and threats to their health will organize and mobilize a community very quickly. The Children's Health

Wild and beautiful places require environmental protection. This public value enhances the credibility of the EPA. (Photograph © by Frank Miller)

Protection Office of the EPA supports and facilitates the EPA's efforts to protect children's health by working with federal agencies, states, and private sector entities. The health of children affected by environmental risks has been a continual concern of the EPA. Children are often more heavily exposed to toxins in the environment. Pound for pound, they breathe more air, drink more water, and eat more food than adults. Their behavior patterns, such as playing close to the ground and engaging in hand-to-mouth activity, increase their exposure to potential toxics. In addition, they may be more vulnerable to environmental hazards because their systems are still developing, often making them less able than adults to metabolize, detoxify, and excrete toxins. Environmental risks to children include asthma-exacerbating air pollution, lead-based paint in older homes, impacts of accumulating industrial emissions, treatment-resistant microbes in drinking water, and persistent chemicals that may cause cancer or induce reproductive or developmental changes.

Protecting children's health from environmental pollutants has been a major concern for the EPA. An EPA-wide policy to ensure that environmental health risks of children are explicitly and consistently evaluated in risk assessments, risk characterizations, and environmental and public health standards was established in 1995. In 1996 the National Agenda to Protect Children's Health from Environmental Threats, which expanded the EPA's activities aimed at ensuring a consistent approach to improving risk assessments to specifically address children's risks, was adopted. The EPA is committed to protecting all children from environmental health threats by fully considering risks to them and addressing those risks, where appropriate, through national health-based environmental standards.

In 1997 the Office of Children's Health Protection (OCHP) was established to implement the EPA's commitment to protect children from environmental health hazards. OCHP's mission is to make protection of the health of children and of the aging a fundamental goal of public health and environmental protection in the United States and around the world.

OCHP meets its mission by building infrastructure and capacity in federal agencies, states, communities, and private sector entities, such as health care providers. These entities must have the knowledge, resources, and capacity needed to institutionalize children's environmental health in the way they do business. OCHP invests substantial effort to assure that protecting children from environmental threats is a continuing effort and is integrated into public health considerations. It also works to increase awareness of environmental hazards that can affect children. OCHP recognizes that while government and other organizations can do much to help protect children from environmental threats, communities, parents, and other caregivers can do much to reduce children's exposure to pollutants. OCHP has worked to raise awareness of environmental threats and has provided information and resources to enable others to take action. OCHP supports and facilitates the EPA's efforts in three primary areas: (1) regulations and standards, (2) science and risk assessment, and (3) public awareness, community-based programs, and education.

In addition to work within the EPA, OCHP plays a vital role working with other federal departments and agencies, and others to protect children from environmental health threats. Its efforts to build community capacity in children's environmental health protection include

- Providing information and tools to the public;
- Supporting community actions to protect children;
- Increasing the ability of health professionals to identify, prevent, and reduce environmental health threats to children;
- Engaging youth in children's environmental health protection;
- Working with states to develop programs to address children's environmental health issues.

The state of the science in children's environmental health is generally regarded to be in its infancy because the information needed to conduct risk assessments is poor. Traditionally, toxicologists have focused on the adult population. Recently, the EPA has begun a research effort to better understand how children differ from adults. The enormous task that faces the EPA and other federal agencies in the next several decades is to expand research on the influence of environmental pollution on children's development and disease.

The EPA and the National Institute of Environmental Health Sciences have established twelve centers for children's environmental health and disease prevention research that are dedicated solely to the study of children's environmental health hazards. These unique centers perform targeted research in children's environmental health and translate their scientific findings into intervention and prevention strategies by working with communities. Four of the twelve centers were established in October 2001 and are focusing their research on neurodevelopmental disorders in children. The original eight centers were established in 1998 and have varied research programs that include childhood pesticide exposures and asthma.

The EPA's National Center for Environmental Research supports extramural research grants and contracts on topics related to children's environmental health. The National Children's Study was proposed and developed through the cooperation of the EPA, the National Institute of Child Health and Development, the National Institute of Environmental Health Sciences, and the Centers for Disease Control and Prevention. It will examine the effects of environmental influences on the health and development of more than 100,000 children across the United States, following them from before birth until age twenty-one. The National Children's Study (then called the Children's Longitudinal Cohort Study) was passed by Congress and signed into law on October 17, 2000, as a part of the Children's Health Bill. That same month the EPA released the Strategy for Research on Environmental Risks to Children. It provides a framework for research needs and priorities to guide programs over the next five to ten years. It also includes a stable, long-term core program of research in hazard identification, dose-response assessment, exposure assessment, and risk management, as well as problem-oriented research that addresses current critical needs identified by EPA program offices and regions.

The EPA developed the *Child-Specific Exposure Factors Handbook*, which lists exposure factors specifically for children up to nineteen years of age. The *Handbook* summarizes key data on human behaviors and characteristics that affect children's exposure to environmental contaminants, and recommends quantitative data values to use in children's health risk assessment. Although *The Exposure Factors Handbook* (EPA/600/P-95/002Fa-c), published in 1997, included exposure factors and related data on both adults and children, the EPA program offices identified the need to consolidate all children's exposure data into one document. The goal of *The Child-Specific Exposure Factors Handbook* is to fulfill this need. It provides a summary of up-to-date statistical data on such factors assessing children exposures as drinking water consumption; soil ingestion; inhalation rates; dermal factors including skin area and soil adherence; consumption of fresh fruits and vegetables, fish, meats, dairy products, homegrown foods, and breast milk; activity patterns; body weight; consumer products, such as soaps, cleaners, cosmetics, and fuels used around the house; and life expectancy.

The National Health and Nutrition Examination Study published *National Report on Human Exposures to Environmental Chemicals.* This study used biomonitoring to assess human exposures to a set of 116 environmental pollutants. Biomonitoring is the assessment of human exposure by measuring the chemicals or their metabolites in human specimens, such as blood and urine. This study included exposures of children as well as adults. The study has become an annual survey, so that in the future it will be possible to determine how environmental exposures are changing over time. An EPA work group has been exploring children's exposure assessment issues. It has concluded that a major issue facing EPA assessors is how to consider age-related changes in behavior and physiology when preparing exposure assessments for children. Children's behavior changes over time in ways that can have an important impact on exposure. Further, children's physiology changes over time in ways that can impact both their exposures and their susceptibility to certain health effects. There are two aspects to these physiological changes. First, there are anatomical changes resulting from physical growth. Second, there are changes in pharmacokinetics and pharmacodynamics that affect the absorption, distribution, excretion, and effects of environmental contaminants. The EPA is examining the pharmacokinetic/pharmacodynamic changes in children through other efforts, and future meetings on this topic are anticipated.

OCHP provides leadership in reshaping the EPA's policy on science and risk assessment for children's environmental health by working with EPA scientists to modify current approaches to accommodate age-specific biological differences when conducting exposure assessments and quantitative risk assessments. The tradition of science and risk assessment merges with a culture and mission of protecting the public health.

To protect the nation's children from harm due to exposure to environmental contamination, the EPA's standards need to consider and address risks to children that are potentially different from risks to adults. The EPA's traditional method of setting human health protection standards has relied almost exclusively on the assessment of risks to adults. This broad focus is understandable, given how little was known about environmental risk before 1970. It was assumed that people were comparable in terms of their response to exposures to pollution. As more was learned about the effects of environmental contaminants on human health, the differences between subsets of the population, particularly differences between children and adults, began to emerge. A 1993 National Academy of Sciences report, *Pesticides in the Diets of Infants and Children,* concluded that scientific and regulatory approaches did not adequately protect infants and children from pesticide residues in food.

The EPA is committed to considering risks to children when developing standards to protect human health and the environment. This commitment is reflected in the development of rules and policies the EPA and other federal agencies and departments use to evaluate the health and safety effects of planned regulations on children under Executive Order 13045, "Protection of

Children from Environmental Health Risks and Safety Risks." In addition, an EPA policy on evaluating health risks to children requires all EPA standards and regulations to explicitly consider risks to fetuses, infants, and children. To help its rule writers apply the executive order and EPA policy, the EPA issued this guidance in November 1998. It typically prepares an analytic blueprint when developing rules, policies, and other actions. An analytic blueprint describes the EPA's plans for data collection and analyses to support developing the action. To ensure that children's health is properly considered, the guidelines identify the need for analyses related to children's health that include determining whether the action may disproportionately affect children, assessing risks to children, and analyzing the distribution of the costs and benefits. The EPA developed *The Children's Health Evaluation Handbook* as a reference tool for analysts conducting economic analyses of EPA regulations and policies that may affect risks to children's health. This handbook focuses on valuing changes in risks to children's health caused by environmental improvement or degradation. It addresses incorporating children's health considerations in efficiency assessments and distributional analyses.

The Children's Health Evaluation Handbook is a companion to the EPA's *Guidelines for Preparing Economic Analyses* (2002). Because the state of knowledge surrounding the valuation of children's health is still in its infancy, this document is designed to be more informative than prescriptive. It presents and discusses issues that may not be satisfactorily addressed by the current state of knowledge. Discussion of these issues should improve economic analyses of effects on children's health by alerting analysts to unresolved areas and by identifying areas for future research. In this way, the *Handbook* will present the EPA's needs for valuing effects on children's health and will encourage research by EPA and non–EPA economists as well as other experts.

The *Handbook* does the following:

- Describes three alternative approaches to a child-determined value for reducing child health risks;
- Provides information on the valuation of effects on children's health by discussing if, when, and how values for children may differ from values for adults for the same effects;
- Gives guidance on qualitatively describing the likely over- or undervaluation of reduced risk to children resulting from the transfer of risk values estimated for adults to children;
- Provides a description of the best way to value risk experienced by children, recognizing that direct estimates of these values are not yet available;
- Discusses how economic methods used to estimate values for adult health effects can be applied to value children's health effects;

- Provides instructions on when and how to transfer value estimates derived for adults to scenarios involving children, as a second best alternative to actual child values.

The main audiences for the *Handbook* are those performing or using economic analysis, including policy makers; the EPA's program and regional offices; and contractors providing economic reports to the EPA. A copy of the *Handbook* can be downloaded from the Internet.

Children's risk issues have been incorporated into the EPA's regulatory policies. Children's health concerns have been important in the development of many EPA programs, such as the following:

- The EPA is developing standards to regulate the emission of hazardous air pollutants from oil- and coal-fired electric utilities' steam-generating units. The pollutant of greatest concern is mercury. Mercury is toxic, and the developing fetus is sensitive to the effects of methylmercury (a form of mercury). Very young children and women of childbearing age are the populations of greatest concern. The EPA has taken several actions to improve ambient air quality in order to help reduce the incidence of asthma in children, including developing and implementing a voluntary air toxics reduction program, issuing guidance documents, and conducting research activities. Also, the EPA is helping to reduce the risks of childhood asthma through rule-makings addressing particulate matter and sulfur dioxide.

- On June 29, 2004, the EPA promulgated new emissions standards for certain off-road diesel engines that will reduce particulate matter emissions by more than 90 percent.

- The EPA established a single comprehensive national control program to regulate heavy-duty vehicles and their fuel. Among other benefits, the rule is estimated to help prevent more than 360,000 asthma attacks and 386,000 cases of respiratory symptoms in asthmatic children every year.

- In January 2004, the EPA proposed a rule to reduce emissions of sulfur dioxide and nitrogen oxides in order to prevent long-range transport of these pollutants, which can cause particulate and ozone pollution hundreds of miles downwind. The EPA is conducting several activities to review this standard, which was set in 1994.

- The EPA is developing a clean air fine particle implementation rule to guide the states in their efforts to attain the national ambient air quality standard (NAAQS) for fine particles.

- The EPA is conducting the next statutorily required review of the NAAQS for fine particles, to assure that it remains fully protective of human health and the environment. Mercury has known adverse effects on human health, particularly in children. The EPA promulgated a final rule on August 25, 2003, to reduce mercury emissions from mercury cell chlor-alkali plants. This rule replaces the previous standard, which was established in 1973 and was developed without considering children's health. The new rule is estimated to reduce nationwide mercury emissions from chlor-alkali plants by over 70 percent.

- The EPA is working with representatives of auto dismantlers, auto shredders, steelmakers, states, environmental groups, and automakers to remove mercury convenience switches from existing vehicle fleets. Stakeholders are working collaboratively to identify the elements needed for a national approach, the goal being to remove as many switches as possible starting in 2005. It is estimated that there are switches containing a total of 200 tons of mercury in automobiles. The EPA's proposed goal for fiscal year 2005 is to remove and retort 7.5 million auto switches—containing 1,600 pounds of mercury—from scrapped automobiles.

- On July 29, 2004, the EPA proposed the first in a series of emissions reduction requirements known as residual risk standards. These standards are intended to reduce health risks remaining after a category of industrial sources has fully implemented technology-based emissions standards for toxic air pollutants. This proposal applies to coke oven batteries. These facilities convert coal to coke, which is used to produce iron at steel mills and foundries. Coke oven emissions include polycyclic organic matter, polycyclic aromatic hydrocarbons, benzene, and other air toxics that are associated with adverse health effects including cancers and disorders of the blood, central nervous system, and respiratory system.

- As suggested by a National Research Council (NRC) study on the application of biosolids (e.g., sewage sludge) to the land, the EPA is investigating the scientific basis of the existing Clean Water Act (Part 503) rules on use and disposal of biosolids, including the risks to children and other sensitive populations. It has published a strategy explaining how it plans to respond to the NRC report.

- The EPA published the Consolidated Animal Feeding Operations final rule in February 2003 to control runoff from agricultural feeding operations, thus preventing billions of pounds of pollutants from entering U.S. waters. The rule will limit nitrate concentrations in surface and drinking water, among other objectives. Excess nitrate reduces the capacity of blood to carry oxygen, turning skin blue, causing shortness of breath, and depriving the brain of oxygen, which impairs metabolism, thinking, and other bodily functions. These symptoms can develop rapidly in infants.

- Under the Clean Water Act the EPA is establishing water quality criteria that states and tribes use to establish enforceable water quality standards. In January 2001, it published a recommended water quality criterion for methylmercury and withdrew its previous, less stringent criterion. The new criterion was the first water quality criterion expressed as a fish and shellfish tissue value rather than as a water column value. The approach is a direct consequence of the scientific consensus that consumption of contaminated fish and shellfish is the primary route of human exposure to mercury.

The EPA's current drinking water standards are designed to protect both children and adults. The standards take into account the potential effects of contaminants on segments of the population that are most at risk. When the EPA sets each standard, it conducts a risk assessment, in which scientists evaluate whether fetuses, infants, children, or other groups are more vulnerable to a contaminant than the general population is. The standard is set to protect the most vulnerable group. The Safe Drinking Water Act (SDWA) requires the EPA to review each standard at least once every six years and to revise standards, if appropriate. Any revision must maintain or increase public health protection. The results of the most recent review were published in July 2003.

SDWA requires the EPA to establish a list of contaminants to aid in setting priorities for the EPA's drinking water program. In establishing the list, the EPA has divided the contaminants into those which are priorities for additional research, those which need additional occurrence data, and those which are priorities for consideration for rulemaking. The EPA considers risks to children and other sensitive populations in developing priorities. Protecting children from potential effects of pesticides is an important aspect of the EPA's program. The EPA regulates pesticides under the Federal Insecticide, Fungicide, and Rodenticide Act (FIFRA), as amended by the Food Quality Protection Act (FQPA). FQPA requires the EPA to place particular emphasis on children in making regulatory decisions about pesticides. The EPA carefully considers the potential for children to be more sensitive to pesticides than adults. Risk assessments include evaluations for children in various age groups, since children's eating and activity patterns change as they grow up. Some examples of regulatory and outreach activities related to children include the following:

- Implementing the FQPA. The EPA has been increasing protections from pesticides for everyone—and especially children—through its implementation of the landmark 1996 FQPA. The EPA has reassessed nearly 70 percent of the existing pesticide tolerances. As a result, many pesticide uses that posed the greatest risks have been taken off the market. An example of the success of the effort is the greatly reduced use of organophosphates—a class of acutely toxic pesticides—in residential settings. It is estimated that 15 million to 20 million pounds of organophosphate pesticides have been removed from use in and around homes.

- Under the FIFRA, the EPA addresses childhood and prenatal exposures to pesticides, including labeling, reentry intervals (the period of time humans must wait after spraying pesticides before reentry to the fields is safe), personal protective equipment, worker education and training, and posting of signs. To minimize the impact of pesticide exposure on children below the age of twelve who work in agriculture or for other reasons are otherwise present in pesticide-treated fields, the EPA has crafted a four-part strategy: enhancing enforcement of the regulations, improving education, developing better exposure data, and using risk assessment methods in making risk management decisions.

- Organophosphate pesticides can cause cholinesterase inhibition in humans, which results in an overstimulation of the nervous system causing nausea, dizziness, confusion, and, at very high exposures, respiratory paralysis and death. Since these pesticide tolerances were first developed, new information has become available on children's differential exposures and unique susceptibilities. Thus, the EPA has chosen the organophosphate pesticides as one of the first groups to go through tolerance reassessment under FQPA.

The EPA has taken action to reduce exposure to organophosphate pesticides. Some examples include eliminating indoor and outdoor residential uses of the following:

- Chlorpyrifos. Prior to the EPA's evaluation and risk mitigation, chlorpyrifos was one of the most widely used organophosphate insecticides in the United States. To reduce the risk associated with this pesticide, the EPA issued its interim reregistration eligibility decision (IRED) for chlorpyrifos in September 2001. The IRED concluded that the FQPA tenfold safety factor should be retained for infants and children for all exposure durations. It identified measures to mitigate the risks to human health and the environment, and determined that children aged one to six were the most sensitive population subgroup.

- Dimethoate. Dimethoate is a systemic organophosphate insecticide used primarily on field and orchard agricultural crops and ornamentals.

It has been applied with ground and aerial equipment. In September 2001, the EPA announced discontinuation of use of dimethoate on cabbage (bok choy and kohlrabi) because of concerns regarding dimethoate residues. The registrants of products containing dimethoate requested that the EPA delete these uses from their registrations. Also in response to requests, in March 2002 the EPA published a cancellation order and label amendments for dimethoate end-use products. The cancellation order removed all uses at residential and public buildings, including areas around these buildings, and certain agricultural uses. These actions will reduce children's exposure to dimethoate.

- Methyl parathion. Methyl parathion is a restricted-use pesticide that is applied aerially and by ground methods on a variety of field and orchard crops. In August 1999, the EPA accepted voluntary cancellation of uses of methyl parathion on crops that were most common in children's diets. The canceled uses represented 90 percent of the dietary risk to children and reduced the acute dietary risk from food below levels of concern. In January 2001, the EPA revoked the methyl parathion tolerances associated with these foods.

- Diazinon. Diazinon, an organophosphate, is the pesticide most widely used by homeowners on lawns, and one of the most widely used pesticide ingredients for products applied around the home and in gardens. It is used to control insects and grubs. The EPA has phased out all residential uses of diazinon as part of the December 2000 memorandum of agreement between the EPA and the technical registrants. This agreement was initiated because of children's risk concerns. In September 2000, the EPA sent a notice to all retailers to implement the final phaseout by December 31, 2004.

Since FQPA was enacted in 1996, the EPA has registered 125 active ingredients that pose less risk to human health and the environment compared with older chemicals. The EPA has also worked closely with other federal agencies, such as the U.S. Department of Agriculture, and growers to ensure that safer alternatives are available for pesticide uses that are being phased out.

- Atrazine reregistration. The EPA is in the process of reviewing the pesticide atrazine, a triazine herbicide. Atrazine has been one of the most widely used agricultural herbicides in the United States and has been detected in drinking water in the Midwest and other parts of the country. In January 2003, the EPA issued an interim reregistration eligibility decision (IRED) which included monitoring requirements to ensure that community water supplies in the most vulnerable watersheds do not reach levels of concern. If levels of concern are exceeded, further action will be triggered. The EPA issued an addendum to the IRED in October 2003, primarily dealing with potential association between atrazine exposure and cancer, and ecological issues. A final reregistration decision will be made in 2006, upon completion of the cumulative assessment of the triazine pesticides.

- Chromated copper arsenate (CCA), a chemical preservative used to treat wood to protect against rotting and insects, is no longer being produced for use in most residential settings, including decks and play sets. Based on the data the EPA has on wood preservative use, an estimated 60 million pounds of CCA (treating nearly 3 billion board feet of lumber) has been removed from the market as a result of the phaseout. The cancellation of treatment of wood with CCA for residential uses became effective December 31, 2003. There are now safer substitutes available in the marketplace. In addition, a two-year study of the effectiveness of sealants in preventing leaching of arsenic from CCA-treated wood is under way. Results from the first year of the study were expected to be released in 2004, but there have been no results yet.

The EPA is working to reach out to population groups that have been underserved in past outreach efforts, including people who primarily speak languages other than English. The EPA has translated outreach materials into Spanish and has developed public service announcements and other tools to reach such groups. For example, it sponsored a campaign on the radio show "Planeta Azul." The announcements included integrated pest management tips, such as preventing cockroach infestation in the home, as well as highlighting the link between cockroaches and asthma. Others provided information about protecting children from exposure to pesticides and responsible use, storage, and disposal of pesticides.

To protect children from poisonings at home, the law requires that certain household pesticides be in child-resistant containers. Pesticide manufacturers can now access on the EPA's Web site to learn criteria for determining whether a pesticide product requires child-resistant packaging and information on the types of child-resistant packaging available and how to obtain the packaging.

The EPA's dynamic priorities of public health, environmental protection, and the economy helped develop new environmental policies for the cleanup of dangerous places and for protection of children's health. Risk assessment and science contributed to this decisional dialogue. Another big push for these priorities at the EPA is the risk of cancer from pollutants.

Cancer

Cancer is one of the most feared events in life. To the extent that environmentally borne chemicals cause cancer, the EPA is compelled to act.

Often at issue is whether the exposure to the chemical was the scientific cause of the specific cancer. Determining this may require certain conditions for statistical analyses, such as adequate sample size, to be met. Many scientific inquiries conclude that they can neither confirm nor deny causality. This type of conclusion is weak evidence for legal liability, but can justify policy exploration. Combined with the fear of cancer that underscores the public health concern evident in contaminated communities, it can create tension between scientific experts and the affected community. (See discussion of Love Canal in Chapter 3.) Often, communities may have heard from non-EPA scientific experts about the safety of various chemicals and industrial practices. When cleanups occur under the EPA's control, when industries want to acquire new sites or to enlarge old ones, and under other permit-issuing conditions, the main question from communities concerns the safety of the chemicals. Fire, police, and sanitation services all need to know the nature of the chemicals they may have to handle. With the rise of right-to-know laws and the toxics release inventory (see discussion in Chapter 5), and the growth of the environmental justice movement, many more people have questions and concerns about chemicals. These now relate to accumulated impacts; synergy between chemicals; movement of the chemicals through land, air, and water; and vulnerable populations. The EPA was involved in developing right-to-know laws, the toxics release inventory, and the Office of Environmental Justice, as well as in risk assessment guidelines for cancer-causing chemicals.

The EPA has completed a draft of the final version of *Guidelines for Carcinogenic Risk Assessment*, which includes *Supplemental Guidance for Assessing Cancer Susceptibility Resulting from Early-Life Exposure to Carcinogens*. The *Supplemental Guidance* contains an analysis of studies and a possible approach to how quantitative scientific data could inform risk assessments when exposure to carcinogens during childhood are considered.

In 1983, the National Academy of Sciences (NAS)/National Research Council (NRC) published a report titled *Risk Assessment in the Federal Government: Managing the Process*. In that report, the NRC recommended that federal regulatory agencies establish "inference guidelines" to promote consistency and technical quality in risk assessments and to ensure that the risk assessment process was maintained as a scientific effort separate from risk management. The EPA responded to this recommendation by publishing a set of risk assessment guidelines in 1986, including *Guidelines for Carcinogen Risk Assessment* (September 24, 1986). The EPA began revising the 1986 cancer guidelines in light of significant advances in our understanding of the processes of carcinogenesis and the modes of action of disease at the cellular level.

Revising the cancer guidelines is in keeping with the EPA's original intent when it issued the first set of final risk assessment guidelines in 1986. The risk assessment guidelines were meant to be dynamic, flexible documents that would evolve to reflect the current state of the science and risk assessment practices. In keeping with this approach, the EPA undertook an effort to revise the cancer guidelines. The drafts of the *Cancer Guidelines* and *Supplemental Guidance* have been subjected to extensive public comment and scientific peer review, including multiple reviews by EPA's Science Advisory Board. The following chronology traces the development of the EPA's tradition of concern about carcinogens. Most of these documents are available on the Web.

1976	EPA issues *Interim Procedures and Guidelines for Health Risk Assessments of Suspected Carcinogens.*
1986	Publication of the first *Guidelines for Carcinogen Risk Assessment.*
1996	EPA publishes for public comment the *Proposed Guidelines for Carcinogen Risk Assessment.* They undergo Science Advisory Board (SAB) review in 1997.
1999	In January the SAB reviews revisions of key sections of the proposed guidelines per previous SAB and public comments. In July, the SAB and Children's Health Protection Advisory Committee review the draft of the *Final Revised Guidelines for Carcinogen Risk Assessment* for its protection of children.
2001	In November the EPA publishes in the Federal Register a notice of intent to finalize the cancer guidelines and extends the opportunity to provide additional information and comment. This notice also identifies the July 1999 draft of the *Revised Guidelines for Carcinogen Risk Assessment* as interim guidance pending issuance of final guidelines.
2003	In March the EPA releases the draft final version of *Cancer Guidelines* and the draft *Supplemental Guidance for Assessing Cancer Susceptibility from Early-Life Exposure to Carcinogens* for public comment. The SAB reviews the draft *Supplemental Guidance.*
2004	In March the EPA receives SAB comments on the *Supplemental Guidance.*
2004/2005	In response to an SAB recommendation, the EPA extends the analysis supporting the *Supplemental Guidance.* The National Institute of Environmental Health Sciences journal, *Environmental Health Perspectives,* peer reviews this analysis and accepts it for publication. A separate peer review of this analysis is also conducted.

2005   In March the EPA publishes the final *Cancer Guidelines* and *Supplemental Guidance*.

The *Guidelines* and *Supplemental Guidance* serve as the EPA's recommendation to its risk assessors preparing cancer risk assessments. As the EPA develops cancer assessments under the Integrated Risk Information System program, as well as in other EPA programs, it intends to begin to use the *Guidelines* and *Supplemental Guidance*.

The SAB reviewed the *Supplemental Guidance* and, in terms of childhood exposures, the 2004 SAB made the following observations and recommendations.

- The review panel agrees with the EPA that the science supports the conclusion that, compared with adult exposures, early-life exposures result in increased susceptibility to carcinogens that act in a mutagenic mode. The review panel notes that a broader look at the scientific literature beyond the studies included in the *Supplemental Guidance* analysis would strengthen that conclusion.

- The review panel notes that for certain groups of nonmutagenic chemicals with known modes of action (e.g., estrogen receptor agonist/antagonist), there is sufficient evidence supporting increased susceptibility to cancer following early-life exposure. The review panel suggests that the EPA include a discussion of these agents in the *Supplemental Guidance*. Nonmutagenic carcinogens with known modes of action should be assessed on a case-by-case basis as suggested by the EPA.

- The review panel supports the use of slope factor adjustments in developing default approaches. Application of an adjustment to the adult cancer slope factor seems to be the most transparent and practical approach for risk assessment.

- The review panel reviews age-specific human vulnerabilities and concludes that it would be useful to include an additional age grouping (ages nine to fifteen) to recognize the potentially important vulnerabilities during puberty. Thus, four age groupings would be appropriate (up to two years, ages three to eight, nine to fifteen, and fifteen-plus) to represent critical periods of human growth and development.

- The review panel suggests that the EPA consider alternative analyses that might allow it to use more of the available data and directly test hypotheses concerning the appropriateness of the adjustment values for predicting the dose response from early-life exposure.

- The review panel recommends that a priority for the near term would be the development of mode-of-action approaches for endocrine disrupters, beginning with estrogenic agents.

- The review panel cannot at this time recommend a feasible method for incorporating transplacental or in utero exposure data. However, it believes this is an important issue that requires further research.

- The review panel recommends that the EPA work more closely with the research community to encourage the evaluation of early-life susceptibilities. For chemical agents that are known to increase cancer risk, carcinogenic potency and the extent of exposure should be used in deciding which chemicals to study first.

- Certain groups of nonmutagenic carcinogens with known modes of action serve as important examples in support of applying a default factor to nonmutagenic carcinogens when the mode of action is unknown. The review panel suggests that the EPA reconsider limiting the application of adjustment factors only to mutagenic agents, and instead apply a default approach to both mutagenic and nonmutagenic chemicals for which mode of action remains unknown or is insufficiently characterized.

In an effort to update key scientific risk assessment methodologies, the EPA has published revised *Guidelines for Carcinogen Risk Assessment*. The *Guidelines* provide a framework for EPA scientists assessing possible cancer risks from exposures to pollutants or other agents in the environment. They will also inform the EPA decision makers and the public about these recommended procedures. Revisions to the *Guidelines* are intended to make greater use of the increasing scientific understanding of processes of cancer development. Major issues considered in finalizing revisions to the *Guidelines* were the following:

- Beginning with an analysis of available information and invoking defaults, if needed, to address uncertainty or the absence of critical information;

- Emphasizing key events and processes, starting with the interaction of an agent with a cell, through functional and anatomical changes, that may result in adverse health consequences (modes of action);

- Considering that certain subpopulations, and childhood and other life stages, may be associated with higher susceptibilities to risk;

- Summarizing the full range of available evidence and describing any conditions associated with conclusions about an agent's hazard potential, using a weight-of-evidence narrative and accompanying descriptors.

The final *Cancer Guidelines* explicitly call for consideration of possible sensitive subpopulations and/or life stages (such as childhood). The consideration of childhood risks in the final *Cancer Guidelines* has been augmented by *Supplemental Guidance for Assessing Susceptibility from Early-Life Exposure to*

Carcinogens. Questions and Answers, Cancer Guidelines Fact Sheet, Issuance Fact Sheet, and *Memorandum on the Application of New Cancer Guidelines* provide additional information regarding both documents.

SCIENCE AND RISK ASSESSMENT

The use of science at the EPA is a fundamental part of its traditions and culture. Most of the rules and regulations developed by the EPA have some type of scientific basis. Because of the many laws implemented by the EPA and the lack of scientific baseline knowledge on the state of the U.S. environment, this is a major, ongoing challenge. To meet this challenge, the EPA has several scientific offices.

Science Advisory Board

The Science Advisory Board (SAB), in its present form, was established in 1978 by the Environmental Research, Development, and Demonstration Authorization Act (ERDDAA). Predecessor bodies date back to the early 1970s. In carrying out the mandate of ERDDAA, the SAB provides scientific advice requested by the Administrator, the Committee on Environment and Public Works of the U.S. Senate, or the Committees on Science and Technology, Interstate and Foreign Commerce, and Public Works and Transportation of the House of Representatives. Because the SAB is a federal advisory committee, it must comply with the Federal Advisory Committee Act and related regulations. Consequently, it has an approved charter, which must be renewed biennially; announces its meetings in the Federal Register; and provides opportunities for public comment on issues before the SAB. As a practical matter, the function of providing credible technical advice to the EPA and Congress antedates ERDDAA and SAB. The roots of SAB can be traced back through predecessor committees within the EPA and—prior to the creation of the EPA—to other agencies, such as the Department of Health, Education and Welfare. Since 1978 the SAB has operated as a staff office, reporting directly to the Administrator.

Members of and consultants to the SAB constitute a distinguished body of scientists, engineers, and economists who are recognized, nongovernmental experts in their respective fields. These individuals are drawn from academia, industry, and environmental communities throughout the United States and, in a few cases, other countries. Increasingly, the EPA has placed a premium on basing its regulations on a solid scientific foundation. Consequently, since 1989 the SAB has assumed growing importance and stature. It is now formal practice that many major scientific points associated with environmental problems are reviewed by the SAB. For example, the Clean Air Act requires that decisions related to the National Ambient Air Quality Standards be reviewed by the Clean Air Scientific Advisory Committee, which is administratively housed within the SAB. Generally, the SAB functions as a technical peer review panel that conducts its business in public view and benefits from public input during its deliberations. Through these proceedings the EPA positions are subjected to critical examination by leading experts in the field in order to test the currency and technical merit of those positions. At the same time, the SAB recognizes that the EPA is sometimes forced to take action to avert an emerging environmental risk before all of the rigors of scientific proof are met. To delay action until the evidence amounts to incontrovertible proof might have irreversible ecological and health consequences. In such cases, the EPA makes assumptions and extrapolations from what is known in order to reach a rational science policy position regarding the need (or lack thereof) for regulatory action. Here, the SAB serves as a council of peers to evaluate the soundness of the technical basis of the science policy position adopted by the EPA. Five committees have historically conducted most SAB reviews: (1) Clean Air Scientific Advisory Committee, (2) Ecological Processes and Effects Committee, (3) Environmental Engineering Committee, (4) Environmental Health Committee, and (5) Radiation Advisory Committee (RAC).

In recent years, the following committees have been added:

- Integrated Human Exposure Committee (IHEC), formerly the Indoor Air Quality/Total Human Exposure Committee, mandated in the Superfund Amendments and Reauthorization Act in fiscal year 1986;
- Drinking Water Committee, which evolved from the IHEC in fiscal year 1990;
- Advisory Council on Clean Air Compliance Analysis (COUNCIL);
- Compliance Analysis Council, mandated in the 1990 Clean Air Act Amendments.

Finally, the executive committee (EC) serves as a board of directors for the SAB. It is composed of the chairs of the standing committees noted above and several members at-large. The EC meets quarterly to discuss relevant issues and SAB policies and procedures, and to provide final review and approval of all SAB reports (except those from the two separately chartered committees— COUNCIL and the EPA's Clean Air Scientific Advisory Committee (CASAC)—which report their findings directly to the Administrator).

Environmental Modeling

The EPA develops, evaluates, and applies a wide variety of highly complex environmental models. These models are used to coordinate and/or predict the environmental consequences of a wide range of activities. Frequently, these models become the basis for environmental cleanup, protection, or regulation. They provide a basis for resolution of issues that involve multiple media. In order to ensure the adequacy of these models in their development, evaluation, and application, it is imperative that the EPA adopt basic principles that will guide its modeling community in performing analyses. The Council on Regulatory Environmental Modeling (CREM) promotes consistency and consensus within the EPA on mathematical modeling issues including modeling guidance, development, and application, and enhances both internal and external communications on modeling activities. It supports and enhances existing modeling activities by the program offices. CREM provides the EPA with consistent yet flexible modeling tools to support environmental decision-making, in particular as they relate to the development and implementation of programs with cross-EPA implications. Further, it provides EPA staff and the public with a central point for inquiring about the EPA's use of modeling. CREM's scope of activity is as follows:

- Promoting consistency in model development and application in order to eliminate duplication, confusion, and uncertainty;
- Providing a point of focus to address cross-EPA modeling issues that are beyond the purview of any single EPA office, including communications within the environmental modeling community.
- Providing an initial point of inquiry regarding the EPA's development and utilization of models through the implementation of a home page with links to program- and region-specific information.
- Strategic planning and priority setting, in consultation with the Science Policy Council (SPC), regarding the possible development of cross-EPA guidance, principles, or activities for issues such as model development and applications, peer review, quality assurance/control, and model performance/evaluation/verification/validation;
- Training, technical support, and identification and penetration of barriers to improved use of models in the EPA.
- Overseeing the activities of cross-EPA action teams set up to tackle issues such as those above.

CREM is headed by the EPA deputy administrator in his role as chair of the SPC. It reports to the deputy administrator through the SPC, which must approve amendments to the framework. CREM reports are referred to the SPC Steering Committee for consideration of policy and procedural issues. CREM products or recommendations become EPA policy upon acceptance by the SPC and concurrence by the deputy administrator as chair of the SPC.

Science and Legislation at the EPA

One of the EPA's problems is that many of the statutes it administers leave little room for scientific judgments. Although science is used extensively in

Protesters rallied by Arizona's Southwest Organizing Project march in solidarity with residents of mostly Latino farmworker communities. They were successful in blocking the siting of a hazardous waste incinerator in Kettleman City, California, 1993. (Photograph by R. D. Bullard)

developing regulatory guidelines, and in risk assessment and measurement, it is not part of the enabling legislation in much of the law the EPA administers. As a result, some things are done that may or may not make scientific sense. Some of the statutes require that certain regulatory actions take place, without regard to any knowledge about the risks involved. Generally, if there is any mismatch between science and what the EPA does, it results from statutory enactments.

Another general issue for the EPA is the role of science in causality models. Science generally relies on a statistical basis for proof of a cause-and-effect relationship. The models predict a certain action will cause another effect to a 10 percent or 5 percent degree of probability that the result is random. If it does not reach this level, the null hypothesis requires scientists neither to confirm nor to deny that a causal relationship exists. In terms of environmental policy development, this can pose problems. The EPA is often faced with inescapable decisions and congressional mandates. For scientists neither to confirm nor to deny causality may not necessarily be helpful in policy development and implementation. Another issue is that statistical tests of causality require a minimum sample size. If the sample is not large enough, no causality can be assumed. Many impacted communities that have cancer clusters, such as among farmworkers, are small communities and their data do not reach causality because of their small sizes.

The causality model of science, keeps many communities from pursuing effective remedies in the courts. This is because the burden of proof rests with the plaintiff. If the scientific model can neither confirm nor deny causality, that criterion is not met and the case will be dismissed or summarily judged against the plaintiff.

One tool that can help foster the evolution of an integrated and targeted national environmental policy is the concept of environmental risk. Each environmental problem poses some possibility of harm to human health, the ecology, the economic system, or the quality of human life. Risk assessment is the process by which the form, dimensions, and characteristics of that risk are estimated, and risk management is the process by which the risk is reduced. The concept of environmental risk, along with its terminology and analytical methodologies, helps people discuss environmental problems with a common language. It allows many environmental problems to be measured and compared in common terms, and it allows different risk reduction options to be evaluated from a common basis. Thus the concept of environmental risk can help the nation develop environmental policies in a consistent and systematic way.

Scientists have made some progress in developing quantitative measures for comparing different risks to human health. Given sufficient data, such comparisons are now possible within limits. Although the current ability to assess and quantify ecological risks is not as well developed, an increased capacity for comparing different kinds of risks more systematically would help determine which problems are most serious and deserve the most urgent attention. That capacity will be even more valuable as the number and seriousness of environmental problems competing for attention and resources increase. An improved ability to compare risks in common terms would also help society choose more wisely among the policy options available for reducing risks. There are a number of ways to reduce the automobile emissions that contribute to urban smog, and there are a number of ways to decrease human exposure to lead.

The evaluation of relative risks can help identify the relative efficiency and effectiveness of different risk reduction options. There are heavy costs involved if society fails to set environmental priorities based on risk. If finite resources are expended on lower-priority problems at the expense of higher-priority risks, society will face needlessly high risks. If priorities are established on the basis of the greatest opportunities to reduce risk, total risk will be reduced in a more efficient way, thereby lessening threats to both public health and local and global ecosystems. This is especially important as the EPA faces the challenges of sustainability, environmental justice, ecosystem approaches, and accumulating emissions. (See discussion in Chapter 6.)

Since the mid-1980s the EPA has put in place extensive and detailed government policies to control a number of environmental problems. Smog in heavily populated areas, the eutrophication of lakes, elevated levels of lead in the blood of millions of children, the threat of cancer from exposure to pesticide residues in food, and abandoned drums of hazardous wastes are a few of the problems that have driven the enactment of more than a dozen major federal laws and the current public and private expenditure of about $100 billion a year to protect the environment. Those efforts have led to very real national benefits. Yet despite the demonstrable success of past efforts to protect the environment, many national environmental goals have not been attained. Factors such as the growth in automobile use and common agricultural practices have caused national efforts to protect the environment to be less effective than intended. Furthermore, with hindsight it is clear that in many cases those efforts have been inconsistent and uncoordinated. The fragmentary nature of U.S. environmental policy has been evident in three ways:

1. In laws. As different environmental problems have been identified, usually because the adverse effects—smog in major cities, lack of aquatic life in streams, declining numbers of bald eagles—were readily apparent, new laws have been passed to address each new problem. However, the tactics and goals of the different laws have not been consistent or coordinated, even if the pollutants to be controlled are the same. Many laws not passed primarily for environmental purposes also have had major effects on the environment.

2. In programs. The EPA was established as the primary federal agency responsible for implementing the nation's environmental laws. It evolved an administrative structure wherein each program was primarily responsible for implementing specific laws. Consequently, the efforts of the various programs rarely were coordinated, even if they were attempting to control different aspects of the same environmental problem. This problem is compounded by the fact that the EPA is not the only agency whose activities affect the environment.

3. In tools. The primary tools used to protect the environment have been controls designed to capture pollutants before they escape from smokestacks, tailpipes, or sewer outfalls, and technologies designed to clean up or destroy pollutants after they have been discharged into the environment. These "end-of-pipe" controls and remediation technologies almost always have been applied because of federal, state, or local legal requirements.

For a number of reasons, this kind of fragmented approach to protecting the environment will not be as successful in the future as it has been in the past.

The most obvious controls already have been applied to the most obvious problems. Yet complex and less obvious environmental problems remain, and the aggregate cost of controlling those problems one by one is rising. Moreover, this country—and the rest of the world—is facing emerging environmental problems of unprecedented scope. Population growth and industrial expansion worldwide are straining global ecosystems. Never before in history have human activities threatened to change atmospheric chemistry to such an extent that global climate patterns are altered.

Given the diversity, complexity, and scope of the environmental problems of concern today, it is critically important that U.S. environmental policy evolves in several fundamental ways. Essentially, national policy affecting the environment must become more integrated and more focused on opportunities for environmental improvement than it has been in the past. The traditions and culture surrounding fragmented program approaches face challenges from the difficulties these approaches pose for cumulative impacts, cross-media transfers, development of environmental baselines, community-based environmental planning, and the development of sustainable policies. (See discussion in Chapter 6.)

The environment is an interrelated whole, and society's environmental protection efforts should be integrated as well. Integration in this case means that government agencies should assess the range of environmental problems of concern and then target protective efforts at the problems that seem to be the most serious. It means that society should use all the tools—regulatory and nonregulatory alike—that are available to protect the environment. It means that controlling the end of the pipe where pollutants enter the environment, or remediating problems caused by pollutants after they have entered the environment, is not sufficient. Rather, waste-generating activities have to be modified to minimize the waste or to prevent the waste from being generated at all. Most of all, integration is critically important because significant sources of environmental degradation are embedded in typical day-to-day personal and professional activities, the cumulative effects of which can become serious problems. Thus protecting the environment effectively in the future will require a more broadly conceived strategic approach, one that involves the cooperative efforts of all segments of society.

Measurement Science

Environmental monitoring is a critical component of EPA decision-making. It is the data gathered when conducting studies that form the basis for the decisions. The qualities of the decisions are directly related to the quality of the information gathered. Measurement science, therefore, is the cornerstone of environmental monitoring. Monitoring plays a critical role in the development and, especially, the implementation of the EPA's regulatory programs. Examples include conducting site-specific risk assessments to identify and prioritize contaminated sites and monitoring to determine compliance with permits and other regulatory requirements.

The EPA develops, evaluates, and applies a wide variety of field and laboratory methods, and assesses data quality to characterize the environment and the materials entering the environment (e.g., wastes), and to support its enforcement activities. These protocols and methods encompass sample collection, sample analysis, quality assurance, and assessment of data quality. EPA policies on environmental measurements influence which data and metadata are collected, what methods are used to collect and evaluate the data, and how the data are used in decision-making. The application of these methods and policies impacts not only the EPA's own data-gathering efforts but also those of the regulated community, the states, and the commercial laboratory sector.

The Forum on Environmental Measurements (FEM) is a standing committee of senior EPA managers established to develop policies to guide the EPA measurement community in validating and disseminating methods for environmental monitoring; for ensuring that monitoring studies are scientifically rigorous and statistically sound, and yield representative data; and for employing a quality systems approach which ensures that the data gathered and used by the EPA are of known and documented quality. FEM was established to promote consistency and consensus within the EPA on measurement issues. Furthermore, it provides the EPA and the public with a central point for addressing measurement methodology issues with multiprogram impacts. Current FEM activities include the following:

- Ensuring and demonstrating the competency of EPA laboratories;
- Identifying and correcting problems with existing measurement methods;
- Validating new EPA measurement methods;
- Consolidating EPA-supported measurement science conferences.

Measurement science will continue to be an important part of the EPA. New challenges arising from cumulative impacts, sustainability, community-based environmental planning, and ecosystem approaches will all incorporate measurement sciences.

Unfinished Business

The EPA squarely faced the question of relative risk for the first time when it established a task force to assess and compare the risks associated with a range of environmental problems. In 1986 and 1987 about seventy-five senior career managers and staff compared the relative risks posed by thirty-one environmental problems within four broad categories of risk: (1) human cancer risk, (2) human noncancer health risk, (3) ecological risk, and (4) welfare risk.

The task force limited its comparison to those risks which remain after currently required controls have been applied (residual risks). The results of this effort were presented in *Unfinished Business: A Comparative Assessment of Environmental Problems*, a landmark study. For the first time, the many environmental problems of concern to the EPA were compared with each other in a nonprogrammatic context. Moreover, the report explicitly pointed out the disparity between residual risk and resource allocation at the EPA. The problems that the authors judged to pose the most serious risks were not necessarily the problems that Congress and the EPA had targeted for the most aggressive action. However, the report did find a correlation between EPA's programmatic priorities and the apparent public perceptions of risk. Congress and the EPA were paying the most attention to environmental problems that the general public believed posed the greatest risks. The authors of *Unfinished Business* recognized that their risk rankings, though based on the judgments of experienced professionals, were limited because they were based on incomplete data and novel risk comparison techniques. But the value of the report rests not so much on the accuracy of the rankings as on the fact that the EPA had begun to see the long-term public policy importance of understanding relative risks. In short, *Unfinished Business* clung to the tradition of examining dynamic priorities of public health and environmental protection.

There are major differences in the perception of risk by race and gender. The perception of risk alone can lead to physiological effects such as hypertension, increased risk of strokes, and heart attacks. People of color and females tend to view most risk events as 30 percent more risky than do white males. This dynamic holds true in population samples with advanced degrees in hard sciences and in British population samples. Some have maintained that these studies underscore the unacknowledged privilege of white males. When the white male cohort was broken down, 15 percent stands out. The higher the income and the greater the education of a white male, the lower his perception of risk. This subgroup also believes it is permissible to expose others to deadly risks without informing them.

The Relative Risk Reduction Strategies Committee

Shortly after he took office early in 1989, EPA Administrator William K. Reilly asked the SAB to review the EPA's 1987 report on relative environmental risk, *Unfinished Business*, evaluate its findings, and develop strategic options for reducing risk. In response to that request, the SAB formed the Relative Risk Reduction Strategies Committee (RRRSC), which in turn was divided into subcommittees on ecology and welfare, human health, and strategic options. The thirty-nine members of the RRRSC and its subcommittees were nationally recognized scientists, engineers, and managers with broad experience in addressing environmental and health issues. Through its combined efforts the RRRSC attempted to achieve four objectives:

1. Critically review *Unfinished Business*, reflecting any significant new information that bears on the evaluation of risks associated with specific environmental problems;

2. To the extent possible, merge the evaluations of cancer and non-cancer risks and ecological and welfare risks;

3. Provide strategies for reducing the major environmental risks;

4. Develop a long-term strategy for improving the methodology for assessing and ranking environmental risks and for assessing the alternative strategies that can reduce risks.

In particular, the Ecology and Welfare Subcommittee and the Human Health Subcommittee were charged with reviewing and updating the risk findings from *Unfinished Business*. They were to provide, to the extent possible, a single aggregate ranking of the risks that each assessed, and recommend a long-term strategy for improving the methodology for assessing such risks. The Strategic Options Subcommittee was charged with (1) identifying strategy options for reducing residual environmental risks and (2) developing and demonstrating analytical methodologies for identifying and selecting risk reduction options.

The RRRSC conducted a lengthy review of the data and methodologies that support risk assessment, comparison, and reduction. This review led to several conclusions about the need for and value of comparative risk assessments and their implications for the national environmental agenda. It highlighted the most important findings and recommendations from the three subcommittee reports, along with insights derived from discussions among the committee members after they reviewed the reports. The report included ten recommendations on approaches to risk management and on the future direction of national environmental policy.

1. The EPA should target its environmental protection efforts on the basis of opportunities for the greatest risk reduction. Since the United States has already taken the most obvious actions to address the most obvious environmental problems, the EPA needs to set priorities for future actions so that it takes advantage of the best opportunities for reducing the most serious remaining risks.

2. The EPA should attach as much importance to reducing ecological risk as it does to reducing human health risk. Because productive natural ecosystems are essential to human health and to sustainable, long-term economic growth, and because they are intrinsically valuable in their own right, the EPA should be as concerned about

protecting ecosystems as it is about protecting human health. (See discussion of ecosystem approaches in Chapter 6.)

3. The EPA should improve the data and the analytical methodologies that support the assessment, comparison, and reduction of different environmental risks. Although setting priorities for national environmental protection efforts will always involve subjective judgments and uncertainty, the EPA should work continually to improve the scientific data and analytical methodologies that underpin those judgments and help reduce their uncertainty.

4. The EPA should reflect risk-based priorities in its strategic planning processes. Its long-range plans should be driven not so much by past risk reduction efforts, or by existing programmatic structures, as by ongoing assessments of remaining environmental risks, the explicit comparison of those risks, and the analysis of opportunities available for reducing risks.

5. The EPA should reflect risk-based priorities in its budget process. Although the EPA's budget priorities are determined to a large extent by the environmental laws that it implements, it should use whatever discretion it has to focus budget resources on those environmental problems which pose the most serious risks.

6. The EPA—and the nation as a whole—should make greater use of all the tools available to reduce risk. Although the nation has had substantial success in reducing environmental risks through the use of government-mandated end-of-pipe controls, the extent and complexity of future risks will necessitate the use of a much broader array of tools, including market incentives and information.

7. The EPA should emphasize pollution prevention as the preferred option for reducing risk. By encouraging actions that prevent pollution from being generated in the first place, the EPA will help reduce the costs, intermedia transfers of pollution, and residual risks so often associated with end-of-pipe controls.

8. The EPA should increase its efforts to integrate environmental considerations into broader aspects of public policy in as fundamental a manner as are economic concerns. Other federal agencies often affect the quality of the environment (e.g., through the implementation of tax, energy, agricultural, and international policy), and the EPA should work to ensure that environmental considerations are integrated, where appropriate, into the policy deliberations of such agencies.

9. The EPA should work to improve public understanding of environmental risks and train a professional workforce to help reduce those risks. The improved environmental literacy of the general

public, together with an expanded and better-trained technical workforce, will be essential to the nation's success in reducing environmental risks in the future.

10. The EPA should develop improved analytical methods to value natural resources and to account for long-term environmental effects in its economic analyses. Because traditional methods of economic analysis tend to undervalue ecological resources and fail to adequately treat questions of intergenerational equity, the EPA should develop and implement innovative approaches to economic analysis that will address these shortcomings. (See discussion of sustainability in Chapter 6.)

These recommendations not only reflect the tradition and culture of the EPA, they also have shaped its direction thus far to engage in the significant challenges of the future.

Release of Environmental Equity Report

The report titled *Environmental Equity: Reducing Risks for All Communities* also reviews existing data on the distribution of environmental exposures and risks across population groups, and includes findings and recommendations. Among the findings are clear differences between racial groups in terms of disease and death rates; the experience of racial minority and low-income populations of higher than average exposures to selected air pollutants, hazardous-waste facilities, contaminated fish, and agricultural pesticides in the workplace; and the existence of great opportunities for the EPA and other government agencies to improve communication about environmental problems with members of low-income and racial minority groups. Among the recommendations in the report are that the EPA should increase the priority it gives to issues of environmental equity; identify and target opportunities to reduce high concentrations of risk to specific population groups; and increase efforts to involve racial minority and low-income communities in environmental policy-making. (See discussions of environmental justice in Chapters 3 and 6.)

"EPA's basic goal is to make certain that the consequences of environmental pollution should not be borne unequally by any segment of the population," said Administrator William K. Reilly. "EPA has a responsibility to identify and target these populations. This report offers EPA and state agencies recommendations for how to address these equity concerns." On the recommendation of the report, Administrator Reilly established the Environmental Equity Cluster, a team of senior staff from all of the EPA's programs and regions. He also established the Office of Environmental Justice to deal with environmental impacts on racial minority and low-income communities. The office's core functions include serving as the EPA's and the public's point of contact for equity outreach, technical assistance and information dissemination, and administering the Minority Academic Institutions Program.

The EPA's expansion of those at risk to include children, minorities, and other vulnerable population groups reflects the tradition of public health and science. It is also driven by increased knowledge of accumulating emissions and impacts.

Cumulative Risks

Several recent reports have highlighted the importance of understanding the accumulation of risks from multiple environmental stressors. These include the National Research Council's 1994 report *Science and Judgment in Risk Assessment* and the 1997 report by the Presidential/Congressional Commission on Risk Assessment and Risk Management, *Risk Assessment and Risk Management in Regulatory Decision-Making*. In addition, legislation such as the Food Quality Protection Act of 1996 has directed the EPA to move beyond assessments of single chemicals and to focus, in part, on the cumulative effects of chemical exposures occurring simultaneously. Further emphasizing the need for the EPA to focus on cumulative risks are the cases filed under Title VI of the 1964 Civil Rights Act, which prohibits discrimination based on race in the disbursement of federal funds. These cases have demanded a population-based approach to assessing human health risks from environmental contaminants.

The framework for cumulative risk assessment is the first step in a long-term effort to develop cumulative risk assessment guidance. Building on the EPA's growing experience with cumulative risk assessment, it identifies the basic elements of the cumulative risk assessment process and provides a flexible structure for conducting and evaluating cumulative risk assessment and for addressing scientific issues related to cumulative risk. Although this framework will serve as a foundation for developing future guidance, it is neither a procedural guide nor a regulatory requirement within the EPA, and it is expected to evolve with experience. It is not an attempt to lay out protocols to address all the risks or considerations that are needed to adequately inform community decisions. Rather, it is an information document focused on describing various aspects of cumulative risk.

The framework benefited from extensive peer input. Earlier drafts of the documents served as background pieces for consultations with state, federal, and other groups. An external peer review, open to the public, was held in June 2002. The document was revised on the basis of input received during the consultation and review processes and from public review and comment. In response to the increasing focus on cumulative risk, the EPA has begun to explore cumulative approaches to risk assessment. Cumulative risk assessment is an analysis, characterization, and possible quantification of the combined risks to human health or the environment from multiple agents or stressors. The EPA will use the framework as a basis for future guidance as it continues with assessment activities related to cumulative risk. Building on the EPA's growing experience with cumulative risk assessment, the framework is intended to foster consistent approaches to cumulative risk assessment, identify key issues, and define terms used in these assessments. It identifies the basic elements of the cumulative risk assessment process and provides a flexible structure for conducting and evaluating such assessment, and for addressing scientific issues related to cumulative risk.

The EPA's continued growth and policy maturation in the area of cumulative risks will lay the foundation for environmental policy in the future. This tradition and culture of taking a hard look at risk will help the EPA overcome some of the problems inherent in fragmented programmatic approaches. (The author was one of the external peer reviewers of the framework.)

ROLE OF FEDERAL ADVISORY COMMITTEES

Since the administration of Theodore Roosevelt, U.S. presidents have used citizen advisory committees to assist in the development of federal policy. An increase in the number of regulatory agencies has been accompanied by a concomitant rise in the number of advisory committees, especially in environmental regulation. Awareness of increased reliance on advisory committees has elicited a mixed response from the legislative and executive branches. Concerned that advisory committees can cross the line between advice and improper influence, in 1972 Congress passed the Federal Advisory Committee Act. Although the act embraced the advisory committee as a "frequently . . . useful and beneficial means of furnishing expert advice, ideas, and diverse opinions to the Federal Government," Congress nonetheless declared that "the need for many existing advisory committees has not been reviewed," and concluded that the creation and operation of advisory committees should be more strictly controlled. Accordingly, the act requires that new advisory committees be kept to a "necessary" minimum; that advisory committees be terminated when they have served their purpose; that the establishment, operation, administration, and duration of advisory committees be subject to uniform procedures; and that relevant information regarding advisory committees be made available to the public.

Throughout their history, advisory committees have served two general functions. First, they have provided the federal government with a means of obtaining expert advice on a wide range of issues at relatively little cost. This function has been of critical importance in the regulation of toxic substances. As the federal government has endeavored to protect the public health through the control of toxic substances, it has entered into an area of complex scientific, technical, and economic decision-making. Advisory committees provide the expertise that such decisions require. Second, by providing a means through which public opinion on a particular issue can be made known to responsible officials, advisory committees have often served a democratic function. For many years the advisory committees used for this purpose were drawn almost exclusively from the more privileged social and economic classes and failed to provide an accurate portrayal of public opinion. Since the administration of Lyndon Johnson, the agencies have broadened the base from which advisory committees are drawn, selecting women and more representatives of diverse social, economic, and ethnic backgrounds. This has been especially true at the EPA as environmental justice has become a prominent policy concern. Since advisory committees are deeply immersed in policy issues, the importance of their including a variety of viewpoints increases.

The Legal Framework for EPA Advisory Committees

As noted above, the Federal Advisory Committee Act sets forth general guidelines and procedures applicable to all federal advisory committees. Not only does it require open meetings, detailed transcripts, a limited right of public participation, and the attendance of a federal government representative at committee meetings, but Sections 5(b)(2) and 5(c) state that committee membership should be "fairly balanced in terms of points of view represented and the functions to be performed." The recommendations of an advisory committee are, except where otherwise specifically authorized by statute, advisory only. These advisory committees and subcommittees fall into three general categories: permanent (created by statute to advise agencies on science), technology, and general.

The EPA established the Science Advisory Board administratively in 1974, and it was subsequently established by statute in the Environmental Research, Development, and Demonstration Authorization Act. The original board consisted of five standing committees and an executive committee. During the Reagan administration the EPA reduced the number of standing committees to three. By statute, these committees must meet periodically with the EPA Administrator "to provide advice . . . on the scientific and technical aspects of environmental problems and issues." Their membership is to be "a body of independent scientists and engineers of sufficient size and diversity to provide a range of expertise required to assess the scientific and technical aspects of environmental issues," and additional ad hoc committees may be drawn from the members.

The EPA's regulation of toxic substances is assisted by an administratively created advisory committee known as the Administrator's Toxic Substance Advisory Committee (ATSAC). This quasi-permanent, "balanced" committee focuses primarily on issues of policy rather than of science. According to its charter, ATSAC is to advise the EPA "on policy, technical and procedural matters relating to the environmental, economic, and social aspects" of implementing the Toxic Substances Control Act, and to "consider and comment on proposals for rules and regulations." However, the committee is directed to "generally defer" on scientific matters to the Science Advisory Board. The committee's sixteen members are to be drawn, "in appropriate balance," from three groups: (1) manufacturers, processors, and users of chemical substances; (2) environmental, health, and public interest organizations; and (3) other interested parties, "including, but not limited to, labor organizations, professional societies, and state and local interests." The committee is also authorized to form ad hoc subcommittees to deal with specific issues. ATSAC must hold from three to six meetings a year; the subcommittees meet "as needed."

Advisory Committee Performance

In general, advisory committees play a constructive role in developing regulatory policies for toxic substances. Members have usually been knowledgeable, and the deliberations valuable and instructive. All things considered, they have dealt well with the science and technology questions presented to them. The committees are part of the executive branch's decision-making process and include members who are scientists, public health officials, business representatives, citizens, persons affiliated with specific communities, and people at all levels of government who are committed to a greater knowledge about the environment and what can be done to protect it. Approximately 1,400 citizens sit on Federal Advisory Committee Act (FACA) committees, bringing a variety of perspectives and expertise to the environmental consensus-building process.

FACA committees can be created by the president, Congress, or federal departments or agencies, and must meet the following basic requirements:

- Their meetings must be open to the public, and the public must be permitted to present their views;
- All meeting minutes and reports must be available to the public;
- The public must be notified of meetings by advertisement in the Federal Register;
- Committee membership must be balanced in terms of points of view.

The Office of Cooperative Environmental Management operates four FACA committees and has responsibility for the oversight and policies of all EPA federal advisory committees.

How the EPA Uses FACA to Achieve Collaboration

The EPA has used federal advisory committees to solicit expert participation and citizen involvement in developing and implementing a wide variety of environmental policies and programs. The advisory committee process has proven to be an effective tool to achieve collaboration and build consensus among the EPA's diverse customers and stakeholders.

The federal advisory committee process should generally be used when the EPA wants advice or recommendations from a group of people who are not solely federal employees and who have expertise or perspectives that can be of value to the decision-making process.

FACA committees operate "in the sunshine," which means that their meetings, deliberations, and reports are open and available to the public. EPA's federal advisory committees range from those with a science focus (Board of Scientific Counselors, Science Advisory Board), to a geographic focus (Good Neighbor Environmental Board), to a functional focus (Environmental Financial Advisory Board, Children's Health Protection Advisory Committee), among others.

The EPA has twenty-four FACA committees and thirty-eight subcommittees managed by virtually every major EPA program office. In a given year, there are about 150 committee meetings that include about 1,000 scientists, public health officials, businesspeople, academics, citizens, and representatives of all levels of government.

An example of how a federal advisory committee works at the EPA is illustrative. In the early 1990s the EPA announced the Common Sense Initiative (CSI), a sweeping effort to fundamentally shift environmental regulation by moving away from the pollutant-by-pollutant, crisis-by-crisis approach of the past to an industry-by-industry approach for the future. This new approach was designed to achieve results that are cleaner, cheaper, and smarter—cleaner for the environment, cheaper for business and taxpayers, and smarter for the nation's future. Administrator Carol Browner allowed six stakeholder groups to be represented—industry, environmental organizations, labor, state environmental regulators, the EPA, and, for the first time, those concerned with environmental justice. CSI was officially established in October 1994 under a FACA charter as the Common Sense Initiative Council (with specialized industrial sector subcommittees). The formal role of the council was to advise and make recommendations to the Administrator on matters falling within the scope of the initiative, either on its own or based on ideas developed by sector subcommittees.

The Administrator's charge to the council underlined its responsibility for identifying crosscutting issues or potential joint projects affecting several sectors. Six industry sectors were selected to test this new tailored approach. These sectors comprised a broad range of experience with a mix of large and small companies, as well as older and newer industries: automobile manufacturing, computers and electronics, iron and steel, metal finishing and plating, petroleum refining, and printing. In the fall of 1998, it was announced that the CSI would conclude in December 1998. Three of the former CSI sectors (metal finishing, printing, and petroleum refining) are continuing as work groups under the Standing Committee on Sectors in the National Advisory Committee on

Environmental Policy and Technology (NACEPT). NACEPT is an EPA advisory committee created in 1988 to provide advice to the Administrator on a variety of environmental policy, economics, finance, and technology issues.

CSI was extremely productive in terms of projects developed and recommendations submitted to the EPA for action. The council and subcommittees worked on over forty projects, including both individual projects and larger, multiproject efforts. Nearly thirty subcommittee recommendations were endorsed by the council and submitted to the Administrator for EPA action. These projects and recommendations addressed all eight of the CSI program elements (regulation, pollution prevention, record keeping and recording, compliance and enforcement, permitting, environmental technology, community involvement, and future issues). Four projects led to recommended rule revisions that are being acted on by the EPA. One project led to the pilot project discussed below. Previous program evaluations showed that the pace of progress in the first two years of CSI was hampered by process-related problems, including inadequacies in the consensus-process ground rules, time lines and facilitation, insufficient technical assistance, and the relationship of the council to the subcommittees.

The pace of development of CSI's recommendations and project implementation increased for most of the subcommittees and the council during the last two years of CSI. This increased productivity can be attributed to the following:

- Increased mutual understanding of participants' issues and concerns;
- Subcommittees' improvements in identifying and focusing on actual opportunities for success;
- Participants' increased familiarity with the use of consensus decision-making;
- Adoption of project deadlines by the subcommittees and council;
- A stronger leadership role by the EPA.

The council mounted three major crosscutting efforts during the last two years of CSI:

1. Commenting on the EPA plans for improving environmental information and reporting through the reinventing environmental information (REI) initiative, which resulted, in part, in the creation of, and action plan on, data gaps, a strategy to address data quality, and the formation of a new information office;

2. Supporting the EPA's efforts to provide effective future stakeholder involvement in environmental decision-making, resulting in the Stakeholder Involvement Plan;

3. Supporting the EPA's integration of the lessons learned from CSI into its core functions through the development of a sector-based approach in the Sector Based Environmental Protection Action Plan.

One recommendation that came out of the printing sector was a project called PrintSTEP. The EPA has implemented the first phase of PrintSTEP—the Printers Simplified Total Environmental Partnership—by awarding co-operative agreements with grants to three states: Minnesota ($150,000), Missouri ($172,157), and New Hampshire ($150,000). PrintSTEP funds will enable these states to test approaches to making the regulatory system more effective and flexible for the printing industry. PrintSTEP was developed as part of the EPA's Common Sense Initiative to allow federal and state governments and interested stakeholder groups to develop consensus recommendations for improving environmental management strategies. The pilot projects will test specialized compliance tools for the printing sector, easier reporting for environmental permit holders, and ways to reduce government oversight of facilities.

PrintSTEP pilot tests do not change the existing emissions or release standards for the printing industry. Instead, they change the process of implementing those standards. The grants will help states establish baseline data and collect data that can be used to measure the pilot programs' success. The goal of PrintSTEP is to help the printing industry and the public achieve cleaner, cheaper, and smarter environmental protection through the creation of a simpler regulatory framework. PrintSTEP is expected to improve environmental performance, to be more efficient, and to make the regulatory process easier. This new approach encourages all stakeholders in the printing industry to become involved and contribute positively. Pilot projects with extensive evaluation (including gathering baseline information before the initiation of the pilot projects) will be the primary means of determining the effectiveness of PrintSTEP.

CSI is one example of an unusually productive and innovative federal advisory committee at the EPA. It was one of the first to include environmental justice representation. (The author was an environmental justice appointment to CSI.) Federal advisory committees to the EPA serve an important role in the traditions and culture of the EPA. As the EPA faces difficult future challenges, these federal advisory committees will continue to serve as incubators of new and needed ideas and solutions.

ENVIRONMENTAL ENFORCEMENT APPROACH TO FACILITATION OF COMPLIANCE

While one of the strongest traditions at the EPA is enforcement of environmental laws, rules, and regulations, one of the strongest cultural norms is to induce compliance with environmental requirements. The EPA's civil enforcement program helps protect the environment and human health by assuring compliance with federal environmental laws. Civil enforcement encompasses the investigations and cases brought to address the most significant violations, and include EPA administrative actions and judicial cases referred to the Department of Justice. The EPA works closely with states (e.g., in joint development of cases) as well as with tribes and with other federal agencies in implementing the enforcement programs. The EPA emphasizes actions that reduce the most significant risks to human health or the environment, and consults extensively with states and other stakeholders in determining risk-based priorities. For over two decades, the EPA's statutory and regulatory enforcement programs have made a measurable contribution to reducing the amount of pollution that goes into the air we breathe or the water we drink, and by encouraging safer handling of hazardous waste and toxic materials.

The mission of the multimedia criminal enforcement program is to identify, apprehend, and assist prosecutors in convicting those who are responsible for the most significant and egregious violations of environmental law that pose substantial risks to human health and the environment. The EPA's criminal enforcement program was established in 1982. Recognizing the growing need to combat environmental crime, Congress granted the EPA full law enforcement authority in 1988 and greatly expanded the program with the enactment of the 1990 Pollution Prosecution Act.

The criminal enforcement program has successfully prosecuted significant violations of all major environmental statutes, including data fraud cases (e.g., private laboratories submitting false environmental data to state and federal environmental agencies); indiscriminate hazardous-waste dumping that resulted in serious injuries and death; industrywide ocean dumping by cruise ships; oil spills that caused significant damage to waterways, wetlands, and beaches; international smuggling of CFC refrigerants that damage the ozone layer and increase skin cancer risk; and illegal handling of hazardous substances, such as pesticides and asbestos, that exposed children, the poor, and other especially vulnerable groups to potentially serious illness.

The criminal enforcement program is made up of well-trained federal law enforcement agents, environmental forensic scientists and engineers, attorneys, and training specialists. With more than forty area and resident offices nationwide, and supported by the EPA's forensics laboratory in Denver, Colorado, and training facilities in Washington, D.C., and Denver, and the Federal Law Enforcement Training Center in Glynco, Georgia, the program works closely with other federal, state, tribal, and local law enforcement authorities, both to investigate and to successfully prosecute criminal violations and to build the criminal enforcement capacity of other units of government.

Compliance assistance helps business, industry, and governments—the regulated community—understand and meet their environmental obligations. The EPA partners with other providers of assistance to develop and deliver compliance assistance resources such as Web sites, compliance guides, fact sheets, and training materials. These partners include state and local governments, trade associations, nonprofit organizations, and academia. The EPA also works with these organizations to help serve as a repository of information on compliance assistance tools and to measure the results of compliance assistance.

Sector-based Approaches at the EPA

Sector-oriented assistance addresses compliance issues or needs for business and industry sectors (e.g., dry cleaning, metal finishers, and furniture manufacturers) and government sectors (e.g., local governments, tribal governments, and federal government facilities). Statute-specific assistance includes compliance assistance activities or tools related to specific EPA statutes or regulations, such as the Clean Air Act. Planning for compliance assistance enables all stakeholders to understand the purpose and timing of planned activities. This allows EPA offices and regions, along with other compliance assistance providers and the regulated community, to identify opportunities for improved coordination, collaboration, or partnerships in developing and delivering compliance assistance.

The EPA often provides compliance assistance on a sector-by-sector basis in order to efficiently reach facilities with similar operations, processes, or practices. To reach members of a sector, the EPA works with sector leaders and organizations, and uses communication channels shared within each sector. Sectors can be broadly defined—construction, manufacturing, agriculture, or government—or more narrowly defined—residential construction, automobile assembly, poultry production, or drinking water supply. Historically the EPA has used the Standard Industrial Codes to categorize and maintain data on sectors. These codes are useful when searching EPA data systems. The EPA is now in the process of converting to the more recent North American Industry Classification System. The International Standards Organization also develops standards for environmental issues.

Compliance assistance centers provide comprehensive, easy-to-understand compliance information targeted to specific industry and government sectors. Sector notebooks are booklets that describe in plain language environmental problems associated with major U.S. industries. Compliance assistance and inspection publications—including guides, manuals, fact sheets, and brochures that pertain to an individual sector or a specific regulation—are also available. The National Compliance Assistance Clearinghouse links public and private compliance assistance materials. Users may post documents and interact with assistance providers, both within and outside of the EPA. The clearinghouse allows users to search for relevant material on new and existing regulations, pollution prevention opportunities, and voluntary programs created by other parts of the EPA, other federal agencies, tribes, state and local agencies, industry, and other organizations.

Compliance Monitoring

A key factor to providing environmental protection is assuring compliance by the regulated community with environmental laws/regulations through effective monitoring and compliance assessment. Unless there is compliance with the requirements that are designed to provide the necessary environmental protection, the promulgation of laws and regulations has little impact. Compliance monitoring consists of actions to do the following:

- Determine compliance with applicable laws, regulations, permit conditions, orders, and settlement agreements;
- Review and evaluate the activities of the regulated community;
- Determine whether or not conditions presenting imminent and substantial endangerment may exist.

Compliance monitoring consists of a wide range of activities in six basic categories, which may overlap.

1. Surveillance is generally a preinspection activity that consists of obtaining general site information prior to entering the facility. Examples include ambient sampling at the property line or observations of activity at the site.
2. Inspections (on-site) may include record reviews, observations, sampling, and interviews, and may be single- or multimedia, facility or industry sector-based, or have a geographic or ecosystem focus.
3. Investigations are generally more comprehensive than inspections, and may be warranted when an inspection or record review suggests the potential for serious, widespread, and/or continuing civil or criminal violations.
4. Record reviews may be conducted at the EPA, state or local offices, or the facility, and may or may not be combined with fieldwork. Records may be derived from routine self-monitoring requirements, inspection reports, citizen/employee tips, or remote sensing.
5. Targeted information gathering may be used to provide or acquire more accurate information on the status of compliance and/or environmental conditions.
6. Remediation compliance monitoring of work required by regulation, permit, order, or settlement includes ensuring timely submissions, review of submittals for adequacy, and oversight of remedial activities. Elements of these activities may include sampling, sample analysis, observations, issuance of information requirement letters or subpoenas, and ensuring data quality.

The EPA works closely with its regulatory partners in carrying out compliance monitoring activities. States with delegated programs conduct the majority of compliance monitoring activities within their jurisdictions. The EPA's role in compliance monitoring includes

- Collecting and analyzing compliance and enforcement data;
- Conducting inspections/investigations for programs not delegated to the states;
- Setting national/regional priorities;
- Assisting states and tribes when they request assistance;
- Overseeing programs and state grants;
- Responding to citizen complaints;
- Developing policy and legal guidance when questions arise as to the interpretation of federal environmental laws, regulations, and policies;
- Providing technical assistance to states and tribal and local governments;
- Managing and overseeing compliance monitoring enforcement grants to states and tribes.

Information about compliance monitoring data can be accessed on the Planning and Results sidebar on the Compliance and Enforcement home page. Data may be viewed in the Sector Facility Indexing Project (SFIP), which brings together environmental and other information from a number of data systems to produce facility-level profiles for five industry sectors (petroleum refining, iron and steel production, primary nonferrous metal refining and smelting, pulp manufacturing, and automobile assembly) and a subset of major federal facilities. SFIP information relates to compliance and inspection history, chemical releases and spills, production, and demographics of the surrounding population.

This compliance-monitoring home page provides access to documents about the EPA's compliance-monitoring program, such as inspection manuals, guides, and strategies for specific regulations or for an industry sector (e.g., woodstoves). Furthermore, on this home page one can find compliance assistance tools and materials that can assist in compliance monitoring.

The culture of enforcement at the EPA is to induce compliance rather than punish noncompliance. The EPA promotes compliance through the use of incentives—policies and programs that eliminate, reduce, or waive penalties under certain conditions for business, industry, and government facilities that voluntarily discover, promptly disclose, and expeditiously correct environmental problems. Information about these incentives, self-disclosure programs, and related tools such as environmental audit protocols, environmental management systems, pollution prevention, and the environmental benefits achieved by such programs are located on the home page.

In connection with the audit policy, the EPA has established programs for promoting environmental compliance and the correction of violations by offering incentives to the regulated community in exchange for agreements to perform self-assessment, disclosure, and the correction of violations. These incentives may involve reduced penalties for violations, extended time for correction, fewer inspections, and/or other considerations. For more information, see the compliance incentives Web pages, which provide information on some of the more important compliance incentive programs and projects.

The EPA supports the use of market-based incentives for improved environmental performance and the prevention of environmental noncompliance. Information about its collaboration with the Securities and Exchange Commission (SEC) is located on the compliance incentives Web pages. The EPA encourages the disclosure of environmental information in accordance with the mandatory corporate disclosure requirements promulgated by the SEC.

Compliance with the SEC's requirement to disclose environmental legal proceedings is important to the EPA because it increases public access to corporate environmental information. Increased corporate environmental disclosure also helps maintain a level playing field for environmentally responsible companies, helps to raise company awareness concerning environmental issues, and enables capital markets to account for environmental matters more fully.

The EPA promotes the disclosure of environmental information in accordance with the SEC's mandatory corporate disclosure requirements as a means of promoting improved environmental performance. In order to increase awareness of those requirements, the EPA distributes "Notice of SEC Registrants' Duty to Disclose Environmental Legal Proceedings" to parties to certain EPA-initiated enforcement actions. The EPA does not determine that each recipient of the "Notice" is necessarily required to make a public disclosure of the environmental legal proceeding at hand, but advises each recipient to consider the applicability of the SEC's requirements. The federal securities regulatory system relies upon SEC registrants to fully disclose material information to actual and potential shareholders in order to ensure that they can make informed investments and to promote proper market functioning. The SEC's regulations do not promote any particular type of investment over another, but facilitate the free flow of information between regulated companies and the public.

The SEC has several regulatory provisions that specifically require registrant companies to publicly disclose environmental information. SEC Regulation S-K, Item 101—Description of Business—requires SEC registrants to disclose the material effects of complying, or failing to comply, with environmental requirements on the capital expenditures, earnings, and competitive position of the registrant and its subsidiaries. SEC registrants are required to disclose pending environmental legal proceedings, or proceedings known to be contemplated, that meet any of three qualifying conditions: materiality, 10 percent of current assets, or monetary sanctions. SEC registrants are required to disclose environmental contingencies that may reasonably be expected to have material impact on net sales, revenue, or income from continuing operations.

The EPA promotes compliance with environmental laws and regulations through its use of incentives with regard to the regulated community. The EPA's audit policy, small business policy, and small community policy, and the incentive programs developed in association with them, are designed to reduce or eliminate penalties under certain conditions for business, industry, and government facilities that voluntarily discover, promptly disclose, and correct environmental violations. In addition to the penalty eliminations and reductions granted under its enforcement response and incentive policies, the EPA grants penalty waivers and reductions under the Compliance Incentive Program (CIP) initiatives. These programs invite companies or industrial sectors to disclose and correct violations in exchange for reduced or waived penalties while increasing the risk of enforcement for those not taking advantage of this opportunity. There is also a specialized type of CIP, commonly called a cap program, that offers a capped penalty or a specified maximum penalty for violations. This is an amount below the normal penalty assessment.

Typically, the CIP proceeds in four steps.

1. The EPA notifies a group within the regulated community that it is, or may be, subject to specific environmental requirements;

2. The notified companies are given an opportunity to disclose and correct violations, subject to a widely publicized and meaningful deadline;

3. Participants that disclose violations within the deadline and commit to return to compliance receive a waived or greatly reduced penalty—in cap initiatives, the penalty limits are advertised in advance, so participants know what the "capped" penalty, if any, will be;

4. The EPA makes it widely known that companies which do not take advantage of this offer face a greater risk of future inspections.

The EPA develops similar programs in the various enforcement areas as the need arises. The need for such programs is based on the finding of abnormally high rates of noncompliance in industrial sectors or industrial groups that may endanger public health or the environment. However, most industries self-report environmental data to the EPA. The rise of citizen monitoring of environmental conditions increases pressure for the EPA to monitor compliance with environmental law as well as whether the conditions of a permit are met.

EPA's Audit Policy

The EPA audit policy, titled "Incentives for Self-Policing: Discovery, Disclosure, Correction and Prevention of Violations," has been in effect since 1995. It safeguards human health and the environment by providing incentives for regulated entities to come into compliance with federal environmental laws and regulations. The policy was designed to provide major incentives for regulated entities that voluntarily discover, promptly disclose, and expeditiously correct noncompliance, rendering formal EPA investigation and enforcement action unnecessary. The audit policy reflects the input of industry, trade associations, state environmental program practitioners, and public interest groups. Disclosures are often preceded by consultations between the EPA and the regulated entity so that mutually acceptable disclosure details, and compliance and audit schedules, can be discussed. If policy conditions are met, most penalties may be waived and further civil or criminal prosecution may not be pursued.

There are four incentives for self-policing under the audit policy.

1. No gravity-based penalties for disclosing entities that meet all nine policy conditions, including "systematic discovery" of the violation through an environmental audit or a compliance management system. Gravity-based penalties are that portion of the penalty over and above the economic benefit. In general, civil penalties that the EPA assesses consist of two elements: the economic benefit component and the gravity-based component. The economic benefit component reflects the economic gain derived from a violator's illegal competitive advantage. Gravity-based penalties reflect the egregiousness of the violator's behavior and constitute the punitive portion of the penalty. The EPA retains its discretion to collect any economic benefit that may have been realized as a result of noncompliance.

2. Reduction of gravity-based penalties by 75 percent may be granted to entities that meet all of the conditions except "systematic discovery" of the violation through an environmental audit or a compliance management system.

3. There may be no recommendation for criminal prosecution of entities that disclose violations of criminal law and meet all applicable conditions under the policy. "Systematic discovery" is not required for an entity to be eligible for this incentive, although the entity must be acting in good faith and adopt a systematic approach to preventing recurring violations. The EPA generally does not focus its criminal enforcement resources on entities that voluntarily discover, promptly disclose, and expeditiously correct violations

unless there is behavior that merits criminal investigation. When a disclosure that meets the terms and conditions under the audit policy results in a criminal investigation, the EPA generally will not recommend criminal prosecution for the disclosing entity, although it may recommend prosecution of culpable individuals and other entities.

4. There are no routine requests for audit reports from entities that disclose under the audit policy. In general, the EPA will refrain from routine requests for audit reports. However, if the EPA has independent evidence of a violation, it may seek the information it needs to establish the extent and nature of the violation and the degree of culpability.

Entities that satisfy the following conditions are eligible for audit policy benefits. Even if they fail to meet the first condition—systematic discovery—they may be eligible for a 75 percent penalty mitigation and for no recommendation regarding criminal violations.

- Systematic discovery of the violation through an environmental audit or a compliance management system;
- Voluntary discovery that is not through a legally required monitoring, sampling, or auditing procedure;
- Prompt disclosure in writing to the EPA within twenty-one days of discovery or such shorter time as may be required by law—discovery occurs when any officer, director, employee, or agent of the facility has an objectively reasonable basis for believing that a violation has or may have occurred;
- Independent discovery and disclosure before the EPA likely would have identified the violation through its own investigation or on the basis of information provided by a third party;
- Correction and remediation within sixty calendar days, in most cases from the date of discovery;
- Prevention of recurrence of the violation;
- Repeat violations, those which have occurred at the same facility within the past three years or have occurred as part of a pattern of violations within the past five years at another facility(ies) owned or operated by the same company, are ineligible—if the facility has been newly acquired, the existence of a violation prior to acquisition does not trigger the repeat violations exclusion;

Certain types of violations, such as those resulting in serious harm, those which presenting an imminent and substantial danger, and those which violate the specific terms of an administrative or judicial order or consent agreement, are ineligible. Cooperation by the disclosing entity is required.

The EPA's audit policy faces dynamic tension from the regulated industries, concerned communities, and state agencies. There are many different kinds of audits of environmental performance and compliance with environmental laws. As emissions accumulate and the EPA faces the challenges of sustainability and community-based environmental planning, it is likely that this tension will increase. The specific manner in which an environmental audit is performed faces increasing scrutiny.

Audit Protocols

The compliance auditing protocol is a collection of tools for use by the regulated community and others in developing programs for individual facilities to evaluate their compliance with environmental requirements under the federal environmental laws and regulations. Audit protocols assist the regulated community in developing programs at individual facilities to evaluate their compliance with federal environmental requirements. The protocols are intended solely as guidance. The regulated community's legal obligations are determined by the terms of applicable environmental facility-specific permits, as well as underlying statutes and applicable state and local laws. Environmental audit reports are useful to a variety of businesses and industries; local, state, and federal government facilities; and financial lenders and insurance companies that need to assess environmental performance. The audit protocols are designed for use by persons with various backgrounds, including scientists, engineers, lawyers, and business owners or operators. They provide detailed regulatory checklists that can be customized to meet specific needs.

There are eleven audit protocols that provide coverage of the Comprehensive Environmental Response, Compensation, and Liability Act; the Clean Water Act; the Emergency Planning and Community Right-to-Know Act; the Federal Insecticide, Fungicide, and Rodenticide Act; the Resource Conservation and Recovery Act; the Safe Drinking Water Act; and the Toxic Substance Control Act. In addition, there is a how-to manual on designing and implementing environmental compliance auditing programs for federal agencies and facilities.

These protocols are very specific, and change frequently. Some audits remain undisclosed to the public.

Traditions and Culture from the National Environmental Policy Act

The National Environmental Policy Act (NEPA) requires federal agencies to integrate environmental values into their decision-making processes by considering the environmental impacts of their proposed actions and reasonable alternatives to those actions. To meet this requirement, federal agencies prepare a detailed environmental impact statement (EIS).

The EPA focuses on three main areas regarding NEPA compliance:

1. Coordinating EPA's review of all EISs prepared by other federal agencies;

2. Maintaining a national EIS filing system and publishing weekly notices of EISs available for review and summaries of EPA's comments;

3. Assuring that EPA's own actions comply with NEPA and other environmental requirements.

Because NEPA passed into law at the same time the EPA was formed, it is strongly ingrained in the EPA's culture and traditions. NEPA represents the highest ideals in U.S. environmentalism, but its policy implementation has greatly narrowed its original goals. Nonetheless, it has served as a model for state and tribal environmental policy acts.

NEPA requirements have been honed in a judicial context. They helped establish the early credibility of the EPA and the practice and policy of examining environmental, social, and economic impacts of a particular decision. EISs are advisory only, and the decision maker is not required to choose the least environmentally damaging alternative. Nonetheless, the public participation aspects of NEPA raised the profile of the EPA in the public mind. (See discussion in Chapter 1.)

Supplemental Environmental Projects

If the EPA believes that an individual or company has failed to comply with federal environmental laws, it may initiate an enforcement action. Enforcement actions are taken in order to compel the individual or company to return to compliance, and to deter others from violating these laws. In settling an enforcement action, the EPA usually requires individuals or companies to pay cash penalties and to take injunctive relief actions needed to eliminate noncompliance, correct environmental damage, and restore the environment. In addition, enforcement settlements may include supplemental environmental projects (SEPs). SEPs are actions taken by an individual or a company that are in addition to what is required to return to compliance with environmental laws. They benefit public health or the environment and offer a unique opportunity to further the EPA's goals of ensuring clean air and water, safe food, and better waste management, and expanding the public's right to know about the environment.

SEP projects have existed since the early 1980s, and their use increased steadily through the 1990s. For instance, while more than 200 SEPs were approved in 1992, a total of 336 SEPs were agreed to as part of 197 case settlements in fiscal year 1999. The total monetary value of these SEPs was over $230 million. Approximately half of these projects were classified as pollution prevention or pollution reduction activities.

Through its SEP policy the EPA allows a violator of environmental laws to do more than simply correct its violation(s). A SEP is an environmentally beneficial project that a violator voluntarily agrees to undertake in addition to actions required to correct the violation(s) as part of an enforcement settlement. Besides showing the ability to complete the project, the company must fully finance the project. The EPA provides oversight to ensure that the company does what it promises to do but does not manage or control the funds.

SEPs are designed to protect and to improve the environment and public health to a level beyond that achieved by compliance with applicable laws. SEPs may directly or indirectly benefit the public by preventing pollution or addressing environmental justice concerns. Community involvement can assure greater consideration of community needs, and also can lead to increased communication and trust between all concerned parties. SEPs have been implemented by large and small companies, hospitals, federal facilities, and state and local governments. If a company performs a SEP, the EPA may reduce the penalty assessed. In addition to receiving this economic incentive, a company may improve the quality of life for the surrounding community and, as a result, build a better relationship with the community.

As described below, the EPA has seven specific categories of projects that are acceptable SEPs. In addition, it allows companies to perform other types of projects that have environmental or public health benefits.

1. Pollution prevention. These SEPs involve changes that reduce or eliminate some form of pollution, or that reduce a pollutant's toxicity prior to recycling, treatment, or disposal. Examples include use of less toxic materials to make products, modifications in the production process to reduce material losses, changes in product design that require less-polluting processes, and improved housekeeping. The EPA places a high priority on pollution prevention approaches, since these reduce the potential for future pollution, and may lead to more widespread, environmentally beneficial changes in business or industry activities. As a result, the EPA may allow greater mitigation of penalties for pollution prevention projects than for other SEPs.

2. Pollution reduction. These SEPs are similar to pollution prevention SEPs in terms of outcome. But instead of eliminating a source of pollution, they reduce the amount or danger of the pollution that reaches the environment. Examples include improved treatment or control of pollutants, and recycling and reuse of chemicals or materials.

3. Public health. Such SEPs include examining residents in the community put at risk by the violation to determine if anyone has experienced health problems related to the violation, as well as providing related medical treatment or rehabilitation therapy.

4. Environmental restoration and protection. These SEPs improve the condition of the land, air, or water in the area damaged by the violation. For example, by purchasing land or developing conservation programs for the land, a company can protect a natural habitat for wildlife or a source of drinking water. Beyond preservation, such a SEP may involve restoring natural areas that are vital to long-term protection of the environment or public health.

5. Assessments and audits. Any violating company may agree to examine its operations for pollution prevention opportunities, and determine if it can reduce the use, production, or generation of hazardous materials and other wastes. These audits go well beyond standard business practices. In addition, small businesses (with fewer than 100 employees) or small communities (fewer than 2,500 residents) can receive credit for agreeing to conduct audits to determine their compliance with environmental laws in order to avoid future violations.

6. Environmental compliance promotion. These are SEPs in which the violator helps other companies achieve compliance and reduce pollution related to the type of violation. For example, a company that violated the Clean Air Act might train other companies on how to comply with the act.

7. Emergency planning and preparedness. These SEPs provide technical assistance and training to state or local emergency planning and response organizations to help them better respond to chemical emergencies. For example, a company may provide a local fire department with additional equipment to deal with a hazardous-waste situation.

8. Other types of projects. Other acceptable SEPs are those which have environmental merit but do not fit the categories listed above. These types of projects must be fully consistent with all other provisions of the SEP policy. While these projects have significant monetary value, their true value lies in their impacts on public health and/or the environment actually or potentially affected by the violation.

SEPs offer a unique opportunity to achieve environmental improvements in addition to what is required for violators to return to compliance with environmental regulations.

In going beyond what is required to settle an enforcement action, SEPs help the EPA meet its long-term, congressionally mandated goals. For example, projects that reduce emissions of pollutants or eliminate their production have a positive effect on the local community's air quality. SEPs that involve health screening and treatment of children affected by pollution can improve public health dramatically. Restoration projects that return wetlands to their natural state not only provide habitat for endangered and other species, but also allow for natural filtration of pollutants and flood control. Because the benefits to the community and the environment that can be obtained through SEPs can be significant, the EPA encourages their use in settlement agreements. Additional information on SEPs and the SEP policy may be found at www.epa.gov/oeca/sep.

The tradition of environmental performance through a culture of inducing compliance remains strong at the EPA. Evidence of this is seen in the EPA's recent emphasis on collaborative approaches to environmental decision-making.

Overall, inducing compliance, auditing environmental performance of industry, and collaborating with environmental wrongdoers on remedies is the EPA's approach to enforcement of environmental laws. Each of these areas is dynamic. Each is also mirrored at the state level. However, enforcement remains an evolving area. Only the permit holder and permit granter may challenge a specific industry permit. This often leaves citizens with evidence of permit violations no option other than to protest to state environmental agencies and to the EPA. The EPA has considered the "any credible evidence rule," which would allow citizens to bring evidence of permit violations more directly to the EPA. This has not been adopted, but, in communities where emissions are accumulating and citizens are doing environmental monitoring, and in an era where ecosystem approaches, community-based environmental planning, and sustainability are growing, the pressure to enforce environmental laws and permit conditions is increasing.

☆ 5 ☆

Organization and Day-to-Day Activities

As a major regulatory and policy-making federal agency, the EPA has various offices to support its day-to-day operations. The following offices within the Office of the Administrator help support the mission of the EPA.

ADMINISTRATIVE LAW JUDGES

Administrative law judges play a very important role at the EPA. Because prospective litigants are required to exhaust their administrative remedies before a court can accept a case, most complaints against the EPA must go through an administrative law judge first. Not only do these judges decide or settle the case, but they also construct the record that may be forwarded to a judicial court. Administrative law judges conduct hearings and render decisions in proceedings brought by the EPA. The EPA's Office of Administrative Law Judges is an independent office in the Office of the Administrator. The administrative law judges conduct hearings and render decisions in proceedings involving the EPA and persons, businesses, government entities, and other organizations that are, or are alleged to be, regulated under environmental laws. They preside over enforcement and permit proceedings in accordance with the Administrative Procedure Act. Most enforcement actions initiated by the EPA are for the assessment of civil penalties.

All litigants are offered the opportunity to resolve enforcement cases through alternative dispute resolution, with an administrative law judge serving as a neutral party, prior to assignment of the case for litigation. Administrative law judges are certified by the Office of Personnel Management and appointed in accordance with 5USC3105. They have decisional independence pursuant to Section 557 of the Administrative Procedure Act, 5USC557, which ensures the fair and impartial resolution of proceedings.

179

Decisions issued by the administrative law judges are subject to review by the Environmental Appeals Board (EAB). The judge's initial decision becomes the final order of the EPA within forty-five days after service upon the parties unless a party appeals to the EAB or the EAB on its own initiative elects to review the decision.

ALTERNATIVE DISPUTE RESOLUTION IN THE OFFICE OF ADMINISTRATIVE LAW JUDGES

In essentially every environmental case filed with it, the Office of Administrative Law Judges offers the parties alternative dispute resolution in the form of mediation. The mediation process is initiated only if it is accepted by all parties. The neutral mediator is one of the office's seven judges, all of whom have had mediation training. There is no charge to either side. Mediation is offered immediately upon arrival of the case in the office and before the case is assigned to a judge for litigation. If litigation has begun, mediation is still available to the parties upon their motion and at the discretion of the presiding judge. Mediation is allowed to continue for sixty days and, at the discretion of the neutral judge, may be extended up to an additional sixty days. When a case is not settled during mediation, it is thereafter handled by one of the office's other judges, who presides over the litigation and renders a decision resolving the case. Confidentiality is strictly observed during and after the mediation process. There is no communication on the substance of the case between the judge who served as mediator and the judge who presides over the litigation, and the notes and written records of the mediator are destroyed. Environmental cases coming before the Office of Administrative Law Judges involve one or more of the major environmental statutes. The office's experience with mediation has been favorable. For this reason the office has expanded the use of mediation from its inception in 1997, when mediation was offered for only a few selected cases, to the present, when it is offered for essentially every case.

The administrative law judges also conduct hearings and render decisions in appeals from determinations of the EPA's Office of Civil Rights regarding complaints of violation of Title VI of the Civil Rights Act of 1964 and of the EPA's implementing regulations (40 CFR7). The EPA's Office of Administrative Law Judges now has access to videoconferencing equipment. In mediation proceedings the neutral judge may use such equipment with the consent of the parties. For proceedings in litigation, videoconferencing equipment may be used for oral arguments, pretrial conferences, and hearings, with the parties' consent and the presiding judge's approval.

CONGRESSIONAL AND INTERGOVERNMENTAL RELATIONS

The Office of Congressional and Intergovernmental Relations (OCIR) coordinates interactions among Congress, states, and local governments. It serves as liaison with these constituencies on the EPA's major programs (e.g., air/pesticides, water, and waste) as well as on intergovernmental issues. The major functions of OCIR include

- Assisting in development and implementation of the legislative agenda for the EPA, including initiatives and proposals;

- Leading the EPA in the review of legislation, coordinating the EPA's formal positions and technical assistance to Congress, and monitoring all relevant legislative actions (e.g., bills, reports, and regulations) related to the EPA's programs;

- Leading the development and implementation of the National Environmental Performance Partnership System between the EPA and the states;

- Managing and monitoring environmental issues with both national associations and individual state and local governments through interactions with governors, state environmental commissioners, the Local Government Resource Center, the Small Community Advisory Committee, and the Local Government Advisory Committee;

- Facilitating communication of the EPA's priorities and policies to Congress;

- Managing and monitoring EPA and public requests for congressional information and maintaining the Legislative Library, which provides reference data and general research services.

- Coordinating EPA appearances at congressional hearings and managing associated testimony. The Office of Regional Operations serves as the regional offices' advocate and ombudsman at headquarters and is a critical link between the Administrator/Deputy Administrator, the assistant administrators, the general counsel, the inspector general, and the regional/deputy regional administrators. OCIR ensures the integration of headquarters' policy and concerns into regional office operations, as well as the incorporation of regional office views and needs in the formulation of EPA and national policy and decision-making processes. It also manages resources and coordinates policy for the regional geographic initiatives and the organizations;

- Providing cooperative environmental management through the Federal Advisory Committee. The EPA's advisory committees bring the concerned public into a productive information-gathering process to assist in the development of national and international environmental policies. (See discussion of federal advisory committees in Chapter 4.)

The major impact of OCIR on day-to-day activities of the EPA is on the relationships the EPA has with Congress, states, local governments, and the public. These change as issues facing these groups change. Given the varying nature of these stakeholder groups, the EPA must have good communication on daily basis. The political will and programmatic ability of state and local governments to implement environmental programs necessary for the mission of the EPA vary. Many states are wary of unfounded mandates from the federal government. Some localities are wary of EPA money for fear of excessive federal entanglement in local government. OCIR must have good relationships inside and outside the EPA.

ENVIRONMENTAL APPEALS BOARD

The Environmental Appeals Board (EAB) is the final EPA decision maker on administrative appeals under all major environmental statutes that the EPA administers. It is an impartial body independent of all EPA components outside the Office of the Administrator. The EAB typically sits in panels of three judges and makes decisions by majority vote. Currently, nine experienced attorneys serve as counsel to the EAB. It was created in 1992 in recognition of the growing importance of the EPA adjudicatory proceedings as a mechanism for implementing and enforcing the environmental laws.

The EAB's caseload consists primarily of appeals from permit decisions and civil penalty decisions. The EAB has authority to hear these appeals in accordance with regulations delegating this authority from the EPA Administrator. Appeals from permit decisions made by the EPA's regional administrators (and in some cases, state permitting officials) may be filed either by permittees or by other interested persons. A grant of review of a permit decision is at the EAB's discretion. Appeals of civil penalty decisions made by EPA's administrative law judges may be filed either by private parties or by the EPA. A substantial additional portion of the EAB's caseload consists of petitions for reimbursement of costs incurred by complying with cleanup orders issued under the Comprehensive Environmental Response, Compensation, and Liability Act of 1980 (CERCLA). The EAB decides these matters pursuant to a delegation of authority from the Administrator. The EAB is also authorized to hear appeals from administrative decisions under the Clean Air Act's acid rain program and appeals of issuance of federal Clean Air Act Title V operating permits. The EAB considers all major environmental laws in its jurisdiction, including the following:

- Clean Air Act;
- Clean Water Act;
- Comprehensive Environmental Response, Compensation, and Liability Act;

- Emergency Planning and Community Right-to-Know Act;
- Federal Insecticide, Fungicide, and Rodenticide Act;
- Marine Protection, Research, and Sanctuaries Act;
- Solid Waste Disposal Act (RCRA);
- Safe Drinking Water Act;
- Toxic Substances Control Act.

Although it is relatively new within the EPA, the EAB still has a significant impact on the day-to-day operations in its functioning and its decisions. Its decisions are final and may not be appealed to the Administrator. However, the parties (other than EPA) have statutory rights of appeal to federal courts under the various environmental statutes. This is important because many courts require potential plaintiffs to exhaust their administrative remedies before the court will exercise its jurisdiction. Absent a special citizen suit provision (see discussion in Chapter 2), the exhaustion of internal EPA appeals can be confusing and time-consuming. One issue is how to tell if one has exhausted all administrative remedies. The EAB definitively answered that question. After it finishes its consideration of a particular issue, the administrative remedies are exhausted and the parties may proceed to judicial forums. The EAB's contribution to the day-to-day functioning of the EPA is also in its streamlining of dispute resolution within the EPA.

HOMELAND SECURITY

The Office of Homeland Security (OHS) focuses on leading and coordinating homeland security activities and policy development across all EPA program areas. This involves ensuring consistent direction, efficient use of resources, and effective communication of homeland security efforts both within and outside the EPA. The OHS is located in the Office of the Administrator and works closely with the Homeland Security Council, the Department of Homeland Security, and other federal agencies as it coordinates overall EPA homeland security strategy.

The disposal of military ordnance is part of the hazardous waste stream. As some bases are closed, the disposal of their waste becomes an issue for the remaining community. (Photograph © by Frank Miller)

As a very new office within the EPA, OHS is developing involvement in the day-to-day activities of the EPA. The EPA has administrative experience in many of the areas of priority for the Office of Homeland Security. For example, the Office of Solid Waste and Emergency Response has experience with environmental responses to chemical incidents.

POLICY, ECONOMICS, AND INNOVATION

The Office of Policy, Economics, and Innovation (OPEI) supports the EPA's mission and serves as its focal point for regulatory analysis, economic analysis, and innovative policy development to achieve greater and more cost-effective public health and environmental protection. In consultation with various internal and external stakeholders and partners, it supports and oversees the testing of new and innovative approaches to environmental protection and related policy changes. OPEI is the focal point for regulatory analyses, policy development, and economic analyses necessary to support the EPA's regulatory development process and changes in business conditions. Its role in the regulatory development process is to manage the process and ensure that the underlying policy analyses are sound. OPEI helps strengthen the analytic foundation of the EPA's decision-making processes by working with the EPA's science adviser to strengthen the integration of scientific and economic analyses.

PUBLIC AFFAIRS

The Office of Public Affairs (OPA) serves as the EPA's primary policy office on all communications, environmental education, and media relations activities. It serves as the Agency-wide point of contact for the planning, development, and review of all electronic and print products intended for the public and ensures that the public has easy access to information on the EPA's Web site. The associate administrator for public affairs is the chief spokesperson for the EPA and principal adviser to the Administrator on all issues concerning short-term and long-term strategic communications. The OPA advances and supports environmental education efforts critical to the EPA's mission. It provides the news media with national-level announcements, press releases, Administrator's speeches, statements, and other key EPA communications. It communicates the EPA's mission, objectives, and goals to the media and is also the key link between the Administrator's Office and the media, providing official spokespeople and expert counsel on press matters to EPA employees at headquarters and in regional offices.

The Office of Multimedia Communications and Technology (MCAT) oversees the development and management of Web content to communicate the EPA's mission and the Administrator's priorities. It is responsible for the news section of the EPA home page and, with the Office of Environmental Information, manages other top-level pages of the EPA Web site. Together both offices monitor and oversee implementation of policies governing Web content (including organization and presentation) and infrastructure management. MCAT also manages the EPA's "Newsroom" and "Activities Update" and the Web site for the Office of the Administrator. In addition, it records EPA events through video and photography, helps set the stage with its graphic production skills and leadership, and provides daily national news from television, radio, Web, and print sources.

The Office of Environmental Education advances and supports education efforts that develop an environmentally conscious and responsible public. Its mission is to ensure that environmental education is a recognized and appropriately utilized tool for protecting human health and the environment, and for improving student academic achievement. This office's goals are to improve and enhance environmental education as a field by providing support, including financial resources as needed, ensuring quality and professionalism in the field, and improving and enhancing envi-

Actual notice requirements of public participation are often filled by telephoning community residents. Communication is an important aspect of public involvement. (Photograph © by Frank Miller)

ronmental education by seeking collaborations that produce consistently high-quality environmental education materials and messages.

The Office of Information and Special Initiatives builds and maintains relationships with a broad range of public and private-sector organizations and manages the print publications review process. The Office of Scheduling processes and responds to the Administrator's scheduling requests, submits proposals to the Administrator regarding events and activities, and works with appropriate offices inside and outside of the EPA to coordinate events. The Office of Long-Range Communication Planning works with EPA regional offices and the Office of Scheduling, as well as the Administrator's speechwriters, to coordinate national and regional events and announcements. It also develops themes to highlight EPA programs.

THE SCIENCE ADVISORY BOARD

The Science Advisory Board assures the scientific and technical basis for EPA rules and regulations, and integrates policies that guide the EPA decision makers in their use of scientific and technical information. Congress established the

Science Advisory Board in 1978 and gave it a broad mandate to advise the EPA on technical matters. Its principal mission includes the following:

- Reviewing the quality and relevance of the scientific and technical information being used or proposed as the basis for EPA regulations;
- Reviewing research programs and the technical basis of applied programs;
- Reviewing generic approaches to regulatory science, including guidelines governing the use of scientific and technical information in regulatory decisions, and critiquing such analytic methods as mathematical modeling;
- Advising the EPA on broad matters in science, technology, and social and economic issues;
- Advising the EPA on emergency and other short-notice programs.

OFFICE OF AIR AND RADIATION

Under the Clean Air Act, the EPA establishes air quality standards to protect public health and the environment. The EPA has set national air quality standards for the six principal air pollutants: carbon monoxide, lead, nitrogen dioxide, ozone, particulate matter, and sulfur dioxide. It tracks air pollution through air quality and emissions.

Trends in air quality are based on actual measurements of pollutant concentrations in the ambient (outside) air at monitoring sites across the country. Monitoring stations are operated by state, tribal, and local governments. Each year the EPA looks at the levels of these pollutants in the air and the amounts of emissions from various sources to see how both have changed over time and to summarize the current status of air quality. Trends are derived from direct measurements at these monitoring stations on a yearly basis. The EPA estimates nationwide emissions of the six principal air pollutants and the 188 toxic air pollutants regulated under the Clean Air Act. These estimates are based on actual measurements, levels of industrial activity, fuel consumption, vehicle-miles traveled, and other estimates of activities that cause pollution.

The Clean Air Act requires the states to develop and implement an operating permit program that meets minimum federal requirements. Most of the significant air pollution sources throughout the country must obtain a permit from the appropriate state, tribal, or local permitting authority. All "major" stationary sources (primarily industrial facilities and large commercial operations) emitting certain air pollutants are required to obtain operating permits. Whether a source meets the definition of "major" depends on the type and amount of air pollutants it emits and, to some degree, on the overall air quality in its vicinity. Generally, major sources include stationary facilities that emit 100 tons or more per year of a regulated air pollutant. Regulated pollutants include compounds such as carbon monoxide, particulates, volatile organics, sulfur dioxide, and nitrogen oxides. Smaller sources are considered "major" in areas that do not meet the national air quality standards for a particular pollutant. For example, certain sources releasing twenty-five or even ten tons of pollutants per year are considered "major" in areas with extreme ozone (urban smog) problems. The operating permit program also covers various other significant operations, such as:

- Large coal-burning utility boilers and industrial boilers subject to control requirements under the acid rain provisions of the Clean Air Act;
- Sources that are subject to requirements under new source performance standards and national emission standards for hazardous air pollutants;
- Sources of toxic air pollutants (any source that emits more than ten tons per year of an individual toxic air pollutant or more than twenty-five tons per year of any combination of toxic air pollutants);
- Sources required to have preconstruction or new source permits (under new source review or prevention of significant deterioration requirements).

Often these facilities are very large, with a wide variety of process operations and hundreds of emission sources. Examples include chemical plants, petroleum refineries, and large manufacturing facilities. The operating permit program covers most significant sources of air pollution in the United States. The more complex sources, such as large petroleum refineries and chemical production plants, can have hundreds or even thousands of emission points. Other key provisions of the operating permit program are the following:

- Sources are required to provide emissions reports to their permitting authorities at least semiannually and must certify their compliance status annually.
- Sources must periodically renew their operating permit, generally every five years.
- To fund their programs, permitting authorities are required to collect permit fees from sources subject to the operating permit program. Fees are most frequently based on the amount of air pollutants that a source may emit.
- Public notification and opportunity for comment must be provided during the permit review process for every new permit and for permits that are renewed or significantly revised.

- The EPA is responsible for overseeing the implementation of permit programs and may object to a permit that fails to comply with program requirements.

- The EPA is required to establish a federal permit program in any area where the permitting authority fails to develop and maintain an adequate program of its own.

It is important to note that state and local governments can and do implement separate requirements that are appropriate for unique local conditions.

The Office of Air and Radiation regulates traditional areas of the EPA on a daily basis. It is so well established that in some ways it is like a mini EPA. It is often involved in challenges and controversies in environmental policy development.

AMERICAN INDIAN ENVIRONMENTAL OFFICE

The American Indian Environmental Office (AIEO) coordinates the EPA-wide effort to strengthen public health and environmental protection in Indian country, with a special emphasis on building tribes' capacities to administer their environmental programs. AIEO oversees development and implementation of the EPA's Indian policy and strives to ensure that all EPA headquarters and regional offices implement their parts of the EPA's Indian program in a manner consistent with the Administration's policy of working with tribes on a government-to-government basis and the EPA's trust responsibility to protect tribal health and environments. AIEO's responsibilities include

- Providing multimedia program development grants to tribes;
- Negotiating tribal/EPA environmental agreements that identify tribal priorities for building environmental programs, as well as direct EPA program implementation assistance;
- Developing tools to assist tribal environmental managers in their decisions on environmental priorities and training curricula for the EPA staff on how to work effectively with tribes;
- Working to improve communication between the EPA and its tribal stakeholders in a number of ways, including assistance to the EPA offices as they consult more closely with tribes on actions that affect tribes and their environments, and support for regular meetings of the EPA's Tribal Operations Committee.

INTERNAL EPA OPERATIONS

For each fiscal year (October through September), the EPA develops a proposed budget that defines the goals and objectives toward which it intends to work within the fiscal year and the funding it believes is necessary to accomplish these goals and objectives. This budget is combined with the budgets of the rest of the executive branch and is then sent by the president to Congress in the first quarter of the calendar year. Congress then acts on the various budgets by developing, amending, and ultimately passing bills that enact the budgets into law (normally prior to the start of the fiscal year covered by the budget). The enacted budget becomes the blueprint for the EPA's activities during the next fiscal year. The "Summary of the EPA's Budget" (also known as the "Budget in Brief") provides an overview of the EPA's budget and of its activities as a whole. The "Summary" is available online for fiscal years going back to 1997.

The "Annual Performance Plan" defines the budget's goals and objectives in greater detail and ties the annual budget to the five-year strategic plan of the EPA. It is available online for fiscal years going back to 1999 (the year in which it was developed). The "Congressional Justification" (sometimes known as the "CJ") is the formal title for the actual budget document that is submitted to Congress. It is available online for fiscal years going back to 1999. The "appropriations links" link to the congressional Web site, where the actual House bills (designated "H.R."), Senate bills (designated "S."), and public laws are available. The EPA's budget is only a portion of the bill that encompasses the Departments of Veterans Affairs and Housing and Urban Development as well as many independent agencies, of which the EPA is one. These bills and laws are available online for fiscal years going back to 1998.

Strategic Plan

The EPA submitted the 2003 strategic plan to Congress and the Office of Management and Budget on September 30, 2003, as required under the Government Performance and Results Act. It will serve as the EPA's road map until 2008. The strategic plan lays out the EPA's five long-term goals and guides them in establishing the annual goals. It will help to measure how much progress has been made toward achieving goals and to recognize how to adjust approaches or directions to achieve better results. Finally, it will provide a basis from which EPA's managers can focus on the highest-priority environmental issues and ensure effective use of taxpayer dollars.

The strategic plan is built around five goals, centered on the themes of air and global climate change, water, land, communities and ecosystems, and compliance and environmental stewardship. These themes reflect the EPA's mission, "to protect human health and the natural environment." In addition, the plan discusses strategies the EPA is applying across all five goals in areas such as science, human capital, innovation, information, homeland security, partnerships, and economic and policy analysis.

The EPA's 1997 and 2000 strategic plans were based on ten goals, both outcome-oriented (e.g., clean air) and functional or support (e.g., effective management). In contrast, the EPA constructed its 2003 strategic plan around five new goals: clean air and global climate change, clean and safe water, land preservation and restoration, healthy communities and ecosystems, and compliance and environmental stewardship. Under this new plan, the EPA treats such critical functions as sound science, quality environmental information, and innovation not as goals in themselves, but as important means to an environmental end. EPA leaders believe that taking this broader approach of establishing goals focused on environmental results and streamlining the EPA's planning and budgeting structure will facilitate the EPA's ability to promote multimedia, cross-program approaches to solving environmental problems. Establishing goals that are less rigorously aligned with EPA programs or organizational units will provide greater flexibility both within the EPA and for state and tribal environmental programs. The EPA regional offices, for example, working with their state and tribal partners, will be better able to conduct regional strategic planning activities and address regional or geographic priorities under the EPA's five national goals.

2003–2008 EPA Strategic Plan: Direction for the Future

Most of the advances in environmental protection that the United States has realized since the mid-1970s would not have been possible without the participation and support of state, tribal, and local governments. The EPA's partnerships with states, tribes, and local governments are essential to achieving human health and environmental protection goals. Over the coming years the EPA will continue to work closely with state partners to strengthen the National Environmental Performance Partnership System, established in 1995 to reflect commitments made by states and the EPA to work together for environmental protection. The EPA is also reviewing the use of performance partnership agreements—negotiated agreements that define EPA and state responsibilities—to make them more useful and definitive and to reduce transaction costs.

The EPA is committed to working with tribes in a government-to-government relationship to improve environmental and human health protection throughout the nation. It is particularly concerned about the poor state of the environment often found in Indian country. As a result, the work described in the EPA's strategic plan that focuses on communities also provides for safeguarding tribes and tribal lands.

The EPA's strategic plan reflects five governmentwide initiatives presented in the president's management agenda: (1) strategic management of human capital, (2) competitive sourcing, (3) expanded electronic government, (4) improved financial performance, and (5) budget and performance integration. In developing plans for each of its five environmental goals—establishing objectives and subobjectives, and developing the means and strategies for achieving them—the EPA has considered opportunities to advance these initiatives. EPA staff has also been alert to opportunities for using competitive sourcing reviews to increase the efficiency and effectiveness of EPA operations. Through its cross-goal strategy for information the EPA is expanding its use of electronic systems for information management and a number of outreach and information-sharing mechanisms to streamline and improve communications with its state and tribal partners and with the public.

In June 2003, the EPA was recognized as the second executive branch federal agency (along with the Social Security Administration) to achieve a "green" rating from the Office of Management and Budget for improved financial performance. The EPA's record of superior accomplishments includes clean audit opinions on annual financial statements, effective internal controls to prevent erroneous payments, and resolving all outstanding material weaknesses for the first time since the Federal Managers Financial Integrity Act became law. Equally important to EPA's financial performance is its financial management system, which promotes integrated information to provide timely and reliable financial and performance data to program managers, who use it to support day-today decision-making. By integrating its planning and budgeting efforts and implementing other systems changes, the EPA has been better able to evaluate its programs, assess its performance, and use the results to make budget and program improvement decisions. The EPA will continue to strengthen links between budget and performance through its new goal structure. In addition, it is enhancing its financial reporting system by further integrating program performance and cost information, and making it available to EPA managers and decision makers in a timely manner.

All federal agencies must comply with the civil rights laws. The Office of Civil Rights (OCR) enforces federal nondiscrimination laws in all of the EPA's internal and external programs and policies. It serves as the principal adviser to the Administrator with respect to the EPA's nationwide internal and external equal opportunity and civil rights programs and policies. It also investigates and resolves complaints of discrimination by either the EPA or its financial assistance recipients. Through the External Compliance Staff, recipients of EPA financial assistance comply with federal nondiscrimination requirements. "Recipients" are, for the purposes of this regulation, any state or its political subdivision; any instrumentality of a state or its political subdivision; any public or private institution, organization, or other entity; or any person to which federal financial assistance is extended directly or through another recipient, including any successor, assignee, or transferee of a recipient, but excluding the ultimate beneficiary of the assistance.

Budget, strategic planning, and civil rights compliance are all part of the day-to-day operations of most federal agencies. Because of the dynamic nature of the EPA's regulatory environment, these activities underlie much of the organizational structure of the EPA.

OFFICE OF ENFORCEMENT AND COMPLIANCE ASSURANCE

The Office of Enforcement and Compliance Assurance (OECA), working in partnership with EPA regional offices, state governments, tribal governments, and other federal agencies, ensures compliance with the nation's environmental laws. Employing an integrated approach of compliance assistance, compliance incentives, and innovative civil and criminal enforcement, OECA and its partners seek to maximize compliance and reduce threats to public health and the environment. The Administration and Resources Management Support Staff is located within OECA. It provides a wide range of administrative support services, including human resources, labor relations, budgets and finance, contracts, grants, information and records management, and the Correspondence Control Unit.

As part of the OECA the Federal Facilities Enforcement Office (FFEO) is responsible for ensuring that federal facilities take all necessary actions to prevent, control, and abate environmental pollution. Federal facilities program managers in all of the regions assist FFEO in fulfilling those responsibilities. The Office of Compliance assists industries and other organizations in improving their compliance with environmental laws. It sets national compliance assurance and enforcement priorities through strategic planning and targeting; collects and integrates compliance data; develops effective compliance monitoring programs to support inspections and self-reporting; builds the capacity for more effective compliance assistance to the regulated community; improves the quality of regulations; works with regions, states, municipalities, citizen groups, and industry; and supports enforcement activities. The Office of Criminal Enforcement, Forensics, and Training directs the EPA's criminal prosecution program, provides a broad range of technical and forensic services for civil and criminal investigative support, and oversees the EPA's enforcement and compliance assurance training programs for federal, state, and local environmental professionals.

The Office of Federal Activities is responsible for coordinating EPA's review of all federal environmental impact statements (EISs) prepared by other agencies under the National Environmental Policy Act (NEPA); maintaining a national EIS filing system and publishing a weekly notice of EIS documents available for review; assuring that the EPA's own actions comply with NEPA and other environmental requirements; providing technical assistance and building capacity for environmental compliance, enforcement, and impact assessment in other countries; and working with federal and state agencies, foreign governments, and international organizations in order to ensure compliance with U.S. environmental laws.

The Office of Planning, Policy Analysis, and Communications (OPPAC) recommends national policy on issues pertaining to enforcement and compliance, and addresses emerging and crosscutting issues in OECA's program that impact various statutes. OPPAC is OECA's lead agency for work on innovations. It participates in the EPA's development and implementation of innovative environmental protection tools, such as environmental auditing and environmental management systems that encourage the regulated community to move beyond compliance.

The Office of Civil Enforcement works with states, EPA regional offices, tribes, and other federal agencies to assure compliance with the nation's environmental laws. It accomplishes its mission by investigating violations, deterring violations of federal environmental laws through civil enforcement actions, and providing appropriate incentives to members of the regulated community that wish to comply with the law. Civil enforcement and compliance incentive programs are integral parts of the compliance assurance framework that also includes assistance to the regulated community and criminal prosecution of intentional misconduct.

The Office of Site Remediation Enforcement facilitates, coordinates, and evaluates the enforcement of the EPA's national hazardous-waste cleanup programs. OECA supports and provides the means for the regions and states to vigorously and effectively enforce these statutes. Their goals are to achieve prompt site cleanup and maximum liable party participation in performing and paying for cleanup in ways that promote environmental justice and fairness.

OECA is the enforcement arm of the EPA. Virtually all environmental laws pass through it, and thus it shapes policy on a daily basis. Much of the workload at the EPA is related to the quality and quantity of the enforcement of environmental law. To this extent much of the EPA's organizational structure is affected by what OECA is enforcing and to what degree it is enforcing it.

OFFICE OF THE INSPECTOR GENERAL

The Office of the Inspector General (OIG) is an independent office within the EPA that helps the EPA protect the environment in a more efficient and cost-effective manner. It consists of auditors, program analysts, investigators, and others with extensive expertise. Although it is part of the EPA, Congress provides the OIG with funding separate from the EPA to ensure independence. It was created pursuant to the Inspector General Act of 1978 and performs audits, evaluations, and investigations of the EPA and its contractors. The OIG's missions are to promote economy and efficiency and to prevent and detect fraud, waste, and abuse. It also provides ombudsmen and hotline services to review public complaints about EPA programs and activities. Personnel of the OIG discuss issues with EPA management and others, including Congress, and provide detailed reports. Twice a year, they provide a semiannual report to Congress that identifies significant EPA deficiencies and proposed corrective actions, as well as profiles of EPA accomplishments. (See Chapter 3.)

The Office of Audit (OA) manages, coordinates, and has overall responsibility to lead the policy and direction of audits in three areas: business systems, contracts, and assistance agreements. It serves as the focal point for all financial, performance, and external audits related to those areas. OA designs long-term, multioffice audit plans; coordinates the implementation of its audits; synthesizes findings from these reviews; and provides for the timeliness, tone, quality, and objective review of the resulting reports.

The Office of Investigations manages, sets policy, coordinates, and has overall responsibility for criminal investigations of allegations of

- Financial fraud involving procurement personnel, contractors, grantees, and other recipients of EPA funds;
- Criminal wrongdoing involving EPA employees and programs, laboratory fraud, and computer crimes;
- Computer forensic examinations and media analysis to identify, investigate, and help counter illegal intrusions into the EPA's computer systems.

The Office of Program Evaluation (OPE) manages, coordinates, and has overall responsibility for leading the design and implementation of program evaluations within the OIG. Its evaluations use design and methodology strategies that maximize innovation, identify new issues, and focus on increased understanding of EPA programs. OPE designs long-term, multioffice program evaluation plans, coordinates the execution of the evaluations, synthesizes findings from these reviews, and provides for the timeliness, tone, quality, and objective review of the resulting reports.

The OIG also compiles the Compendium of Environmental Programs. The Compendium allows the EPA, inspectors general, the Government Accountability Office, the Office of Management and Budget, and other stakeholders in environmental programs use its database to view data on specific environmental activities. To appreciate and quantify the impact of EPA's programs, the Compendium's 2005 update sought to combine the benefit of the EPA's efforts with those undertaken by other federal agencies and departments. The EPA's Annual Performance Plan and Congressional Justification, as well as OIG research, identified twenty-three federal agencies that collectively share responsibility for clean air and global climate change, clean and safe water, land preservation and restoration, and healthy communities and ecosystems. The Compendium represents a collaborative effort among federal agencies to identify future opportunities for joint audits, evaluations, and investigations.

Investigations of wrongdoing and constant program evaluation are also part of most federal agencies' day-to-day activities. Given the controversial issues that the EPA must confront, these activities are intrinsic to its day-to-day operations.

OFFICE OF POLLUTION PREVENTION AND TOXICS

The Office of Pollution Prevention and Toxics (OPPT) was formed in 1977 with the primary responsibility for administering the Toxic Substances Control Act. This law covers the production and distribution of commercial and industrial chemicals in the United States. OPPT has the responsibility for assuring that chemicals available for sale and use in the United States do not pose any adverse risks to human health or to the environment. Its responsibility was expanded with the passing of the Pollution Prevention Act of 1990. This act established pollution prevention as the national policy for controlling industrial pollution at its source. In addition, OPPT manages the right-to-know initiatives, the Design for the Environment, "green" chemistry programs, and the lead, asbestos, and polychlorinated biphenyls programs. Its missions are the following:

- Promoting pollution prevention as the guiding principle for controlling industrial pollution;
- Promoting safer chemicals through a combination of regulatory and voluntary efforts;
- Promoting risk reduction so as to minimize exposure to substances such as lead, asbestos, dioxin, and polychlorinated biphenyls;
- Promoting public understanding of risks by providing understandable, accessible, and complete information on chemical risks to the broadest audience possible.

The OPPT is part of the organizational structure of the EPA insofar as protecting the public and environmental health from hazardous chemicals is part of the EPA's mission. Chemical compounds can represent the cutting edge of technology, but they also challenge environmental policy makers and regulators. What, exactly, does "toxic" mean? Placing that label on a particular chemical can affect its entire market structure. However, failure to do so can expose vulnerable populations to increased environmental risks. Other challenges include protection of chemical compositions that are patented. An industry may have invested in research and development for a new chemical and patented it, and wishes to protect it against patent infringements. Another major challenge is the chemical interactions that result from the accumulated effects of chemical emissions. Emissions are broadly classified as a by-product of manufacturing processes. These emissions and discharges can mix with waste from communities. These chemicals can move through air, water, and land ecologically over time. Some of these chemicals are dangerous for humans and persist throughout ecosystems; there is no way of telling how these chemicals will interact with each other. Do they synergize, catalyze, antagonize, or do nothing? What effects do these chemicals have on bioaccumulation? Since the EPA uses the additive principle of risk—that is, they add the risks of different chemicals in a compound to ascertain overall risk—it may be under- or overrepresenting risks. This becomes a problem when seeking a baseline of accumulated risks, especially those which bioaccumulate. Meeting these challenges is part of the day-to-day activities of the OPPT. (See discussion of cumulative risk assessment in Chapter 6.)

OFFICE OF RESEARCH AND DEVELOPMENT

The EPA relies on sound science to safeguard both human health and the environment. The Office of Research and Development (ORD) is the scientific research arm of the EPA. ORD's leading-edge research helps provide the solid underpinning of science and technology for the EPA. ORD conducts research on ways to prevent pollution, protect human health, and reduce risk. The work at its laboratories, research centers, and offices across the country helps improve the quality of air, water, soil, and the way we use resources. Applied science at ORD builds understanding of how to protect and enhance the relationship between humans and the ecosystems of Earth.

ORD has initiated a multiyear effort to plan the direction of its research program in selected areas over five or more years. This approach promotes its focus on the highest-priority issues and provides coordination for achieving long-term research goals. To understand ORD's research program, it helps to be familiar with the "risk paradigm," an important EPA organizing principle. The risk paradigm consists of two interrelated phases: risk assessment and risk management.

Risk assessment is the process used to evaluate the degree and probability of harm to human health and the environment from such stressors as pollution and habitat loss. The risk assessment process, as proposed by the National Academy of Sciences in 1983, consists of

- Exposure assessment—describing the populations or ecosystems exposed to stressors and the magnitude, duration, and spatial extent of exposure;
- Hazard identification—identifying adverse effects (e.g., short-term illness, cancer) that may occur from exposure to environmental stressors;
- Dose-response assessment—determining the toxicity or potency of stressors;
- Risk characterization—using the data collected in the first three steps to estimate and describe the effects of human or ecological exposure to stressors.

Risk management entails determining whether and how risks should be managed or reduced. It is based on the results of the risk assessment as well as other factors (e.g., public health, social, and economic factors). Risk management options include pollution prevention or control technologies to reduce or eliminate the pollutant or other stressor on the environment. The environmental or public health impacts resulting from risk management decisions must be monitored so that any necessary adjustments can be made.

Risk assessment and management have become part of the culture and tradition at the EPA, and thus have permeated its day-to-day operations. (See discussion of risk reports in Chapter 4.)

OFFICE OF WATER

The Office of Water (OW) is responsible for implementing the Clean Water Act and Safe Drinking Water Act, and portions of the Coastal Zone Act Reauthorization Amendments of 1990; the Resource Conservation and Recovery Act; the Ocean Dumping Ban Act; the Marine Protection, Research and Sanctuaries Act; the Shore Protection Act; the Marine Plastics Pollution Research and Control Act; the London Dumping Convention; the International Convention for the Prevention of Pollution from Ships; and several other statutes. Its activities are targeted to prevent pollution wherever possible and to reduce risk to people and ecosystems in the most cost-effective ways possible.

OW staff relies on the ten EPA regions, other federal agencies, state and local governments, Indian tribes, the regulated community, organized professional and interest groups, landowners and land managers, and the public at large. OW often provides guidance; specifies scientific methods and data collection requirements; performs oversight; and facilitates communication among those involved. As soon as OW and regional staff have helped the states and Indian tribes to build the capacity, many water programs are delegated to them to implement.

Since the EPA was established in 1970, it has made great progress in improving surface water quality and ensuring safe drinking water. Under the provisions of the Clean Water Act, the nation has invested over $75 billion to construct municipal sewage treatment facilities, nearly doubling the number of people served with secondary treatment to almost 150 million. Through federal and state actions issuing permits, the EPA has controlled over 48,000 individual industrial facilities and thousands more through general permits. By establishing nationwide discharge standards for over fifty industrial categories, industrial loadings have been reduced by as much as 90 percent. Industrial waste and sewage sludge—at their peaks 5.9 million tons and 8.7 million tons, respectively—are no longer dumped into coastal waters. Since 1986 the EPA has more than tripled the number of contaminants governed by drinking water standards, bringing the total to ninety-four. Through the Safe Drinking Water Act and parts of other laws, the EPA is regulating many high-risk sources of groundwater contamination, including pesticides, underground storage tanks, underground injection wells, and landfills, thereby helping to ensure the safety of drinking water supplies.

Significant risks to our waters remain. They include difficult and controversial regulatory problems such as pollutant runoff from agricultural lands and storm water flows from cities, seepage into groundwater from nonpoint sources, and the loss of habitats such as wetlands. Microbial contamination of drinking water still presents problems in many communities.

The OW will continue to increase the capacity of states, local governments, and tribes to manage water programs, and to provide nationwide baseline controls and standards as well as science leadership. The OW is committed to developing science, methods, models, and other tools to better identify, assess, and quantify risks caused by exposure, chemical and biological dangers, fate, and transport of contaminants.

Several organizations make up the OW: the Office of Wetlands, Oceans, and Watersheds; the Office of Science and Technology; the Office of Wastewater Management; and the Office of Groundwater and Drinking Water. Policy, communications, and budget staffs support the overall operation of the OW. In addition, water divisions in all ten regional offices work with stakeholders to implement all programs.

Water quality was one of the fundamental environmental issues the EPA was designed to handle. The standards for water quality are still in the development stage. However, as our population increases, so does our need for water. As standards for water quality become developed, the EPA will promulgate the necessary rules and regulations to enforce them. Water issues will continue to dominate the organization of the EPA and its day-to-day activities. Like air, water is a foundational aspect of the EPA as well as part of every future challenge to it, such as sustainability. (See discussion in Chapter 6.)

EPA REGIONS AND RELATIONSHIPS WITH STATES

The EPA and the states share responsibility for environmental protection. In 1995, state and EPA leaders recognized that they needed to work together more effectively—as partners—to solve the nation's environmental challenges. They agreed to put in place a new approach to EPA–state partnerships, the National Environmental Performance Partnership System. The goal is to build an environmental management system that is focused on achieving the best results possible, taking full advantage of the unique strengths of each partner.

The system of intergovernmental relations between federal agencies, their federal regions, state agencies, their state regions, localities and their municipalities, and communities and their neighborhoods is very important in implementing environmental law and policy. Generally, the revenue allocated to EPA headquarters is distributed to its regions, and sometimes directly to states and localities. From the EPA regions the revenue is allocated to state environmental agencies, and sometimes to localities and communities, within the region. This can be a substantial part of a state agency's budget.

One gaping hole in environmental intergovernmental relations is between local control of land use and any other state or federal agency. Municipalities control land use through the power delegated to them by the state. They do not usually need to inform the state environmental agency or the EPA of land-use actions such as permits or variances. Likewise, the state environmental agency and the EPA generally do not have to inform municipalities of any environmental permits they are granting, modifying, or extending. Since all implemented environmental policy is local, affecting the land, air, and water, the lack of communication regarding environmental management between municipalities and state environmental agencies and the EPA will continue to challenge growth of environmental policy in ecosystem approaches, sustainability, and environmental justice.

Through performance partnerships, the EPA and states are working to

- Promote joint planning and priority-setting based on information about environmental conditions and program needs;
- Give states greater flexibility to direct resources to the most pressing environmental problems;
- Foster use of innovative strategies for solving water, air, and waste problems;
- Use a balanced mix of environmental indicators and traditional activity measures for managing programs;
- Improve public understanding of environmental conditions and protection efforts.

To implement performance partnerships, many states develop performance partnership agreements (PPAs) with the EPA regions. In this process the EPA and state officials sit down together to discuss environmental conditions and program needs, agree on goals and priorities, devise strategies for addressing priority needs, decide what the roles and responsibilities of each partner will be, and decide how they will measure progress.

These agreements set out priorities and how the partners will work together to solve environmental problems. The process of developing these written agreements will help assure that the EPA and the state have a mutual understanding of priorities and of their respective roles and responsibilities. The performance partnership framework outlines suggested topics to be considered in developing the agreement. The ideal PPA explains the following:

- The goals and objectives for environmental protection in the state;
- Strategies that will be employed in meeting them;

- Roles and responsibilities of the state and EPA in carrying out the strategies;
- The measures that will be used to assess progress.

Priorities should be based on an assessment of national and local environmental conditions as well as of the performance of the individual state's protection programs. The framework calls on states to assess their environmental conditions as well as the performance of their protection programs. The EPA brings its own perspective about the state to the table as well as information that explains and supports national and regional priorities. This information is the starting point for negotiating priorities and other elements of the PPA. The scope and coverage of a PPA can be very broad—covering all the programs in which the EPA and the state have parallel responsibilities as well as environmental programs where only the state has jurisdiction. The PPA may cover just the programs the state wants to have funded through a performance partnership grant, or it can be a comprehensive statement of the state's work with the EPA.

The long-range goal is to provide strong public health and environmental protection by developing a system in which the states and the EPA work together to achieve continuous gains in environmental quality and productivity. This system builds on each party's comparative strengths and compensates for each party's relative weaknesses. The states should serve as the primary frontline delivery agents: managing their own programs, adapting to local conditions, and testing new approaches for delivering more environmental protection for less money. Among its other responsibilities, such as ensuring good science and strong national health and environmental standards, the federal government should provide analysis of environmental and compliance trends, provide expertise to and facilitate learning among the states, work in a collaborative and more flexible partnership with states, address interstate issues, and serve as a backstop, ensuring that all states provide fundamental public health and environmental protection. At times, however, direct federal involvement is necessary. Environmental problems do not respect political boundaries, and some important issues require a regional/national/international perspective. Even exemplary state programs cannot be expected to solve these problems independently. In such cases the federal government needs to exercise its authority or offer appropriate facilitation. This system does not change federal authority, but serves as a guide to the judicious and more effective exercise of that authority.

This system has seven principal components:

1. Increased use of environmental goals and indicators;
2. New approach to program assessments by states;
3. Environmental performance agreements;

4. Differential oversight;

5. Performance leadership programs;

6. Public outreach and involvement;

7. Joint system evaluation.

These indicators are used by the states and the EPA to assess long-term program effectiveness and to select near- and long-term program activities. These indicators are collected regularly for all states and made available not only to the EPA but also to other states and to the public. Many of the indicators and measures initially used will be changed over time as the states and the EPA learn their value through experience. The states work with the EPA in an equal partnership in selecting, testing, developing, and adopting the indicators and measures. It is also recognized that greater emphasis on a strong data quality assurance program is essential to the success of this new approach.

The performance partnership system places greater reliance on an annual environmental and programmatic self-assessment by the state. The state provides information identifying the following:

- What the state sees as its key environmental problems, opportunities, and priorities;
- The recent performance of the state's programs, based on available measures of program success;
- An analysis of current program weaknesses, from the state's perspective;
- An assessment of basic fiscal accountability, along with an identification of any areas needing capacity building;
- The state's proposed action plan for maintaining and improving its environmental program performance, identifying specific actions and approaches it plans to take in the coming year, and suggestions for the EPA to assist the state in improving performance or achieving stated goals;
- A report on how well the state has carried out the plan agreed to in its environmental performance agreement.

Increased reliance on environmental indicators is essential for ensuring a sustained focus on environmental outcomes. Activity measures such as the number of inspections conducted may provide valuable insight into program effectiveness, and therefore be worth collecting. A basic goal of these agreements is to shift the primary focus of the EPA and state dialogue from "bean-counting" to identification of environmental priorities for each state and the appropriate actions to address those priorities. Under the traditional system, too much attention has been directed to the number of permit reviews, inspections, and enforcement actions taken by a state, rather than to the outcomes and value of those actions and to alternative actions that might be pursued to achieve the same objective.

This system offers unprecedented opportunity for constructive public involvement in the management of environmental programs and improved understanding of national environmental performance. Informal discussion is held with stakeholders (associations, environmental groups, and the regulated community). In implementing the PPAs, three distinct aspects of the process can benefit from sharing information with the public:

1. Environmental conditions, problem identification, and setting of goals and priorities;

2. Consideration of alternative approaches for addressing the problems;

3. Evaluation of the effectiveness of the new approach to joint EPA/state environmental management.

Reporting this information to the public will help inform local citizens about their environmental conditions and challenges.

Overall, it is the relationship that the EPA has with its stakeholders and constituents that determines the degree to which many environmental policies are implemented. States are traditional and necessary stakeholders in the process, fed by a strong revenue stream from EPA regional offices (depending on the specific program and EPA regional priorities). Often this revenue is to aid permit issuance and enforcement in air, water, waste, or other programs where the EPA has delegated this authority to the state.

PERMIT ISSUANCE AND ENFORCEMENT

One of the duties of the EPA is issuance, renewal, modification, and enforcement of the terms of the permit. The EPA's policy stance is to seek industry's compliance with the law. Many state agencies, as well as the EPA, employ a number of resources to aid regulated industries in their permit actions. However, when the EPA cannot get compliance with the law, it turns to the Department of Justice for assistance in the prosecution of environmental crimes. Operating air permits are legally enforceable documents that permitting authorities issue to air pollution sources after the source has begun to operate. Most Title V permits are issued by state and local authorities. These permits are often called Part 70 permits because the regulations that establish minimum standards for state permit programs are found in the Code of Federal Regulations (40 CFR 70). However, the EPA issues Title V permits, called Part 71 permits, to sources in Indian country and in other situations as needed.

The purpose of Title V permits is to reduce violations of air pollution laws and improve enforcement of those laws. Title V permits do this by recording in one document all of the air pollution control requirements that apply to the source. This gives members of the public, regulators, and the source a clear picture of what the facility is required to do to keep its air pollution under the legal limits. Title V permits also require the source to make regular reports on how it is tracking its pollution emissions and the controls it is using to limit its emissions. These reports are public information. They also require addition of monitoring, testing, or record-keeping requirements where needed to assure that the source complies with its emission limits or other pollution control requirements. The EPA also requires the source to certify each year whether or not it has met the air pollution requirements in its Title V permit. These certifications are public information. Many states were issuing operating permits before Title V was enacted. Some states continue to issue these permits, which are generally less comprehensive than Part 70 permits.

The EPA has maintained a strong federal enforcement program directed at violations of state implementation plan requirements, new source performance standards, and national emission standards for hazardous air pollutants. The EPA also has increased its emphasis on enforcement of prevention of significant deterioration and nonattainment new source review requirements.

The new Clean Water Act amendments gave the EPA the authority to administratively assess penalties against violations of water pollution requirements. In some circumstances an administrative order with penalties may be a more appropriate enforcement tool than a civil referral.

The Hazardous and Solid Waste Amendments of 1984 required, among other things, that land disposal facilities for which owners and operators did not (1) certify compliance with groundwater monitoring and financial responsibility requirements and (2) submit a final (Part B) permit application, would lose interim status on November 8, 1985. This loss of interim status (LOIS) provision requires that all noncomplying land disposal facilities be closed. The EPA's response to the LOIS violations that are potentially the most harmful to the environment—the continued operation of facilities lacking adequate groundwater monitoring, insurance, or closure resources— has been comprehensive. Enforcement actions have been taken to address 97 percent of these violations, and the prosecution of these actions has remained a high priority for the EPA. With the support of the increased funding and strong enforcement and settlement provisions in the statute, the EPA increased the number of injunctive actions under Section 106 and the number of cost recovery cases under Section 107.

Permit issuance and enforcement are two important daily activities that span more than one office within EPA. Permit issuance puts the EPA directly in the regulatory role. The EPA and many state environmental agencies employ compliance assistance specialists to assist the regulated industry with compliance and permit requirements. With the advent of environmental justice and growth of the right to know and toxics release inventory, the regulatory role of permit issuance has expanded to include broader public involvement via the EPA's permitting authority. Enforcement of environmental laws puts the EPA in court, often as the complaining party. The level of enforcement of a particular environmental law strongly influences the day-to-day activities at the EPA in terms of permits and other regulatory activities. Permit issuance and enforcement will continue to be the operating vehicles for the EPA's strongest environmental policies.

ENVIRONMENTAL IMPACT STATEMENTS

The National Environmental Policy Act (NEPA) requires federal agencies to integrate environmental values into their decision-making processes by considering the environmental impacts of their proposed actions and reasonable alternatives to those actions. To meet this requirement, federal agencies prepare a detailed statement known as an environmental impact statement (EIS). In terms of the EPA's internal operations, the focus is on three main areas regarding NEPA compliance:

1. Coordinating the EPA's review of all EISs prepared by other federal agencies;

2. Maintaining a national EIS filing system and publishing weekly notices of EISs available for review and summaries of EPA's comments;

3. Assuring that the EPA's own actions comply with NEPA and other environmental requirements.

Many federal agencies have their own NEPA requirements. Although the EPA does have an overarching role, it is often more important to comply with the particular NEPA requirements of the EPA. (See discussion of NEPA in Chapter 4.)

Since NEPA is often considered part of the formation of the EPA and its requirements are so often litigated, it is part of the day-to-day operations of the EPA.

POLICY DEVELOPMENT

The Office of Policy, Economics, and Innovation (OPEI) supports the EPA's mission by promoting innovation that achieves greater and more cost-effective public health and environmental protection. In consultation with its internal and external stakeholders and partners, OPEI supports and oversees the testing of new and innovative approaches to environmental protection and related policy changes. It is the focal point for regulatory analyses, policy development, and economic analyses necessary to support the EPA's regulatory development process and changes in business conditions. OPEI's role in the regulatory development process is to manage the process and ensure that the underlying policy analyses are sound. OPEI helps strengthen the analytic foundation of the EPA's decision-making processes and works with the EPA's science adviser to further the integration of scientific and economic analyses.

Many offices within the EPA have their own policy components. However, to begin to implement any policy, the EPA often tests it. This can take the form of research and development, a demonstration grant, or a contract. It often involves testing the proposed environmental policy in operation, which requires collaboration among several regulatory agencies at the federal, state, and local levels, as well as stakeholders external to the government, such as landowners. The OPEI functions to provide coordinated underlying support for innovation in environmental policy development. Given the relative newness of the EPA, and of environmental policy generally, the need for innovation is high. Add to that the growing U.S. population, increasing and complicated waste flow and decreasing waste sites, and an emerging societal consensus about sustainability—creating a very dynamic EPA environment becomes a strongly desired objective. Innovation is part of a rapidly developing policy that has characterized many of the policies of the EPA, especially the first ones. (See discussion in Chapter 8.) The OPEI helps the EPA develop sound environmental policy and is an important part of how the EPA will meet challenges in the future.

PUBLIC INVOLVEMENT

The EPA started with a stronger engagement of the idea of public notice, participation, and involvement than most federal agencies. Many environmental laws require some type of public notice and opportunity to be heard when rules and regulations are developed. Environmental impact statements require public involvement if there are significant impacts on the environment. The Federal Register publishes the notices of proposed rules and regulations being considered by the EPA and all other federal agencies. It also lists records of decision of environmental impact assessments. It is issued daily and is required reading for all national advocacy groups. All states have their own version, sometimes called the State Register.

Public involvement has been a constant focus of the EPA, both because it is a policy and a legal issue, and because of the controversial nature of the many environmental issues. Perhaps it is in the nature of environmental problem solving to involve those closest to the problem. Public involvement encompasses the full range of activities that the EPA uses to engage the public in the EPA's decision-making processes. It is a progression that starts with outreach to build awareness and interest. It evolves to information exchange, through collaboration and recommendation, to agreement and decision-making. Public involvement begins when individuals and organizations seek information from the EPA about a topic or issue or when the EPA identifies them as a potentially affected party. The EPA's outreach activities serve and engage these individuals and organizations. Information exchange is the next step. Here EPA staff and management, and members of the public share data, options, issues, and ideas. In the next step, individuals and groups may collaborate with each other and with the EPA to provide the EPA with recommendations for action. Some continue on to engage EPA management in reaching agreement by consensus.

Access to information is crucial throughout the progression. As individuals and groups move through its steps, they seek more detailed information, increased access to decision makers, and more influence on the ultimate decisions. The EPA's goal is to provide opportunities for people to engage at every point along the progression. Individuals and groups decide whether, when, and how to participate.

Four categories are defined in terms of the purpose of the interaction and the expectation of how the EPA and the stakeholders will use the information to help clarify the roles for all involved.

Outreach activities and products enable the EPA to raise public awareness and inform interested or affected individuals about what the EPA is doing or planning, and what the EPA's needs are. Outreach is the first step in basic communication. Examples of outreach include the following:

- Hotlines;
- Web sites;
- Newsletters;
- E-mail list servers;
- Distribution lists;
- Federal Register notices;
- Exhibits;
- Documents;
- Electronic bulletin boards;
- Fact sheets;
- Brochures;
- Briefings;
- Formal public meetings;
- News releases;
- Radio or television public service announcements;

- News conferences and press kits;
- EPA visitor centers and libraries;
- Informing through cooperating organizations;
- Open houses;
- Information meetings.

Information exchange activities build and share a broad knowledge base for all interested parties. Information exchange activities include

- Workshops and forums;
- Small, interactive public meetings;
- Roundtable discussions;
- Focus groups;
- Question-and-answer sessions;
- Availability/listening sessions;
- Surveys, polls, interviews, and door-to-door canvassing;
- Joint fact-finding;
- Internet-based dialogues;
- Interactive radio and television talk shows;
- Public hearings and meetings.

These information exchanges seek to enhance participants' understanding of the issues. The participants are not expected to reach agreement.

Recommendation activities are those in which participants, either individually or collectively, urge the EPA to pursue specific actions. Recommendations may be in the form of written comments or be made through collaboration, which involves a smaller number of individuals who work with each other and with EPA staff on a set of recommendations that reflect the majority or consensus. The EPA is not bound to implement recommendations, nor are the parties. (See discussion of FACAs in Chapter 4.) The outside parties are free to criticize or take legal actions.

Agreement activities involve affected parties or stakeholder representatives, including the EPA, negotiating a specific agreement that each is expected to abide by and implement. Examples of agreement activities include the following:

- Negotiated rulemaking committee efforts;
- Settlement agreements;
- Mediated agreements;

- Negotiated or consensus permits;
- Memoranda of understanding.

Many enforcement activities also result in agreements, such as consent orders and consent decrees. In some cases, parties other than those involved in the enforcement action may have an opportunity to provide input to these types of agreements. The Office of Policy, Economics, and Innovation coordinates the development of, and provides support for implementing, the EPA's public involvement policies.

Many environmental policies are locally implemented, and therefore require buy-in from communities. Trust needs to be established between institutional stakeholders such as the EPA, the state environmental agency, and the community. Trust is difficult to create and easy to destroy in these circumstances. It requires that the stakeholders have some credibility with each other. In a speech to the American Chemical Society, Administrator William D. Ruckelshaus said:

> If a decision regarding the use of a particular chemical is to have credibility with the public, and with media who may strongly influence the public judgment, then the decision must be made in the full glare of public limelight. . . . People want to know the risk involved in the use of a certain chemical, as well as the benefits. They want to know what these risks and benefits are before a decision is made as to the chemical's use.

Despite the emotion that sometimes accompanies public discussion of environmental issues, Ruckelshaus said his obligation is to make a public accounting of a decision and to explain why he has taken or refused to take certain action: "To fail to publicly support a wise decision may well be to concede defeat in the battle to convince the public of the credibility of the decision, and without such credibility, neither you nor I will long be entrusted with decisions that the public considers vital to their lives." Ultimately the mission of the EPA—to protect the land, air, water, and public health—needs the credible buy-in of the public in order to achieve its mission. This is particularly true if EPA is to meet its future challenges of community-based environmental planning, environmental justice, sustainability, and ecosystem approaches. (See the discussion of future challenges in Chapter 6.)

Emphasis is given in the regulations to the public hearings process, a chief tool of public participation, with particular attention focused on the following requirements:

- Sufficient advance notice mailed to interested persons or groups that supplies the agenda and other elements of the hearing;

- Location and time of the hearing, which must be set with accessibility in mind, and facilitate attendance and testimony by a cross section of interested and affected persons or organizations;

- Availability of material pertinent to the action to be discussed, in advance of the hearing;

- Availability of hearing records for public inspection for enough time to allow for submission of supplementary statements.

Definitions of the Stakeholder Involvement Terms

The term "the public" is used in EPA policy in the broadest sense, meaning the general population of the United States. Many segments of "the public" may have a particular interest or may be affected by EPA programs and decisions. In addition to private individuals, "the public" includes, but is not limited to, the following:

- Representatives of consumer, environmental, and other advocacy groups;

- Environmental justice groups;

- Indigenous peoples;

- Minority and ethnic groups;

- Business and industrial interests, including small businesses;

- Elected and appointed public officials;

- News media;

- Trade, industrial, agricultural, and labor organizations;

- Public health, scientific, and professional representatives and societies;

- Civic and community associations;

- Faith-based organizations;

- Research, university, education, and governmental organizations and associations.

"Affected parties" are stakeholders who are or may be impacted by EPA decisions.

"Consensus building" is a process in which people agree to work together to resolve common problems in a relatively informal, cooperative manner. It is a technique that can be used to bring together representatives from different stakeholder groups early in a decision-making process. A neutral third party helps the people design and implement their strategy for developing group solutions to problems.

"Convening" (also called conflict assessment) involves the use of a neutral third party to help assess the causes of the conflict, to identify the persons or entities that would be affected by the outcome of the conflict, and to help these parties consider the best way (for example, mediation, consensus building or a lawsuit) for them to deal with the conflict. The convener may also help the parties prepare for participation in a dispute resolution process by educating them on what the selected process will be like.

"Facilitation" is a process used to help a group of people or parties have constructive discussions about complex or potentially controversial issues. The facilitator helps the parties set ground rules for these discussions, promotes effective communication, elicits creative options, and keeps the group focused and on track. Facilitation can be used even where parties have not yet agreed to attempt to resolve a conflict.

"Fair treatment" means that no group of people, including a racial, ethnic, or a socioeconomic group, should bear a disproportionate share of the negative environmental consequences from industrial, municipal, and commercial operations or the execution of federal, state, local, and tribal programs and policies.

"Meaningful involvement" means that

- Potentially affected community residents have an appropriate opportunity to participate in decisions about a proposed activity that will affect their environment and/or health;
- The public's contribution can influence the EPA's decision;
- The concerns of all participants involved will be considered in the decision-making process;
- The decision makers seek out and facilitate the involvement of those potentially affected.

"Mediation" is a process in which a neutral third party (the mediator) helps disputants reach a mutually satisfying settlement of their differences. Mediation is voluntary, informal, and confidential. The mediator helps the disputants to communicate clearly, to listen carefully, and to consider creative ways to reach resolution. The mediator makes no judgments about the people or the conflict and issues no decision. Any agreement that is reached must satisfy all parties.

"Stakeholders" are individuals or representatives from organizations or interest groups that have a strong interest in the EPA's work and policies.

"Timely information" means distributing information far enough in advance that the interested public has time to review relevant material, decide whether to become involved, and make plans for that involvement. "Timely" applies to the availability of background information on particular issues as well as notice of public meetings, public comment periods, or other critical involvement activities.

As the EPA evolves to face new challenges and as more members of the public become engaged in environmental decisions, the role of public involvement at the EPA will continue to expand.

How the Public Can Learn About Waste and Chemicals

One activity that engages the EPA's organization and day-to-day activity is informing the public about the risk from waste or chemicals. Society is very concerned about the risks of getting and dying from cancer, and it places a high value on children. Despite lack of scientific consensus regarding cause and effect, these concerns and values exert a strong influence on the policy discourse around environmental considerations in waste and chemical regulation. Congress is one place where this influence has exerted itself.

Title III of the Superfund Amendments and Reauthorization Act of 1986 (SARA) authorized the Emergency Planning and Community Right-to-Know Act (EPCRA). EPCRA, also referred to as SARA Title III, created a program with two basic goals: (1) to increase public knowledge of and access to information on the presence of toxic chemicals in communities, releases of toxic chemicals into the environment, and waste management activities involving toxic chemicals; and (2) to encourage and support planning for responses to environmental emergencies.

To meet these goals, EPCRA created the toxics release inventory (TRI) and the hazardous chemical inventory. This information enables state and local governments and the community to identify what needs to be done at the local level to better deal with pollution and chemical emergencies.

The public has the right to information about the amounts, location, and potential effects of hazardous chemicals present in the community. Under the hazardous chemical reporting provision of EPCRA, facilities storing hazardous chemicals in amounts exceeding specified thresholds must report the chemical type and amount stored to local emergency planning committees (LEPCs) and state emergency response commissions (SERCs). The LEPC and SERC must make the hazardous chemical inventory and accidental release information submitted by local facilities available to the public. EPCRA also created the toxic release inventory (TRI) program. Under Section 313 of EPCRA, covered facilities are required to submit annual reports to the EPA and the state on the amounts of toxic chemicals they have released into the environment, either routinely or accidentally. The EPA compiles these reports into a database that provides governments and the public with information about releases of toxic chemicals into the air, water, and land. The EPA encourages citizens, government entities, and facilities to use these data to establish a chemical profile of their community and to initiate and direct pollution prevention activities and risk reduction analyses. Pollution prevention avoids the creation of waste, as opposed to pollution control, which concentrates on managing and disposing of waste.

EPCRA's emergency planning provisions are designed to help communities prepare for and respond to emergencies involving hazardous substances. These functions are carried out by each state SERC and by the LEPCs under each SERC's jurisdiction. On tribal lands, the equivalent of the SERC is the Tribal Emergency Response Commission. These organizations encourage prevention, preparedness, and quick response to chemical emergencies.

Emergency plans help facilities and local and state governments respond to accidents quickly and efficiently. Careful emergency planning can make the difference between disaster and slight inconvenience. Emergency plans outline the procedures a facility and the community should follow in responding to a chemical release. The planning process has a greater impact than the plan itself, encouraging awareness, communication, and coordination of efforts.

EPCRA's emergency planning provisions also require facilities to immediately notify SERCs and LEPCs of accidental chemical releases. This notification will activate emergency plans. EPCRA is implemented by two offices within the EPA. The Chemical Emergency Preparedness and Prevention Office (CEPPO) carries out the emergency planning, emergency response notification, and inventory reporting provisions of the law. The Office of Environmental Information (OEI) implements the TRI aspects. CEPPO is part of the Office of Solid Waste and Emergency Response. Its mission is to help local and state authorities assemble the necessary information for chemical emergency prevention, preparedness, and response activities.

The division of OEI primarily associated with the TRI is the TRI Program Division, within the Office of Information Analysis and Access. This division oversees the collection of facility release reports and management of the TRI database. It also administers right-to-know components of the program, and provides a toll-free hotline for the public at 1-800-424-9346. A third EPA office, the Office of Enforcement and Compliance Assurance, is responsible for the enforcement of EPCRA, producing compliance with U.S. environmental laws while promoting pollution prevention activities to the regulated community.

Section 313 of EPCRA established the TRI program, a national database that identifies facilities; chemicals manufactured, processed, and used at the identified facilities; and the annual amounts of these chemicals released (in routine operations, including spills, and in catastrophic accidents and other one-time events), and otherwise managed on- and off-site in waste. In 1990, Congress passed the Pollution Prevention Act. Among its requirements was a mandate to expand TRI to include additional information on toxic chemicals in waste and on source reduction methods. Beginning in 1991, covered facilities were required to report quantities of TRI chemicals treated on-site, recycled, and burned for energy recovery. This waste management data has strengthened TRI as a tool for providing information on facilities' handling of TRI chemicals in waste as well as for analyzing progress in reducing releases. The TRI program has been tremendously successful. Governments—federal, state, and local—have used it to set priorities, measure progress, and target areas of special and immediate concern.

The public has used the TRI data to understand the local environment, to participate in local and national debates about the choices being made that may affect their health and the health of their children, and, ultimately, to exert their influence on the outcome of these debates. The release estimates are an input to determine exposure or calculate potential risks to human health and the environment, but by themselves do not represent risk. Given the potential for using TRI data in these ways, it is important for the public to understand the limitations as well as the benefits of TRI data and factors that should be considered in drawing conclusions from it about risks to human health or the environment. The determination of potential risk depends on many factors, including toxicity, chemical fate after release, release location, and population concentrations.

Since TRI began in 1987, the program has grown. For the reporting year 2000, it was expanded to include certain new persistent bioaccumulative toxic (PBT) chemicals. In addition, reporting thresholds were lowered for both the newly added PBT chemicals and certain PBT chemicals already on the TRI list. The year 1998 marked the first reporting by seven additional industry sectors: metal mining, coal mining, electrical utilities that burn coal and/or oil, hazardous-waste treatment and disposal facilities, chemical wholesale distributors, petroleum bulk stations and terminals, and solvent recovery services. Since 1994, federal facilities have been added to TRI and the number of reportable chemicals has nearly doubled.

Many challenges in the right-to-know program remain to be met. TRI was designed to evolve, over time, to meet the changing needs of an informed and involved public. As new chemicals of concern are identified, they will be added. Sectors that appear to contribute to environmental loadings will be added. Data collection will be modified to meet new information needs, and access technologies will be developed to assure enhanced public access to the TRI data.

The 2001 TRI public data release report (EPA 260-R-03-001) provides a detailed view of the information collected through TRI. It summarizes data collected for calendar year 2001, along with changes since 1988. The 2001 public data release: state fact sheets (EPA 260-F-03-002) supplies TRI data in greater detail for each state and territory. The online TRI Explorer, a Web tool for searching TRI data, available at www.epa.gov/triexplorer, includes data collected for all years. The 2001 TRI public data release report contains three chapters plus an executive summary. Chapter 1 provides background information, as well as important factors and assumptions that need to be considered when using TRI data. Chapter 2 examines TRI data by industry sectors. It gives an overview of on- and off-site releases, management of TRI chemicals in waste, and transfers off-site for further waste management for 2001, 2000, and 1998 through 2001. Chapter 3 presents TRI data for 2000 and

2001 for PBT chemicals. Federal facility data are also examined in Chapters 2 and 3.

Each year, facilities that reach certain thresholds must report their releases and other waste management activities for listed toxic chemicals to EPA and to the state or tribal entity in whose jurisdiction the facility is located. The TRI list for 2001 included more than 600 chemicals and 30 chemical categories. Each facility submits a TRI reporting form for each TRI chemical it has manufactured, processed, or otherwise used during a year in amounts exceeding the thresholds. Reports for each calendar year are due by July 1 of the following year. After completion of data entry and data quality assurance activities, the EPA makes the data available to the public in printed reports, in a computer database, and through various other information products. States also make available to the public copies of the forms filed by facilities in their jurisdiction, and some states produce their own data release report. Facilities with Standard Industrial Classification (SIC) primary codes 20 through 39 have been required to report to TRI since 1987. Federal facilities have been required to report since 1994, regardless of their SIC code.

Facilities in the specified industries that have the equivalent of ten or more full-time employees and meet the established thresholds for manufacturing, processing, or "other use" of listed chemicals, must report their releases and other waste management quantities (including quantities transferred off-site for further waste management). For most chemicals, thresholds for manufacturing and processing are currently 25,000 pounds for each listed chemical, and the threshold for other use is 10,000 pounds per chemical. For PBT chemicals these thresholds have been lowered.

Each year, facilities report to TRI the amounts of toxic chemicals released on-site to air, water, and land and injected underground, and the amounts of chemicals transferred off-site for recycling, energy recovery, treatment, and disposal. They also report quantities of production-related waste recycled, burned for energy recovery, treated, released, or otherwise disposed of, both on- and off-site, and catastrophic or other one-time releases (Section 8 of Form R).

SIC codes are used throughout the federal government to classify economic activity by industry. On TRI Form R and on TRI Form A certification statements, facilities list the four-digit SIC codes that define their operations. A facility might report, for example, SIC code 2873, nitrogenous fertilizers, which at the two-digit level is in the chemicals and allied products major group, SIC code 28. Industrial facilities often conduct interrelated operations that result in products or services that are classified in different SIC codes.

Facilities provide specific identifying information, such as name, location, type of business, contact names, name of parent company, and environmental permit numbers. They also provide information about the manufacture, process, and other use of the listed chemical at the facility and the maximum amount of the chemical on-site during the year. Facilities report information about methods used to treat waste streams containing toxic chemicals at the site and the efficiencies of those treatment methods. In addition to information about the amount of toxic chemicals sent off-site for waste management, facilities must specify the destination of these transfers.

Beginning with the 1991 reports, facilities were required to provide information about source reduction and other pollution prevention activities, along with the quantities managed in waste by activities such as recycling. Companies must provide a production index that can help relate changes in reported quantities of toxic chemicals in waste managed to changes in production. Such additional data facilitate tracking of industry progress in reducing waste generation and moving toward safer waste management alternatives. Though current TRI data cannot provide an absolute measure of pollution prevention, they can offer insights into the complete toxics cycle.

TRI facilities may file their reports either electronically, using the TRI reporting software, or in hard copy. Each facility submits a Form R for each TRI chemical for which it meets the reporting requirements. Starting with the 1995 reporting year, facilities with lower levels of reportable amounts that do not manufacture, process, or otherwise use more than 1 million pounds of the chemical can certify that they are not required to report on the Form A certification statement. Information reported by facilities includes

- Basic information identifying the facility;
- Name and telephone number of a contact person;
- Environmental permits held;
- Amount of each listed chemical released to the environment at the facility;
- Amount of each chemical sent from the facility to other locations for recycling, energy recovery, treatment, or disposal;
- Amount of each chemical recycled, burned for energy recovery, or treated at the facility;
- Maximum amount of chemical present on-site at the facility during the year;
- Types of activities conducted at the facility involving the toxic chemical;
- Source reduction activities.

Form R is the TRI reporting form that must be submitted annually by the owner or operator of a covered facility. Reports are submitted on or before July 1 and cover activities at the facility during the previous calendar year. The EPA provides instructions and technical guidance on how to calculate toxic chemical releases from facilities.

While expanding chemical and industry coverage, the EPA has also provided a burden-reducing option for facilities with relatively low quantities of listed toxic chemicals in waste. Beginning in 1995, when the expanded chemical list went into effect, facilities whose total annual reportable amount of a listed toxic chemical does not exceed 500 pounds can apply a higher activity threshold in determining their reporting obligations. The total annual reportable amount is defined as the sum of the waste management categories that would be reported to TRI: quantities released (including disposal); recovered as a result of on-site recycling operations, combusted on-site for energy recovery, and treated at the facility; and amounts transferred off-site for recycling, energy recovery, treatment, and disposal. These amounts add up to total production-related waste. If the facility does not exceed a total production-related amount of 500 pounds, it is eligible for a "manufacture, process, or other use" threshold of 1 million pounds of the listed chemical. If it does not exceed either the reported amount or 1-million-pound threshold, the facility does not have to file a Form R and instead can submit a certification statement (Form A), which certifies that the facility has met the conditions outlined above and is not required to report the TRI data for that chemical.

The TRI program has given the public unprecedented direct access to toxic chemical release and other waste management data at the local, state, regional, and national levels. Use of this information can enable the public to identify potential concerns, gain a better understanding of potential risks, and work with industry and government to reduce toxic chemical releases and the risks associated with them. When combined with hazard and exposure data, this information can allow informed setting of environmental priorities at the local level.

Federal, state, and local governments can use the data to compare facilities or geographic areas, to identify hot spots, to evaluate existing environmental programs, to set regulatory priorities more effectively, and to track pollution control and waste reduction progress. TRI data, in conjunction with demographic data, can help government agencies and the public identify potential environmental justice concerns. Industry can use the data to obtain an overview of the release and other waste management of toxic chemicals, to identify and reduce costs associated with toxic chemicals in waste, to identify promising areas of pollution prevention, to establish reduction targets, and to measure and document progress toward reduction goals. Public availability of the data has prompted many facilities to work with communities to develop effective strategies for reducing environmental and human health risks posed by releases and other waste management of toxic chemicals. Completion of three major efforts in the EPA's strategy to enhance TRI's effectiveness has significantly increased the usefulness of TRI data. These actions are the TRI chemical expansion for the 1995 reporting year, facility expansion to include new industries for the 1998 reporting year, and expanded coverage of PBT chemicals through lower reporting thresholds and addition of PBT chemicals to the TRI chemical list beginning with the 2000 reporting year. The EPA's expansion strategy has given TRI users a substantially greater range and depth of valuable information. The EPA's action on chemical expansion nearly doubled the number of chemicals that TRI addresses.

As a result of the addition of seven industries, nearly 2,000 additional facilities have submitted reports. Beginning with the data for reporting year 2000, communities have additional information on releases and other waste management of PBT chemicals that may pose threats to human health and the environment.

TRI reports reflect releases and other waste management of chemicals, not exposures of the public to those chemicals. Release estimates alone are not sufficient to determine exposure or to calculate potential adverse effects on human health and the environment. Nevertheless, TRI data can be used to identify areas of potential concern and, in conjunction with other information, can be a starting point in evaluating exposures that may result from releases and other waste management activities for toxic chemicals. The determination of potential risk depends upon many factors, including the toxicity of the chemical, the fate of the chemical after it is released, the locality of the release, and the human and other populations that are exposed to the chemical after its release. While TRI provides the public, industry, and state and local governments with an invaluable source of key environmental data, it has some limitations that must be considered.

Even with the expanded industry coverage, TRI does not address all sources of releases and other waste management for TRI chemicals, although the EPA has increased the number of industries that must report and has added PBT chemicals to the Section 313 list of toxic chemicals. In addition, facilities that do not meet the TRI threshold levels (those with fewer than ten full-time employees or those not meeting TRI quantity thresholds) are not required to report. The new PBT chemicals reporting thresholds expand the information TRI will collect, but only for a subset of the TRI chemicals. Thus, while the TRI includes 95,513 reports from 24,896 facilities for 2001, the 6.16 billion pounds of on- and off-site releases reported represent only a portion of all toxic chemical releases nationwide. The TRI does not include data on toxic emissions from cars and trucks, or from the majority of sources of releases of pesticides, volatile organic compounds, fertilizers, and many other nonindustrial sources.

Though many facilities base their TRI information on monitoring data, others report estimates to TRI because the program does not mandate additional release monitoring. Various estimation techniques are used when monitoring data are not available, and the EPA has published guidance for the regulated community. Variations between facilities can result from the use of different estimation methodologies. These factors should be taken into account when considering data accuracy and comparability. TRI data reflect chemical releases and other waste management activities that occur in a given calendar year. It must be recognized that patterns of releases and other waste management activities can change dramatically from one year to the next.

In 1987, when Congress passed EPCRA, more than 300 chemicals and chemical categories were included in the TRI chemical list and manufacturers in SIC codes 20–39 were required to report under EPCRA Section 313. Further, data coverage was initially confined to information on releases and certain transfers off-site for further waste management. Passage of the Pollution Prevention Act in 1990 expanded the TRI to include information on toxic chemicals in waste and on source reduction methods. Beginning in 1991, covered facilities were required to report quantities of TRI chemicals recycled, burned for energy recovery, and treated on- and off-site. Over time, the EPA has expanded the TRI to cover other industrial sectors and chemicals. To that end it has pursued a strategy that has enlarged TRI in several ways.

The original TRI chemical list combined two existing lists: New Jersey's environmental hazardous substance list and Maryland's chemical inventory report list. Over time, through the EPA's petition process, the original list has been modified in response to requests to add and delete chemicals, given the law's toxicity listing criteria, which focus on both acute and chronic health effects as well as environmental effects, as outlined in section 313(d) of EPCRA. The first expansion occurred in 1993 with the addition of certain chemicals that appear on the Resource Conservation and Recovery Act list of hazardous wastes and certain hydrochlorofluorocarbons (HCFCs) to EPCRA Section 313. The second expansion was the addition on November 30, 1994, of 286 chemicals and chemical categories. The additional chemicals can be characterized as high or moderately high in toxicity, and they are currently manufactured, processed, or otherwise used in the United States. Many are produced in high volume. This list expansion raised the number of chemicals and chemical categories reported to TRI to more than 600. Specifically, the rule added more than 150 pesticides, certain Clean Air Act chemicals, certain Clean Water Act priority pollutants, and certain Safe Drinking Water Act chemicals. Many of the chemicals are carcinogens, reproductive toxicants, or developmental toxicants. Of particular note is the addition of industrial chemicals such as di-isocyanates, N-hexane, N-methyl-2-pyrrolidone, and polycyclic aromatic compounds that result from the combustion of fuels.

Since the enactment of EPCRA, the TRI program has focused on the releases and other waste management activities of the manufacturing sector—facilities primarily in SIC codes 20–39. To provide the public with a more complete picture of the toxics in their community, the EPA undertook a detailed examination of nonmanufacturing industries to determine which may be significant generators of toxic chemical releases and other wastes. This effort focused particular attention on sectors linked to manufacturing—those providing energy, further managing products, or further managing waste from the manufacturing sector. Factors used to evaluate industries for this expansion included available data on toxic chemical releases and other waste management activities, the relationship of nonmanufacturing operations to manufacturing operations, the degree to which reporting would be expected to occur, and the potential burden that TRI reporting might impose on these facilities. On May 1, 1997, the EPA published a final rule adding seven industry sectors to TRI: metal mining, coal mining, electrical utilities that burn coal and/or oil, hazardous-waste treatment and disposal facilities, chemical wholesale distributors, petroleum bulk stations and terminals, and solvent recovery services. Of the 286 chemicals, 20 were di-isocyanates and nineteen were polycyclic aromatic compounds. These are reported not as individual chemicals but as two chemical compound categories. Not individually counting the members of these two categories reduces 286 to 247. Furthermore, three other chemicals have been remanded and one chemical was not reportable because of an administrative stay. Thus, the number of chemicals added to TRI, beginning with the 1995 reporting year, was 244. The EPA has also conducted an aggressive outreach campaign, including guidance, training, and technical assistance, to assist these industries in understanding their reporting obligations. Final guidance documents for these industries are available from the EPA's Web site at www.epa.gov/tri.

Beginning with the reporting year 2000, lower reporting thresholds apply to TRI facilities that manufacture, process, or otherwise use certain PBT chemicals. Also, additional PBT chemicals that TRI had not previously covered were added to the Section 313 toxic chemical list. Two types of PBT chemicals are substances such as mercury, lead, and polychlorinated biphenyls (PCBs), already on the TRI list, and dioxin and similar compounds, which were among the chemicals added for the 2000 reporting year. PBT chemicals are of particular concern not only because they are toxic but also because they remain in the environment for long periods of time and are not readily destroyed (i.e., they are persistent), and accumulate in body tissue (i.e., they bioaccumulate). Relatively small releases of PBT chemicals can pose human and environmental health threats. Consequently, these chemicals warrant recognition by communities as potential health threats, and information about their releases and other waste management activities need to be captured by the TRI.

In the October 1999 PBT chemical rulemaking, the EPA created three separate thresholds for PBT chemicals: 10 pounds for certain highly persistent, highly bioaccumulative toxic chemicals; 100 pounds for other PBT chemicals; and a special threshold of 0.1 gram for dioxin and similar chemicals. The threshold for a PBT chemical is the same for manufacturing, processing, and other uses. Under the existing thresholds of 25,000 pounds for manufacture or processing of a listed chemical and 10,000 pounds for otherwise using a listed chemical, important information on the releases and other waste management activities of the PBT chemicals were not reported.

In addition to the chemical category of dioxin and similar compounds (a total of seventeen substances), six other PBT chemicals were added to TRI:

benzo(g,h,i)perylene, benzo(j,k)fluorine (fluoranthene, as part of the PACs category), 3-methylcholanthrene (as part of the PACs category), octachlorostyrene, pentachlorobenzene, and tetrabromobisphenol A. New reporting thresholds apply to the following PBT chemicals already on the TRI list: aldrin, chlordane, heptachlor, hexachlorobenzene, isodrin, methoxychlor, pendimethalin, polycyclic aromatic compounds, polychlorinated biphenyls, toxaphene, trifluralin, lead and lead compounds, mercury and mercury compounds.

Users of TRI information should be aware that it reflects releases and other waste management activities of chemicals, not whether (or to what degree) the public has been exposed to those chemicals. TRI data, in conjunction with other information, can be used as a starting point in evaluating exposures that may result from releases and other waste management activities that involve toxic chemicals. The determination of potential risk depends upon many factors, including the toxicity of the chemical, the fate of the chemical, and the amount and duration of human or other exposure to the chemical after it is released. The lower reporting threshold and requirements for lead and lead compounds have been in effect since the 2001 reporting year, and apply to all lead and lead compounds except for lead in stainless steel, brass, or bronze alloys.

The TRI list consists of chemicals that vary widely in their toxic effects. Some high-volume releases of less toxic chemicals may appear to be more serious problems than lower-volume releases of more toxic chemicals, when just the opposite may be true. For example, phosgene is toxic in smaller quantities than methanol. A comparison of these two chemicals when setting hazard priorities or estimating potential health concerns that is based solely on volumes released may be misleading.

Degradation or persistence of the chemical in the environment is another variable factor. The longer the chemical remains unchanged in the environment, the greater the potential for exposure. Microorganisms readily degrade some chemicals, such as methanol, into less toxic chemicals; volatile organic compounds, such as ethylene and propylene, react in the atmosphere and contribute to the formation of smog; metals will not degrade upon release to the environment. Thus, smaller releases of a persistent, highly toxic chemical may create a more serious problem than larger releases of a chemical that is rapidly converted to a less toxic form.

Another important variable is bioconcentration of the chemical in the food chain. As a chemical becomes incorporated into the food chain, it may concentrate or disperse as it moves up the food chain. Some chemicals, such as mercury, accumulate as they move up the food chain. Small releases of a chemical that bioaccumulates may result in significant exposures. The environmental medium (air, water, land, or underground injection) into which the toxic chemical has been released affects the actual exposure of a population and the types of exposures possible, such as inhalation, dermal exposure, or ingestion. Releases of a chemical to the air can result in exposures for organisms nearby and downwind. Persistent toxicity of the chemical also varies, and the potential for exposure may be greater, the longer the chemical remains unchanged in the environment. Chemicals may fall from the air onto land or into bodies of water, resulting in exposures via these environmental media. Exposures that result from releases into water (streams, lakes, etc.) depend in part on the downstream uses of the water, including drinking, cooking, and bathing.

Releases to underground injection wells are regulated by the EPA's Underground Injection Control Program to provide safeguards so these wells do not endanger current and future underground sources of drinking water. When wells are properly sited, constructed, and operated, underground injection is an effective and environmentally safe method to dispose of wastes.

Land disposal units, such as Resource Conservation Act (RCRA) Subtitle C landfills and surface impoundments, must comply with stringent requirements for liners, leak detection systems, and groundwater monitoring. Land disposal restrictions provide that a hazardous waste cannot be placed on the land until the waste is treated (or meets specific treatment standards) to reduce the mobility or toxicity of the hazardous constituents in the waste. The amount of a toxic chemical that ultimately enters the environment depends on how the chemical is handled during treatment, energy recovery, or recycling activities. The efficiency of recycling operations depends on the method of recycling and the chemical being recycled. Use of a combustible toxic chemical for energy recovery typically results in the destruction of 95 percent to 99 percent or more of the chemical. The remainder may be either released to the air or disposed of as ash on land.

The efficiency of the treatment of toxic chemicals in waste sent to sewage treatment plants depends on the chemical and the sewage plant. Some high-volume pollutants, such as methanol, are readily degraded by most treatment plants. Other chemicals, such as methyl ethyl ketone, may be partially treated and partially released. Still other high-volume chemicals, such as ammonia, are not readily treated by most plants and will pass into the aquatic environment. In addition, metals sent to sewage treatment plants may be removed with solid wastes and sent to landfills, or they may pass through the plant and be discharged into surface waters without being destroyed.

The efficiency of other treatment methods, such as incineration, also depends upon the specifications of the treatment facility and the nature of the chemical. Toxic chemicals in waste sent off-site for disposal are typically released to land or injected underground. As with on-site waste management, the amount of the toxic chemical released to the environment depends on how the chemical is handled during treatment, energy recovery, or recycling. However, since the waste management is off-site, any amount of the chemical that enters the environment after waste management is reported to TRI as part of that facility's releases.

Data on off-site releases have included additional details about off-site transfers of metals and metal compounds since reporting year 1997. The EPA's methodology seeks to avoid duplication of amounts released off-site (transfers to land and underground injection disposal) through their also being reported as on-site releases by facilities that receive such transfers. This potential for duplication arises now that RCRA Subtitle C hazardous-waste treatment and disposal facilities report to TRI.

The Pollution Prevention Act (PPA) of 1990 requires facilities to report the quantities of TRI chemicals they manage in waste, both on-site and off-site. The PPA established as national policy that source reduction is the preferred approach to managing waste. Source reduction is defined as an activity that prevents the generation of waste. The PPA also established as national policy a hierarchy of waste management options for situations where source reduction cannot be implemented feasibly: recycling, energy recovery, treatment, and release (including disposal).

Although source reduction is the preferred method of reducing risk, environmentally sound recycling shares many of its advantages. Like source reduction, recycling reduces the need for treatment or disposal of waste and helps conserve energy and natural resources. Where source reduction and recycling are not feasible, toxic chemicals in waste can be treated. Release (including disposal) of a chemical is viewed as a last resort, to be employed only if the preferred methods of waste management cannot be implemented. The PPA did not specifically address the burning of waste for energy recovery as a waste management option. However, because energy recovery shares aspects of recycling and treatment, the EPA chose to list this activity separately in the waste management hierarchy.

The amount of TRI chemicals in waste reported includes both waste generated by the originating facility and waste received by the facility for further waste management. Facilities report these data as estimates for the reporting year (e.g., 2001) and the previous year (e.g., 2000) and as projections for the two following years (e.g., 2002 and 2003). The PPA requires this projection to encourage facilities to consider their future waste generation, opportunities for source reduction, and potential improvement in waste management.

A release is a discharge of a toxic chemical to the environment. On-site releases include emissions to the air, discharges to bodies of water, and releases at the facility to land, as well as releases into underground injection wells. Releases are reported to TRI by type of medium. On-site releases are reported in Section 5 of Form R. Releases to air are reported either as point source emissions or fugitive emissions. Point source emissions, also referred to as stack emissions, occur through confined air streams, such as stacks, vents, ducts, or pipes. Fugitive emissions are all releases to air that are not through a confined air stream. Fugitive emissions include equipment leaks, evaporative losses from surface impoundments and spills, and releases from building ventilation systems. Releases to water include discharges to streams, rivers, lakes, oceans, and other bodies of water from contained sources, such as industrial process outflow pipes or open trenches. Releases due to runoff, including storm water runoff, are also reportable to TRI. Underground injection is the placement of fluids in wells. TRI chemicals associated with manufacturing, the petroleum industry, mining, commercial and service industries, and federal and municipal government-related activities may be injected into Class I, II, III, IV, or V wells if they do not endanger underground sources of drinking water, public health, or the environment. The types of authorized injection are available at the EPA.

On-site releases to land occur within the boundaries of the reporting facility. Releases to land include the following:

- Disposal of toxic chemicals in landfills, in which wastes are buried;
- RCRA Subtitle C landfills, which are landfills that comply with stringent requirements for liners, leak detection systems, and groundwater monitoring, and other landfills;
- Land treatment/application farming, which are management techniques in which a waste containing a listed chemical is applied to or incorporated into the soil;
- Surface impoundments that are uncovered holding areas used to volatilize and/or settle waste materials;
- Other land disposal methods, which include waste piles, spills or leaks.

Beginning with the 1996 reporting year, facilities separately report amounts released to RCRA Subtitle C landfills and amounts released to other on-site landfills. This change was made to recognize the difference in management and regulatory oversight provided for RCRA Subtitle C landfills. In Section 6.2 of Form R, facilities report the amount sent to each off-site location to which the facility ships or transfers wastes containing the reported toxic chemical for recycling, energy recovery, treatment, or disposal.

An off-site release is a discharge of a toxic chemical to the environment that occurs as a result of a facility's transferring a waste containing a TRI chemical off-site for disposal, as reported in Section 6 of Form R. Certain other types of transfers are categorized as off-site releases because, except for location, the outcome of transferring the chemical off-site is the same as releasing it on-site. Toxic chemicals in waste may be transferred off-site to landfills or other types of land disposal areas, or to sites that inject the wastes underground. A toxic chemical for which there is no known disposal method is generally sent off-site for storage. An example is toxic chemicals in mixed hazardous and radioactive waste. The EPA considers such storage an off-site release because it is being used as a form of disposal and the toxic chemical will remain there indefinitely. The "unknown" category of disposal indicates that a facility does not know the type of waste management used for the toxic chemical that is sent off-site. Therefore, the EPA has categorized this method as the environmentally least desirable type of waste management and has included it as a type of disposal for reporting purposes. Transfers of metals and metal compounds to solidification/stabilization sites, to privately owned wastewater treatment plants, and to publicly owned treatment works (municipal sewage treatment) also are classified as off-site releases (transfers to disposal).

The individual waste management quantities are reported in a way designed to avoid double-counting. For example, an incinerator may destroy 99 percent of a chemical in the waste; in this case, the amount reported as treated on-site would be the amount destroyed by the incinerator, not the amount that entered the incinerator. The amount not destroyed in incineration (1 percent) would be reported as released. The sum of the individual quantities in a given year is the total quantity of TRI chemicals in waste resulting from routine production operations at a facility during that year. For the reporting year, facilities must also report the quantity of waste released (including disposal) as a result of activities other than routine production operations. This quantity is labeled "nonproduction-related waste managed." It includes waste released to the environment at the facility or transferred off-site because of catastrophic events or remedial (cleanup) actions at the facility. Nonproduction-related waste is considered less amenable to source reduction because facilities cannot reasonably anticipate the quantity. Because the EPA has not yet specifically issued regulations defining the reporting requirements for these data, some facilities may include in their reports amounts that other facilities do not believe they must include. Thus, higher quantities of TRI chemicals in waste for a particular state or industry may reflect not only differences in actual quantities but also different interpretations of the reporting requirements.

TRI facilities transfer chemicals in waste to other facilities for disposal. These recipient facilities can dispose of the wastes in on-site landfills, surface impoundments, land treatment facilities, or other types of land disposal methods. They may also dispose of wastes in underground injection wells, or, if metals and metal compounds are sent to a wastewater treatment facility, they may be discharged to surface waters. The receiving facilities generally are treatment, storage, and disposal (TSD) facilities regulated under the federal Resources Conservation and Recovery Act (RCRA). Such facilities are among the industries that must, beginning with the 1998 reporting year, report their releases, transfers, and other waste management activities to TRI. Thus, the facility that sends these transfers report the amounts to TRI as transfers to disposal (off-site releases), and the TSD facility reports the amounts as on-site releases to land, surface waters, or underground injection. Off-site transfers to these TSD facilities must be omitted from tables that compare or summarize on-site and off-site releases for all industries, including the industries added in 1998. Only the on-site releases from the TSD facilities are included in such analyses.

The RCRA ID number that facilities report is used to identify such transfers and match them to on-site releases reported by TSD facilities. A TRI facility must report its own RCRA ID number as well as the RCRA ID number of the TSD facility receiving the transfer. If the two RCRA ID numbers match, and the two facilities report on-site releases of the same chemical (or the same metal and its compounds) that are greater than or equal to the sum of the off-site transfers received, then the off-site transfer amount is omitted from the analysis. If the TRI facility receiving the waste reports on-site releases of the chemical less than the total reported as transferred to it, the amount omitted from the analysis is reduced proportionally.

For example, if Facility A reports 20,000 pounds transferred to Facility C and Facility B reports 80,000 pounds transferred to Facility C, but Facility C reports only 90,000 pounds released on-site (90 percent of the total amount of 100,000 pounds reported as transferred), then the amount of transfers omitted from the analysis for Facility A is 18,000 pounds (90 percent of 20,000 pounds) and for Facility B is 72,000 pounds (or 90 percent of 80,000 pounds). In tables that present off-site transfers but not on-site releases, these amounts are not omitted in order to present complete data on off-site transfers. Tables that present data on the amount of waste managed do not omit any reported data in order to present complete data on how waste is being managed.

Information about facilities' management of TRI chemicals in waste is reported in Section 8 of Form R. Recycled on-site waste is the quantity of the toxic chemical recovered at the facility and made available for further use. To avoid double-counting, the amount reported represents the amount exiting the recycling unit, not the quantity that entered. For example, 3,000 pounds of a listed chemical enters a recycling operation. Of this, 500 pounds are in residues from the recycling operation that are subsequently sent off-site for disposal. The quantity reported as recycled on-site would be 2,500 pounds. Recycled off-site waste is the quantity of the toxic chemical that leaves the facility for recycling, not the amount recovered at the off-site location. This quantity includes the amount(s) reported in Section 6 of Form R as transferred off-site for recycling, less any amount(s) associated with nonroutine events.

Waste used for energy recovery on-site is the quantity of the toxic chemical that is burned in some form of energy recovery device, such as furnaces (including kilns) or boilers. The toxic chemical should have a heating value high enough to sustain combustion. To avoid double-counting, the amount reported represents the amount destroyed in the combustion process, not the amount that entered the energy recovery unit. For example, 100,000 pounds of toluene enters a boiler that, on average, burns 98 percent of the toluene. Any remaining toluene is discharged to air. A total of 98,000 pounds is reported as burned for energy recovery (the remaining 2,000 pounds is reported as released). When waste is used for energy recovery off-site, the quantity of the toxic chemical that left the facility for energy recovery, not the amount burned at the off-site location, is reported. Requirements for the waste and for recovery equipment are the same as for on-site recovery.

When waste is treated off-site, the quantity reported is the amount of the toxic chemical that leaves the facility and is sent to privately owned treatment works (POTWs) or other off-site locations for treatment, not the amount that is destroyed at the off-site location(s). This quantity includes the amount(s) reported in Section 6 of Form R as transferred to POTWs or other off-site locations for treatment, less any amount(s) associated with nonroutine events and not including quantities of metals and metal compounds. Waste released on- and off-site is the total quantity of the toxic chemical released to the environment or disposed of at the facility (directly discharged to air, land, or water, or injected underground) or sent off-site for disposal. This quantity is the sum of the amounts reported in Sections 5 and 6 of Form R (releases plus transfers to disposal and transfers to POTWs of metals and metal compounds), less any amount(s) associated with nonroutine events.

The amount released to the environment due to one-time events (nonproduction-related waste) is the quantity released to the environment or sent off-site for recycling, energy recovery, treatment, or disposal due to one-time events not associated with routine production practices—catastrophic events, such as accidental releases, as well as remedial actions (cleanup). This quantity is separate from the quantities recycled, used for energy recovery, treated, and released, in order to distinguish between quantities that are routinely associated with production operations, and thus are more amenable to source reduction, and those which are not routinely associated with production processes, and thus are not so amenable to source reduction because they are not readily anticipated. This separation is important in assessing progress in source reduction at facilities.

Year-to-year comparisons must be based on a consistent set of reporting requirements to assure that any changes in releases or waste management data do not simply reflect expansion of TRI's chemical and industry coverage or other modifications in reporting requirements. Therefore, trend analyses are very difficult.

Through source reduction, risks to people and the environment can be lessened, financial and natural resources can be saved that would otherwise have to be expended on environmental cleanup or pollution control, and industrial processes can become more efficient. Source reduction is defined in the Pollution Prevention Act (PPA) of 1990 as any practice that reduces the amount of any hazardous substance, pollutant, or contaminant entering any waste stream or otherwise released into the environment (including fugitive emissions) and reduces the hazards to public health and the environment associated with the release of such substances, pollutants, or contaminants. Source reduction practices include modifications of equipment, process, procedure, or technology; reformulation or redesign of products; substitution of raw materials; and improvements in maintenance and inventory controls. Under this definition, waste management activities, including recycling, treatment, and disposal, are not considered forms of source reduction.

Some reported increases and decreases do reflect changes in the amounts of TRI chemicals actually released or otherwise managed in waste. Other reported increases and decreases are accounting or "paper" changes that do not reflect changes in releases or other waste management techniques. Source reduction activities, such as process changes, elimination of spills and leaks, inventory control, improved maintenance, chemical substitution, and alternative methods of cleaning and degreasing, can cause real reduction in the amount of waste generated and/or managed. The installation of pollution control equipment does not reduce the amount of waste generated, but may lead to real reductions in TRI chemicals released. However, if the pollution control does not destroy the reported chemical, it may merely shift the chemical from one type of waste management to another. Production changes can cause real changes in the quantities of TRI chemicals released or otherwise managed as waste by facilities.

Production-related waste is likely to increase when production increases and to decrease when production decreases, although the relationship is not necessarily linear. One-time events unrelated to normal production processes, such as accidental releases or cleanup operations, can cause a real but anomalous increase in the reporting year in which they occur and then a decrease from that abnormally high level the following year. Changes in estimation or calculation techniques can cause a change in the amount reported without a corresponding change in actual quantities of the chemical released or otherwise managed as waste. Clarifications of reporting instructions or changes in the way a facility interprets those instructions may cause a change in reported amounts without an actual change in quantities of the chemical released or otherwise managed as waste. Changes in the reporting definition of a particular chemical may cause a change in the reported amounts without an actual change in quantities released or otherwise managed as waste. For example, revising the definitions of sulfuric acid and hydrochloric acid to include only aerosol forms, as occurred in the reporting years 1994 and 1995, resulted in lower reports of releases.

Similarly, a facility's use of the alternative threshold may result in a reported decrease without an actual reduction in releases if the facility begins to take advantage of an alternative manufacture, process, or other use threshold of more than 1 million pounds. Since the 1995 reporting year, some facilities whose total annual reportable amount of a reportable chemical does not exceed 500 pounds may employ an alternative manufacture, process, or other use threshold of more than 1 million pounds of the chemical. If they do not exceed this threshold, they no longer need to report amounts of releases or other waste management activities. Apparent increases or decreases can occur if a facility makes a reporting error one year and does not submit a revision for that year, but does not repeat the error the following year. Reasons for changes in facility estimates of releases and other waste management changes include actual source reduction projects undertaken to reduce a facility's generation of waste of a particular chemical, increases or decreases in production levels, changes in a facility's methods of estimating or calculating reportable amounts (that do not indicate a corresponding change in actual releases and waste management), and reporting errors in previous years for which the facility has not filed a revised submission. Apparent increases and decreases among industries can also result when facilities change the SIC codes they report from one year to another, reflecting new or discontinued facility operations or indicating a different understanding of how SIC codes relate to the facility's business.

As noted above, the PPA of 1990 requires facilities to report the quantities of TRI chemicals they manage in waste, both on- and off-site. The PPA also requires facilities to provide information about the efforts they have made to reduce or eliminate those quantities. Since the 1991 reporting year, facilities have been reporting information about any source reduction activities implemented during the year. Source reduction activities are undertaken to reduce the amount of a toxic chemical that enters a waste stream or is otherwise released to the environment. By reducing the generation of toxic chemicals in waste, source reduction activities reduce the need to recycle, treat, or dispose of toxic chemicals. A reported source reduction activity may have been implemented at any time during the reporting year. This is important to consider when analyzing the impact that source reduction activities may have had on the total quantity of waste that a facility has managed during the year. Undertaking a source reduction activity late in the reporting year has a smaller impact on the amount of waste managed during the year than implementing the same activity earlier in the year would have.

The TRI data are available in online databases and in a variety of computer and hard copy formats to ensure that everyone can easily use the information. The TRI User Support Service (202-566-0250; tri.us@epa.gov) can provide assistance in accessing and using the TRI data. Online services include the TRI Explorer, the EPA's Envirofacts, the National Library of Medicine's TOXNET system, and the Right-to-Know Network (RTK NET). To request copies of TRI and EPCRA documents or to obtain further information about the program, contact the EPCRA call center at 1-800-424-9346. TRI information is also available on the TRI Web site, www.epa.gov/tri. Other sources of TRI information include the state EPCRA Section 313 contacts, the EPA regional offices, and the facilities themselves.

Although it is not always good news, knowledge about the environment is very empowering for all stakeholders. It helps make large environmental transactions more transparent (i.e., more observable by such outside stakeholders as the public). Given the lack of environmental baseline data and the increasing need for citizens, state and local governments, and international agencies to know about accumulating emissions and impacts, it is essential that this information be collected and that it be accessible, especially by those most impacted by the chemicals described in the TRI listing. Citizen knowledge can fill in some of the holes in TRI coverage discussed above. Community knowledge may, for example, reveal where the old underground petrochemical storage tanks were before there were regulations or the regulations were enforced.

☆ 6 ☆

Future Challenges for the EPA

The EPA is designed to handle the challenges of meeting its statutory missions for the future. It can adjust its missions to the legal limits of its administrative discretion but is still limited to laws passed by Congress and by executive orders. The challenge is to handle some of the environmental issues in society within the scope of current missions. Some areas the EPA is examining include community-based environmental planning, environmental justice, sustainability, cumulative impacts, and ecosystem approaches.

COMMUNITY-BASED ENVIRONMENTAL PLANNING

Community-based environmental planning (CBEP) integrates environmental management with human needs, considers long-term ecosystem health, and highlights the positive correlations between economic prosperity and environmental well-being. It is coordinated by the Office of Policy, Economics, and Innovation at the EPA. CBEP is a new approach to environmental protection for the United States.

Traditionally, environmental protection programs have focused on a particular medium or problem by incorporating a "command and control" approach to environmental protection. These "command and control" programs have been effective in reducing point source pollution and improving environmental quality since the early 1980s. However, some environmental problems, such as nonpoint source pollution, that may involve several media types and diffuse sources are less amenable to "command and control" programs. Instead, a solution that seeks to address the various causes of the problems and to understand the relationships between human behavior and pollution in a specific area may be more appropriate. CBEP supplements and complements the traditional environmental protection approach by focusing on the health of an ecosystem and the behavior of humans who live within its boundaries.

The CBEP approach has several other qualities that complement and supplement traditional environmental protection. Under a place-based protection scheme, the number and diversity of stakeholders tends to increase. For example, whereas an air pollution program may bring together a few industry representatives and groups interested in air quality, a place-based program affects all individuals, groups, and industries concerned with the health and sustainability of a certain geographic area. Collaboration between diverse public and private stakeholders within a specific geographic area facilitates comprehensive identification of local environmental concerns, the setting of priorities and goals that reflect overall community concerns, and the forging of comprehensive, long-term solutions. It includes a much broader range of stakeholders. Typical CBEP stakeholders include the following:

- EPA headquarters officials;
- EPA regional officials;
- State officials;
- City planners;
- Environmental groups;
- Nongovernmental organizations;
- Tribal leaders;
- Regulated communities;
- Community groups;
- Academics;
- Concerned citizens.

The CBEP approach also connects and broadens the issues dealt with by environmental protection programs. Often a particular environmental problem, such as nonpoint source pollution, is affected by and related to several other environmental and resource issues in a geographic area. In order to solve one environmental problem, the related and connected environmental concerns must also be addressed. This is very difficult under the current single-medium regime of environmental protection.

Additionally, the CBEP approach recognizes the place of humans in ecosystems. Humans are the main agents of change in an ecosystem, and in order for ecosystem change to be benevolent and beneficial, the agents of change need to feel healthy and productive. Therefore, human economic and social needs must be addressed in concert with environmental solutions to promote a sustainable future. A place-based focus allows stakeholders to identify the interrelated problems and forge a comprehensive, long-term plan that addresses the needs of the environment and its inhabitants. Therefore, the CBEP approach to environmental protection is holistic, not linear and isolated.

Finally, the CBEP approach can improve environmental program management. A large, diverse group of stakeholders can provide a wide array of expertise and knowledge when properly informed of an area's interrelated problems. This encourages the development of effective and appropriate problem-solving tools. For example, a tool that may improve air quality levels but exacerbate other ecosystem pollution problems would be avoided under a CBEP approach. Widespread stakeholder collaboration also improves environmental protection management by providing a means and forum for adaptive problem solving. If a problem-solving method is not working, the relationships established under collaborative work should facilitate discussion and implementation of alternative approaches. Therefore, the CBEP approach, by tapping into a high level of expertise and collaborative relationships, is an effective management tool. Currently the CBEP approach at the EPA uses six principles:

1. Focus on geographic area;
2. Work collaboratively with stakeholders;
3. Protect and restore quality of air, water, land, and living resources in a place as a whole;
4. Integrate environmental, economic, and social objectives;
5. Take action using the most appropriate tools;
6. Use adaptive management.

CBEP is based on the ideas first explored in comparative risk assessment, ecosystem management, the EPA's geographic programs, the Office of Water's "watershed approach," sustainable development, and reinventing government initiatives. These diverse programs have several elements in common, including an exploration of relationships among different environmental media in ecosystems, a holistic approach to problem solving, and examination of stakeholder participation. The issues that drive CBEP include sprawl, or unrestrained urban development; watersheds and their management; and sustainable development.

The EPA's involvement in place-based, collaborative, and holistic environmental protection includes geographic programs such as the National Estuary Program, the Chesapeake Bay Program, and the Great Lakes Program. These programs and others have demonstrated on a large scale the advantages of a CBEP approach. In particular, the Office of Water has been at the forefront of ecosystem-based protection with its watershed approach, which, like CBEP, emphasizes collaborative partnerships, a geographic focus, and sound management techniques.

Finally, government reinvention initiatives have encouraged a CBEP approach. By placing problem-solving responsibility with stakeholders and local governments and by searching for holistic solutions, CBEP improves federal government performance in ways that include:

- Customer service and responsive government—policies and initiatives endorsed by the EPA are created by citizens themselves;
- Government efficiency—by searching for holistic solutions at the community level instead of the media level, economies of scale can be achieved by pooling diverse stakeholder resources, avoiding duplicative efforts, utilizing local expertise, and forging lasting solutions.

CBEP is also growing in states and in municipalities. As a policy it faces several challenges. One criticism is that communities will not protect natural resources if that protection interferes with short-term economic gain. For example, a community may choose to log all its old growth trees to ensure full employment. Another criticism is that many communities currently lack the capacity to make fully informed environmental decisions. CBEP will need much greater public involvement than current EPA requirements. Another major issue in U.S. environmentalism and environmental policy that CBEP must face is land use control. Currently, the EPA and many state environmental agencies do not control land use. Private property is a highly held public value in the United States. However, without adequate land use control, many environmental policies falter at the point of implementation. CBEP will need to address all these issues as it moves toward implementation.

ENVIRONMENTAL JUSTICE

Environmental justice refers to the distribution of environmental burdens and benefits. It also refers to procedural fairness and cultural perspectives in the development, implementation, and enforcement of environmental laws, many administered by the EPA. It is driven by the practicalities of cleanup.

In 1983, the General Accounting Office issued a report that correlated race and other socioeconomic characteristics with hazardous-waste sites in EPA Region 3. Prodded into doing a study by District of Columbia Representative Rev. Walter E. Fauntleroy, who had been arrested in Warren County, North Carolina, for protesting the siting of a hazardous-waste landfill in an African American community. (See discussion in Chapter 3.) This report found significant correlations. However, correlation is not considered to prove causality. Robert Bullard's *Dumping in Dixie: Race, Class, and Environmental Quality* was published at the same time and exploded the issue into national consciousness. In the early 1990s the first law review article was published in the *Virginia Environmental Law Review*—my "Environmental Equity: A Law

Northeast Houston residents protest the construction of the Whispering Pines landfill in their neighborhood, 1979. (Photo by R. D. Bullard)

and Planning Approach to Environmental Racism." Both were widely circulated in academia and in government.

Also in the early 1990s environmental advocacy groups began to address environmental issues. For example, Greenpeace, an environmental group noted for being at actual sites of environmental concern, issued a report, *Playing with Fire*, in 1993. This report was a hazardous-materials incinerator siting study exclusive of Indian reservations. It found that demographic indicators showed race was more important than low income in incinerator siting. Also in 1991 the first People of Color Environmental Leadership Summit was held in Washington, D.C. It was here that the principles of environmental justice were developed. (See Appendix 2.) It convened again in 2001.

The best predictor of where an uncontrolled hazardous-waste site is located in the United States is not the condition of the land, air, or water. It is the race of the nearby population, with low-income groups both paired with race and considered separately. This is actual field data tested to a 99.9 percent degree of certainty (1 chance in 10,000 of being random). The best use of the EPA's resources is in terms of cleaning up the worst environmental areas first is predominantly in communities of color. In the United States there are startling differences in rates of cleanup, penalties, enforcement in general, regulatory oversight, and accumulated and accumulating emissions, by race and by income. Over time these accumulated emissions can produce accumulated impacts on nearby communities. These emissions also begin to migrate through the ecosystem via water, land, and air. This causes them to be discernible in communities farther from the source. As communities with good environmental protection began to explore sustainability, they became aware of the magnitude and source of many of these emissions. This awareness, combined with surging EPA cleanup policy development and a burgeoning public right-to-know movement, created fertile ground for the rapid institutionalization of the environmental justice movement. For this reason it is both a controversy (discussed in a case form in Chapter 3) and future challenge.

The environmental justice movement was started by people, primarily people of color, who needed to address the inequity of environmental protection services in their communities. Its mantra is that communities speak for themselves. The environmental concerns of communities of color were unable to find expression in the U.S. environmental movement, at the EPA, or in state or local governments. Grounded in the struggles of the 1960s civil rights movement, these citizens emerged to protest the environmental inequities accumulating in their communities. These communities were very concerned about the public health dangers that posed an immediate peril to the lives of their families, their communities, and themselves. With the Love Canal controversy in the public eye and with the EPA developing policies that prioritized cleanup, many of these communities suddenly had a new ally and forum with the EPA.

Early in 1990, the Congressional Black Caucus, a bipartisan coalition of academicians, social scientists, and political activists, met with EPA officials to discuss their findings that the EPA was unfairly applying its enforcement inspections and that environmental risk was higher in racial minority and low-income populations. In response, the EPA Administrator created the Environmental Equity Work Group in July 1990 to address the allegation that "racial minority and low-income populations bear a higher environmental risk burden than the general population." The group produced a final two-volume report, *Reducing Risk in All Communities* (June 1992), which supported the allegation and made ten recommendations for addressing the problem. (See discussion of this report in Chapter 4.) One of the recommendations was to create an office to address these inequities. The Office of Environmental Equity was established on November 6, 1992, and was renamed Office of Environmental Justice in 1994.

On February 11, 1994, President Bill Clinton signed Executive Order 12898, Environmental Justice: Federal Actions to Address Environmental Justice in Minority Populations and Low-Income Populations, which focused federal attention on the environmental and human health of minority and low-income populations with the goal of achieving environmental protection for all communities. (See Appendix 1.)

The order directed federal agencies to develop environmental justice strategies to identify and address disproportionately high and adverse human health or environmental effects of their programs, policies, and activities on minority and low-income populations. It was also intended to promote non-discrimination in federal programs substantially affecting human health and the environment, and to provide minority and low-income communities with access to public information on, and an opportunity for public participation in, matters relating to human health or the environment. The presidential memorandum accompanying the order underscored certain provisions of existing law which could help ensure that all communities and persons live in a safe and healthful environment.

One of the provisions of the executive order established an interagency working group (IWG) on environmental justice chaired by the EPA Administrator and composed of the heads of eleven departments/agencies and several White House offices. These include the EPA; the Departments of Justice, Defense, Energy, Labor, Interior, Transportation, Agriculture, Housing and Urban Development, Commerce, and Health and Human Services; the Council on Environmental Quality; the Office of Management and Budget; the Office of Science and Technology Policy; the Domestic Policy Council; and the Council of Economic Advisers. The IWG meets monthly to continue the collaborative projects. Fifteen demonstration projects have been selected, and additional projects will be selected each year.

The statutes that the EPA implements provide it with the authority to consider and address environmental justice concerns. These laws encompass the breadth of the EPA's activities, including setting standards, permitting facilities, making grants, issuing licenses or regulations, and reviewing proposed actions of other federal agencies. These laws often require the EPA to consider a range of factors that generally include one or more of the following: public health, cumulative impacts, social costs, and welfare impacts. Moreover, some statutory provisions (under, for instance, the Toxic Substances Control Act) explicitly direct the EPA to target low-income populations for assistance. Other statutes direct the EPA to consider vulnerable populations in setting standards. In all cases, how the EPA chooses to implement and enforce its authority can have substantial effects on the achievement of environmental justice for all communities.

Since the Office of Environmental Justice (OEJ) was created, there have been significant efforts across EPA to integrate environmental justice into how the Agency conducts its day-to-day operations. Information on these activities can be found throughout the EPA. Every headquarters office and region has an environmental justice coordinator. This network of individuals plays a key role in outreach and education to both external and internal individuals and organizations.

The OEJ is the entity within the EPA with the primary responsibility for coordinating the EPA's efforts to integrate environmental justice into all policies, programs, and activities. The EPA's environmental justice mandate encompasses the breadth of the EPA's work, including setting standards, permitting facilities, awarding grants, issuing licenses or regulations, and reviewing proposed actions of the federal agencies. The OEJ works with all stakeholders to constructively and collaboratively address environmental and public health issues and concerns. It also provides information and technical and financial resources to assist and enable the EPA to meet its environmental justice goals and objectives.

The EPA's definition of environmental justice is the fair treatment and meaningful involvement of all people, regardless of race, color, national origin, or income, with respect to the development, implementation, and enforcement of environmental laws, regulations, and policies. Fair treatment means that no group of people should bear a disproportionate share of the negative environmental consequences resulting from industrial, governmental, and commercial operations or policies. Meaningful involvement means that

- People have an opportunity to participate in decisions about activities that may affect their environment and/or health;
- The public's contribution can influence the regulatory agency's decision;
- The public's concerns will be considered in the decision-making process;
- The decision makers seek out and facilitate the involvement of those who may be affected.

The EPA has this goal for all communities and persons. It will be achieved when everyone enjoys the same degree of protection from environmental and health hazards and equal access to the decision-making process in order to have a healthy environment in which to live, learn, worship, and work.

The Federal Interagency Working Group on Environmental Justice

The federal Interagency Working Group on Environmental Justice (IWG), established under executive order 12898 in 1994, is composed of members from eleven federal agencies and several White House offices. Each agency, with leadership from EPA, is working to integrate environmental justice into its individual programs. On August 9, 2001, EPA Administrator Christine Todd Whitman reaffirmed the EPA's, and affirmed the Bush administration's, commitment to environmental justice.

The IWG currently has three active task forces—Health Disparities, Revitalization Demonstration Projects, and Native American—that focus on its priority issues. In October 2002, the IWG created the Health Disparities Task Force to identify and work to address many of the issues that pertain to concerns over both health disparities and environmental justice. The task force is working to develop partnerships, under the leadership of federal entities, between agencies and organizations working to eliminate health disparities and/or address environmental justice. It is clear that many of the populations which suffer health disparities are also facing other environmental justice issues. In May 2000, the IWG identified fifteen revitalization demonstration projects in environmental justice communities. The IWG created the collaborative models for environmental decision-making that are being tested at the state level.

The Native American Task Force was established in November 1999, as a result of the unique political status of tribes as sovereign entities and the existence of the "federal trust responsibility." It works to address environmental justice issues (e.g., environmental, health, and economic) of concern to federally recognized tribes, nonfederally recognized tribes, tribal organizations, and tribal members.

The protection of sacred places and cultural resources is a significant concern for many tribes. The difficulties in protecting these places and resources, and the lack of understanding of the legal re-

The protection of sacred places and cultural resources is a significant part of environmental protection for many tribes. Shoshone spiritual leader, medicine man, and elder Corbin Harney visiting the Grand Ronde Reservation circa 1990. (Photograph by Brent Merrill)

quirements to protect them, have been identified by some tribes as environmental justice issues. The task force is supporting the efforts of tribes and tribal organizations to bring attention to these concerns. It has created a compendium of existing federal policies/documents on Native American sacred places and cultural properties. To further the understanding of the importance of this issue to tribes, and to identify ways these resources can be better protected, the task force is working with various tribal organizations and other interested groups to develop a training module on cultural resources and environmental justice. It has the primary responsibility to work with tribes to identify potential interagency environmental justice demonstration projects. The task force members are working with their regional counterparts to encourage greater interagency coordination in addressing the environmental, public health, and economic concerns of tribes.

In May 2000, the IWG released the Integrated Federal Interagency Environmental Justice Action Agenda, which identified fifteen model demonstration programs. The action agenda ensures the targeting of coordinated federal initiatives and resources to help environmentally and economically distressed communities. The anticipated result will be a dramatic improvement in the quality of life in fifteen minority and low-income communities that suffer from disproportionate environmental impact. The action agenda seeks to build dynamic and proactive partnerships among federal agencies to benefit environmentally and economically distressed communities. Increased coordination and cooperation among federal agencies will enhance identification, mobilization, and utilization of federal resources. Increased coordination and cooperation also will enable distressed communities to improve environmental decision-making and to access and leverage federal government initiatives more efficiently. The action agenda will result in improved quality of life for minority and/or low-income populations suffering disproportionate environmental impacts. These populations may include indigenous/tribal communities. The action agenda intends to accomplish the following:

- Ensure that no segment of the population, regardless of race, color, national origin, or income, suffers disproportionate adverse human or environmental effects, and that all people live in clean, healthy, and sustainable communities;

- Create opportunities for building partnerships between specific federal agencies to promote comprehensive solutions to environmental justice issues;

- Promote models based on an integrated approach to addressing environmental, public health, economic, and social concerns of distressed communities;

- Ensure that those who live with environmental decisions (community residents; state, tribal, and local governments; and the private sector) have meaningful opportunity for public participation in the decision-making process;

- Provide a lasting framework for the integration of environmental justice into the missions of federal agencies.

As follow-up to the action agenda, the IWG has been examining the demonstration projects as they are implemented. The Status Report on Environmental Justice Collaborative Model recounts the lessons learned and successful elements of the fifteen action agenda projects and begins to define a collaborative problem-solving model that is emerging from the experiences. The collaborative efforts described in this report have as a theme the federal government's responsibility for assuring that all Americans live in high-quality environments. This theme follows a key principle of the National

Environmental Policy Act (NEPA) of 1969, which states that it is the continuing responsibility of the federal government to assure that all Americans live in "safe, healthful and aesthetically and culturally pleasing surroundings." This congressional mandate is also clearly reflected and referenced in EPA Administrator Christine Todd Whitman's August 9, 2001, memorandum regarding the EPA's continuing commitment to environmental justice: "Environmental justice is achieved when everyone, regardless of race, culture, or income, enjoys the same degree of protection from environmental and health hazards and equal access to the decision-making process to have a healthy environment in which to live, learn, and work." As chair of the IWG, Administrator Whitman stated that the OEJ is dedicated to ensuring that the mandate is fulfilled within the EPA and to supporting the efforts of other federal agencies that compose the IWG to pursue the same mandate.

Most important, the IWG demonstration projects and the collaborative model have received enthusiastic and widespread endorsement from all stakeholder groups. For example, according to the National Environmental Policy Commission's report to the Congressional Black Caucus and Congressional Black Caucus Foundation Environmental Justice Brain Trust (September 28, 2001), "The IWG demonstration projects are particularly significant. They point to the potential to problem-solve across stakeholder groups in a constructive, collaborative manner, building relationships, avoiding duplicated efforts, and leveraging instead of wasting resources." The IWG's work on the demonstration projects has forged an important new integrated prototype for federal agencies and stakeholders in the area of creative, collaborative, and constructive problem solving.

Starting in 2001, the EPA's Evaluation Support Division began conducting an evaluation (Evaluating the Use of Partnerships to Address Environmental Justice Issues) that looked at six IWG projects to determine the value of using partnerships to address environmental justice issues. This effort included six case studies and an analysis that examined project processes, activities, and outcomes; key factors influencing project success; the value of partnering to address environmental justice issues; and the value of federal agency involvement in partnership efforts. A core set of findings and recommendations was also included. Findings indicate that the partnerships are producing important results, including the improved opportunity for local residents and community organizations to have a genuine say in efforts to revitalize their communities, enhancement of relationships between stakeholders, implementation of environmental protection and other programs, and improved delivery of community assistance by public service organizations.

In regard to the overall value of partnering, most interviewees indicated that the issues facing the affected communities either wouldn't have been addressed, or wouldn't have been addressed to the same extent, if at all, without a collaborative approach. Interviewees also saw federal involvement in these efforts as critical. In addition to the many positive points voiced, interviewees noted that the partnerships are facing challenges, including difficulties associated with partnership maintenance and operational support, and the implementation of partnership-specific initiatives. Overall, this evaluation shows that use of these approaches can be an effective means for addressing environmental justice issues in communities.

Individual Case Studies

The Barrio Logan Partnership is based primarily in an inner city community near downtown San Diego. It was formed in 2001 after discussions between a senior EPA official and representatives of the Environmental Health Coalition, a local environmental justice organization with a long-standing history of working in the Barrio Logan community. Barrio Logan faces several challenges, most notably incompatible land uses resulting from lack of proper zoning restrictions that led to the emergence of industrial land uses near residential neighborhoods. Through a structured, facilitated partnering process, the Barrio Logan Partnership has brought long-standing adversaries together to discuss, form goals, and implement actions to address some of the numerous quality-of-life issues facing the community.

The Bridges to Friendship Partnership emerged in 1998 out of concerns that a major redevelopment effort in a distressed Washington, D.C., neighborhood would fail to benefit local residents and could eventually result in their displacement. Initiated by community organizations and officials at the Washington Navy Yard, a structured but flexible partnership involving numerous community nonprofits, several federal agencies, and the government of the District of Columbia was formed to ensure that local residents would benefit from the redevelopment through better coordination, communication, and pooling of expertise and resources. There are over forty partners today, and partnership members view this coordinated approach as an effective way to conduct business and continue to search for opportunities to better serve local residents.

The Metlakatla Peninsula Cleanup Partnership is an emerging collaboration between the Metlakatla Indian Community (MIC), federal agency field staff in Alaska, and federal headquarters staff based primarily in Washington, D.C. Its purpose is to ensure the cleanup of over eighty primarily government-contaminated sites on the MIC's home island in southeast Alaska. Through these coordinated efforts, the parties hope to clean up the sites in a manner that is satisfactory to the tribe, make more efficient use of resources, and map out a process for cleanup of complex, multiparty sites. The issues are complex, given the numerous agencies and other parties involved in the contamination, the different parties' policies and procedures for contaminated site cleanup, and disagreements over who should clean up the sites and to what level. The partnership effort began in 2000 after its designation by the IWG as a national demonstration pilot project and built upon an ongoing local collaboration primarily between the MIC and Alaska federal agency field staff.

The Metro East Lead Collaborative is an effort that emerged after a local hospital and government officials determined that high lead levels in children in East St. Louis, Illinois, and surrounding communities may be a result of lead-contaminated soil. In early 1999, recognizing the need for a comprehensive approach to reduce the threat of lead poisoning, an EPA representative brought several groups already at work on lead and related issues together to form a structured partnership. Although initially focused on East St. Louis, the project soon expanded to nearby neighborhoods. In addition, the enthusiasm over its lead reduction efforts spurred the partnership to begin addressing brownfields redevelopment.

The New Madrid Tri-Community Partnership was formed in 1998 after residents of a rural community in southern Missouri requested the assistance of the Natural Resources Conservation Service (NRCS) to help it tackle numerous social, economic, and environmental challenges. Responding to the call, NRCS joined with the EPA, a regional nonprofit, and two additional communities in the area to begin addressing common concerns. Soon after the partnership was designated by the EPA as a Child Health Champion national demonstration project, these groups began taking a structured approach to addressing asthma, lead, and water quality issues in the three communities. The partners have made significant progress in meeting the objectives outlined under their program.

The ReGenesis Partnership emerged in 1999 after the leader of a 1,400-member group representing two distressed adjacent neighborhoods in Spartanburg, South Carolina, brought together numerous stakeholders in an effort to clean up and revitalize the area. By building a shared vision for redevelopment, the energy and enthusiasm surrounding the effort brought together approximately seventy organizations representing a range of interests that include the cleanup and redevelopment of two Superfund equivalent sites, the building of a health clinic, creation of a recreational greenway, new road construction, and new affordable housing.

The Environmental Justice Directory, a comprehensive listing of the contacts in the federal agencies that make up the IWG, was published in October 2000. With this resource, the OEJ hopes to enhance coordination and communication among federal agencies, state and local governments, and the public in addressing environmental justice issues.

The EPA is continually attempting to improve its approach to environmental protection. Traditionally, environmental programs at all levels of government have set broadly applicable standards for individual pollutants released by specific types of sources, with the goal of protecting the environment and all people. Recognizing that not everyone is affected in the same way by pollution, these standards have often ignored the most susceptible groups, such as asthmatics, children, and pregnant women.

Environmental protection has progressed from this initial strategy to include risk-based priority setting. The EPA Science Advisory Board, in its report "Reducing Risk: Setting Priorities and Strategies for Environmental Protection," urged the EPA to target its environmental protection efforts on the basis of opportunities for reducing the most serious remaining risks. (See discussion in Chapter 4.) In response, the EPA began to examine and to target its efforts on environmental problems that pose the greatest risks to human health and the environment nationwide, using comparative risk analyses to rank these problems according to severity. One approach the EPA now employs to prioritize environmental efforts based on risk is geographic targeting, in which attention is focused on the problems faced by cities or by regions, such as the Chesapeake Bay, the Great Lakes, and the Gulf of Mexico.

In the context of a risk-based approach to environmental management, the relative risk burden borne by low-income and racial minority communities is a special concern. A low-income community that is surrounded by multiple sources of air pollution and by waste treatment facilities and landfills, and that has lead-based paint in the residences is clearly a community that faces higher than average potential environmental risks. A racial or cultural group whose children commonly have harmful levels of lead in their blood is living with a greater environmental risk. In addition, as a result of factors affecting health status, such communities may be more likely than the general population to experience disease or death due to a given level of exposure. Poor nutrition, smoking, inadequate health care, and stress contribute to an increased rate of health effects at a given pollutant level. To the extent that these communities are subject to these factors, they are more likely to experience harm due to these exposures.

Issues such as these, and how government agencies respond, are known as issues of environmental equity. Environmental equity refers to the distribution of environmental risks across population groups and to policy responses to these distributions. The EPA has begun to assess how patterns of environmental problems converge on different places, how people who live in those places are affected, and how environmental programs should be further refined to address identified differences. The causes of these differences are often complex and deeply rooted in historical patterns of racial and economic oppression, commerce, geography, state and local land use decisions, and other factors that affect where people live and work. With respect to some types of pollutants, race and income appear to be strongly correlated with these distributions. (See the discussion of the Office of Inspector General Report in Chapter 3.)

Clearly, environmental equity is important to those who might bear high risks, but everyone has a stake in environmental equity because it results in better environmental protection. Environmental justice is an important goal in a democratic society. It involves ensuring that the benefits of environmental protection are available to all communities and that there is an environmental policy-making process that allows the concerns of all communities to be heard, understood, and addressed. Without environmental justice, the other challenges facing the EPA, such as sustainability and ecosystem approaches, will be insurmountable.

The EPA Environmental Equity Work Group

In response to concerns raised by EPA staff and the public, in July 1990, EPA Administrator William K. Reilly formed the EPA Environmental Equity Work Group with staff from all EPA offices and regions. The work group was directed to assess the evidence that racial minority and low-income communities bear a higher environmental risk burden than the general population, and to consider what the EPA might do about any identified disparities. The work group helped lay the foundation for the executive order regarding projects discussed above.

The work group's report to the Administrator reviewed existing data on the distribution of environmental exposures and risks across population groups, and also summarized the group's review of EPA programs with respect to racial minority and low-income populations. Based on the findings from these analyses, the work group made initial recommendations. Because of the specific nature of the group's assignment, the report did not deal with important related subjects, such as the EPA's minority recruiting programs. The report was intended to contribute to the national dialogue on environmental equity and to suggest further steps for the EPA. Here is a summary of the findings of the report.

- There are clear differences between racial groups in terms of disease and death rates. There are limited data to explain the environment's contribution to these differences. In fact, there is a general lack of data on environmental health effects by race and income. For diseases that are known to have environmental causes, data typically are not disaggregated by race and socioeconomic group. The notable exception is lead poisoning: A significantly higher percentage of black children compared with white children have unacceptably high levels of lead in their blood.

- Racial minority and low-income populations experience higher than average exposures to selected air pollutants, hazardous-waste facilities, contaminated fish, and agricultural pesticides in the workplace. Exposure does not always result in an immediate or acute health effect. High exposures and the possibility of chronic effects are nevertheless a clear cause for concern.

- Environmental and health data are not routinely collected and analyzed by income and race. Nor are data routinely collected on health risks posed by multiple industrial facilities, cumulative and synergistic effects, or multiple and different pathways of exposure.

Risk assessment and risk management procedures are not in themselves biased against certain income or racial groups. However, risk assessment and risk management procedures can be improved to better take equity considerations into account.

- Great opportunities exist for the EPA and other government agencies to improve communication about environmental problems with members of low-income and racial minority groups. The language, format, and distribution of written materials, media relations, and efforts at two-way communication all can be improved. In addition, the EPA can broaden the spectrum of groups with which it interacts.

- Since they have broad contact with affected communities, the EPA's program and regional offices are well suited to address equity concerns. The potential exists for effective action by such offices to address disproportionate risks. These offices currently vary considerably in terms of how they address environmental equity issues. Case studies of the EPA program and regional offices reveal that opportunities exist for addressing environmental equity issues and that there is a need for environmental equity awareness training. A number of the EPA regional offices have initiated projects to address high risks in racial minority and low-income communities.

- Native Americans have a special relationship with the federal government and distinct environmental problems. Tribes often lack the physical infrastructure, institutions, trained personnel, and resources necessary to protect their members.

- Although large gaps in data exist, the work group believes that enough is known with sufficient certainty to make several recommendations to the EPA. These recommendations are also applicable to other public and private groups engaged in environmental protection activities.

- The EPA should increase the priority given to issues of environmental equity.

- The EPA should establish and maintain information that provides an objective basis for assessment of risks by income and race, beginning with the development of a plan for research and data collection.

- The EPA should incorporate environmental equity into the risk assessment process. It should revise its risk assessment procedures to ensure, where practical and relevant, better characterization of risk across populations, communities, or geographic areas. These revisions could be useful in determining whether there are any population groups at disproportionately high risk.

- The EPA should identify and target opportunities to reduce high concentrations of risk to specific population groups, employing approaches developed for geographic targeting.

- The EPA should, where appropriate, assess and consider the distribution of projected risk reduction in major rulemakings and initiatives.

- The EPA should selectively review and revise its permit, grant, monitoring, and enforcement procedures to address high concentrations of risk in racial minority and low-income communities. Since state and local governments have primary authority for many environmental programs, the EPA should emphasize its concerns about environmental equity to them.

- The EPA should expand and improve the level at and forms with which it communicates with racial minority and low-income communities, and should increase efforts to involve them in environmental policy-making.

- The EPA should establish mechanisms, including a center of staff support, to ensure that environmental equity concerns are incorporated into its long-term planning and operations.

In response to public concerns, the EPA created the Office of Environmental Justice in 1992 and implemented a new organizational infrastructure to integrate environmental justice into EPA's policies, programs, and activities. The Executive Steering Committee, made up of senior managers, represents each headquarters office and region, and provides leadership and direction on strategic planning to ensure that environmental justice is incorporated into agency operations. The most active group is the Environmental Justice Coordinators Council, which serves as the frontline staff specifically responsible to ensure policy input, program development, and implementation of environmental justice through the EPA. This new structure has established a clear commitment from EPA's senior management to all personnel that environmental justice is a priority.

National Environmental Justice Advisory Council Overview

The National Environmental Justice Advisory Council (NEJAC) was established September 30, 1993. Its functions cannot be performed within the EPA. This council is the first bringing together of community, academia, industry, and environmental, indigenous, and state/local/tribal government groups to engage in a dialogue to define or "reinvent" solutions to environmental justice problems. In addition, NEJAC provides a valuable forum for integrating environmental justice with other EPA priorities and initiatives.

The NEJAC is made up of twenty-six members and one designated federal officer from the EPA who serve on a parent council and an additional twenty-seven individuals who serve on the seven subcommittees. Subcommittees of the NEJAC meet independently of the full NEJAC and present their findings for review. The Executive Council membership is rotated to provide the greatest possible opportunity for a variety of individuals to serve. To ensure that all views are represented, membership is composed of a balanced representation of the following groups: academia; community groups; industry/business; nongovernment organizations/environmental organizations; state/local governments; and tribal governments/indigenous groups. NEJAC has published important and pioneering reports on permitting, public involvement, pollution prevention, and other topics.

For example, one NEJAC recommendation deals with permitting of industrial emissions. NEJAC recommended that the EPA Administrator direct permit writers to issue only permits consistent with the EPA's mission: protecting the health of all citizens. Specifically, permit writers should ensure that any permit complies with all applicable provisions of law, including state and local health, environmental, and zoning laws (where such laws are not preempted), and adequately protects health and the environment. Factors that academicians and community groups believe the EPA should consider in determining the bases for modifying or denying permits in low-income or minority communities include the following:

- Negative health risks;
- Racially disproportionate burdens;
- Cumulative and synergistic adverse impacts on human health and the environment;
- High aggregation of risk from multiple sources;
- Community vulnerability based on the number of children, elderly, or asthmatics;
- Cultural practices, including tribal and indigenous cultures and cultural reliance on land;
- Water that may become pathways of toxic exposure;
- Proximity to residential areas and adequacy of buffer zones;
- Health and ecological risk assessment;
- The economic burden of medical costs and lost productivity;
- Access to health care;
- Psychological impacts;
- Physical impacts;
- The risk of chemical accidents;
- Emergency preparedness;
- Community right-to-know in permitting;

- The impact on the quality of life in the surrounding community;
- An applicant's compliance history.

Another product of the NEJAC was a report titled "Environmental Justice and Community-Based Health Model Discussion." Its recommendations included the following:

- The EPA and other federal agencies need to promote better understanding of the approach and usefulness of community-based participatory research models and the importance of including prevention and intervention components in these models.

- The EPA and other federal agencies may fail to act on a problem because of an inability to "prove" a casual relationship to health disparities. Greater emphasis needs to be placed on translating current scientific knowledge into positive action at the policy and community levels (i.e., what the government can do to help, even though it doesn't have absolute proof).

- The EPA and other federal agencies should establish more extensive formal and informal interagency mechanisms to help assure that the necessary expertise and other resources are brought to bear on eliminating health disparities and disproportionate exposures. This process should better define responsibilities and available resources for dealing with specific problems and issues.

- The EPA and other federal agencies need to examine the impact and significance of socioeconomic factors, as well as cultural and traditional values and practices, on health disparities. Then, as appropriate, these factors should be included in developing health assessment, intervention, and prevention strategies.

- The EPA and other federal agencies need to further examine the most significant needs of medically underserved communities. The mechanisms established above should then be used to eliminate or reduce disparities in access to health care and to improve environmental health education.

The EPA has developed some tools to assist in determining which communities face environmental justice issues. The Environmental Justice Geographic Assessment Tool, now available, was produced by an EPA-wide work group and provides information relevant to any area in the continental United States. Factors relevant to environmental justice assessments generally fall into four sets of indicators: environmental, health, social, and economic. The conditions these indicators seek to illuminate include, but are not limited to, adverse health or environmental impacts, aggregate or cumulative impacts, unique exposure pathways, vulnerable or susceptible populations, and lack of capacity to participate in the decision-making process. As these data become available, they may be incorporated into the Environmental Justice Geographic Assessment Tool, which, when fully developed, will provide the information necessary to conduct a comprehensive preliminary analysis of any area of concern. Use of buffers is incorporated into the Environmental Justice Geographic Assessment Tool, and population estimation is accomplished through an area-weighted methodology. The smallest unit of geographic resolution is the census block. The Environmental Justice Geographic Assessment Tool is meant to serve as a module to be incorporated on the front end (e.g., screening) of all appropriate EPA assessments. This Web-based technology is accessible at www.epa.gov/enviro/ej.

Environmental justice is a grassroots driver of significant change within the EPA. Communities facing the burden of weak environmental protection are highly motivated to develop new policies and programs that protect them where they live, work, and play. Environmental justice at the EPA faces several challenges in policy implementation. One is that it is not among the statutory missions of the major laws that the EPA administers. Another is the historical exclusion of people of color from the environmental movement and the complexities of race in the institutional practices and policies of the EPA. Like community-based environmental planning, environmental justice is challenged by the current exclusion of municipal land use control by state environmental agencies and the EPA. Information about land use decisions with environmental impacts is not communicated to the state environmental agency. The state environmental agency is often delegated permitting power over air and water by the EPA. They do not communicate with municipalities about environmental decisions. However, as emissions continue to accumulate, as cities become part of U.S. environmentalism, and as public knowledge increases, the distribution of environmental benefits and burdens becomes clearer. These forces not only organize communities around environmental issues, they mobilize communities to increase the political saliency of unequal distributions of environmental risks. The environmental justice movement existed before EPA recognition, and will continue to do so because all the factors that increase its political saliency continue to increase.

SUSTAINABILITY

Sustainability is the ability to achieve economic prosperity while protecting the natural systems of the planet and providing a better quality of life for its residents. Individuals, communities, and institutions are developing and implementing sustainability practices with the help of dozens of EPA programs, partnerships, and policy tools.

The EPA recognizes that shaping a sustainable future calls for using innovative science and technology in a cost-effective, participatory way. It is refining and coordinating current programs that aim to improve industrial practices, help states and local governments to manage their resources effectively, and promote innovate and interdisciplinary environmental programs.

The term "sustainability" has achieved both cachet and controversy since the World Commission on Environment and Development's 1987 report, "Our Common Future." This document, better known as the Brundtland Report, specifies that development is sustainable when it "meets the needs of the present without compromising the ability of future generations to meet their own needs." Though sustainability has been described in diverse and conflicting ways, a broad consensus supports its basic principle of balancing economic prosperity, environmental responsibility, and social fairness so as to support rewarding lives for people living today and for future generations.

The relevance of this core meaning of sustainability cannot be ignored. In the next half-century, world population is expected to increase by 50 percent, manufacturing activity and energy consumption to triple, and global gross domestic product to reach five times current levels. These projected trends will lead to environmental, economic, and social catastrophes unless better ways to use Earth's resources are found. The concept of sustainability has been gaining global acceptance since the Brundtland Commission described it. As a philosophical and policy imperative, it has inspired institutions and individuals to strive for environmental stewardship while promoting economic growth and social objectives.

In the United States, commitment to sustainability has prompted planning and action by federal, state, and local governments; tribes; universities; large corporations and small firms; consumers; and civic groups. There is broad agreement not only that substantial expansion of environmental regulation is not politically feasible, but also that reliance on governmental regulations cannot produce sustainable development. The required changes in product design, industrial processes, use and reuse of materials, and citizen behavior are too extensive and complex to be enforced by prescriptive regulation. The 2004 Sustainability Summit heard testimony from federal managers that many U.S. agencies are seeking to advance sustainable development, assist state- and community-led initiatives, develop new tools and methodologies, and support research and educational activities. Summit participants worked to define relevant issues and coordinate sustainability efforts among their agencies.

The EPA is among the frontline federal agencies recognizing that shaping a sustainable future calls for using innovative science and technology in a cost-effective, participatory way. It is refining and coordinating current programs that improve industrial practices, manage resources more economically and effectively, and help states and local governments to manage their resources effectively. Today the EPA has policy tools and voluntary, incentive-based programs that encourage and foster a sustainable future. While not all of these programs explicitly refer to sustainability, together they encourage sustainable development. The EPA sustainability Web site provides easy access to many of these resources for institutions, communities, and individuals.

While recognizing the momentous progress on environmental issues since its founding in 1970, the EPA has begun to assess how it can enhance its current approaches to meet ever more daunting challenges. Its Science Advisory Board, composed of distinguished non–EPA scientists, has been prodding the evolution of sustainability at the EPA, urging the agency to support advances in science and engineering as the foundation of a sustainable future. The EPA's Office of Research and Development (ORD) is leading the EPA's efforts to understand sustainability, create solutions, and measure progress. ORD is committed to advancing science and crafting decision tools for long-term environmental solutions.

Toward this end, ORD has begun to outline a new research strategy for sustainability. A key element of this emerging strategy is the development of new materials and industrial processes to enhance economic growth and minimize environmental risks. Progress is being made in the development of safer chemicals, products that are less material-intensive, and more efficient manufacturing processes designed through "green" chemistry and engineering. Research in these areas can lead to resource conservation and reduced reliance on hazardous substances.

ORD has also undertaken several initiatives to make science and technology more effective elements in decision-making. As it identifies and develops the science and technology for sustainability, ORD has the potential to provide the framework for the EPA's future decision-making. In 2004 ORD launched the following initiatives in institutional collaboration, technology, and education.

- In partnership with the EPA's Office of Policy, Economics, and Innovation and the Office of Regional Operations, ORD created the Collaborative Science and Technology Network for Sustainability (CNS). This program of grants encourages innovative thinking about practical applications of science and engineering to planning and decision-making. Projects are regional in scale and focus on the long-term sustainability of resources in a broader systems context, such as a watershed, urban built environment, and industrial network. Projects address the environmental, economic, and social dimensions of sustainability. The CNS program leverages the growing enthusiasm for sustainable solutions throughout the country by supporting cooperative efforts among government agencies at all levels, academic institutions, nonprofit groups, and private firms.

- The Environmental Technology Council was established to shape and coordinate the EPA's technology programs. It facilitates innovative technological solutions to environmental problems and challenges. It has identified ten priority environmental problems in which a focus on technology can bring improved results, and is collaborating with industry and other stakeholders to advance technology solutions that are most likely to lead to significant environmental improvement.

- In early 2004, the EPA launched the P3 national student design competition for sustainability, emphasizing considerations for people, prosperity, and the planet.

- The EPA has solicited proposals to benchmark the integration of sustainability into engineering curricula at U.S. institutions of higher education. This project will identify and recognize engineering administrators and faculty who have significantly contributed to advancing engineering education for sustainability. This program will encourage the integration of sustainability into higher education by spotlighting successful programs and effective leaders.

- International collaboration and international cooperation will be an important element of the EPA's research strategy for sustainability. These activities reflect the view that sustainability can be a positive stimulus for innovation and a means to foster integrated decision-making. Striving for sustainable development pushes the frontiers of science and business management and encourages collaborative decision-making. The goal of sustainability can therefore advance U.S. science and technology and be an important driver to shape future environmental policy.

Regional Environmental Vulnerability Assessments at the EPA

Human activities often place severe strains on the ecological systems of which people are an integral part. The impacts are not uniformly distributed across landscapes and regions (defined here as multistate areas). Better planning requires the development of an overview of the environmental condition of regions and how ecological resources are likely to change as a result of society's actions. The EPA's Regional Vulnerability Assessment (ReVA) program is designed to produce the methods needed to understand a region's environmental quality and its spatial pattern. The objective is to assist decision makers in making more informed decisions and in estimating the large-scale changes that might result from their actions. Its Web site (http://amethyst .epa.gov/revatoolkit/welcome.jsp) includes an introduction to the ReVA approach and an overview of the ReVA tools and their applications.

Vulnerability is the degree to which a system is likely to experience harm as a result of exposure to perturbations or stress. For example, degraded stream water quality and polluted air are analogous to harm to human health in that there are a bewildering number of factors that contribute to problems in complex ways that are difficult to understand. A doctor monitors the health of a person through indicators such as blood pressure, blood tests, or other examinations. Taking into account factors such as family history, obesity, and smoking, the doctor can determine the most probable health risks a person faces. Precise predictive models do not exist, but given a large enough group, the likelihood of developing health problems can be determined.

Regional vulnerability can be assessed in much the same way. Sensitivities to particular stressors—inherent properties that predispose an organism or an ecological system to problems—can be identified by studying places in which similar organisms or systems were affected by those same stressors in the past. Based on this information, one can determine the likelihood of future problems even if there are no precise predictions that the exact conditions will occur in any specific location.

Regional vulnerability assessment is an approach used to evaluate the risk of harm to human health and the environment from such stressors as pollution and habitat loss. Vulnerability considers both the quality of the valued resources and the intensity of the stressors. For example, heavily urbanized areas are not considered to be vulnerable because they have already lost most of their valued natural resources, and therefore are not sensitive to further loss. (This may also reflect the antiurban bias of the EPA and the environmental movement generally.) Highland areas that are inaccessible to most human activities retain high levels of resources, and are unlikely to be seriously damaged by continued human land use changes. Those involved in environmental and resource management are always confronted by more problems than they can address with available time and resources. The type of information that ReVA provides can assist managers in concentrating their limited time and money on areas that still support valued resources and are already subjected to stress. Action in these areas can produce real improvements in ecological system health.

For the pilot study, the watershed was chosen as the spatial unit for all analyses. This was a logical unit for assessing environmental quality because there are defined boundaries. It would also be possible to deal with the data by using the county as the spatial unit if the end point of an assessment was socioeconomic in nature. Smaller spatial units are not uniformly available across a region and could be overly sensitive to limits in the spatial accuracy of many variables. Larger spatial units would decrease the ability to discern spatial patterns of environmental quality.

Once the data set was assembled, a correlation analysis was performed to screen the data. The analysis identified highly related variables. High correlation coefficients may indicate that two variables are actually two different measurements of the same underlying ecological process. If this occurs, one of the variables can be dropped from the data set. In other cases high correlation may simply indicate that high values of two variables tend to co-occur in the same watershed. If the variables measure different aspects of the underlying ecology, they are kept in the data set. However, it must be remembered that statistical analysis of the data set will be affected by these high correlations because it is usually assumed that variables are independent.

The next step was to code the data so that they could be combined in various ways. Some variables, such as the number of exotic species, may range from 0 to 10. Other variables, such as human population density, may range from 50 to 2,000 people per acre. To facilitate integration across different variables, ReVA codes all data from 0 to 1. A value of 0 indicates the best possible environmental conditions. Thus the highest value for each resource across the region is assigned a value of 0 and the lowest value of each stressor is assigned a value of 0. A value of 1 indicates the worst conditions. Thus, the lowest value for resources and the highest value for stressors are assigned a value of 1.

The assessment approaches developed by ReVA enable decision makers to view changing environmental conditions from a number of perspectives, ranging from a broad overview to focused views held by stakeholders with varying priorities. There is value in looking at the broad view, even for local decision-making. A broad-scale view provides context for local problems, provides information about the extent of the problems, and helps to identify how to address them (strategic planning). The broad scale also helps to focus on where problems may occur in the future, especially those related to broad-scale changes that progress across the landscape, such as land use change, regional air quality, and the spread of exotic pests. These approaches also allow identification of potential opportunities for improving conditions on the ground. For example, it is possible to identify areas where restoration efforts will best enhance habitat connectivity, thus protecting native migratory species. And, perhaps most important, these approaches can help identify where closer looks are needed, making it possible to focus limited resources in areas where they can do the most good.

Both human communities and ecological systems can be stressed as a consequence of human actions. For example, poorly planned economic development can cause exposure to pollution, pests, and diseases. A healthy, resilient ecological system or human community can absorb a lot of stress and continue to function fairly normally. However, an ecological system or human community that has been stressed by past events will be more vulnerable to future disturbances. For example, a wetland that is already stressed from a drought will have a harder time surviving an influx of toxic chemicals introduced by upstream agricultural activities. A forest that has been damaged by acid rain will have difficulty recovering from overuse by humans and overbrowsing by deer. A child who has been exposed to pesticides or other toxic chemicals in the home will be more susceptible to health problems caused by poor air quality.

There are so many environmental problems and so little time, money, and staff available to deal with them. To make real progress in addressing these problems, efficient use of limited management resources must be focused.

Some way to prioritize competing problems in order to get a good return on management investments is needed. Environmental vulnerability assessment is a promising approach to prioritization.

Different stresses have different impacts on the vulnerability of a region's watersheds to radical change. These impacts can be identified by using different assessment strategies. When seeking compromises among different interest groups, decision makers commonly have to deal with different views of the environment. For example, fishing interests may be primarily concerned with maintaining high aquatic biodiversity. Hikers and bird-watchers may be most interested in preserving areas of intact forest. Still others may be most concerned about dealing with urban sprawl and population growth. It may be possible to reach a compromise using the ReVA tool kit if it evolves to include urban areas. The decision maker might, for example, survey the interest groups and ask them to rate various factors. Based on the results, the decision maker can produce a map identifying areas of greatest concern to all groups. Environmental policy makers may be faced with decisions about where to focus conservation efforts. The ReVA tool kit can assist in the planning effort by locating areas in greatest need of protection.

Different conservation actions may be needed to protect terrestrial versus aquatic resources. Terrestrial systems may require zoning regulations to control development or forest harvest regulations to prevent fragmentation. In contrast, aquatic systems may require control of nutrient inputs or elimination of invading exotic species. It is useful, therefore, to look at both the overall regional pattern and to focus separately on the terrestrial and aquatic systems.

The ReVA tool kit produces a map showing the watersheds in greatest need of conservation in blue. The user is encouraged to explore the following options:

- Assessing the condition of regional components. The ReVA assessment of the Mid-Atlantic region emphasized the integration of all available data to provide an overview of environmental conditions. However, the decision maker may be dealing with a problem that emphasizes only one of the functional components, such as the terrestrial, aquatic, or social system. The ReVA tool kit permits isolation of each of these components and examination of them separately, using two complementary methods. Greatest confidence can be placed in the results when the methods agree.

- Estimating the effects of restoration. The decision maker may be attempting to motivate community cooperation in restoration efforts. The ReVA tool kit can help by showing how much environmental quality will improve through restoration activities.

- Evaluating the effects of individual stressors. Environmental degradation results from the simultaneous impact of many different stressors. Planning requires strategies for addressing all of the potential impacts. The ReVA tool kit can help by allowing the planner to estimate how each stressor will affect future conditions.

- Estimating the improvements through mitigation. Mitigation is a complex issue for the regional decision maker that may involve negotiation and compromise as much as enforcing legal restrictions. The ReVA tool kit can assist in this complex process by estimating how various mitigation strategies will affect both regional and local environmental quality. Often such information is needed to motivate cooperative responses from individuals and commercial enterprises.

Sustainable Environmental Systems is the management of environmental problems at the systems level in a way fully accounting for the multidimensional nature of the environment. This includes socioeconomic dimensions as well as the usual physical and life science aspects of environmental problems. The environment and any problems that arise in relation to it are complex and multidimensional, and their management must be at an appropriate level of sophistication. The point is that there is no environmental problem that has a single causative source. For instance, air pollution is not due only to the existence of automobiles, but to the existence of automobiles coupled with the need to drive long distances. The long-term management of environmental problems including air pollution must, therefore, encompass not only technological approaches (e.g., less polluting automobiles) but other aspects as well. These other aspects can be appropriate economic incentive systems to discourage excessive automobile driving, location of services and employment so as to minimize the need to drive long distances, and legal structures that support these measures. Sustainable Environmental Systems is at its core an effort to create the necessary methodology for multidimensional environmental management. A protocol for a particular problem might include the use of technology (e.g., less polluting automobiles) coupled with a market incentive system (e.g., tradable permits for air emissions) that are cognizant of existing law (e.g., in terms of freedom of movement and environmental regulations), and an ecological system that is in a publicly and biologically acceptable state.

The Sustainable Environmental Systems Research Program is the logical and natural outgrowth of the pollution prevention research effort that has been under way at the EPA for a number of years. As such it draws on the spirit of the pollution prevention research strategy and much of the research work done in pollution prevention. Pollution prevention is chiefly concerned with the development and implementation of environmentally better technologies and procedures. The socioeconomic aspect is mainly focused on efforts to encourage the public to adopt environmentally better practices. Sustainable Environmental Systems simply takes the next logical step by considering the full complexity of the interactions between the different parts of the system (socioeconomic, technological, and ecological) that lead to environmental problems, and then attempting to develop a strategy to address the problems.

Sustainable Environmental Systems is important because environmental problems do not respond well to one-dimensional environmental management approaches. As discussed in Chapter 4, this can be the case in many environmental difficulties. For example, in the case of air pollution, the development of less polluting automobiles can lead, and has led, to an initial and significant drop in air pollution. But then pollution levels slowly rise as the number of miles driven by more and more automobiles continues to increase, necessitating further measures. This cycle can continue, rather like a race. This would probably not be the case if modest improvements in automobile technology were coupled with economic incentives to reduce driving, appropriate land use planning to reduce the need to drive, and legal structures to support these (as already discussed). The problems with one-dimensional environmental management are particularly evident in the case of more subtle problems such as nonpoint source pollutants (nutrients), ecological restoration efforts, and excessive storm water flows. The need for multidimensional environmental management is painfully clear in these cases.

Although storm water management ostensibly occurs in many jurisdictions, the design criteria employed may exacerbate stream degradation—for example, channel scouring and ecological (aquatic habitat) degradation along with serious water quality problems. In areas with combined sanitary sewers, the water quality problem has led to EPA enforcement action in most metropolitan areas. One reason why nonpoint environmental problems are difficult to regulate is that the legal responsibility is diffused throughout a region involving many municipalities and many property owners. These are cases where there is a pressing need for strategies that cost-efficiently manage and prevent the problem over the long term.

The goal of the Sustainable Environmental Systems Research Program is to construct the knowledge base necessary to engineer stable management schemes for environmental problems. The chief goal is development of generic methodology in a way that can address entire classes of environmental problems. This effort will span about nine years. The core of the program is the Sustainable Environments Branch in the Sustainable Technology Division at the National Risk Management Research Laboratory in the Office of Research and Development. The research program is structured so that it taps into physical and human resources from other divisions within the National Risk Management Research Laboratory and other laboratories within the Office of Research and Development, other EPA offices, and other government agencies.

Specifically, there is a collaborative relationship between the EPA grants program at the National Center for Environmental Research and the Sustainable Environments Branch. Essentially, the latter will tap into research efforts being conducted under other programs so as to minimize duplication of effort. There are also collaborative relationships with the Mid-Atlantic Integrated Assessment Group in EPA Region 3, the Critical Ecosystems Team in EPA Region 5, and the Canaan Valley Institute, the Agricultural Research Service, and several local government agencies in Ohio, including the Hamilton County engineer, the Metropolitan Sewer District of Greater Cincinnati, and the Hamilton County Soil and Water Conservation District. The Sustainable Environments Branch is organized into five research teams representing five research areas: environmental economics, sustainable technology, law, hydrology and land use, and sustainability theory. Each of these research teams has collaborations in various states of progress.

The mission of the Sustainable Environments program at the EPA (http://www.epa.gov/ORD/NRMRL/Std/seb) is to construct a strategy for sustainable environmental systems management using economics, water resource and land use planning, physical and ecological theory, law, and technological methods and knowledge implemented through computer-based tools, field data, and human experience to reduce risks to human health and the ecology.

Although this may seem like a very broad mission, it is important to note that the objective is not to solve every problem, but to develop the knowledge base necessary for solving a class of problems. To accomplish this mission, the branch will use models, measured data, and other methods, including case studies. The case studies, however, are not so much intended to provide solutions to actual problems as to illustrate the use of methodologies developed under the research program.

The research staff in the Sustainable Environments Branch is organized into five research teams based on a single discipline or a cluster of related disciplines. However, they function in a collaborative fashion such that any of the projects within any given team will typically involve staff members from other teams (as needed). These five research teams are the primary groups responsible for meeting the annual performance goals and annual deliverables under the Sustainable Environmental Systems Multiyear Plan. This collaborative network is being systematically and deliberately constructed through contacts at the researcher, branch, division, and laboratory levels. The work from completely different disciplines is incorporated in a systematic and comprehensive way, with all materials on an equal footing. Every discipline commonly uses results from other disciplines; for example, engineers use results from economics, economists use engineering, and they all consider the law. But this is not the same as merging methodologies on an equal footing. The integration of methodologies from different disciplines will, therefore, pose a significant challenge, but it is the heart of the research program.

More generally but perhaps more important, the Sustainable Environmental Systems Research Program will establish the basis of a new and badly needed science. There seems to be a wide consensus on the need for multidisciplinary or multidimensional environmental management, but the necessary methodologies and ideas for actually doing it are not available. This is, therefore, a research program where a deliberate effort is being made to simultaneously provide practical tools and create new knowledge.

Current EPA Programs Related to Sustainability

The EPA has integrated some aspects of sustainability into its present programs. To the extent that the protection and preservation of the environment is part of its legal mission, the EPA does move in the general direction of sustainability. Water is one example.

The storm water pollution problem has two main components: the increased volume and rate of runoff from impervious surfaces, and the concentration of pollutants in the runoff. Both are directly related to development in urban and urbanizing areas. Together these components cause changes in hydrology and water quality that result in a variety of problems, including habitat modification and loss, increased flooding, decreased aquatic biological diversity, and increased sedimentation and erosion. Effective management of storm water runoff offers a multitude of possible benefits, including protection of wetlands and aquatic ecosystems, improved quality of receiving bodies of water, conservation of water resources, protection of public health, and flood control. In addition to chemical pollutants in storm water, the physical aspects related to urban runoff, such as erosion and scour, can significantly affect a receiving water's fish population and associated habitat. Alterations in hydraulic characteristics of streams receiving runoff include higher peak flow rates, increased frequency and duration of bankfull and subbankfull flows, increased occurrences of downstream flooding, and reduced baseflow levels. Traditional flood control measures that rely on the detention (storage) of the peak flow (referred to as peak shaving) have characterized many storm water management approaches, have generally not targeted pollutant reduction, and in many cases have exacerbated the problems associated with changes in hydrology and hydraulics. The EPA recommends an approach that integrates the control of storm water peak flows and the protection of natural channels to sustain the physical and chemical properties of aquatic habitat.

Since its inception in 1995, the EPA's brownfields program has grown into a proven, results-oriented program that has changed the way contaminated property is perceived, addressed, and managed. It is designed to empower states, communities, and other stakeholders in economic redevelopment to work together in a timely manner to prevent, assess, safely clean up, and sustainably reuse brownfields. A brownfield is a property the expansion, redevelopment, or reuse of which may be complicated by the presence or potential presence of a hazardous substance, pollutant, or contaminant. It is estimated that there are more than 450,000 brownfields in the United States. Cleaning up and reinvesting in these properties increases local tax bases, facilitates job growth, utilizes existing infrastructure, takes development pressures off undeveloped, open land, and both improves and protects the environment. Initially, the EPA provided small amounts of seed money to local governments that launched hundreds of two-year brownfield pilot projects. Through passage of the Small Business Liability Relief and Brownfields Revitalization Act, effective polices that EPA had developed over the years became law. The brownfields law expanded the EPA's assistance by providing new tools for the public and private sectors to promote sustainable brownfields cleanup and reuse. (See discussion of brownfields in Chapter 3.)

Energy powers homes, businesses, and industries. The energy decisions made every day encourage the development of new power sources, each with a different impact on the environment. Today, more than ever, electricity consumers have the ability—and the interest—to choose clean, low-impact energy options, including renewable energy and highly efficient combined heat and power. The EPA's clean energy programs are designed to help consumers improve their knowledge about their clean energy options by providing objective information, creating networks between the public and private sectors, and providing technical assistance. The EPA also offers recognition to leading organizations that adopt clean energy practices.

Consumers increasingly have a choice when they buy electricity. Green power is an environmentally friendly electricity product that is generated from renewable energy sources. Buying green power is easy, and it offers a number of environmental and economic benefits over conventional electricity. The EPA's Green Power Partnership provides assistance and recognition to organizations that demonstrate environmental leadership by choosing green power. Combined heat and power (CHP) is an efficient, clean, and reliable approach to generating power and thermal energy from a single fuel source. By installing a CHP system designed to meet the thermal and electrical base loads of a facility, CHP can increase operational efficiency and decrease energy costs while reducing emissions of greenhouse gases that contribute to the risks of climate change.

The CHP Partnership is a voluntary program that seeks to reduce the environmental impact of power generation by promoting the use of CHP. It works closely with energy users, the CHP industry, state and local governments, and other stakeholders to support the development of new projects and to promote their energy, environmental, and economic benefits.

The EPA also has the Emissions and Generation Resource Integrated Database (eGRID), which provides information on the air quality attributes of almost all the electric power generated in the United States. eGRID provides many search options, including information on individual power plants, generating companies, states, and regions of the power grid.

Another program designed to move sustainable practices forward at the EPA is the Clean Materials Initiative. Part of the initiative is the Orphaned Sources Program, a cooperative effort with the Conference of Radiation

Control Program Directors (CRCPD) that is designed to assist states in retrieving and disposing of radioactive sources that find their way into nonnuclear facilities. Radioactive waste is antithetical to sustainability because it is very damaging to life for a very long time. The EPA is funding the first national program to systematically address the problem of "orphan" radioactive sources. The Orphan Sources Initiative is a cooperative effort with the CRCPD that is designed to assist states in retrieving and disposing of radioactive sources that find their way into nonnuclear facilities, particularly scrap yards, steel mills, and municipal waste disposal facilities. The program will also help people at these facilities recognize and safely secure radioactive sources. One goal of the program is to establish a nationwide disposal system that provides quick and effective identification, removal, and disposal of orphan sources that, if undetected, can present health hazards and cost facilities millions of dollars in lost production and decontamination expenses. Disposal may include recycling, reuse, or disposal. Another goal for the program is to provide technical assistance to those who may dissolve unwanted radioactive sources at their facilities.

Radioactive sources are found in some types of specialized industrial devices, such as those used for measuring the moisture content of soil or density or thickness of materials. Usually, a small quantity of the radioactive material is sealed in a metal casing and enclosed in a housing that prevents the escape of the radiation. As long as the sources remain sealed, the housing remains intact, and the devices are handled and used properly, there is no health risk from the radioactive source within. In fact, manufacturers of these devices must demonstrate their safety in order to receive a license to manufacture and sell them. Purchasers of the devices must be licensed to use the device in the intended manner, and are required to dispose of the sources safely and legally.

"Orphan" equipment contains a sealed source that is disposed of improperly or sent for recycling as scrap metal. Or the sealed source may have been lost and have ended up in a metal recycling facility, or may be in the possession of someone who is not licensed to handle it. Specially licensed sources bear identifying markings that can be used to trace these sources to their original owners. However, some sources do not have these markings or the markings have become obliterated. In these cases, the sources are referred to as "orphan sources" because no known owner can be identified. They are one of the most frequently reported radioactive contaminants in shipments received by scrap metal facilities. If a steel mill melts a source, it contaminates the entire batch of metal, the processing equipment, and the facility. More important, it can result in the exposure of workers and community members to radiation.

Sources have contaminated recycled metal. There have been at least twenty-six recorded accidental meltings of radioactive material in the United States since 1983. Contamination of the recycled metal produced by the steel mill and subsequently used in consumer products also could occur. Decontaminating a steel mill once this has happened is extremely expensive, averaging

$12–15 million, and causes unnecessary human health risks. One such case happened in Texas in 1996 when a cobalt-60 source was stolen from a storage facility and sold as scrap metal. Workers at and customers of the scrap yard and law enforcement officers who conducted investigations at the scrap yard were exposed to the source and may have received dangerous doses of radiation. No measurement of community exposure was taken.

Scrap yards and disposal sites attempt to detect orphan sources and other contaminated metals by screening incoming materials with sensitive radiation detectors before they can enter the processing stream and cause contamination. Unfortunately, the protective housings that make the sources safe also make detection extremely difficult. Further, if the source is buried in a load of steel, the steel acts as further shielding, making detection nearly impossible. Consequently, there is always a potential for sources to become mixed with and to contaminate scrap metal. The EPA is following research into improved detection capabilities that can help scrap recyclers detect sources before they cause harm.

Better training in identification of and response to orphan radioactive sources will result in a reduction of individuals' radiation exposure. Making information on disposal and reuse options available to as wide an audience as possible will increase the likelihood that sources will be captured before falling out of regulatory control. The Nuclear Regulatory Commission is planning to expand its existing database to include radioactive sources nationwide. It will contain information that will facilitate the reuse of sources by companies who need them and will combine several sources for more cost-effective disposal. The collection and disposition of orphan sources will prevent individuals from inadvertently being exposed to radiation.

The EPA is very concerned with finding and securing lost "orphaned" sources. However, in order to address this problem completely, it is necessary to prevent radioactive sources from falling out of regulatory control in the first place. The EPA is investigating the feasibility of tracking high-activity stationary sources to prevent inadvertent or intentional loss. It is also promoting prevention of losses by identifying legal and economical methods for disposal of unwanted radioactive sources. As more devices involving nonradioactive technologies become available as alternatives to the radioactive source devices, there will be a need for these disposal options.

The EPA tries to ensure that imported metal is not contaminated with radioactivity. Scrap metal recycling is an increasingly international industry. Because the United States imports millions of tons of scrap metal, semifinished metal, and metal products each year, it is important to ensure that this metal is not contaminated with radioactivity.

With the breakdown of the economy and of controls at nuclear facilities in the former Soviet Union, and increasing cross-border trade, the potential for contaminated metals to enter the international steel supply is increasing. In some cases, radioactive scrap metal from foreign facilities is manufactured into intermediate or finished products before export to the United States. For example, a steel fabrication plant in Mississippi detected small amounts of radioactive contamination in steel plates imported from Bulgaria. Fortunately, reported incidents are isolated and the radiation that has been detected in imported metals to date has not been at levels that are currently considered dangerous (that is, levels are below the threshold requiring Superfund action). However, there is always the possibility that more highly contaminated materials could be exported to the United States, and the EPA is working on several approaches to prevent their entry.

The EPA is working with the International Atomic Energy Agency (IAEA) and other federal agencies to ensure that a consistent standard is applied to all materials released internationally. This will facilitate the goal of protecting the U.S. public against contaminated material from foreign countries. Through the IAEA, the EPA is collaborating with representatives of other industrialized countries to develop international radiological screening guidelines to ensure that metals will not contain harmful levels of radioactive contamination. Although the IAEA recommendations will be voluntary, many countries are concerned about radioactively contaminated metal. Thus, the EPA anticipates broad adoption of the IAEA recommendations. When finalized by the IAEA, these guidelines will form the first of three protective barriers against the potential for radioactively contaminated metal imports. The second barrier is formed by U.S. Customs officials who use radiation detection equipment to screen incoming materials. The final barrier is formed by the detection equipment used by scrap metal recyclers to screen incoming shipments of metal.

Facilities operated by the federal government and private industry currently generate scrap metal from routine operations as well as from facility closure (decommissioning). Metal from these facilities falls into one of the following three categories:

1. Metal that has never been exposed to radiation and can be recycled like any other scrap metal;

2. Metal that has been exposed to some radiation, but can be cleaned to natural background levels, with its cleanliness verified before its release to scrap metal dealers;

3. Metals that have been exposed to high levels of radiation, cannot be cleaned, and are not candidates for recycling. The only appropriate disposition for these metals is isolation and burial. The preparation of contaminated scrap metal from domestic nuclear facilities for recycling is conducted under guidance developed by the Nuclear Regulatory Commission (NRC) and the Department of Energy (DOE) in the early 1970s. These guidelines contain clearance levels for individual radionuclides. The clearance levels

were set at the lowest level that could be distinguished from background by detection equipment, and thus are technology-based guidelines. They apply to materials being cleaned that have only surface contamination, but not to metals that have been contaminated throughout (volumetrically contaminated metals).

In the United States, the release of materials (including scrap metal) with radioactive surface contamination from commercial facilities, such as power plants, is controlled by the NRC's Regulatory Guide 1.86, "Termination of Operating Licenses for Nuclear Reactors." The DOE incorporated most of the NRC guidance for use by DOE facilities in DOE Order 5400.5, "Radiation Protection of the Public and the Environment." The clearance levels in the NRC guidelines for surface contamination are based on the detection capabilities of existing measurement technologies. These existing guidelines apply only to exposure from single types of radionuclides and do not limit the cumulative exposure that might be of concern when more than one radionuclide is present. None of the available standards for releasing materials for general use address materials that are "volumetrically contaminated," meaning that they have become contaminated throughout. However, DOE or NRC may analyze volumetrically contaminated materials from the facilities that they regulate on a case-by-case basis to determine if the materials are sufficiently clean to be released. Nuclear facilities also can recycle surface or volumetrically contaminated materials for their own internal use. Materials may be decontaminated or recycled to make new products acceptable for use on-site under an NRC license or DOE order.

Future environmental solutions to current problems will require imagination and creativity. Photograph of "Imagine," Central Park, New York City. (Photograph by Brent Merrill)

The EPA will need to devote greater effort to understanding risks posed by cumulative exposures and by interactions between hazardous agents, including combined exposures to chemicals and radiation. There is a significant but necessary challenge to harmonize radiation and chemical regulatory approaches based on the careful walking of a tightrope between chemical and radiation models, parameters, risk calculations, and measurement techniques. Over time, these principles can bridge the historical separation between radiation protection and the larger area of environmental protection that the EPA oversees.

The EPA has developed a relatively new culture around its programs for considering sustainability. This focus seems to be developing in isolation from other important challenges, such as environmental justice and community-based environmental planning. Even wonderful environmental concepts such as sustainability are not immune from human foibles of racism and unrestrained, short-term economic development. Storm water management, urban revitalization and cleanup, energy regulation, and radiation control may be important bridges between these inescapable challenges.

CUMULATIVE EMISSIONS AND RISKS

The United States has had industrial emissions since the mid-1800s. Spewing smokestacks were once seen as a sign of progress and economic development. Since that time, technology has vastly increased both industrial productivity and industrial pollutants. When the EPA was created in 1970, many emissions had had over a century to accumulate, especially in populated areas. In many communities, population growth and sprawl such as land development had both increased waste creation and brought people closer to waste sites. In many states (e.g., Virginia) it was not until the late 1980s that "dumps" became regulated as landfills. These constantly accumulating by-products of industrial expansion never go away, and remain in place unless they are disposed of properly.

As these wastes have increased in volume and begun to infiltrate other parts of ecosystems through both vertical and horizontal geological migration, dissipation into air, and following water pathways, more people have been exposed to them, creating cumulative risks. This has increased public consciousness and uncovered disparities in exposure by race and income. (See discussion of environmental justice above.) It also exposes regulatory gaps in environmental protection policies and pushes the policies to continue evolving. For example, under the National Environmental Policy Act (NEPA) it is not necessary to provide a full-blown environmental impact statement unless there is a finding of significant impacts on the environment. Most accumulated emissions do have a significant impact on the environment, and therefore require the full environmental impact assessment. Further, the political process has categorically excluded many activities that have a significant impact on the environment from NEPA environmental impact assessments. Many of these exclusions apply to urban areas. As time passes, the EPA will face significant challenges to most of its policies as emissions, impacts, and risks accumulate.

The Beginning

The Food Quality Protection Act, which became law in August 1996, requires the EPA to consider the cumulative effects on human health that can result from pesticides and other substances that have a common mechanism of toxicity (i.e., act the same way in the body). Through cumulative risk assessment the EPA will be able to determine if the risks posed by a group of pesticides that act in the same way in the body meet the current safety standard of "reasonable certainty of no harm." Pesticides that meet this standard may successfully complete tolerance reassessment under the Federal Food, Drug, and Cosmetic Act, now closely intertwined with completing reregistration under the Federal Insecticide, Fungicide, and Rodenticide Act.

The Office of Pesticide Programs has developed a framework for conducting cumulative risk assessments. Achieving this framework has required the development of new methods and tools. The EPA began with consideration of what constitutes a common mechanism of toxicity, then moved on to methods for conducting aggregate exposure and risk assessments, and finally examined the cumulative risk assessment process. A common "mechanism of toxicity" group consists of chemicals for which scientifically reliable data demonstrate that the same toxic effect occurs in or at the same organ or tissue by essentially the same sequence of major biochemical events.

Aggregate Exposure and Risk Assessment

As part of the individual chemical risk assessment the EPA performs an aggregate risk assessment, which includes consideration of exposures to the pesticide from food, drinking water, and residual/nonoccupational sources. Basically, aggregate risk assessments simply add up the risks and do not consider issues of synergy, antagonism, or catalysis. Further, it is very difficult to perform an aggregate risk assessment because many emissions into the environment are not regulated unless they exceed a specific, self-reported threshold. The EPA has published guidance on aggregate risk assessment, drinking water exposure assessment, and conducting residential exposure assessments. It also has consulted regarding various aspects of its approach to aggregate risk assessment.

Assessing Cumulative Risk

Assessing cumulative risk involves developing ways to combine exposures to different substances that may have differing degrees of toxicity and be used in various ways at various times of the year. The EPA's guidance has to address how these factors will be handled. The EPA has pursued an open, peer-reviewed process to develop cumulative risk assessment methods and approaches. (The author was one of twelve external peer reviewers.) The EPA has published guidance on cumulative risk assessment, and most of these documents are available on the Web (http://www.epa.gov/osa/spc/htm/2cumrisk.html). They include draft guidance published for comment on June 30, 2000, and revised guidance on cumulative risk assessment published on January 16, 2002.

The EPA has held technical briefings to help explain the methods and issues addressed in the guidance. These represent some of the best sources of information on cumulative risk assessment in the United States.

1999

September 21–24	Proposed Guidance on Cumulative Risk Assessment of Pesticide Chemicals That Have a Common Mechanism of Toxicity
	Issues Pertaining to Hazard and Dose-Response Assessment
December 8–9	Issues Pertaining to Exposure Assessment and Estimating Cumulative Risk: Chapter 4, "Exposure Assessment and Characterization"; Chapter 6, "Estimation and Characterization of Cumulative Risk"

2000

July	Technical briefing on the draft cumulative risk assessment guidance
September 26–29	End Point Selection and Determination of Relative Potency in Cumulative Hazard Assessment: A Pilot Study of Organophosphate Pesticide Chemicals
	Assessing Aggregate and Cumulative Risk Using Life-Line (Hampshire Research Institute)
	CALENDEX Calendar-Based Dietary and Nondietary Aggregate and Cumulative Exposure Software System (Novigen Sciences, Inc.)
December 7–8	Case Study of the Cumulative Risk of 24 Organophosphate Pesticides; Cumulative Risk Assessment Method for Dietary (Food) Exposure; Cumulative Risk Assessment for Residential Exposure; Cumulative Risk Assessment for Drinking Water; Integrated Cumulative Risk Assessment

2001

March 28	LifeLine system operation review and users manual
August 22	Technical briefing on background and hazard methodology—revised relative potency factor paper
September 5–6	Preliminary Cumulative Hazard and Dose-Response Assessment for Organophosphorus Pesticides; Determination of Relative Potency and Points of Departure for Cholinesterase Inhibition
October 3	Technical briefing on background, methods, and data proposed for use in the organophosphate pesticide cumulative exposure assessment for drinking water.
November 15	Technical briefing on food and residential exposure methodologies and approaches to integration of multiple pathways of exposure

2002

January 15	Technical briefing on the preliminary cumulative risk assessment
February 5–8	Organophosphate Pesticides: Preliminary Cumulative Risk Assessment

There is no escape from accumulating emissions, risks, and impacts. Those who are most vulnerable in terms of age, environmental exposure, health, and pregnancy tend to be the first who are impacted by the risks. The EPA's model of risk assessment was originally based on one of the healthiest segments of the U.S. population—the 150-pound white male. Only recently, prompted by demands from the environmental justice movement, have issues of vulnerability have been included in risk assessments at the EPA. Complicating the issue of when accumulated emissions become risks is the dose-response variance in human populations. This is the question of what dose, or what amount of exposure, causes a particular response. There can be large differences in dose-response rates between human populations. There are better cumulative risk assessment models in other countries, such as Canada. Cumulative impacts will be a driving and inescapable challenge to the EPA for the foreseeable future. The stakes are high because cumulative risk assessments may drastically increase industrial, commercial, and municipal environmental regulation. Failure to accurately assess cumulative emissions will hamper policy development in sustainability, environmental justice, and ecosystem approaches.

ECOSYSTEM APPROACHES

As the EPA grows to meet new challenges in environmental protection, questions are raised about the single-medium approach to environmental regulation. The EPA bases its risk assessment on single-pathway, single-medium, and single-chemical human health risk assessment. However, as human populations continue to grow and more emissions continue to accumulate—and sometimes bioaccumulate—questions focus on better ways to analyze risk and to control it. This is particularly true in most approaches to sustainability. Currently, managed ecosystems such as croplands, estuarine aquacultural systems, and forest plantations are used for producing necessary consumer goods. These intensively managed ecosystems are embedded in the matrix of less managed ecosystems. A good way to track accumulating pollutants from less managed ecosystems in order to minimize their effect on managed ecosystems is to incorporate an ecosystem risk analysis.

With limited understanding of the importance of diversity and complexity in ecological systems, utilitarian management has generally proceeded on the notion that it is possible to simplify the structure and composition of ecosystems in order to achieve efficient production of specific goods—such as timber, fish, or agricultural crops—at no risk to sustainability. The grossly inadequate understanding of the important role of natural disturbance processes for sustained ecosystem function certainly supports "object oriented" management protocols for wilderness parks, which deny that their ever-changing ecological understanding and models of ecosystem functioning are provisional and subject to change. However, mechanisms for adjustment of management goals and strategies as ecosystems change are often limited or absent. No fewer than eighteen federal agencies have committed to the principles of ecosystem management. Elements of ecosystem management are mandated for federal lands in a number of important pieces of legislation. Ecosystem-level science, such as studies of entire watersheds, estuaries, or oceans, has provided many important basic concepts for ecosystem management. However, an understanding of populations, communities, and landscapes is no less relevant.

Ignorance of the importance of processes operating over wide ranges of spatial and temporal scales has permitted definition of the boundaries of management jurisdictions with little or no reference to such processes. Rivers may provide convenient boundaries between countries, counties, and other political jurisdictions but, because they divide watersheds, they are very poor boundaries for managing most ecosystem processes. The 200-mile territorial fishing limits were established with little reference to the behavior of the resources to be managed or the processes affecting those resources. Budgeting strategies that are focused on fiscal years or the timing of political elections often drive short-term decisions regarding natural resource use that is not congruent with processes that operate over decades and centuries.

Ecosystem function depends on the ecosystem's structure, diversity, and integrity. While human interests may focus on a relatively small subset of the organisms or processes operating in an ecosystem, the overall complexity of such a system is critical to its sustainability. Thus, maintenance of biological diversity is an integral component of ecosystem management plans. Biological diversity is the variety of life and its processes, including the variety of living organisms and the genetic differences among them, as well as the variety of habitats, communities, ecosystems, and

Some species are indicators of ecosystem degradation and are used in ecological risk assessment. (Jupiter Images)

landscapes in which they occur. Included in this definition of biological diversity is recognition of the importance of biotically derived physical structures such as logs and corals.

Some principles of ecosystem management include the following:

- Transparency. Operate in an open and accountable manner, providing the public with accurate, understandable information it can use to make decisions and evaluate the performance of organizations. Assure easy public access to up-to-date information on the state of chemicals and radiation in the environment. Avoid unnecessary secrecy, carefully balancing any risks to security that open access to information may pose with the social advantages of greater transparency.

- Inclusive science and policy. Maintain a balanced approach that insists on the importance of sound science but also acknowledges the importance of inclusiveness. Engage a variety of disciplines, viewpoints, and stakeholders, involve younger scientists, and bring to the table people with nonmainstream views as long as their approach is evidence-oriented. Employ alternative dispute resolution techniques to reach greater agreement on especially contentious issues.

- Pollution and exposure prevention. Adopt practices to reduce at the source the amount of any hazardous substance or pollutant being released into the environment. Whenever feasible, eliminate the use of hazardous materials. Adopt practices that reduce exposures to hazardous substances and pollutants whose presence cannot be eliminated.

The ecosystem approach chafes under the political and legal basis for the EPA and current systems of establishing political boundaries. Land, air, and water do not follow the political boundaries of municipalities, states, EPA regions, or nations. There have been proposals for changing the EPA regions to bioregions. This would allow the EPA to carry out its current regulatory and statutory missions and would enable ecosystem approaches to move toward implementation. A full ecosystem approach would also require a substantial advancement in intergovernmental relationships in environmental policy-making, among them the inclusion of land use planning and urban areas. It would also require changes in current patterns of consumption by most people. Current environmental policy coerces behavior change by threats of punishment, such as permit revocation or fines. This would be difficult to enforce on an individual level. Individuals must be persuaded, and for them to do so, they must both have the capacity to understand their behavior and must be included in the forums and venues of environmental policy-making. A full ecosystem approach will be a major challenge for the EPA and for society.

Biographies of Important EPA Administrators

Because of the power, authority, and potential for creative leadership, the EPA has attracted some charismatic individuals to its head position of administrator.

This position requires leadership and vision as well as significant engagement with Congress, the president, and several other political constituencies. Some EPA administrators have had strong industry relations. Others have worked in government and in nonprofit environmental advocacy groups. As the EPA has grown and evolved, so has its management and the requirements for administrator. The EPA that was created by President Nixon was not politicized at first because Democrats and Republicans agreed on environmental policy. The EPA became politicized when the Reagan administration attempted to reorient it. Such politicization involved both increasing the number of political appointees and altering career–noncareer relations in government. Before Reagan, the people who worked for Gerald Ford's administrator, Russell Train, had kept working for Jimmy Carter's administrator, Douglas Costle. After Reagan, polarization has continued. For example, until the Clinton administration, the U.S. Forest Service had only a single political appointee, traditionally from its career ranks. Some suggest that President Clinton's selection of the chief of the Forest Service and the deputy chief in charge of the National Forest System from outside the organization represented "politicization," even though these officials were career federal employees. The Clinton administration, particularly Vice President Al Gore, made a legitimate political decision to change the Forest Service by emphasizing the preservation mission and deemphasizing timber harvesting. The administrator and his or her Schedule C political appointees now operate in a very political environment with an occasionally hostile Congress.

There have been eleven administrators of the EPA since it was formed. Two of them served two terms. There have been eleven acting administrators, who serve when there is no appointed administrator. The Office of the Administrator provides the overall supervision of the EPA. The administrator is responsible to the president and is assisted by the deputy administrator and staff offices, including Administrative Law Judges, Civil Rights, Small and Disadvantaged Business Utilization, Science Advisory Board, Executive Support, Executive Secretariat, Cooperative Environmental Management, Pollution Prevention Policy Staff, and Environmental Appeals Board. In addition, the administrator is assisted by associate administrators for congressional and intergovernmental relations; communications, education, and media relations; and policy, economics, and innovation. (See discussion in Chapter 1.) Biographies of six administrators who left their indelible mark on the EPA follows.

CAROL M. BROWNER (1993–2001)

From 1991 to 1993, Carol Browner was secretary of Florida's Department of Environmental Regulation, one of the nation's largest state environmental agencies. She won praise for dealing effectively with difficult issues involving wetland protection, hazardous-waste disposal, and cleanup of the Everglades. From 1986 to 1988, she worked in Washington, D.C., for Senator Lawton Chiles. She also served as legislative director for Senator Al Gore.

Carol M. Browner grew up near the Everglades. Her parents were professors at Miami-Dade Community College. Browner graduated from the University of Florida in 1977 and then earned a degree from its law school. She served as general counsel for the Florida House of Representatives Government Operations Committee in 1980. She then worked for Citizen Action, a grassroots consumer group in Washington, D.C., where she met her husband, Michael Podhorzer. They have a son, Zachary. In April 1997, Browner received the Mother of the Year Award from the National Mother's Day Committee for her dedication to preserving a safer, healthier world for America's children. She also has received *Glamour* magazine's Woman of the Year Award, the South Florida Chapter of the Audubon Society's Guy M. Bradley Lifetime Achievement Award, and the Lifetime Environmental Achievement Award from the New York State Bar Association.

Carol M. Browner. (U.S. Environmental Protection Agency Archives)

Appointed by President Clinton in January 1993, Browner was the longest-serving administrator in the history of the EPA. As EPA administrator, her mission was to protect public health and the environment by safeguarding the nation's air, water, and land from harmful pollution. She was guided by the philosophy that safeguarding the environment means protecting where people live and how they live. It means protecting the health of families and communities. It means providing Americans with real, everyday benefits: fresh air to breathe, clean water to drink, safe food to eat, land on which it is safe to live.

Browner also was guided by the philosophy that the environment and the economy go hand in hand. Tough standards can be set to protect the environment and public health—but this must be done in ways that promote innovation, flexibility, and competitiveness. Guided by these principles, Browner successfully fended off repeated attempts by some in Congress to undermine environmental and public health protections, and secured funding for the Clinton administration's new generation of more commonsense, cost-effective, and protective environmental standards.

Browner made it a top priority to protect the public from breathing polluted air. Under the president's and vice president's leadership, she took the toughest action in a generation to safeguard public health with updated standards for particulate matter (soot) and ozone (smog). The new standards together will provide health benefits to 125 million Americans, including 35 million children. Every year, they will prevent 350,000 cases of aggravated asthma, nearly a million cases of significantly decreased lung function in children, and approximately 15,000 premature deaths. Browner was able to engage the American Lung Association in her advocacy efforts after the petrochemical companies fought hard against this legislation. She expanded the role of the EPA to engage cities, public health, and children on an unprecedented scale.

Browner took a number of other actions to reduce air pollution in cost-effective, commonsense ways, including new partnerships with the automobile industry to produce cleaner cars. She worked closely with Midwestern and Southern states to address the airborne transport of smog, a serious problem in the eastern United States. Browner also approved the Chemical Manufacturing Rule, which will reduce air toxics by 500,000 tons per year and smog-producing chemicals by 1 million tons per year.

Browner moved against one of the nation's most serious threats: global warming. She believes the country, working together, can address this problem in ways that grow the economy and improve U.S. competitiveness. For example, under her leadership, the EPA built partnerships with thousands of businesses and organizations to use energy more efficiently. In 1997 alone, these partnerships prevented the release of nearly 60 million tons of carbon dioxide, the primary contributor to global warming. At the same time, these measures saved businesses and consumers more than $1 billion.

Another priority was protecting the nation from unhealthy drinking water. During Browner's tenure 10 million more Americans received water that meets the EPA water quality standards. In 1996, President Clinton signed the new Safe Drinking Water Act, which includes strong new standards to safeguard public health and the release of consumer confidence reports to update consumers on the health of their water system. President Clinton announced the first public health standards under the act to protect against cryptosporidia, other disease-causing microbes, and potentially harmful by-products of the water treatment process. These standards will strengthen drinking water protection for 140 million Americans—and meet the challenges of the twenty-first century.

Browner led the Clinton administration's efforts for the first comprehensive restoration plan for the Florida Everglades, which will replumb half a century of misguided waterworks to balance future development with the preservation of natural areas, as well as the needs of farms, urban areas, and the natural system. She also established broad protection for the Great Lakes and helped lead the administration's efforts to develop and implement President Clinton's Clean Water Action Plan, the nation's blueprint for finishing the job of cleaning up and restoring all the nation's rivers, lakes, and coastal areas.

To protect people from toxic waste, Browner made cleanups of the nation's hazardous-waste sites 20 percent faster and significantly less expensive. In her last six years, more Superfund toxic-waste sites were cleaned up than in the entire history of the program. Today, 90 percent of Superfund sites are either cleaned up or being cleaned up. She also made the cleanup of brownfields a priority. (Brownfields are abandoned, contaminated urban property.) So far, the program has leveraged more than $1 billion in public and private funds for brownfields redevelopment, and created thousands of new jobs. This brings new hope, new prosperity, and new development to inner city communities across the country while helping to protect the green areas outside the cities.

Through enforcement of President Clinton's new food safety production law, Browner set protective, comprehensive, health-based standards that limit pesticide risks in the foods American children eat. Through this law the first cumulative risk assessments are being performed. (See discussion in Chapter 6.)

Every action the EPA took to protect the American people from environmental hazards reflected Browner's deep commitment to children's health issues. Browner recognized that an awareness of children's unique susceptibility and exposure to toxic threats must guide the EPA's actions to protect public health and the environment. She established the Office of Children's Health Protection at the EPA, and developed and implemented new EPA policies that ensure—for the first time ever—that children's health risks will be consistently and explicitly evaluated in all scientific and standard-setting activities. (See discussion in Chapter 4.)

To promote better understanding of children's health risks, Browner worked with other federal agencies to establish eight federal children's health research centers at premier research institutions. She also convened a federal conference on possible links between childhood cancer and environmental hazards, and coordinated federal research into this issue. She developed a new federal strategy to protect children from lead-based paint, and launched the Child Health Champion pilot program to jump-start community efforts to identify and eliminate local environmental risks to children.

Browner believed that one of the best ways to protect children and all Americans from environmental hazards is to ensure the public's right to know about pollution in neighborhoods and communities. During her tenure the EPA doubled the number of chemicals for which facilities must report releases and required thousands more facilities to report. (See discussion in Chapter 5.) The public now has access to information about smog levels in their communities and when levels pose a significant health risk. The EPA has joined in partnership with the environmental community and the chemical manufacturing industry to provide the American people with public health data on 3,000 of the most widely used chemicals. Browner also directed the establishment of a new office of information to coordinate information and data programs to ensure that they are timely, accurate, and widely accessible, including on the Internet.

To ensure that tough public health standards are met, Browner established a vigorous enforcement and compliance assistance program. Under her leadership, the EPA collected the largest environmental fines in history from irresponsible polluters—while also offering a new level of compliance assistance to honest business owners. The EPA has nine compliance assistance centers to help small businesses understand and comply with environmental requirements as easily and cost effectively as possible. The EPA also has implemented a self-audit policy that waives penalties for companies that voluntarily identify, disclose, and correct violations. Since 1996, more than 1,600 facilities have voluntarily disclosed and corrected violations. Following Vice President Al Gore's mandate, Browner worked to "reinvent" environmental protection, to achieve the very best public health and environmental protection for the least cost. Her Common Sense Initiative was an industry-by-industry approach to environmental regulation that moved beyond the old piecemeal approach. (See discussion in Chapter 4 and 8.)

Browner led the Clinton administration's successful fight against annual congressional barrages of antienvironmental riders and legislation. She secured funding for environmental protection and preserved the nation's commitment to health, air, water, communities, and children's future.

Browner was one of the ablest administrators ever to lead the EPA. Completely fearless in her engagement with controversial environmental issues, she developed sector-based approaches, defended integration of environmental justice into all environmental policies, and made environmental transactions transparent to all citizens. She based her leadership on commonsense approaches that resonated with the public. With vision, intellect, perseverance, and diplomacy she created the foundation for the EPA to move forward to meet the challenges of the future.

ANNE M. GORSUCH (1981–1983)

Anne McGill Gorsuch was sworn in as the administrator of the EPA by Vice President George H. W. Bush. The first woman to head the EPA, she said, "I am grateful that President Reagan has asked me to assume a frontline position on his new team with responsibility for one of the largest and most important government agencies in this country.... I share the president's deep concern that our quality of life be protected, and I pledge the full commitment of my energies and that of my staff to this critical task."

Gorsuch, thirty-nine, from Denver, Colorado, was unanimously confirmed by the Senate on May 5 to head the EPA—the executive branch watchdog for the protection of air, water and land resources. It would be the first time the EPA would become politicized. She was the daughter of a conservative Denver physician, a graduate of the University of Colorado Law School at age twenty (and at the time the youngest woman ever admitted to the Colorado bar), a former Fulbright Fellow in India (where she studied criminal law), a former assistant district attorney, and, from 1976 to 1980, a member of the Colorado House of Representatives.

Gorsuch had no experience managing environmental or public health programs or, for that matter, any large organization. During her two terms, in the Colorado House of Representatives, she also worked as an attorney for the

Anne M. Gorsuch. (U.S. Environmental Protection Agency Archives)

Mountain Bell phone company. As a legislator she was a member of a clique that called itself "The Crazies" and had an agenda that consisted mainly of states' rights and opposition to federal energy and environmental policies. For example, "The Crazies" fought the EPA Denver regional office over the use of strict sanctions to bring the Denver area into compliance with federal clean air statutes. The group was often allied with such organizations as the Mountain States Legal Foundation, a coalition made up mainly of private energy companies and run by James Watt, Reagan's pick for secretary of the interior. Mountain States' avowed purpose was to "fight in the courts those bureaucrats and no-growth advocates who create a challenge to individual liberty and economic freedoms." Gorsuch was by all accounts an effective if not universally admired legislator. She won an award for "outstanding freshman legislator," and in her second term was appointed by House Speaker Robert Burford—subsequently Reagan's pick to head the Bureau of Land Management—to the State Affairs Committee chairmanship.

A rival described her as "sharp, poised and super-controlled," and she once told a reporter, "Whether you contact my friends or my enemies, they'll tell you two things: "I'm intelligent and I'm capable of making hard decisions."

While a legislator, Gorsuch led or played a prominent role in efforts to enact a determinate sentencing bill (limiting the discretion of judges in sentencing criminals). She also fought to leave decisions on the siting of hazardous-waste dumps in the hands of local authorities and to prevent the adoption of a state hazardous-waste bill. She also worked to abolish the Colorado Commission on Women. Gorsuch sponsored a state auto emissions inspection and maintenance bill while at the same time adamantly opposing the use of federal sanctions to require Colorado to implement such a program. Her argument was for voluntarism. She felt that states would achieve better environmental protection than would be possible under federal control. She was also known for her fierce advocacy of the doctrine of strict statutory construction (i.e., of not prescribing in regulation that which was not explicitly called for in statute or in a constitution).

Gorsuch was brought to the attention of the Reagan White House transition team by James Watt and Joseph Coors, the latter a Colorado beer brewing and energy magnate who was both a prominent Reagan supporter and the founder of Watt's Mountain States Legal Foundation and other conservative organizations. The transition team first had Gorsuch in mind for the deputy administrator post, upgrading her because better-known and more experienced candidates turned down the top job and because the team was so impressed with her intelligence, poise, and commitment to Reagan's agenda. The agenda was no secret, consisting of budget cuts and force reductions, regulatory relief/reform, and greater delegation of responsibility to the states. This plan encompassed not only the EPA but also many other federal agencies and, by all accounts, the key federal agency advancing it was the Office of Management and Budget (OMB). Since the election, OMB Director-designate David Stockman had been carefully scrutinizing the EPA's regulations. His widely circulated November memo to Reagan, "Avoiding a GOP Economic Dunkirk," stressed that EPA regulations could become a drag on a Reagan economic recovery program. At the time, the EPA had some 400 separate rules under consideration.

Shortly after his inauguration, Reagan established a vice presidential task force on regulatory relief under the direction of James C. Miller III, a political appointee to OMB and deregulation enthusiast. An executive order provided OMB with veto authority over all EPA regulations, and by March 25 the deregulation group had targeted several key rules relating to hazardous-waste disposal and auto emissions for possible deferral or cancellation. Gorsuch, who was unfamiliar with Washington and whose nomination came late for a major appointment, did not play a major role in this planning effort. While awaiting her Senate nomination hearing (which was delayed due to a prolonged security check by the Environment and Public Works Committee), she worked in Watt's Interior Department offices, meeting only infrequently with the EPA's career staff and surrounding herself instead with a small group of special assistants, most of whom had connections to Watt, Coors, or the Reagan campaign. The EPA core group of senior management was dedicated and experienced, but at the time Gorsuch's view of the EPA and its staff was apparently fairly skeptical.

Watt kept telling Gorsuch that she could not allow herself to be captured by the people she supervised. He felt that in terms of organizational dynamics, if you know people, you begin to make compromises, and see things more in tones of gray than in sharp black and white. Though Watt wasn't her boss, Gorsuch had a great deal of respect for him—they were both conservative Republicans and Coloradoans.

At her long-delayed nomination hearing on May 1, Gorsuch sought to dispel the widespread perception that the EPA was a rudderless agency under the direction of OMB and also provided a long recitation of her goals and commitments:

> As a long-term Coloradoan I come before you with a deep appreciation of the unique beauties which we enjoy in our environment—the majesty and grandeur of the Rocky Mountains, the openness and sense of space of our eastern plains, a climate which enjoys the variety and change afforded by each season of the year.... The president is committed to the preservation and enhancement of environmental values, and that is a commitment I share. The president is committed to achieving a new federalism in which the decisions and the power to implement those decisions will be shifted from the banks of the Potomac back to the level of government which is closest and most accountable to the people it serves. I share that commitment. The president is committed to regulatory reform, and here I believe it is important to emphasize that the reform is not limited to withdrawal of unnecessary or overly burdensome singular regulations, but envisions a much broader scope involving the process by which new regulations are formulated and current regulations evaluated.... We must recognize that EPA is affected today by economic, energy and environmental considerations largely unknown when many of the laws were passed. The public is no less committed to environmental protection, but increasingly aware of the need to balance all of these interests. EPA's programs must reflect this public awareness.

This eloquent opening statement ended with Gorsuch advocating a "nonconfrontational" approach by the EPA to achieving its mission and saying she was "confident" that Reagan did not choose her based on "any advocacy position" she had taken. "I have not made my living fighting for or against environmental laws and regulations." Although an environmental group lobbyist called Gorsuch an "administrative novice" lacking "necessary technical experience," the Senate approved her in a voice vote on May 5.

Almost no segment of Anne Gorsuch's twenty-two-month tenure at the EPA lacked controversy. In short order there were reports that she was "aloof" and "frosty" in her dealings with the career staff, many of whom were already apprehensive over rumors that she had been meeting with a steady stream of industry representatives at Interior and was planning to revamp the EPA. There were allegations that the Gorsuch team had in hand a "hit list" of career employees to be fired or transferred. This was a favorite tactic of the Reagan administration—to remove protected civil servants from their areas of expertise. There were questions about the fact that the majority of her appointees were former lawyers, lobbyists, or consultants for industries heavily regulated by the EPA. Many other powerful appointments were individuals with experience in Reagan's campaign but not the environmental arena. A mid-June reorganization of headquarters, which, among other things, abolished the enforcement office and sent most of its segments to corresponding program offices, created great concern because of the weakening effect it would have had on the enforcement of environmental laws. Following the reorganization came reports of infighting between Gorsuch's special assistants and the line appointees in charge of program and support offices; these appeared to be confirmed in September 1981 when two line appointees resigned after barely more than two months on the job. During Gorsuch's tenure there was a sharp decline in the number of enforcement cases sent by the EPA to the Justice Department. Many members of Congress, including Republicans, did not display much enthusiasm either for Gorsuch's agenda or for her manner in carrying it out. Gorsuch was increasingly dogged by charges, based on leaked internal documents, that she was planning to level massive fiscal year (FY) 1983 force reductions and budget cuts that would put operating expenditures at 40 percent below their FY 1981 level. Amid much publicity, William Drayton, the influential head of the planning and management office in the Carter administration, formed a "Save EPA" organization. The budget/force reduction flap finally abated in early February 1982 when Gorsuch issued an open letter to the staff promising no further reductions in FY 1982 and (probably) none in FY 1983.

Midway through February, however, Gorsuch suspended a regulatory ban on the disposal of containerized hazardous-waste liquids in landfills. Although the ban had only recently gone into effect, one member of Congress called the decision "a glaring and outrageous example" of EPA's "inactivity" in the hazardous-waste area and another, at a hastily called hearing, said that "even as we sit here . . . the trucks are rolling into 900 landfills all over America carrying a deadly legacy that our children and grandchildren will have no choice but to accept." Both Republicans and Democrats were concerned about the effect of hazardous materials in the environments of their constituencies. The chemical industry offered no public support for the action, and the story received prominent play in both national and local news media. After just eighteen days Gorsuch issued a new rule tightly restricting the disposal of those liquids. The flip-flop on the liquids-in-landfills issue actually ushered in a relatively quiet period for Gorsuch and the EPA. Over the following several months the EPA, among other things, tightened lead-in-gasoline standards (another reversal of a previous position), issued stiff new regulations on asbestos, and settled several Superfund cases with hazardous-waste dumpers. Although relations with Congress remained extremely poor, Gorsuch did make strides in developing better working relations with the career staff.

However, more trouble was brewing for Gorsuch in the House Energy and Commerce Committee, whose powerful chairman, John Dingell (D-MI), was conducting an investigation of the EPA's use of Superfund monies. Dingell began the inquiry late in the summer of 1982, out of concern about the slow progress of a program for which (unlike most other EPA programs) money was readily available. Particularly suspicious was the conduct of Rita Lavelle, Gorsuch's assistant administrator for solid waste and emergency response and a former California corporate public relations specialist.

In September, Dingell requested a number of documents relating to specific Superfund enforcement cases. The Justice Department intervened, however, asking for all copies of the documents and instructing the EPA to withhold them from Congress. On October 21, an angry Dingell issued a subpoena requiring Gorsuch to appear before the panel with the records, and a month later another congressional panel with Superfund jurisdiction issued a second subpoena to Gorsuch. On November 30, the president, acting on the advice of the White House counsel and the attorney general, instructed Gorsuch not to comply with the subpoena, explaining that "sensitive documents found in open law enforcement files should not be made available to the Congress or to the public except in extraordinary circumstances."

Apparently, Gorsuch had strongly questioned the legal as well as the political rationale for a claim of "executive privilege," but both the White House (which was feeling confident due to a good Republican showing in the November 1982 elections) and the Justice Department (which had suffered embarrassment in late 1981 after backing down on a similar case involving James Watt) were ripe for a showdown. The strategy quickly backfired. Leaders of both parties in Congress bridled at the administration's action, and Dingell said publicly that leaked documents suggested political manipulation of a specific Superfund enforcement case. On December 16, with public interest in the confrontation rapidly mounting, the House, by a wide margin, voted Gorsuch in contempt of Congress. The Justice Department immediately filed suit in U.S. district court to halt the contempt proceedings.

At Christmastime freak floods led to a hazardous waste spillage and the evacuation of homes in Times Beach, Missouri, spurring what one account labeled a "feeding frenzy" among the media. The administration's suit was dismissed in court and Rita Lavelle was fired by Reagan (after she turned down a Gorsuch request to resign). Also at this time fresh conflict of interest allegations were leveled against James Sanderson, a close Gorsuch adviser. Old controversies, such as the one involving the "hit list," resurfaced, and more top EPA employees resigned. In early March, apparently to her disbelief, the Justice Department told Gorsuch that its responsibility to investigate the fresh conflict of interest allegations and other charges of improprieties precluded its continued representation of her in the contempt/executive privilege proceedings. On March 9, the president reluctantly accepted her resignation. Gorsuch announced that the Congress would have full access to the documents in question. On March 21, Reagan nominated William Ruckelshaus, the EPA's first administrator, to take Gorsuch's place. The move was widely praised by Congress, environmental groups, and a number of industry groups.

Gorsuch presided over the first extensive politicization of the EPA. Never before had the EPA been thrown into such a political maelstrom. The collective experience of many senior environmental managers was lost due to job insecurity and confrontations between their administrator and Congress. Nonetheless, events in the environment continued to occur and drive social awareness of environmental issues. Environmental advocates sought judicial resolution of environmental complaints and did not pursue dialogue with the EPA. The EPA had matured under Gorsuch to realize another aspect of its dynamic organizational structure.

WILLIAM K. REILLY (1989–1993)

The U.S. Senate unanimously confirmed the nomination of William K. Reilly to be administrator of the EPA on February 2, 1989. His appointment had been announced on December 22, 1988, and he was officially nominated by President George H. W. Bush on January 20, 1989.

Reilly had held five environment-related positions during the previous two decades, the latest as president of the World Wildlife Fund–US and of the Conservation Foundation. An alumnus of Yale University, he holds a law degree from Harvard University and a master's degree in urban planning from Columbia University. He was born in Decatur, Illinois, on January 26, 1940, and grew up in Fall River, Massachusetts. He is married to Elizabeth Bennett Buxton, and they have two daughters.

William K. Reilly. (U.S. Environmental Protection Agency Archives)

Reilly was widely respected as the president of World Wildlife Fund and of the Conservation Foundation. He was appointed at a pivotal moment in the EPA's then short but eventful history. President George H. W. Bush had promised to be more of an environmentalist than his predecessor, and many interpreted his choice of Reilly as the EPA administrator as a sign of sincere commitment to that goal.

Reilly's proclivity for drawing people together was not just directed outward, toward the regulated community. It was expected to bring new cohesion to the internal operations of the EPA. In September 1988, two months before his appointment, Reilly criticized the "heavily fragmented system" of environmental regulation that then prevailed at the EPA. Also in 1988, he sponsored a Conservation Foundation proposal for a "model" omnibus Environmental Protection Act that would reflect the cross-media realities of today's environment. Although such a law was unlikely in the foreseeable future, a push toward a simpler and better coordinated regulatory apparatus was certainly one of Reilly's major goals. He was a man of vision and foresight on many environmental issues.

Reilly's personal style—gentlemanly and soft-spoken—made him the ideal mediator, effective at bridging differences even when antagonisms were intensely felt and there seemed to be no common ground for agreement. He was also known for his firm grasp of facts and his commitment to principle. The importance of ethical "values" was a theme to which Reilly referred frequently in conversation, and he attributed that facet of his thinking—like so much else—to his tutelage under Russell Train.

Reilly had compiled an impressive professional record. After attending public high school in Fall River, Massachusetts, he completed his undergraduate studies at Yale in 1962. He then moved on to Harvard for his law degree, which he received in 1965. That same year he married Elizabeth Bennett Buxton, the mother of his two daughters. After serving for two years as a captain in the U.S. Army, Reilly earned a master's degree in urban planning from Columbia University in 1971. At the time, Columbia University was known as an inclusive Ivy League institution that embraced the diversity of the city. The Urban Planning Department there had had an African American departmental chair in the 1930s.

While studying at Columbia, Reilly received his first exposure to the burgeoning field of environmentalism. As associate director of the Urban Policy Center at Urban America, he was coauthor of a report for the Public Land Law Review Commission that predicted what future demands cities would make on public land. Ever since, land use and land conservation have remained among Reilly's keenest interests.

As a senior staff member at the CEQ (1970–1972), Reilly had responsibilities in land use, public lands, urban growth policy, and historic preservation. From 1972 to 1973, he headed the Task Force on Land Use and Urban

Growth, chaired by Laurence S. Rockefeller, which produced a popular report titled "The Use of Land."

Reilly's career moved into high gear in 1973 when he was named president of the Conservation Foundation, a high-profile Washington-based think tank committed to steering public policy in the direction of decisions that improve the quality of the environment and ensure wise use of natural resources. Reilly's land use concerns found creative application at the foundation, which sponsors action-oriented research into a wide variety of matters related to environmental policy. Since the mid-1980s the foundation has taken an unusually strong interest in toxics and pollution control. For example, Reilly was instrumental in the 1984 founding of Clean Sites, the public–private partnership that broke the logjam in hazardous-waste site cleanups. He has maintained an active interest in Third World environmental concerns and has traveled extensively in developing countries.

Reilly had been successful in his efforts to secure dialogue and cooperation among business and environmental leaders. One such widely applauded breakthrough occurred in November 1988 when twenty-five previously warring environmentalists, industrialists, and developers made a public commitment to a "no net loss" goal for U.S. wetlands, a resource previously subject to dangerously rapid depletion. These same people, so harmonious by late 1988, had scarcely been on speaking terms when Reilly first coaxed them to convene for a meeting in July 1987. He also allowed the EPA to develop controversial studies, programs, and policies on environmental justice.

Another facet of Reilly's background deserves mention. In 1985, the Conservation Foundation merged with the World Wildlife Fund, a major organization with a budget of $30 million, six times greater than that of the foundation. Reilly became the president of the merged organization, and Train is now chairman of the board. Today, as before 1985, the World Wildlife Fund is committed to the preservation of endangered species and their habitats all over the globe. Under Reilly's brief stewardship, its membership underwent a spectacular rise, tripling in four years.

Since Reilly was already a frequent visitor to the Third World for the Conservation Foundation, his experiences with the WWF have amplified his pronounced international orientation. During an era in the EPA's history when international issues are suddenly a top priority—whether acid rain or the greenhouse effect of CFCs—Reilly's hands-on experience made him a valuable contributor.

Reilly is more ecologically oriented than many of his predecessors. Because of his working background, he is interested in protecting the health not just of people and wildlife but also of the biospheres in which they live. Reilly is committed to continuing the quest for a sounder balance between human health goals and the long-term challenge of preserving for future generations both the ecosphere and our natural resources.

WILLIAM D. RUCKELSHAUS
(1970–1973; 1983–1985)

William Doyle Ruckelshaus served as the first EPA administrator (December 1970–April 1973). During the EPA's formative years he concentrated on developing its organizational structure, enforcement actions against severely polluted cities and industrial polluters, setting health-based standards for air pollutants and for automobile emissions, requiring states to submit new air quality plans, and the banning of the general use of the pesticide DDT.

Ruckelshaus left the EPA in 1973 to serve as acting FBI director, following the breaking of the Watergate scandal, and then served briefly as deputy attorney general. From 1973 to 1975, he was an attorney with the firm of Ruckelshaus, Beveridge, Fairbanks, and Diamond. In 1975 he moved with his family to Seattle, Washington, where he served as a senior vice president of the Weyerhaeuser Company from 1976 to 1983.

During President Reagan's first term, White House Chief of Staff James Baker asked Ruckelshaus to return to the EPA following Anne Gorsuch's departure as administrator. In his 1983–1985 term as administrator, Ruckelshaus worked to improve staff morale and public perceptions of the EPA, and advanced the process of risk-based decision-making for environmental risks subject to EPA regulation. He also oversaw removal of the pesticide ethylene dibromide (EDB) from U.S. agricultural use, reaffirmed the EPA commitment to a federal–state partnership to restore and protect Chesapeake Bay, and helped the EPA institute tighter controls on hazardous-waste management.

Earlier in his career, Ruckelshaus had served as assistant attorney general in the Civil Division of the U.S. Department of Justice (1969–1970), as a member of the Indiana House of Representatives (1967–1969), and as deputy attorney general of Indiana (1960–1965). He had begun his career in law with the Indianapolis firm of Ruckelshaus, Bobbitt, and O'Connor (1960–1968).

After completing his second term as EPA administrator, Ruckelshaus joined the Seattle law firm of Perkins Coie (1985–1988), then served as CEO of Browning-Ferris Industries (BFI) (1988–1995) and as chairman of the board of BFI from 1988 to

William D. Ruckelshaus. (U.S. Environmental Protection Agency Archives)

1999. He is now a principal in Madrona Investment Group, a private investment firm in Seattle, and a strategic partner for the Madrona Venture Group (formed in 1999).

Ruckelshaus has served as chairman of the board of the World Resources Institute (since 1999), special envoy to the Pacific Salmon Treaty between the United States and Canada (1997–1998), chairman of Enterprise for the Environment (1996–1997), and as a member of the President's Council for Sustainable Development (1993–1997). He has been a member of the boards of directors of Cummins Engine, Monsanto, Nordstrom, Weyerhaeuser, Gargoyles, Coinstar, Solutia, and Pharmacia. Ruckelshaus has been a member of the World Commission on Environment and Development, and he currently serves as the chairman of the Salmon Recovery Funding Board for the State of Washington, chairman of World Resources Institute in Washington, D.C., and as a member of the Board of the University of Wyoming Institute for Environment and Natural Resources. In June 2001, he was appointed by President George W. Bush as a member of the Commission on Ocean Policy, created by Congress in 2000.

Ruckelshaus was born in 1932 in Indianapolis, Indiana, and is a graduate of Princeton University (B.A., 1957) and Harvard University (LL.B., 1960). He is married and has five children.

He is highly respected by both political parties for his efficient administrative and management styles. His extensive connections with both industry and environmental advocacy groups have given him an unusual range and depth of experience with many, often complex, environmental issues. His work in setting up the EPA was monumental and pathbreaking.

RUSSELL E. TRAIN (1973–1977)

Russell Errol Train was the second EPA administrator, serving from September 1973 to January 1977. During this time he supported the EPA's expansion of interest in international affairs, the approval of the catalytic converter to achieve Clean Air Act automobile emission reductions, the implementation of the Toxic Substances Control Act and the National Pollutant Discharge Elimination System, and the EPA's work to balance the demands of the energy crisis with environmental issues. He was also one of the masterminds who helped create the EPA.

Before working at the EPA, Train, a member of a highly respected military family, graduated from Princeton University in 1941, then served in the military from 1941 to 1946. Upon returning to civilian life, he entered Columbia Law School. Train served from 1949 to 1956 as attorney, chief counsel, or minority adviser for various congressional committees, then from 1956 to 1957 as assistant to the secretary and head of the Legal Advisory Staff for the Treasury Department.

After leaving the EPA, Train was president of the World Wildlife Fund–US (WWF–US) from 1978 to 1985, and its chairman from 1985 to 1994. During

Russell E. Train. (U.S. Environmental Protection Agency Archives)

1988 he also was cochairman of Conservationists for Bush, and from 1990 to 1992 as chairman of the National Commission on the Environment. Since 1994 Train has been chairman emeritus of WWF–US.

Train was a judge of the U.S. Tax Court from 1957 to 1965; president of the Conservation Foundation from 1965 to 1969; undersecretary of the interior from 1969 to 1970; and chairman of the Council on Environmental Quality from 1970 to 1973. Train has served as trustee emeritus for the African Wildlife Foundation, which he founded in 1961, and as a member of the Council on Foreign Relations, the Washington Institute on Foreign Affairs, and the Atlantic Council. He was born in 1920 in Jamestown, Rhode Island, and grew up in Washington, D.C. He is married to the former Alleen Bowden and has four children.

Train spent the first part of his career in government service as an attorney and jurist. From 1948 to 1965 he was successively legal adviser for the Congressional Joint Committee of the House Ways and Means Committee (where he became an expert on tax law); chief counsel, then minority adviser to the same committee; and Assistant to the secretary of the treasury and chief of the Treasury Department's tax legislative staff. In 1957 President Dwight Eisenhower asked the thirty-seven-year-old Train to complete an unexpired term as U.S. Tax Court judge, following which President John F. Kennedy appointed him for a full twelve-year term.

At this point, Train's path in life seemed clear. He could look forward to life tenure on the bench, a highly sought-after position. Nevertheless, he radically changed the course of his career. The change began during safaris to East Africa in 1956 and 1958. After observing the fragility of the African wilderness in the face of encroachment, Train founded the Wildlife Leadership Foundation in 1959. Through it he attempted to help the emerging nations of Africa build an infrastructure of professional resource management in order to establish effective wildlife parks and reserves. These parks have become essential to the preservation of wildlife diversity in Africa, and Train's foundation continues to offer expertise along these lines.

Train's final environmental awakening occurred in 1965. From 1959 until then his involvement in conservation had deepened and he had met many figures associated with it. At age forty-five he decided to abandon the safety of a lifetime position on the tax court and accepted an offer to be president of the nonprofit Conservation Foundation, a research, education, and information-oriented institution. During his tenure the foundation stressed citizen participation, supported demonstration projects that infused ecological considerations into development planning, and sponsored a major conference on environmentalism in international economic growth. Train also focused the foundation on finding methods to insert greater environmental awareness into federal policy-making processes.

After three years in private life, Train found himself back in government. In 1968 President Lyndon Johnson appointed him to the seven-member National Water Commission. With the election of Richard M. Nixon to the presidency in November of that year, Train figured prominently on one of the many task forces established by the new president to review all executive functions. Nixon asked him to chair a group on resource and environmental issues, which he did between November 1968 and January 1969. The group's report proposed a White House office of environmental policy, which laid the foundation for the creation of the EPA. This report also led to the National Environmental Policy Act (NEPA), which took effect on January 1, 1970. In the meantime, President Nixon appointed Train undersecretary of the interior. In this post he headed the Alaska Pipeline Intergovernmental Task Force, a difficult job that took almost one year. With the passage of NEPA, the president established the Council on Environmental Quality (CEQ) and named Train its first chairman.

Train and his small White House staff quickly defined the environmental role of the CEQ. They assumed the duties of advising the president on policy, drafting legislation, coordinating all federal activities, and preparing an annual report on the state of the nation's environment. These activities continue to be the responsibility of the CEQ. (See discussion in Chapter 1.) Train also carved out important international responsibilities for himself, such as, becoming chairman of the NATO Committee on the Challenges of Modern Society. No sooner had the CEQ established its own mission than a second federal environmental institution came into being. The EPA opened its doors in December 1970, and its administrator, William D. Ruckelshaus, found himself following Train's recent example by defining the role of the new EPA. From the early stages, it became evident that while the two organizations would work closely together, Train and his staff would concentrate on policy formulation and international environmental activity, while William Ruckelshaus and the EPA would focus on implementation of environmental laws.

By 1973 the main tenets of environmental policy had been established, and the EPA began to assume the dominant position. In April of that year, as the Watergate crisis grew more intense, Ruckelshaus resigned from the EPA to become acting FBI director. Realizing the EPA had become the "principal arena" for environmental activities, Train declared his interest in becoming EPA administrator, and in May 1973 President Nixon nominated him for the position. He served as the second administrator from September 1973 to

January 1977, during which time the EPA expanded its interest in international affairs and turned to risk assessment as an instrument of policy-making. More important, at a time when the supply and cost of energy became paramount in the United States, Train and the EPA succeeded in "holding the environmental line." Train's personal commitment to conservation survived the rigors of eight full years as a federal environmental leader.

Looking back on his service to the EPA, Train reflected on an intangible but vital contribution of his tenure. He felt that his most important achievement involved building the credibility of the EPA. "We didn't have any major setbacks insofar as public confidence was concerned. We were able to resolve political problems within the administration and the White House in a way that did not diminish respect for the EPA. We had good Congressional relations. . . . The important thing we did was to build the credibility of the EPA with the public."

Train was a principled intellectual leader committed to government service and to the environment. He solved many difficult issues of implementation of environmental policy and developed the conceptual framework for the implementation of environmental law.

CHRISTINE TODD WHITMAN
(2001–2003)

Christine Todd Whitman took office with the Bush administration in January 2001. Among the achievements of her two years in office were the introduction of President Bush's Clear Skies Initiative to ensure cleaner air; the establishment of a watershed-based approach to protecting our nation's lakes, streams, and rivers; and the passage of landmark brownfields legislation bringing economic and environmental vitality back to neighborhoods marred by abandoned industrial sites.

Administrator Whitman tried to advance the goals of economic success and environmental progress by encouraging public-private partnerships and market-based incentives. Programs such as Climate Leaders, Energy Star, SmartWay Transport, and the new Water Quality Trading Policy encourage voluntary actions from governments, corporations, small businesses, and nonprofit groups. Under Administrator Whitman's leadership, the EPA also undertook efforts to clean up the Hudson River, protect children from environmental health hazards such as asthma and sun exposure, and require cleaner-burning diesel engines and lower-sulfur diesel fuel to reduce emissions from the dirtiest mobile sources.

Christine Todd Whitman brought substantial experience with her to the position of EPA administrator. She had been the first female governor of New Jersey, one of the most urban and most polluted of the fifty states. With its history of waste and pollution came a history of intergovernmental cooperation around environmental issues. State, regional, urban, municipal and local efforts had experience working together to solve some of New Jersey's difficult pollution problems. Whitman offered much to the EPA in terms of urban inclusion in federal environmental policy. This facilitated the development and adoption of brownfields legislation.

Whitman is a millionaire who made much of her money on Wall Street. She is descended from a well-to-do family with strong ties to the Republican party and her siblings have also been involved in politics. She grew up in Hunterdon County, New Jersey, and earned a bachelor's degree in government from Wheaton College in 1968. She is married to John R. Whitman, who also has ties to the Republican party, and has two children.

Whitman was not a career politician when she ran for the New Jersey governor's office. Her only previous political experience had been winning election to the Somerset County Board of Chosen Freeholders, the governing body of that county; she served there for five years. Republican governor Thomas H. Kean subsequently appointed her to the New Jersey Board of Public Utilities, where she served until 1990.

But Christine Todd Whitman defeated her opponent, James Florio, the incumbent governor of New Jersey, with very little political experience. In her campaign she advocated sweeping tax cuts, as well as abortion rights. Whitman's gubernatorial campaign was not without problems. She hired Larry McCarthy as her media consultant in August of 1993, to the outrage of many—he was responsible for the racist "Willie Horton" advertisements that aired during George Bush's campaign against Michael Dukakis. In response, Whitman countered that someone else had been in charge of the infamous ads; however, McCarthy soon quit. While the controversy simmered, Whitman removed herself to go on a biking trip in Idaho.

Another scandal broke after she released her tax returns, which indicated that she and her husband had grossed an impressive $3.7 million in 1992. Journalists also called into question her use of two rural homes as working farms. Finally, a short time after the votes were in, Rollins, her campaign manager, told the press that the reason they had won was because they had paid African American ministers to suppress the vote among their parishioners. Money was also supposedly paid to election workers in Democratic neighborhoods (who were supposed to be getting people to the polls) to stay home. Rollins bragged that these measures were important in Whitman's election victory. A federal judge ruled that an investigation would be necessary. Whitman assured the voters that she would agree to a new vote if any illegalities were uncovered. It turned out that no proof could be found to substantiate Rollins's initial claims, and by November 29, 1993, the Democrats abandoned their campaign to have the election results decertified. On January 12, 1994, state and federal investigators ended their investigation into the campaign and deemed Whitman innocent of the charges.

As governor, Christine Todd Whitman faced serious challenges. The size of New Jersey's deficit had swelled to $1 billion. She stopped a proposal to use taxpayer's money to bring the Philadelphia 76ers professional basketball team from their home in Pennsylvania to Camden, New Jersey. In her inaugural address, she asked the legislature to put into effect a 5 percent tax cut retroactive to January 1. Her campaign promise had been to start cutting taxes by July 1, but she felt it necessary to start her proposals immediately. Whitman's ultimate goal was to see state income taxes reduced by 30 percent within her first three years in office. She went on record as saying that she hoped these cuts would not force municipalities to raise taxes to cover missing state aid, but also said that she would not be responsible if this did happen.

Under her environmental leadership, the number of days New Jersey violated the federal one-hour air quality standard for ground-level ozone dropped from forty-five in 1988 to four in 2000. Beach closings reached a record low, the state earned recognition by the Natural Resources Defense Council for instituting the most comprehensive beach monitoring system in the nation, and a new watershed management program was instituted that resulted in New Jersey leading the nation in opening shellfish beds for harvesting. Governor Whitman also won voter approval for the state's first stable funding source to preserve 1 million more acres of open space and farmland. By 2010, New Jersey—the most densely populated state in the country—will have permanently preserved 40 percent of its total landmass.

During her short tenure as EPA administrator, Whitman championed "free market environmentalism," voluntary initiatives promoted by conservative think-tanks and industry lobbies as an alternative to regulatory measures. Some of these programs are briefly described below. It is too early to tell if any of these initiatives will last into the next presidential administration. Some of these initiatives continue the policies of the past, such as the Clean Water initiative.

Under her administration the EPA began promoting hemispheric environmental partnerships. At the meeting of the Council of the Commission for environmental cooperation in Guadalajara, Mexico on June 29, 2001, Administrator Whitman secured a pledge from the environmental ministers of Mexico and Canada "to explore further opportunities for market-based approaches for carbon sequestration, energy efficiency and renewable energy in North America."

Whitman continued to seek cleaner air through cleaner diesel fuel. She affirmed a rule to reduce emissions from large trucks and buses and to reduce sulfur levels in diesel fuel. This action will result in significant health benefits to the American people, including saving as many as 8,300 lives a year, as well as enhancing the health of children suffering from asthma by preventing more than 360,000 asthma attacks and 386,000 cases of respiratory symptoms annually. This action continued the general development of air pollution policy in the United States and in the tradition of the EPA.

Another interesting policy initiative was to improve the views in America's national parks. The EPA proposed a rule to control the emissions from older power plants and other industrial facilities that contribute to haze that, too often, spoils the scenic views that once captivated park visitors. Parks whose vistas will be improved include Yellowstone, the Grand Canyon, and Sequoia. However, this policy should be considered in the context of a large increase in coal-fired power plants being permitted by state and federal environmental agencies.

With the bombing of the World Trade Center, all federal agencies were directed to prepare a post-9/11 strategy. The EPA emergency response was criticized at the time as somewhat slow to account for all potential hazardous exposures. Because access to the site was limited to security agencies at first, the EPA had to wait. Whitman did prepare the EPA with post-9/11 strategies in response to these new priorities.

Administrator Whitman worked closely with Congress to secure passage of brownfields legislation to meet the president's promise to give state and local governments greater flexibility and necessary resources to turn local environmental eyesores into productive community assets. She also joined with members of the U.S. Conference of Mayors to accept its endorsement of the administration brownfield's proposal. In addition, the administrator announced the awarding of more than $38 million in grants for a total of thirty-six new brownfield pilot projects in communities across the country.

Another goal was the elimination of persistent organic pollutants. To protect the American people from the dangers of chemicals that persist in the environment long after their use, the administrator represented the United States in Stockholm, Sweden, for the signing of the Convention on Persistent Organic Chemicals. This treaty bans or restricts the production, use, and/or release of twelve chemicals that have been linked to numerous adverse effects in humans and animals, including cancer, central nervous system damage, reproductive disorders, and immune system disruption.

She also sought to protect America's wetlands. Whitman affirmed a rule to protect America's wetlands by more closely regulating construction activities in wetlands. This rule, known as the Tulloch Wetland Rule, will help prevent loss of wetlands to construction practices that were being conducted under a loophole in regulations previously promulgated. The environmental impacts of construction can be very damaging to the environment, but are seldom counted toward long-term impacts.

In line with the general course of environmental reporting policy development, Whitman increased reporting on lead. She affirmed a rule to lower the threshold for reporting of industrial lead use. The new standard will require any company that manufactures, processes or uses 100 pounds of lead or more annually to report such use to the EPA as part of the Toxics Release Inventory. This will significantly increase the information available to the public about the uses of lead in America's communities. Past practice has shown that such information generally leads to decreased emissions of reportable toxics by companies, leading to public health and environmental benefits.

Under Whitman the EPA was severely criticized by many mainstream environmental groups on the following grounds:

- Gutting key sections of the Clean Water and Clean Air acts, laws that have traditionally had bipartisan support and have done more to protect the health of Americans than any other environmental legislation.

- Crippling the Superfund program, which is charged with cleaning up millions of pounds of toxic industrial wastes such as arsenic, lead, mercury, and vinyl chloride in more than 1,000 neighborhoods in forty-eight states.

- Cutting the EPA's enforcement division by nearly one-fifth, its lowest level on record. Fines assessed for environmental violations dropped by nearly two-thirds in the administration's first two years, and criminal prosecutions—the government's weapon of last resort against the worst polluters—are down by nearly one-third.

- Abdicating the decades-old federal responsibility to protect native animals and plants from extinction, becoming the first administration to fail to voluntarily add a single species to the endangered species list.

- Endorsing commercial whaling by reversing a U.S. ban in place since 1986.

- Opening millions of acres of wilderness—including some of the nation's most environmentally sensitive public lands—to logging, mining, and oil and gas drilling. Under one plan, loggers could take 10 percent of the trees in California's Giant Sequoia National Monument; many of the monument's old-growth sequoias, 200 years old and more, could be felled to make roof shingles.

- Opening other national treasures for development including the million-acre Grand Canyon–Parashant National Monument in Arizona; the 2,000-foot red-rock spires at Fisher Towers, Utah; and dozens of others.

- Withholding EPA support of Environmental Justice, trying to terminate the National Environmental Justice Advisory Board, and being criticized for its narrow interpretation of Executive Order 12898 by the Office of the Inspector General. Whitman insisted that treating everyone exactly the same was enough to comply with the Executive Order. She would not account for racial or economic disparities. She said she supported the intent and spirit of EO 12898, but subject to her narrow interpretation; the Office of the Inspector General has concluded that her interpretation is too narrow. (See discussion in Chapter 3.)

Whitman resigned in 2003 and has since criticized the Bush administration for being too ideological. In 2004, Whitman formed the Whitman Strategy

Group, a lobbying and consulting group whose first client was FMC Corporation, "a chemical company negotiating with the EPA over the cleanup of arsenic-contaminated soil at a factory near Buffalo, N.Y." In a May 2005 interview, Whitman said she had not worked directly with FMC, but would likely advise them on how to improve their image and gain access to people. FMC is responsible for 136 Superfund sites across the country and has been subject to forty-seven EPA enforcement actions.

Emergency environmental response policy at the EPA is part of her current legacy. It is likely that some form of brownfields urban revitalization will continue to be the subject of some policy focus. In her short tenure at EPA, Whitman kept the primary policies steady, although with reduced enforcement. She increased the urban focus and developed an emergency response strategy.

☆ **8** ☆

Chronology of Key Events

In many ways the chronology of the EPA is a chronology of an important part of the U.S. environmental movement. The laws passed by Congress and the rules and regulations developed by the EPA define the areas of public concern for the environment. Behind each rule and regulation is the research and work of many EPA employees, citizens, and environmental organizations. Most were controversial at the time they passed into law and again when the EPA developed the rules and regulations implement them. (The laws and controversies themselves are discussed in other chapters of this book.)

By chronicling the major pieces of federal legislation that are administered by the EPA, highlighting significant rules and regulations developed and enforced by the EPA, and observing the social contexts of the environmental problems faced by the EPA, the development and growth of a powerful federal agency become clear.

1970–1979: FIRST STEPS

The first steps of the EPA were basic ones. The EPA was to implement the Clean Air Act, the Clean Water Act, and a host of other foundational statutes. Standards needed to be developed, rules and regulations needed to be promulgated, and research studies needed to be started.

William Doyle Ruckelshaus served as the first EPA administrator, from December 1970 to April 1973. During the EPA's formative years, he concentrated on developing the new agency's organizational structure; enforcement actions against severely polluted cities and industrial polluters; setting health-based standards for air pollutants and for automobile emissions; requiring states to submit new air quality plans; and banning the general use of the pesticide DDT.

1970

Clean Air Act Passed

The Clean Air Act is the comprehensive federal law that regulates air emissions from area, stationary, and mobile sources. This law authorizes the EPA to establish national ambient air quality standards (NAAQS) to protect public health and the environment. The goal of the act was to set and achieve NAAQS in every state by 1975. The setting of maximum pollutant standards was coupled with directing the states to develop state implementation plans applicable to appropriate industrial sources within each state. The act was amended in 1977 primarily to set new goals (dates) for achieving attainment of NAAQS because many areas of the country had failed to meet the deadlines. The 1990 amendments to the Clean Air Act in large part were intended to meet unaddressed or insufficiently addressed problems such as acid rain, ground-level ozone, stratospheric ozone depletion, and air toxics.

1971

EPA Sets National Air Quality Standards

The EPA defined, for five of the most common air contaminants, the levels at which "significant harm" to the health of persons might occur during episodes of high air pollution. The five pollutants are sulfur dioxide, particulate matter, carbon monoxide, photochemical oxidants, and nitrogen dioxide. The danger levels were stipulated in an amendment to regulations, issued by the EPA on August 14, 1971, to guide states in planning to clean the nation's air to healthful levels by mid-1975. These regulations require each state plan to spell out steps to be taken to prevent dangerously high air pollution. Such steps would become progressively more stringent as air pollution concentrations increased toward the danger points. The EPA emphasized that state action should assure that air pollution never reaches the levels at which significant harm to health may occur. Under the Clean Air Act, the administrator of the EPA is empowered to bring suit on behalf of the United States in a federal district court when air pollution presents an imminent and substantial danger to the health of persons.

Ocean Dumping Act Passed

The act formally known as the Marine Protection, Research, and Sanctuaries Act gives the EPA the responsibility for regulating the dumping of all materials except dredged material. The Corps of Engineers has the responsibility for regulating the ocean dumping of dredgings, but it must do so using criteria promulgated in consultation with the EPA. The act provides for control of both the transportation of material to be dumped and the dumping itself. Banned entirely are the ocean disposal of radiological, chemical, and biological warfare agents and high-level radioactive wastes.

James L. Agee, assistant administrator for water and hazardous materials, told the House Committee on Merchant Marine and Fisheries in 1975 that in the period 1973–1974 there had been a total increase in ocean dumping of about 2.1 million tons. He added that while there had been an overall decrease in dumping of industrial wastes during this period, the net increase was caused by a rise in the dumping of sewage sludge and construction and demolition debris. The volume of industrial wastes being discharged at sea is on the decline, and the EPA has denied seventy permit applications, mostly for chemical dumping, since the Ocean Dumping Act became effective. Eleven dumping sites in the Atlantic Ocean and the Gulf of Mexico are now used for municipal and industrial wastes by approximately 100 permit holders. There is no dumping in the Pacific, but municipal sewage sludge is discharged to the ocean through outfall lines. The outfall discharges of sludge on the West Coast and elsewhere are controlled under the National Pollutant Discharge Elimination System.

The problem is how to dispose of sewage sludge. As more and more cities upgrade their sewage treatment facilities from no treatment to primary, secondary, or advanced waste treatment processes, more and more sewage sludge is generated. The more advanced degrees of treatment produce greater quantities of sludge, and this sludge tends to contain large quantities of trace metals and persistent organic compounds, which may have adverse environmental consequences whether they are incinerated, put on the land or dumped in the ocean. All present dumping of municipal sewage sludge originates from the New York and Philadelphia metropolitan areas. The total volume of the sludge from these two metropolitan areas is almost equal to the volume of all other materials discharged under the ocean dumping program. Both New York and Philadelphia are dumping under interim permits which stipulate that they must seek some way of reducing concentrations of harmful pollutants and must find alternative methods of disposal.

EPA Administrator William D. Ruckelshaus announced that he had approved portions of several regional air pollution control plans for sulfur oxides and particulate matter. The plans were prepared by state governments prior to the Clean Air Act Amendments of 1970. His action marked the first time that the EPA has approved such state plans.

Twenty-one implementation plans submitted in 1971 by fifteen states for thirteen air quality control regions were originally required to meet state air quality standards under the Clean Air Act before it was amended. However, under the 1970 amendments, state plans must satisfy a number of new requirements. The approved portions of the state plans included regulations judged adequate for attainment and maintenance of national primary (health-related) air quality standards for particulate matter or sulfur oxides or both. In some instances, the plans provided for the achievement of the national secondary standards for these pollutants that the EPA promulgated on April 30, 1971. In each case, the states were advised of needed revisions and were given six months to comply with the new requirements as part of more comprehensive implementation plans due from all states by the end of January 1972. These plans called for attaining and maintaining national standards for carbon monoxide, hydrocarbons, nitrogen dioxide, and photochemical oxidants as well as sulfur oxides and particulate matter.

1972

New Pesticides Law

The Federal Environmental Pesticide Control Act was signed into law by President Nixon on October 21. Under the new legislation, federal control would be extended to actual application of pest control chemicals by the purchaser, with penalties provided for misuse. The old law regulated only the interstate marketing of pesticide products, whereas the new act not only covered misuse but also required federal registration of products distributed within a single state. All pesticide products would ultimately be registered and classified for general use or restricted use. The restricted category would contain chemical toxicants that pose a high risk to humans or the environment. Such compounds could be used only with special restrictions, such as use by or under the supervision of certified applicators.

DDT

Following the EPA's 1972 ban on production, sale, or use of DDT in the United States, investigations were initiated to evaluate the extent of environmental contamination at places where DDT had been manufactured, stored, or used. The general use of DDT would no longer be legal in the United States, ending nearly three decades of application during which the chemical was used to control insect pests on crop and forest lands and around homes and gardens, and for industrial and commercial purposes. An end to the continued domestic usage of the pesticide was decreed on June 14, 1972, when William D. Ruckelshaus, administrator of the EPA, issued an order canceling nearly all remaining federal registrations of DDT products. Public health, quarantine, and a few minor crop uses were excepted, as was export of DDT. The cancellation decision culminated three years of intensive governmental inquiries into the uses of DDT, the first of modern insecticides. DDT was developed early in World War II and was initially used with great effect to combat malaria, typhus, and the other insect-borne diseases among both military and civilian populations. A persistent, broad-spectrum compound often termed the "miracle" pesticide, DDT came into wide agricultural and commercial usage in the late 1940s. During the succeeding thirty years, approximately 675,000 tons had been applied domestically. The peak year for use in the United States was

1959, when nearly 80 million pounds were applied. From that high point usage declined steadily to about 13 million pounds in 1971, most of it applied to cotton. The decline was attributed to a number of factors, including increased insect resistance, development of more effective alternative pesticides, growing public and user concern over adverse environmental side effects—and governmental restriction on DDT use since 1969.

Water

The 1972 amendments changed the thrust of enforcement from water quality standards regulating the amount of pollutants in a given body of water, to effluent limitations regulating the amount of pollutants being discharged from particular point sources. Ambient water quality requirements could still dictate the amount of pollutants permitted for a discharge. The administrator was directed to publish regulations establishing guidelines for effluent limitations by October 18, 1973. Factors for consideration were the costs and benefits of applying such technology, the age of equipment and facilities involved, and the process employed. Industrial dischargers must meet these standards by July 1, 1977. Public treatment works must meet effluent limitations based on secondary treatment by this same date. Industrial dischargers were obliged to meet these standards by July 1, 1983, the date also given for achieving the second national goal designed to protect fish, shellfish, wildlife, and recreation. They must meet zero-discharge requirements if the administrator determined that such a requirement was economically and technologically feasible. By July 1, 1983, public treatment works were to use the best practicable waste treatment technology over the life of the works. New sources of discharge were required to use the best available technology as determined by the administrator and published in the regulations. Zero-discharge by 1985 was a goal, not a requirement under the law.

1973

The EPA Issues First Wastewater Permits

In the first such action in the nation, the Indiana Stream Pollution Control Board issued permits approved by the EPA to five Indiana companies for authority to discharge treated wastewater into navigable waters. Indiana was one of eighteen states in the nation granted interim authority by the EPA to issue National Pollutant Discharge Elimination System permits under the provisions of the Federal Water Pollution Control Act Amendments of 1972. The act required cities, industries, and agricultural operations to have permits for the discharge of wastewater.

The EPA Begins Phaseout of Leaded Gas

The new regulations restricted the average lead content, measured quarterly, in all grades of gasoline produced by any refinery to 1.7 grams per gallon (gpg) by July 1, 1975, 1.2 gpg by July 1, 1976, 0.9 gpg by July 1, 1977, and 0.6 gpg by July 1, 1978. A significant portion of the urban population, particularly children, was overexposed to lead through a combination of sources including food, water, air, leaded paint, and dust. Although leaded paint was a primary source of exposure for lead poisoning in children, leaded gasoline was also a significant source of exposure that could be readily controlled. The total amount of lead used in gasoline amounted to well over 200,000 tons a year. Lead from gasoline was the most ubiquitous source of lead found in the air, dust, and dirt in urban areas. The new lead limits prescribed by the EPA were based on "total pool averaging," a method that allowed refiners to average lead usage over all grades of gasoline produced, including the unleaded grade.

On January 10, 1973, the EPA required the general availability of one grade of unleaded gas by July 1, 1974, in order to protect the catalytic converters that were to appear on many new cars in 1975. Lead in gasoline may cause disintegration of the converters, which control auto air pollution emissions. Also on January 10, the EPA again proposed annual reductions of the lead content in all other grades of gasoline in order to protect public health. The reproposal, based on a pool averaging of only the leaded grades of gasoline, would reduce lead content to 1.25 gpg by January 1, 1978.

1974

Fuel Economy Labeling

The EPA announced a program asking auto manufacturers to post fuel economy information on new cars. It also published fuel economy data for most vehicle models sold in the United States. The intent of this program was to educate consumers regarding the importance of fuel economy differences in lifetime costs of cars and to provide them with data from which to make fuel-saving decisions. Knowledge of this information was expected to immediately accelerate the current trend to smaller, more efficient cars.

Safe Drinking Water Act passed

The Safe Drinking Water Act (SDWA) was originally passed by Congress to protect public health by regulating the nation's public drinking water supply. It was amended in 1986 and 1996, and requires many actions to protect drinking water and its sources: rivers, lakes, reservoirs, springs, and groundwater wells. SDWA authorized the EPA to set national health-based standards for drinking water to protect against both naturally occurring and man-made contaminants. The EPA, states, and water systems then worked together to make sure that these standards were met.

1975

The EPA Requires Pollution Control on Cars

The EPA announced that any American or foreign automobile that had a catalytic converter and had been driven outside the United States, Canada, or Mexico (where unleaded gasoline was not generally available), would have to be fitted with a new catalytic converter before it could enter the United States. Canada and Mexico were the only countries besides the United States that sold unleaded gasoline. A catalytic converter-equipped vehicle that had been continuously operated on leaded fuel was presumed not to be in compliance with federal emission standards.

Federal Government Cuts Aid to Polluters

The EPA published final regulations specifying that federal agencies must withhold contracts, grants, or loans to industrial and manufacturing plants, and other facilities, found to be in violation of the Federal Water Pollution Control Act of 1972 or the Clean Air Act of 1970.

The program dealt with both air and water pollution violations. Regulations published in December 1973 had established similar rules for air pollution violations only. The new regulations were designed to implement Section 307 of the Clean Air Act, Section 508 of the Federal Water Pollution Control Act, and Executive Order 11738. Under the new regulations, the EPA with assistance from the states, would place on its list of violating facilities those which were in violation of the air and water acts. The EPA would begin listing facilities after July 1, 1975. They would be listed upon a determination by the EPA of continuing or recurring violation of air or water standards. Federal, state, or local criminal convictions, civil court decisions, or administrative decisions of violation would serve as a basis for listing. Listed facilities would be prohibited from receiving federal contracts, subcontracts, grants, subgrants, loans or subloans. The program would apply to any contract, grant, or loan in excess of $100,000 as well as any contract of a lesser amount involving a facility with a federal criminal conviction.

The EPA planned to use the list of violating facilities primarily as a tool to bring about voluntary compliance with clean air and water standards by any organization desiring to receive federal funds. The listing procedure would supplement other enforcement provisions in the two acts. No facility would be listed without a proceeding at which its representatives had the opportunity to consult with the EPA about the alleged violation. A facility listed on the basis of a federal criminal conviction would be delisted only if the condition giving rise to the listing had been fully corrected. Facilities listed on any other basis would be delisted upon completion of an approved schedule of compliance for abating the condition. Delisting would also occur if the conviction or other form of ruling that was the basis for the listing was reversed.

1976

Toxic Substances Control Act Passed

The Toxic Substances Control Act (TSCA) was enacted by Congress to give the EPA the ability to track the 75,000 industrial chemicals currently produced in or imported into the United States. The EPA would repeatedly screen these chemicals and could require reporting or testing of those which could pose an environmental or human health hazard. The EPA could ban the manufacture and import of chemicals that posed an unreasonable risk. TSCA supplemented other federal statutes, including the Clean Air Act and the Toxic Release Inventory.

Resource Conservation and Recovery Act Passed

The handling and disposal of hazardous wastes, which are generated mainly by industry, came under regulation. The law also requires that open dumping of all solid wastes be brought to an end throughout the country by 1983.

The Resource Conservation and Recovery Act also called for research, demonstration projects, studies, training, information dissemination, and public participation to enlarge the base of knowledge and public involvement necessary for developing strong state and local programs. Partly as a result of pollution controls that kept wastes out of the air and water, growing amounts of solid wastes were being generated and deposited on the land. Disposal on land had gone largely uncontrolled, resulting in numerous serious effects on human health and environmental quality. The contamination of groundwater by substances leaching from disposal sites was a primary concern. The most urgent objective of the new law was to prevent this and other environmental effects of improper disposal.

1977

The EPA Sets Safe Drinking Water Standards

National safe drinking water standards went into effect this year across the country. EPA regulations required that the 40,000 community drinking water systems and 200,000 other public water systems test their water on a routine basis to make sure it was safe to drink. The law required utilities to notify consumers if the health standards or sampling requirements were not being met.

The regulations set health standards for microbiological contaminants, ten inorganic chemicals, six organic pesticides, turbidity (murkiness), and radiological contamination. These were the first health-related drinking water standards to apply to virtually all public water systems coast to coast. Some types of water supplies had more time than others to start monitoring for certain contaminants. Monitoring began immediately for coliform bacteria and turbidity, both of which relate to the possible transmission of immediate illness through drinking water. Monitoring for the chemical contaminants was to be phased in, according to a specified schedule.

The law provided for a system of variances and exemptions for individual water supplies. Thus a local water system could obtain an extension of compliance deadlines if serious economic or other problems were encountered. However, variances and exemptions would not be granted where there was an unreasonable risk to public health, and the public must be notified when variances and exemptions were granted.

Clean Water Act Passed

The Clean Water Act of 1977 amended the Federal Water Pollution Control Act of 1972 and culminated three years of hard work by Congress to make the necessary midcourse corrections in the national water pollution control program. Congress agreed to long-term funding for the municipal sewage treatment construction grant program. This would help states and communities plan and implement programs to clean up backlogs of municipal pollution. The bill also emphasized the importance of controlling toxic pollutants that endanger the public health. It allowed the federal and state governments to recover their costs in mitigating damages from spills of oil and other hazardous substances.

The EPA Promotes Scrubbers for Coal-fired Power Plants

In 1971 the EPA had set national health standards for SO_2, which can irritate the upper respiratory tract and damage lung tissue, as well as turn plant leaves yellow and eat away iron, steel, marble, and other solid materials. The approximately 1,000 power plants that burn oil and coal to produce electricity in the United States are the major sources of this pollutant.

An unfortunate by-product of scrubber use is the production of sulfur waste material or sludge. Lime and limestone scrubbers—the most widely used types—produce large quantities of sludge, but several commercial methods are now available to solidify this waste material. This solid sludge can be disposed of in landfills without significant adverse effect on the environment. Other disposal methods are being evaluated.

1978

Lead Is Regulated

In 1975 the Natural Resources Defense Council and others brought suit against the EPA to control lead as a national ambient air quality standard under Section 109 of the Clean Air Act. As a result of court action on this suit, the EPA began developing a lead standard. Lead enters the human body principally through ingestion and inhalation, is absorbed into the bloodstream, and distributed to all body tissues. Exposure to airborne lead can occur directly by inhalation, or indirectly by ingestion of lead-contaminated food, water, or nonfood materials including dust and soil. Lead accumulates in the human body throughout life, to a large extent immobilized in bone. A significant amount of body lead is in the blood and soft tissues. Numerous studies have demonstrated that exposure to lead adversely affects human health. Lead has its most pronounced effects on the blood-forming and nervous systems and the kidneys, but may also harm the reproductive, endocrine, hepatic, cardiovascular, immunologic, and gastrointestinal systems. Exposure to high levels of lead may have severe and sometimes fatal consequences, such as brain disease, colic, palsy, and anemia.

There are multiple sources of lead exposure besides air pollution. Lead is found in paint, inks, water supply and distribution systems, pesticides, and fresh and processed foods. Besides the ambient air standard proposed, the EPA had taken other actions to control lead in the environment. In 1975, it had set national drinking water standards for lead, and by 1979 it would develop industrial water pollution rules. The EPA had also issued regulations controlling lead arsenate pesticides and requiring safe disposal procedures for all lead-containing pesticides. In addition, the Resource Conservation and Recovery Act of 1976 authorized the EPA to regulate the recycling and disposal of used crankcase oil, acid batteries, and other wastes containing lead. Other EPA regulations for control of air emissions of sulfur dioxide and particulate matter required pollution control technology that also reduced lead emissions from industrial facilities.

The EPA Bans Aerosol Fluorocarbons

In March 1977, the Food and Drug Administration, the EPA, and the Consumer Product Safety Commission ordered the phaseout of "nonessential" uses of fluorocarbons in spray products, such as deodorants, hair sprays, household cleaners, and pesticides. The agencies' prohibition followed studies by the National Academy of Sciences and other researchers which concluded that the gases could seriously damage the atmospheric ozone layer, which protects Earth's surface from ultraviolet rays that can cause human skin cancer and harm animals and plants. Starting October 15, 1978, manufacturers of bulk fluorocarbons could no longer make them for use in most aerosol products. The other steps in the phaseout were an end to the manufacture of spray products containing fluorocarbons on December 15, 1978, and a ban on interstate shipment of existing stocks of these products on April 15, 1979. Products already on the shelf or in commercial distribution after April 15, 1979, could be sold.

Great Lakes Water Quality Agreement Passed

The 1978 Great Lakes Water Quality Agreement built on experience under the Great Lakes Water Quality Agreement of 1972, under which there has been a significant improvement in understanding of the technical and scientific aspects of water quality, the presence and effects of toxic substances in the Great Lakes system, and the extent of nonpoint source pollution. The 1978 agreement contained the following significant revisions or improvements of the 1972 agreement:

- Provision of revised and new water quality objectives, both general and specific, to largely eliminate discharge of toxic substances into the Great Lakes and to establish warning systems to point up those which may become evident;

- Dates on which municipal (December 31, 1982) and industrial (December 31, 1983) pollution control programs were to be completed and operating were set, and improved monitoring and surveillance requirements to enable assessment of the effectiveness of remedial programs were established;

- Provisions for dealing with pollution from land use activities and for examining the problem of airborne pollutants;

- A definition of new, interim phosphorus loadings with provision for an eighteen-month review and new strategies for controlling phosphorus as necessary input for an annual public inventory of discharges and pollution control requirements.

The agreement stated the purpose of the two signatories to be a commitment to a maximum effort to obtain a better understanding of the basin ecosystem and to reduce or eliminate the discharge of pollutants into the system, with a prohibition on the discharge of toxic pollutants. This purpose was to be met through programs that, as under the original agreement, had general and specific objectives. General objectives were broad descriptions of desirable water quality conditions, and specific objectives were designations of maximum or minimum desired levels of a substance or effect, to protect the beneficial uses of the waters. Among the general objectives were keeping the waters free from the following:

- Sewage discharges, oil, and other debris;
- Materials that adversely affect color, odor, taste, or other conditions;
- Materials that produce toxic conditions or provide nutrients for the growth of algae which interfere with the beneficial uses of the Great Lakes.

Based on work by experts in both countries under the auspices of the Great Lakes Water Quality Board of the International Joint Commission, the specific objectives of the 1978 Agreement were far more comprehensive and stringent than those of the 1972 agreement.

1979

The EPA Bans PCB Manufacture

The EPA issued final regulations banning the manufacture of poly-chlorinated biphenyls (PCBs) and phasing out most PCB uses. PCBs are toxic and persistent chemicals used primarily as insulating fluids and coolants in machinery and heavy-duty electrical equipment in power plants, industries, and large buildings across the country. The EPA rules would gradually end many industrial uses of PCBs over the next five years, but would allow their continued use in existing enclosed electrical equipment under carefully controlled conditions. Valued for chemical stability and fire resistance, PCBs were manufactured and processed from 1929 to 1977. They had caused birth defects and cancer in laboratory animals, and were a suspected cause of cancer and adverse skin and liver effects in humans. The EPA estimated that 150 million pounds of PCBs were dispersed throughout the environment, including air and water supplies; an additional 290 million pounds were in landfills in the United States. PCB waste must be destroyed by incineration or disposed of in approved landfills. In addition, PCB containers and products must be labeled.

Up to 1979, the EPA had taken enforcement actions for illegal PCB disposal. One case resulted in the convictions of three persons for illegally dumping PCBs along 210 miles of roadway in North Carolina. (See discussion of environmental justice in Chapter 3.) Two other cases resulted in fines totaling $28,600 against two companies for improper disposal of PCBs.

The EPA would allow use and servicing of most existing large electrical equipment containing PCBs (representing nearly 578 million pounds of the 750 million pounds of PCBs then in use) under controlled conditions for the life of the equipment. A requirement to immediately replace all of this equipment would have been prohibitively expensive. The manufacture of new PCB electrical equipment (transformers and capacitors) was entirely prohibited. The EPA would stop use of waste oil containing any level of PCBs for dust control. PCB-contaminated waste oil was then used extensively to control dust on roadways, providing a direct source of environmental contamination. Other products to control dust on roadways were available and cost-effective. Between 1982 and 1984, the EPA would reduce existing PCB uses in electrical equipment in railroad and public transit systems, and phase out or reduce its uses in mining machinery, in hydraulic and heat transfer systems, and in paints and pigments.

The economic impact on electric utilities, most affected by the ban, was expected to be between $3.2 million and $17.0 million a year in disposal costs for burning PCB-contaminated mineral oil used in transformers and large capacitors. These costs were significantly less than the $80 million it would have cost utilities under the earlier high-temperature incineration requirement. All of the expenses incurred by the utilities, including replacement of some PCB transformers, were expected to have a negligible effect on consumers' electric bills. The total first-year cost of this rule was expected to range between $58 million and $105 million. By 1985, the annual costs would drop to about $34 million, and should continue to diminish after 1985 as the use of PCBs was discontinued. The ban on the manufacturing, processing, distribution, and use of PCBs, as well as the PCB disposal and marking regulations, were issued under the Toxic Substances Control Act.

United States Sues for Love Canal Cleanup

In one of largest environmental complaints ever lodged by the federal government against a major corporation, the EPA announced that the Department of Justice—acting on behalf of the EPA—filed four suits against Hooker Chemical Company and its parent corporation, Occidental Petroleum, to force the company to clean up four chemical waste dump sites in Niagara Falls, New York, that were posing substantial danger to residents of the area.

The suits sought a total of $117,580,000 in cleanup costs from Hooker as well as reimbursement for more than $7 million spent by federal agencies in emergency measures at Hooker's Love Canal waste disposal site, as well as unspecified civil penalties. (See discussion of Love Canal in Chapter 3.)

The EPA Establishes Hazardous-Waste Enforcement and Emergency Response System

The EPA gave the cleanup of hazardous-waste dump sites threatening public health the "highest Agency priority," and established the agency-wide Hazardous Waste Enforcement and Emergency Response System to respond to hazardous-waste emergencies. The EPA was then in the process of evaluating potential hazards at 111 sites known to contain hazardous wastes. These evaluations could result in legal actions or emergency federal actions to contain the spread of contaminants where there was an imminent hazard and existing local authority and funding was insufficient.

1980–1989: THE CLEANUP BEGINS

The 1970s saw the development of standards, rules, regulations, and enforceable environmental law. In implementing these new laws, the EPA observed how much emissions had built up in the environment. The 1980s were to be the decade of cleaning up toxic threats to the environment and to public health.

1980

The EPA Supervises Three Mile Island Cleanup

The EPA was designated by the White House as the lead federal agency responsible for the monitoring of off-site radiation levels around Three Mile

Island, and for the implementation of a comprehensive program to keep the local elected officials and the public fully informed of near-term and long-term cleanup activities. The EPA, as the independent environmental regulatory arm of the federal government, would be kept informed of the status of the disabled reactor #2 and proposed on-site cleanup actions by the Nuclear Regulatory Commission. The commission would work with the EPA to provide the public and state and local officials with all the necessary information on cleanup operations in a manner that would allow full and open discussions prior to any final action.

Actions included establishment of an environmental radiation monitoring information office by the EPA. This office, to be located in Middletown, Pennsylvania, was to collect information on radiation levels in the environment around the plant and communicate this information directly and promptly to the general public and to the news media. An extensive radiation monitoring system had been in place around Three Mile Island since 1979. With the establishment of an EPA office on-site, residents would be able to telephone a central information desk to obtain specific information, and to arrange briefings for community groups, on overall cleanup activities. (See discussion in Chapter 3.)

Superfund Passes

The Superfund program (the Comprehensive Environmental Response, Compensation, and Liability Act, passed by Congress in December 1980) is the principal federal program to clean up hazardous substances in the United States. The existing evidence strongly suggests that the Superfund program has very substantial benefits.

1981

The EPA Authorizes First State Hazardous-Waste Programs

The EPA regulated the management of hazardous waste by requiring producers to keep records of what waste they produced and where they stored or disposed of it. Its waste tracking system recorded the person who transported the waste and where the waste was delivered for storage or disposal. Waste could be stored or disposed of at any site whose operators had filed with the EPA and had qualified for "interim status" to operate. This meant that they had officially notified the EPA that they operated such a facility, that they were in existence as of November 19, 1980, and that they were expected to comply with general facility standards issued by the EPA in May 1980. To qualify to manage its own hazardous-waste program, a state must develop a program "substantially equivalent" to federal requirements. State programs must be as stringent as the federal requirements, and, if necessary, could be more stringent. The EPA must

approve the program. The EPA's program for consistent nationwide management of hazardous waste under the Resource Conservation and Recovery Act of
1976 was implemented in two phases. Phase I activities, described in regulations
issued on May 19, 1980, included

- Identification and listing of hazardous waste;
- Standards for generators of hazardous waste;
- Standards for transporters of hazardous waste;
- Interim status standards for owners and operators of facilities that
  treated, stored, or disposed of hazardous waste.

The sixteen state programs authorized for Phase I would, in lieu of the
federal program, regulate those aspects of hazardous waste management. Phase
II of the federal regulations would establish permanent standards for facilities
that treat, store, or dispose of hazardous waste. As these regulations were issued,
states could apply for authorization to issue state permits, in lieu of federal
permits, for these facilities. The EPA would operate the federal hazardous-waste
control program in states that did not apply for authorization or were not authorized to operate their own programs.

The EPA Identifies First 114 Top-Priority Superfund Sites

The EPA announced 114 top-priority hazardous waste sites targeted for
action under Superfund (the Comprehensive Environmental Response, Compensation, and Liability Act, passed by Congress in December 1980), a five-
year, $1.6 billion federal cleanup program. It provides funds from industry and
the federal government to clean up hazardous-waste sites where responsible
parties cannot be determined or cannot afford to pay for cleanup. The ranking
of sites was based on a hazard-scoring system developed by the EPA and one of
its contractors, with extensive input from states and industry. (See discussion
in Chapter 4.) The greatest emphasis was on potential threat to public health,
but the threat to the environment was also taken into account. Pollution via
three pathways—air, groundwater, and surface water—was measured for potential impacts. Fire, explosions, and the possibility of direct contact received
separate evaluation as more appropriate for emergency action. In some cases,
the EPA authorized an emergency removal action based on information uncovered during the hazard-scoring process.

The list of 114 sites was developed from an initial list of 282 sites evaluated
by the states and the EPA's ten regional offices. The final quality assurance
phase of the process was conducted by EPA headquarters. The sites announced would be candidates for inclusion on the list of 400 national priority
"response targets" that the Superfund law required the EPA to identify. Under
Superfund, states must contribute at least 10 percent of the actual long-term

costs of cleanup per site unless the site is publicly owned. On publicly owned sites the state was required to pay or assure at least 50 percent of the costs. Cleanup could occur through three mechanisms: direct federal contracts, cooperative agreements under which the state takes the lead in directing cleanup, and private cleanup through voluntary or court-ordered action.

1982

In 1982 a PCB landfill protest in North Carolina begins the environmental justice movement. Dioxin contamination forced the government to purchase homes in Times Beach, Missouri, and relocate the residents. The federal government and the responsible polluters shared cleanup costs. In 1994, President Bill Clinton ordered government agencies to make environmental justice part of their missions.

Asbestos School Hazard Abatement Act Passes

The EPA announced a rule requiring all public and private elementary and secondary schools in the United States to identify any friable asbestos-containing materials in their buildings. Previously these rules had been only voluntary. This new rule would make it mandatory for school officials to maintain records of their findings, notify employees of the location of the friable asbestos-containing materials, provide employees with instructions on reducing exposures to asbestos, and notify parents or the school's PTA if friable asbestos was found. Asbestos is a known human carcinogen. Asbestos-containing materials have been used widely for fireproofing, thermal and acoustical insulation, and decoration in building construction and renovation. The potential for release of asbestos fibers depends in part upon the characteristics of the material contains them. This regulation addressed friable materials (materials that, when dry, may be crumbled, pulverized, or reduced to powder by hand pressure).

Superfund Pays for Love Canal Cleanup

In one of largest environmental complaints ever lodged by the federal government against a major corporation, the EPA announced that the Department of Justice—acting on behalf of EPA—had filed four suits against Hooker Chemical Company and its parent corporation, Occidental Petroleum, requesting that the company clean up four chemical waste dump sites in Niagara Falls, New York, that were posing substantial danger to residents of the area. The suits sought a total of $117,580,000 in cleanup costs from Hooker, reimbursement for more than $7 million spent by federal agencies in emergency measures at Hooker's Love Canal waste disposal site, and unspecified civil penalties. EPA scientists found eighty-two toxic chemicals in air, water, and soil samples near the dumps. The numerous toxic chemicals—a dozen of which are carcinogenic—discarded at Love Canal over a period of thirty years caused health problems, including miscarriages, among the area's residents. Love Canal gained national attention in 1978 when the New York State Department of Health announced a medical emergency there. President Carter later declared a national emergency for the area. Hundreds of families living near the dump site were forced to leave their homes.

The suits charged that the four Niagara Falls disposal sites were an "imminent and substantial endangerment to health and the environment" and violated the Resource Conservation and Recovery Act, the Clean Water Act, the Safe Drinking Water Act, the Refuse Act, and the common law of nuisance. Although none of the landfills was then being used as a disposal site, the suits alleged that hazardous chemicals stored there were migrating from the sites, contaminating the environment, and endangering persons exposed to the chemicals. Hooker disposed of 199,900 tons of chemical waste at the four sites between 1942 and 1975, and Olin disposed of 66,000 tons of chemical waste at the 102nd Street landfill. Dioxin, a deadly chemical, had been found in high concentrations in Bloody Run, a creek that flows from the Hyde Park disposal site, the suit said, and workers and residents in that area had complained of noxious fumes coming from the dump.

In addition, Hooker would be required to take remedial action to ensure the safety of all homes in the Love Canal area affected by the wastes and to pay for the temporary relocation of affected residents until all environmental indicators showed that chemical contamination had been reduced to the normal levels found in nearby unaffected areas. Or, as an alternative to paying for the temporary relocation, Hooker would be required to purchase all homes within the area affected by migration of the Canal wastes, and pay the relocation costs of the persons residing in those homes.

1983

The EPA Relocates Times Beach Residents

In a joint federal-state action, the EPA, the Federal Emergency Management Agency, and the state of Missouri permanently relocated residents of Times Beach, Missouri. The action was necessary after the Centers for Disease Control completed analysis of extensive soil samples from the area and advised that the hazard posed by dioxin contamination was a continuing threat to the health of citizens in the area. The action was taken to protect the health and safety of the people in a flood hazard area and was not in itself an environmental solution to the dioxin contamination of Times Beach. The EPA entered into a cooperative agreement with the state of Missouri to do a remedial investigation and feasibility study of the area to determine the appropriate environmental solution.

Olin Agrees to Clean Up DDT in Triana, Alabama, Area

The Olin Corporation formally agreed to a multimillion-dollar cleanup of DDT contamination around its former manufacturing facility, the Redstone Arsenal in Alabama, and to provide health care for the residents of the nearby community of Triana. The agreement marked the first time an EPA enforcement action had provided for health care for an affected population. This unique provision provided $5 million to establish the Triana Area Medical Fund, which would provide primary health care and monitoring of the residents. This was to be a nonprofit corporation whose board of trustees would consist of representatives of both local citizens groups and the federal government. Many of Triana's 1,000 residents had elevated levels of DDT in their blood, primarily from the consumption of DDT-contaminated fish caught in Indian Creek, which runs near the plant site. The EPA announced general terms of the agreement on December 30, 1982. The final agreement was lodged with the U.S. District Court in Birmingham, Alabama, on April 15, 1983.

DDT had been manufactured at the Redstone Arsenal site from 1947 to 1971 by Olin and the predecessor lessee of the site, the Calabama Chemical Company. In 1972 the EPA banned the use of DDT in the United States except for limited situations. In the late 1970s, widespread DDT contamination was discovered at the plant site, in nearby waterways (the Huntsville Spring Branch-Indian Creek, a tributary of the Tennessee River), and on more than 1,400 acres of the Wheeler National Wildlife Refuge, the largest and oldest national refuge in Alabama. Elevated levels of DDT had also been detected in wildlife in the area. In 1980, the Justice Department, at the EPA's request, sued Olin, asking it to clean up the contamination. In October 1981, the site was designated one of the EPA's top-priority hazardous-waste sites for cleanup under the new Superfund program.

Under the settlement, Olin was to clean up the DDT residue from the nearby Wheeler Refuge and from the sediment of the Huntsville Spring Branch–Indian Creek tributary in order to reduce DDT levels in fish within a ten-year period. In addition to paying for the cleanup, Olin would provide $24 million to assist residents of the contaminated area, including $19 million to satisfy personal injury claims of over 1,000 private parties, including local residents and local commercial fishermen. Under the agreement, Olin must submit a comprehensive remedial cleanup plan for the area to a review panel of federal, state, and local government representatives by June 1, 1984. The review panel would approve or recommend changes to the plan and provide complete oversight of the cleanup. As part of the environmental cleanup Olin also was to provide short- and long-term environmental monitoring for all affected areas. The EPA-Olin agreement also settled related suits against Olin by the state of Alabama and three citizens groups.

1984

The EPA Supports Chesapeake Cleanup

The agreement regarding cleanup of the Chesapeake the first major step toward implementing a cleanup plan based on a seven-year study of the condition of the bay. In 1983, $10 million in federal funds was appropriated for the bay in addition to sewer grants. This money was going to the states primarily for programs to control pollution from fertilizer runoff and other nonpoint sources. These funds also supported a permanent, professional staff in Annapolis, Maryland, that would help plan activities in the bay area as well as coordinate the work of all the parties to the agreement. Formal agreements pledging cooperation and resources also were signed with five other federal agencies: the Army Corps of Engineers, the Fish and Wildlife Service, the U.S. Geological Survey, the National Oceanic and Atmospheric Administration, and the Soil Conservation Service. The Department of Defense agreed to concentrated action to protect the bay from pollution originating from military bases in the watershed.

Hazardous-Waste and Solid-Waste Amendments Pass

In 1976 Congress passed the landmark Resource Conservation and Recovery Act (RCRA), which authorized the EPA to set standards for generators and transporters of hazardous wastes and for operators of hazardous-waste treatment, storage, and disposal facilities. These standards were to be applied through a permitting program, a manifest system, and other administrative mechanisms to track and deal with the wastes "from the cradle to the grave." There were new requirements governing generators, transporters, and disposers of small quantities of hazardous wastes who generally had not been subject to full regulation under RCRA.

The law required that land disposal of a hazardous waste must be banned unless the EPA determined that the prohibition of such disposal was not necessary to protect human health and the environment. The bill also prohibited the landfilling of bulk or noncontainerized liquids, the placement of bulk liquids in salt domes, use of oil contaminated with hazardous waste as a dust suppressant, and the injection of hazardous waste into or above an underground drinking water source. The law further required persons who produce, burn, and distribute or market fuel derived from hazardous waste to notify the EPA and for the EPA to promulgate record-keeping requirements and technical standards for them. In addition, the law strengthened federal enforcement of RCRA by expanding the list of prohibited actions that may constitute criminal offenses and by raising the maximum criminal penalties. Finally, this law required the EPA to issue regulations for and to establish a program to control underground tanks containing petroleum, hazardous wastes, and other designated substances.

1985

The EPA Sets New Limits on Lead in Gasoline

The new standard will limit the lead content of gasoline to 0.10 gram per gallon. The current standard allows 1.10 grams per gallon. The administrator also set an interim standard of 0.50 grams per gallon, effective July 1, 1985. Adverse health effects from elevated levels of lead in blood range from behavior disorders and anemia to mental retardation and permanent nerve damage. The EPA estimated that between 1985 and 1992, the new standards would result in almost 1 million fewer incidences of blood lead levels exceeding 25 micrograms per deciliter, the figure established by the Centers for Disease Control as a measure of elevated blood lead levels.

The EPA Expands Air Toxics Program

The EPA's strategy for controlling the air toxics problem called for

- Expanding the focus of the national air toxics control program from solely regulating individual pollutants to also regulating multiple pollutants from different source categories;
- Expanding the program to reduce risks in specific communities with air toxics problems;
- Increasing federal support of state programs so that states could improve their capability to deal with air toxics within their borders;
- Improving emergency preparedness and response for sudden, accidental releases at all levels of government;
- Beginning new efforts that would give the public the information they need to prevent, prepare for, and respond to toxic accidents.

Along with focusing on emissions of single pollutants from major industrial point sources, the EPA also would evaluate air toxics problems by source category. The strategy called for the EPA to reduce public exposure by targeting widespread sources—such as degreasing operations, motor vehicles and fuels, and small combustion sources, as well as hazardous-waste treatment, storage, and disposal facilities and publicly owned sewage treatment works.

The EPA also would consider other source categories that may require control and, to the extent possible, evaluate entire emission streams rather than isolated chemical constituents. To control toxic emissions from mobile sources, the EPA set standards for lead in gasoline, evaporative hydrocarbons from trucks, and particulate emissions from cars and trucks. It also was considering a total ban on lead in gasoline and proposing standards for fuel volatility and diesel fuel quality.

The agency also might propose health-effects testing of fuel and fuel additives, propose standards for methanol-fueled vehicles, and decide on controls of vehicle refueling. Under this strategy the agency would regulate source categories of multiple pollutants, including the synthetic organic chemicals industry and residential woodstoves, under new source performance standards. In addition, the EPA also was considering the need for national regulation of gasoline distribution and sales to reduce volatile organics emissions during automobile refueling. These regulations could require placement of gasoline vapor controls on gas pumps or the placement of a vapor canister on new automobiles to capture those emissions.

Parts of the strategy were based on regulations or activities already in place to reduce exposure to toxic air pollutants. Control of conventional pollutants had reduced by more than half the number of cancer cases caused by exposures to certain air toxics between 1970 and 1980.

The EPA would expand its program to devise air toxics regulations tailored to the particular problems of individual communities. It also would identify those areas most likely to benefit from site-specific approaches and, in conjunction with state and local governments in those areas, it would design comprehensive, integrated control approaches taking risk and cost considerations into account. Because local problems may best be evaluated and controlled by state and local agencies, the EPA devoted funds to assist state air toxic control programs, developing a model state air toxics program as a guide, and creating the Air Toxics Information Clearinghouse to exchange information more easily. As of 2003 twenty-two state and local governments had air toxics control programs under way. Under the strategy, states were deemed to be in a better position to deal with small areas of high risk caused by individual plants or sources. The EPA would set criteria to identify pollutants that would be referred to states for appropriate action. By the end of 1985, the EPA was to identify the first group of pollutants by source categories to be referred to the states and make available financial support and extensive technical guidance on all aspects of the referred pollutants. The EPA would also audit state activities in the program, provide public information, and monitor the states to make sure their responses were vigorous and consistent.

The EPA's air toxics strategy called for expanding emergency preparedness and response programs at all levels of government. The tragedy at Bhopal, India, in December 1984 focused national attention on episodic releases of hazardous substances to the air and the health consequences for the communities surrounding the source of the accident. The EPA was to take several steps to build on the existing framework of local, state, private, and federal programs. Because emergency preparedness and response begin at the local level—where the initial reaction to an incident takes place—the EPA would help state and local governments improve their capabilities by providing them with assistance in contingency planning, developing, and review; expanded training; exercise of contingency plans through simulations; and identification of chemicals (which can aid in developing prevention and mitigation procedures).

The EPA also was strengthening its reportable quantities regulations under the Superfund law. This provision applied to those who failed to report toxic releases. Reportable quantity levels had been set for approximately 700 substances. Similarly, under the Toxic Substances Control Act the EPA was stepping up implementation and enforcement of its programs that required manufacturers, processors, and distributors of a wide variety of chemicals to maintain records of significant adverse reactions to chemicals. Manufacturers, processors, importers and distributors were required to notify the EPA when they learned that a chemical substance or mixture might present a substantial risk of injury to health or damage to the environment.

1986

The Superfund Amendments and Reauthorization Act (SARA) of 1986

Reauthorized the Superfund to continue cleanup activities around the country. Several site-specific amendments, definitions clarifications, and technical requirements were added to the legislation, including additional enforcement authorities. The Emergency Planning and Community Right-to-Know Act (EPCRA), also known as Title III of SARA, was enacted by Congress as the national legislation on community safety. It was designated to help local communities protect public health, safety, and the environment from chemical hazards. To implement EPCRA, Congress required each state to appoint a state emergency response commission (SERC). The SERCs were required to divide their states into emergency planning districts and to name a local emergency planning committee (LEPC) for each district. Broad representation of fire fighters, health officials, government and the media, community groups, industries, and emergency managers ensured that all necessary elements of the planning process are represented. Public concern about explosions and leaks of toxic chemicals, such as occurred in Bhopal, India, helped lead to passage of the first community right-to-know law directing manufacturers, users, and storers of certain chemicals to keep records about the location, quantity, use, and any release of those materials, and for the EPA to make such information available to the public. (See discussion in Chapter 3.)

Chernobyl

Chernobyl was a secret disaster at first. The initial evidence that a major nuclear accident had occurred came not from Soviet sources but from Sweden, where on April 27 workers at a nuclear power plant were found to have radioactive particles on their clothes. It was Sweden's search for the source of radioactivity that led to the first hint of a nuclear problem in the Soviet Union.

The EPA first learned about a possible radiological incident from press and citizen inquiries on Monday, April 28. The agency's Offices of Press, Radiation, and International Activities began fielding calls while working with the State Department, the Nuclear Regulatory Commission, and the Department of Energy to find out what was happening. The Soviet news agency, TASS, finally issued a terse statement that evening confirming the accident at the Chernobyl plant but offered no details.

The EPA was confirmed as the lead agency for coordinating the federal response. During the next few weeks both the facts and the radioactive clouds from Chernobyl spread slowly westward. EPA's Environmental Radiation Ambient Monitoring System—continuously operated by the Office of Radiation Programs (ORP) and augmented by reports from the Department of Energy labs, the military, U.S. diplomatic missions abroad, and commercial nuclear power plants in the country—provided daily radiation measurements based on samples from hundreds of monitoring posts in the United States and abroad. EPA's Office of International Activities (OIA) also was heavily involved. Radioactive debris from Chernobyl was monitored around the world, and concern was high in most countries. OIA worked closely with the State Department to get radiation data on fallout. This information was used to inform the public of worldwide radiation levels and potential health risks for travelers.

Safe Drinking Water Act Amendments

These amendments created a demonstration program to protect aquifers from pollutants, mandated state-developed critical wellhead protection programs, required the development of drinking water standards for many contaminants previously unregulated, and strengthened the EPA's enforcement powers in dealing with recalcitrant operators of water systems and underground injection wells. It also imposed a ban on lead-containing plumbing materials. (Studies have found that excessive levels of lead in drinking water can harm the central nervous system in humans, especially children.) The measure also provided substantial new authority to the EPA to enforce the law, including increased civil and criminal penalties for violations. The new law did the following:

- Required the EPA to regulate more than eighty contaminants in drinking water within three years and, after that, at least twenty-five more by 1991;
- Required certain water systems using surface water sources to employ filtration treatment under appropriate circumstances;
- Required certain water systems using groundwater sources to use disinfection treatment;
- Called for the EPA to impose new monitoring requirements on public water systems for contaminants not yet regulated;
- Provided for a demonstration program to protect critical portions of designated aquifers;

319

- Required states to develop programs for protecting areas around wells supplying public drinking water systems;

- Required the EPA to issue new rules for monitoring wells injecting wastes below drinking water sources, and to report to Congress on other types of injection wells;

- Prohibited use of lead solders, flux, and pipes in public water systems, a provision to be enforced by states;

- Authorized the EPA to treat Indian tribes as states and to delegate primary enforcement responsibility for safe drinking water to them.

1987

The EPA Mandates Sanctions against States Not Meeting Air Standards

The mandating of sanctions involves both state and federal reviews of approved plans, offered the possibility that some approved plans might be inadequate and have to be revised, and announced the EPA's intent to disapprove a number of pending plans that could not provide a persuasive demonstration that they would attain the standard in the near term. The EPA estimated that about seventy areas of the country were not meeting the ozone standard as of 1987. The EPA estimated that about twenty major metropolitan areas would have to reduce volatile organic emissions by 50 percent or more to attain the ozone standard of 0.12 parts per million. Ozone is a photochemical oxidant and the major component of smog. While ozone in the upper atmosphere is beneficial by shielding the Earth from harmful ultraviolet radiation given off by the sun, high concentrations of ozone at ground level are a major health and environmental concern.

Ozone is not emitted directly into the air but is formed through complex chemical reactions between precursor emissions of volatile organic compounds such as hydrocarbons and nitrogen oxides in the presence of sunlight. Both volatile organics and nitrogen oxides are emitted by transportation and industrial sources. Volatile organics are emitted from sources as diverse as automobiles, dry cleaners, bakeries, auto body paint shops, and other sources using solvents. Oxides of nitrogen are emitted in the combustion of fossil fuels. The health threat from ozone is particularly serious for those who suffer from respiratory illnesses, but even healthy people can experience adverse effects. High levels of ozone can also substantially injure animals and damage crops, forests, and man-made materials.

Hazardous Chemical Reporting Rule Passed

The final rule for hazardous-chemical reporting requirements under Superfund Title III, Sections 311 and 312, was the Emergency Planning and

Community Right-to-Know Act. Section 311 applied to owners or operators of facilities required to prepare or make available material safety data sheets (MSDS) for hazardous chemicals under the Occupational Safety and Health Administration regulations. An MSDS for each hazardous chemical on site or a list of MSDS chemicals must be provided to the state emergency response commission, the local emergency planning committee, and the fire department with jurisdiction over the facility by October 17, 1987. The first-year minimum reporting is for hazardous chemicals that are produced, used or stored in amounts of 10,000 pounds or more. Materials designated "extremely hazardous substances" because of their importance in terms of planning have a reporting threshold of 500 pounds or the threshold planning quantity, whichever is less. The rule also consolidates the originally proposed twenty-three health and physical categories into five: acute health hazards, chronic health hazards, sudden release of pressure, reactivity, and flammability. The Section 312 requirements apply to all facilities that must comply with the Section 311 MSDS reporting requirements. Inventory reporting forms containing aggregate information by hazard category, according to the same thresholds, must be submitted by March 1, 1988, and annually thereafter, to the same entities as the Section 311 submissions.

1988

The EPA Sets Standards for Underground Storage Tanks

The EPA issued comprehensive and stringent requirements for nearly 2 million underground storage tanks, half of which were used to store gasoline at service stations. Its new rules require owners and operators of underground tanks containing petroleum products or certain hazardous chemicals (not hazardous wastes, which are regulated separately) to monitor tanks for leaks and, in the event of a leak, to notify appropriate authorities and clean up the contamination. In October 1988 the EPA expected to issue financial standards requiring owners and operators to maintain the financial capability to clean up contamination and to compensate third parties for damages. Underground storage tanks are those with 10 percent or more of their volume, including pipes, underground. The Resource Conservation and Recovery Act (RCRA) excluded a number of tanks from federal requirements, including farm and residential tanks storing less than 1,100 gallons of motor fuel for noncommercial purposes, tanks storing heating oil for use on the premises, and tanks on or above floors in underground areas, such as basements or tunnels. The EPA estimated that over 95 percent of the nation's 2 million underground storage tanks hold petroleum products.

Of all tanks in use, an estimated 80 percent were unprotected bare steel tanks, the most likely to corrode and leak. The other 20 percent were protected tanks of steel, fiberglass, or some combination of both. Based on a study of the causes of releases from underground storage tanks, the EPA determined that corrosion of bare steel accounted for almost all leaks from underground tanks and a significant portion of the leaks from connected bare-steel pipes. Improper installation and structural failure due to accidents also caused leaks. The most frequent types of leaks were caused by spills and overfills. Some standards concerning underground storage tanks were already in effect. Under a congressional mandate effective May 7, 1985, under RCRA all newly installed tanks must be protected from corrosion, either through "cathodic" protection (preventing the electrical charge that leads to the corrosion of bare steel placed in the ground) or through the use of corrosion-resistant materials such as fiberglass. In addition, the materials must be compatible with the stored products, and the tanks must be installed using certain procedures to prevent damage. Notification requirements required information about the age, size, type, location, and use of each tank.

Tank owners installing new, corrosion-protected tanks had to certify that the tank was installed correctly, to ensure the structural integrity of the system and thus provide leak-free performance. Owners of existing tanks (defined as tanks in service before December 1988) had to provide corrosion protection within ten years. Leak detection methods would have to be developed or installed at all tanks. Leak detection could be accomplished by methods ranging from tank testing with inventory controls (requiring daily measurements) to the installation of monitoring wells around the tank.

Underground tanks holding one or more of 701 chemicals listed under the Superfund law were affected. There were an estimated 54,000 such tanks, accounting for nearly 4 percent of the total tank population. New chemical tanks were required to have dual containment (called secondary containment), through the installation of either a double-walled tank or concrete vaults or impenetrable liners around the tank. In addition, they must have lead-detection systems installed between the two layers of containment. Spill and overfill equipment also was required. Some variances are allowed.

The EPA required certain actions by tank owners to ensure that leaks and any resulting contamination were cleaned up. Petroleum tank owners and operators who discovered a leak, or an above-ground spill of more than twenty-five gallons were required to report the leak to state regulatory authorities within twenty-four hours. Chemical tank owners must report all leaks; spills and overfills must be reported in accordance with Superfund requirements. In all cases the owner was to check with the local fire department to ensure there was no fire hazard. Any fire or explosion threats and free product must be removed and, under certain circumstances, a more thorough investigation must be conducted to confirm the leak and whether there was any damage to nearby soil and groundwater. All additional information on the leak or spill must be reported to the appropriate regulatory agency within twenty days, and again at forty-five days from the spill. At forty-five days, the owner must report whether or not groundwater had been contaminated and, if necessary, submit a plan for recovering any free product. More extensive examination of soil and groundwater contamination might be required, as well as a plan of corrective action for cleaning up groundwater.

Federal Insecticide, Fungicide, and Rodenticide Act Amendments Pass

On October 25, 1988, the president signed into law the Federal Insecticide, Fungicide and Rodenticide Act (FIFRA) Amendments of 1988, which strengthened the EPA's authority in several major areas. Among other things the amendments required a substantial acceleration of the pesticide reregistration process and authorized the collection of fees to support reregistration activities. The law also changed the EPA's responsibilities and funding requirements for the storage and disposal of suspended and canceled pesticides and the indemnification of holders of remaining stocks of such canceled pesticides. FIFRA governed the regulation of pesticides in the United States. Under FIFRA, all pesticides must be registered (licensed) by the EPA before they could be sold or distributed in commerce. FIFRA set an overall risk/benefit standard for pesticide registration, requiring that pesticides perform their intended function when used according to labeling directions and without posing unreasonable risks of adverse effects on human health or the environment. In making pesticide registration decisions the EPA was required by law to take into account the economic, social, and environmental costs and benefits of pesticide uses.

FIFRA was first enacted in 1947, and thousands of pesticide products had been registered since then. However, the standards for pesticide registration had not remained the same, but evolved in tandem with science and public policy. In particular, test data requirements for pesticides became increasingly stringent in light of advances in toxicology, analytical chemistry, and other areas. Under FIFRA, pesticide registrants were responsible for providing all test data necessary to satisfy the EPA's registration requirements. To ensure that previously registered pesticides measured up to current scientific and regulatory standards, FIFRA required the review and reregistration of all existing pesticides. This proved to be a massive undertaking. A combination of factors impeded the Agency's progress in carrying out the reregistration mandate, including inadequate resources and the sheer magnitude of the task. Of the approximately 600 active ingredients, the EPA had issued registration standards for about 185. A registration standard included a comprehensive review of all the available data on the chemical, a list of additional data needed for full reregistration, and the EPA's current regulatory position on the pesticide. FIFRA authorized the EPA to cancel the registration of an existing pesticide if new test data showed that it caused unreasonable adverse effects on human health or the environment. In addition, under certain circumstances the EPA could take action to suspend the registration of a pesticide to prevent an imminent hazard. Until the amendments of 1988, the EPA was required under FIFRA to accept certain suspended and canceled pesticides and dispose of them at government expense. In addition, an indemnification provision required the EPA to reimburse holders of suspended and canceled pesticides for financial losses suffered, up to the cost of the pesticide.

As indicated above, reregistration provisions were the principal focus of the 1988 amendments. These provisions established requirements with very tight deadlines. A sequence of deadlines applied to pesticide registrants, who were responsible for supplying the complete test data necessary for the EPA to make pesticide reregistration decisions. The EPA also had to meet very specific deadlines in analyzing data submissions and reaching decisions whether to reregister currently registered pesticides.

The 1988 amendments also required the EPA to give expedited consideration to applications for initial or amended registration of products similar to pesticides already registered with the EPA. "Similar" products included not only those identical in composition to currently registered products, but also those which differed from registered products only in ways that would not significantly increase the risk to public health and the environment. In addition, the EPA was required to expedite certain minor amendments to existing product registrations.

The 1988 amendments expanded the EPA's authority to regulate the storage, transportation, and disposal of pesticides. In addition to the authority to require data on storage and disposal methods, the 1988 amendments authorized the EPA to establish labeling requirements for transportation, storage, and disposal of the pesticide and its container. The new law also enabled the EPA, for the first time, to take direct enforcement action against violations of storage, disposal, and transportation requirements. The EPA might require registrants and distributors to recall suspended and canceled pesticide products. To facilitate any recalls of this kind, the EPA could require all persons who sell, distribute, or commercially use pesticides to notify the EPA and state and local officials concerning the quantities and location of suspended and canceled pesticides in their possession. The 1988 amendments also authorized the EPA to regulate procedures for storage, transport, and disposal of containers, rinsates, or other materials used to contain or collect excess or spilled pesticides.

Ocean Dumping Ban Act

President Ronald Reagan signed into law the Ocean Dumping Ban Act of 1988, which prohibited dumping of municipal sewage sludge and industrial waste into the ocean after December 31, 1991. This amended the Marine Protection, Research, and Sanctuaries Act, commonly called the Ocean Dumping Act. The new law did the following:

- Made it unlawful for any person to dump, or transport for the purpose of dumping, sewage sludge or industrial waste into ocean waters after December 31, 1991;

- Prohibited any person from dumping, or transporting for the purpose of dumping, sewage sludge or industrial waste into ocean waters unless the person: (1) entered into a compliance or enforcement agreement and (2) obtained a permit issued by the EPA under authority of Section 102 of the Marine Protection, Research, and Sanctuaries Act (MPRSA);

- Provided for the payment of special fees for dumping and any penalties incurred by a dumper to be deposited into certain funds for use in finding alternatives to ocean dumping.

1989

The EPA Tracks Medical Waste

The EPA's two-year pilot tracking program to ensure that medical waste was sent to proper disposal authorities went into effect in Connecticut, Louisiana, New Jersey, New York, and Rhode Island, as well as in the District of Columbia and Puerto Rico. Most medical experts and public health officials, including those from the federal Centers for Disease Control, believed that medical waste does not present a public health threat, especially after it has been exposed to air and water and washed ashore. The tracking system would be jointly implemented and enforced by the EPA and the participating states. Nearly 3.2 million tons of medical waste was generated by hospitals each year. The EPA estimated that 10 to 15 percent of all medical waste was potentially infectious. Large health care facilities already followed very strict procedures in handling medical waste—most medical waste generated by these facilities was incinerated on-site and only 15 percent was transported off-site and 10 percent of that transported off-site was incinerated. The tracking system would apply to a wide range of medical waste generators, including physicians, dentists, veterinarians, and small clinics, as well as hospitals. Congress specifically exempted medical waste generated by individuals or families, most of which was thrown away in ordinary trash. The EPA's regulations establishing the tracking system defined affected medical waste and established uniform standards for segregation, packaging, labeling, and reporting.

The EPA Responds to Exxon Valdez Oil Spill

Shortly after midnight on March 24, 1989, the 987-foot oil tanker *Exxon Valdez* struck Bligh Reef in Prince William Sound, Alaska. What followed was the largest oil spill in U.S. history. The oil slick spread over 3,000 square miles and onto over 350 miles of beaches in Prince William Sound, one of the most pristine and magnificent natural areas in the country. Experts are still assessing the environmental and economic implications of the incident. The very large spill size, the remote location, and the character of the oil tested spill preparedness and response capabilities. Government and industry plans, individually and collectively, proved to be wholly insufficient to control an oil spill of the magnitude of the *Exxon Valdez* incident. Initial industry efforts to get equipment on scene were unreasonably slow, and once it was deployed, the equipment could not cope with the spill. Moreover, the various contingency plans did not refer to other plans or entities, or establish a workable response command hierarchy. This resulted in confusion and delayed the cleanup. (See discussion in Chapter 3.)

Alar Banned for Food Uses

The EPA announced that it intended to approve the request of Uniroyal Chemical Company of Bethany, Connecticut, to voluntarily cancel all food-use registrations of the pesticide daminozide (trade name Alar). The EPA would order a prohibition on all sales, distribution, and use of daminozide products labeled for use on food crops, including existing stock. The cancellation order would require Uniroyal to complete and submit final reports of three cancer studies involving a breakdown product of daminozide, unsymmetrical dimethylhydrazine (UDMH).

The EPA Releases Toxic Inventory Data

The EPA announced the results of an inventory of chemicals released to the nation's water, air, and land. A summary of the toxic release inventory (TRI) data, which were collected under the Emergency Planning and Community Right-to-Know Act (EPCRA), indicated that in 1987, 9.7 billion pounds of chemicals were released to streams and other bodies of water; 1.9 billion pounds were sent to municipal wastewater treatment plants for processing and disposal; 2.7 billion pounds went into the air; 2.4 billion pounds were put into landfills; and 3.2 billion pounds were injected into underground wells. An additional 2.6 billion pounds were sent to off-site treatment and disposal facilities. Much of the reported emissions were currently managed under EPA or state regulations. The inventory also included accidental or unregulated releases. Under Section 313 of EPCRA, certain manufacturing facilities were required to submit annual toxic release inventory reports to EPA and the state. Facility owners and operators were required to report their annual emissions of each listed chemical to water, air, and land. The first reports were due on July 1, 1988, and the data released in 1989 were from the first annual submission of the toxic release reporting forms. More than 75,000 reports were submitted to the EPA and 17,500 facilities submitted reports, one for each listed chemical that was manufactured, processed, or used.

Water

Of the reported chemical releases into water, sodium sulfate constituted 95 percent. Under EPCRA, anyone may petition the agency to add or delete a substance from the TRI reporting list. The agency received a petition from

Hoechst Celanese Corporation on August 9, 1988, to delete sodium sulfate from the list of toxic chemicals because it did not present potential adverse human health or environmental effects. After reviewing the petition, the agency determined that sodium sulfate did not cause significant adverse human health or environmental effects. In February 1989, the EPA proposed to delete sodium sulfate from the toxic emissions reporting list. Almost 5 percent of substances released into water consist primarily of twelve chemicals that are regulated by the EPA and the states: phosphoric acid, sodium hydroxide, sulfuric acid, nitric acid, and hydrochloric acid, which are regulated for industrial and municipal discharges into water; ammonium sulfate, ammonia, ammonium nitrate, chlorine, and arsenic compounds, for which the EPA has issued water quality criteria; aluminum oxides, which break down into toxic forms of aluminum for which a water quality criterion has been issued; and methanol, which biodegrades readily and is toxic only at high levels.

Air

The air emissions data reported, provided a rough estimate of the potential magnitude of toxics released. While many of the reported compounds were known to be toxic to humans at certain exposure levels, the data available from the toxic release inventory were not sufficient to determine with any certainty the magnitude of the potential public health risk that might be associated with the emissions from a particular source. The data were being used in assessing and ranking sources and categories of sources.

Land

Most of the land releases reported in the inventory were waste disposal. These wastes fall into several categories with different levels of regulatory control. The largest volumes of toxic chemicals released to the land resulted from mining activities. The EPA was currently developing a regulatory program under the Resource Conservation and Recovery Act (RCRA) for the large volumes of this waste. Many of the other chemicals reported were RCRA hazardous wastes when they were discarded products or they might be constituents of designated RCRA hazardous-waste streams. These releases were subject to permitting and management standards under federal and state hazardous-waste laws. The EPA was evaluating the land release data to determine if additional control is needed under federal or state programs.

Emergency Planning and Community Right-to-Know Act

Under the Emergency Planning and Community Right-to-Know Act (EPCRA), manufacturing facilities with ten or more employees that produced, processed, or used certain amounts of any one of more than 300 toxic chemicals were required to report their annual releases of those chemicals to the EPA and states by July 1, 1988. The law also required contingency planning for chemical emergencies. Local facilities must submit to their state and local emergency planning committees their inventories of extremely hazardous chemicals and other substances. This information, along with the TRI data, provided a basis for communities to plan for responses to chemical emergencies and to work together to reduce risk. (See discussion in Chapter 5.)

1990–1999: POLLUTION PREVENTION POLICIES

After the 1980s, when its focus was on cleanup of the environment, the EPA developed policies that were designed to prevent the need for cleanup.

1990

Clean Air Act Amendments

Acid rain emissions were cut in half, 30 million tons of toxic chemicals were prevented from entering the air, and the sulfate-induced haze in some national parks was reduced.

Pollution Prevention Act Passed

The Pollution Prevention Act focused industry, government, and public attention on reducing the amount of pollution through cost-effective changes in production, operation, and raw materials use. Opportunities for source reduction were often not realized because of existing regulations, and the industrial resources required for compliance focused on treatment and disposal. Source reduction is fundamentally different from and more desirable than waste management or pollution control. Pollution prevention includes other practices that increase efficiency in the use of energy, water, or other natural resources, and protect our resource base through conservation. They include recycling, source reduction, and sustainable agriculture.

The EPA Restricts Land Disposal of Hazardous Wastes

The EPA announced the completion of a national program restricting the land disposal of hundreds of hazardous wastes that would both reduce the toxicity of hazardous wastes and protect the nation's groundwater supplies. Most hazardous wastes managed under the Resource Conservation and Recovery Act (RCRA) must be treated to reduce their toxicity and mobility before they could be disposed of on land. When fully effective in May 1992, this rule, combined with the previous rulings, was expected to require treatment of a total of 7 million tons of hazardous waste disposed of on the surface in RCRA-regulated facilities.

Under the law, if treatment capacity was not available for a particular hazardous waste at the time the EPA issued the regulation, the EPA could grant an extension of up to two years for generators of those wastes while they acquired adequate treatment capabilities.

1991

In the largest environmental criminal damage settlement in history, Exxon Corporation and Exxon Shipping agreed to pay $25 million in fines and $100 million to the U.S. and Alaska governments for restoration work, and to establish a $900 million remediation fund arising from the 1989 *Exxon Valdez* oil spill. (See discussion of *Exxon Valdez* in Chapter 3.)

The EPA Commits to Environmental Education

The EPA recognized that environmental education is a recognized and appropriately utilized tool for protecting human health and the environment and improving student academic achievement. One of its goals was to improve and enhance environmental education by providing support including financial resources, and ensuring quality and professionalism in the field. Other strategies included

- Linking to the goals and objectives of education reform to increase the quality and quantity of environmental education in the formal education system;
- Supporting state capacity-building programs and activities that would ensure long-term effectiveness and sustainability of environmental education programs;
- Catalyzing research that assessed the effectiveness of environmental education in environmental protection and student achievement;
- Improving communication and the quality, access, and coordination of environmental education information, resources, and programs both within the EPA and external to it.

Acid Rain Emission Sales Rule Passed

The EPA issued a rule for the auctions and direct sales of rights to emit sulfur dioxide (SO_2). This marked the first time it had allowed the buying and selling of emission rights.

The centerpiece of the acid rain program was an innovative market-based trading system of SO_2 "allowances." An allowance gave affected sources (mainly existing electric power plants) the right to emit one ton of SO_2 per year. A plant's total annual SO_2 emissions could not exceed its allowances, and only the EPA could create an allowance. Existing SO_2 sources (110 plants in Phase I, about 700 more units in Phase II) would receive allowance allocations from the EPA based on their emission rates and previous level of coal, oil, or other fuel use. The new act also mandated significant nitrogen dioxide reduction to control acid rain, but this program would probably not use al-lowances. Allowances were transferable, allowing market forces to determine their price. If a source reduced its SO_2 emissions more than required, it would have leftover allowances it could sell to another utility or bank for its future use.

1992

EPA Announces New Standards to Limit Contamination of Drinking Water

This action increased the total number of federal drinking water standards rose from sixty-one to eighty-four when the new standards went into effect in 1993. Required by the Safe Drinking Water Act, the standards had a pre-ventive thrust because most of the contaminants were rarely found in drinking water. As the safe drinking water program matured, the EPA, the states, and communities would focus more attention and resources on the most serious risks to public health. Small communities, in particular, faced extraordinary financial burdens for this and other public services.

These national standards would guide groundwater protection and cleanup actions and help prevent pollution. Monitoring requirements provided an extra layer of protection for all community drinking water supplies. The newly regulated chemicals included nine pesticides, five inorganic chemicals, and nine synthetic organic chemicals. Five of the contaminants were probable human carcinogens, and seven of the nine pesticides were still in use as of 2005/2006. Dioxin, beryllium, cyanide, and antimony were among the af-fected chemicals.

The final standards would require 80,000 public drinking water systems nationwide to meet the new criteria and to monitor for the contaminants. The EPA estimated that when the regulations became effective, 260 of those systems, serving approximately 340,000 people, will have to treat their water for excess levels of any of the twenty-three contaminants. Public water systems would have to monitor for these contaminants regularly, to ensure that the standards were being met.

The 1986 Amendments to the Safe Drinking Water Act required the EPA to publish maximum contaminant levels (MCLs) for eighty-three specific contaminants. The original Safe Drinking Water Act was passed by Congress in 1974, and the EPA began setting national standards in 1975. The regula-tions established federally enforceable MCLs for the original twenty-three pollutants named in 1975. They also set nonenforceable health goals, called maximum contaminant level goals (MCLGs) at a level at which no known or anticipated health effects occurred, thus allowing an adequate margin of safety. The law required that the MCLs be set as close to the MCLGs as feasible to ensure adequate protection of public health. These standards also identified the best available treatment technologies that could achieve the MCLs; stipulated language that public water suppliers must use to notify customers of standards violations; and established requirements for monitoring, reporting, and state implementation of the federal requirements.

The EPA generally delegated the authority to enforce all federal drinking water standards to the states, but could intercede when necessary. States could set standards more stringent than federal ones or establish standards for contaminants not regulated by the EPA. States could not set standards less stringent than the EPA's. These regulations were among a series of rules mandated by the 1986 Amendments to the Safe Drinking Water Act. The EPA's development and promulgation of these rules was coordinated with a number of other EPA activities to ensure protection of public health while addressing the cumulative economic burden of the growing list of regulatory requirements on states, localities, and water systems.

The EPA and New York City Mark End of Sewage Sludge Dumping

The EPA marked the end of dumping sewage sludge in the ocean. New York City met the terms of its agreement to stop transporting and dumping its sludge in the ocean. New York City produced almost 5 million wet tons of sludge annually as a by-product from fourteen sewage treatment facilities. The city's Department of Environmental Protection was completing the construction of eight sludge dewatering facilities, and had contracted with private vendors to manage the resulting sludge cake on an interim basis by transporting it to several sites across the country selected by the vendors. The sites were either landfills or facilities for pelletization, composting, and land application. The city's long-term alternatives—chemical stabilization, pelletization, and composting—were to be implemented fully by 1998. Since sludge is over 90 percent water, dewatering by centrifuges and presses produces a more transportable sludge cake. Pelletization, or thermal drying, further treats sludge by intense heat that inactivates pathogens and volatile chemicals. Chemical stabilization also inactivates pathogens and volatile chemicals, as well as metals. Land application could include landfill cover, land reclamation, and soil enhancement. Compost from sludge could be used as a soil additive or fertilizer.

Since the 1920s many cities had dumped sludge at sea. By 1981, through consolidations and alternative methods, only nine dumpers—six in New Jersey and three in New York—remained, averaging over 8 million wet tons annually. The Ocean Dumping Ban Act prohibited all ocean dumping of industrial waste and municipal sludge after December 31, 1991. Through a court order New York City and other dumpers were given schedules to end the practice. Because of the need to construct dewatering facilities, New York City's schedule allowed it to dump until June 30, 1992. The six New Jersey authorities—Bergen County Utilities Authority, Joint Meeting of Essex and Union Counties, Linden Roselle Sewerage Authority, Middlesex County

Utilities Authority, Passaic Valley Sewerage Commissioners, and Rahway Valley Sewerage Authority—ceased by March 17, 1991. By December 31, 1991, Nassau and Westchester counties in New York ended ocean dumping completely, and New York City reduced its dumping by 20 percent. The EPA estimates that nationally, municipalities now disposed of sludge by land application and other beneficial use alternatives (49 percent), incineration (15 percent), and other methods (1 percent). Before New York and New Jersey authorities ceased ocean dumping, this method accounted for 5 percent of the national total.

From 1924 through 1987, sludge was disposed of at a site about twelve miles offshore in waters about eighty-eight feet deep. The EPA shut down this site because of elevated bacterial levels, closed shellfish beds, and accumulated toxic organic compounds and heavy metals in bottom sediments that caused changes in diversity and abundance of marine life. No impact on human health or on coastal beaches was detected from the site. Beginning in 1986, the EPA required sludge dumpers to phase in use of a site designated as the Deepwater Municipal Sludge Dump Site (also called the 106-Mile Site), located off the Continental Shelf, approximately 115 nautical miles east of Atlantic City, New Jersey, with water depths of about 7,500 feet. The Ocean Dumping Ban Act required conditions at the site to be monitored carefully by the EPA, the Coast Guard and the National Oceanic and Atmospheric Administration. Preliminary monitoring results indicated that the sludge was not being transported onto the Continental Shelf, which is rich with marine life, but that a small percentage was reaching the sea floor southwest of the dump site, raising concern about what might happen if dumping of large amounts of sludge continued. As with the twelve-mile site, there was no impact detected on shoreline beach water quality or on human health.

The EPA Commits to Reducing Environmental Risks to Minorities

The EPA released its final environmental equity report. The report, *Environmental Equity: Reducing Risks for All Communities*, requested by Administrator William K. Reilly, reviewed existing data on the distribution of environmental exposures and risks across population groups and included a series of findings and recommendations. Among the findings were that there are clear differences between racial groups in terms of disease and death rates; racial minority and low-income populations experienced higher than average exposures to selected air pollutants, hazardous-waste facilities, contaminated fish, and agricultural pesticides in the workplace; and great opportunities existed for the EPA and other government agencies to improve communication about environmental problems with members of low-income and racial minority groups. Among the recommendations in the report were that the EPA should increase the priority given to issues of environmental equity, identify and target opportunities to reduce high concentrations of risk to specific population groups, and increase efforts to involve racial minority and low-income communities in environmental policy-making. (See discussion of environmental justice in Chapters 3 and 6.)

1993

Federal Facilities Ordered to Reduce Toxic Emissions

Emphasizing that the federal government should set an example and become the leader in pollution prevention, President Clinton signed an executive order that by 1999 would reduce by half toxic emissions from federal facilities and would require them to report any release of toxic pollutants to the public.

In his speech commemorating Earth Day, the president directed federal agencies to prepare an executive order that would set a voluntary goal of a 50 percent reduction of their release of toxic pollutants by 1999. This goal should be achieved by reducing or eliminating the use of toxic chemicals during production, before they became waste. By stopping pollution at its source, rather than waiting for it to become waste that must somehow be disposed of, the federal government could make a significant contribution to protecting the public health and the environment. The initiative also required federal facilities that manufacture, process, or use toxic chemicals to publicly report their wastes and releases under the Emergency Planning and Community Right-to-Know Act. Under the toxics release inventory requirements of this new law, federal facilities would report their toxic emissions to the EPA and to the states where the chemicals were emitted. The public could obtain this information from a national computer database and from their respective states.

In addition to the establishment of voluntary reduction goals and right-to-know reporting of toxic emissions, the executive order also required review and, where necessary, revision of existing procurement practices. This provision would help eliminate or reduce procurement of extremely hazardous substances and chemicals used by federal facilities in manufacturing and processing. The executive order would provide the public and local governments with information concerning potential chemical hazards present in their communities. Federal facilities would develop emergency response plans with community participation.

The EPA Announces the Common Sense Initiative

In an effort to reenergize its environmental policy-making creativity, the EPA announced the Common Sense Initiative, a sweeping effort to fundamentally shift environmental regulation—moving away from the pollutant-by-pollutant, crisis-by-crisis approach of the past to an industry-by-industry approach for the future. This new approach was designed to achieve cleaner, cheaper, and smarter results—cleaner for the environment, cheaper for business and taxpayers, and smarter for the environment.

The EPA Requires Full Phaseout of CFCs and Other Ozone Depleters

The EPA announced a final rule to fully phase out domestic production and imports of chlorofluorocarbons (CFCs) and six other substances which deplete the stratospheric ozone layer that deflects dangerous ultraviolet radiation and is vital to the protection of human life. Phasing out products that deplete ozone will prevent millions of cases of skin cancer and cataracts.

The Clean Air Act Amendments of 1990 required the EPA to phase out the production and importing of five ozone depleters—CFCs, halons, carbon tetrachloride, methyl chloroform (all Class I substances) and hydrochlorofluorocarbons (Class II substances). The amendments also gave the EPA the responsibility to add other ozone depleters to the phaseout list.

The 1990 Amendments originally set more lenient phaseout deadlines, but required the EPA to accelerate these deadlines under certain circumstances. This accelerated deadline rule was based on recent scientific information regarding unanticipated increases in the rate of stratospheric ozone depletion and on adjustments made to the Montreal Protocol at the Copenhagen meeting. The Montreal Protocol is an international agreement which controls, among the 126 nations that are currently parties, the production and trade of ozone depleters. The EPA emphasized that the phaseout deadlines affected only domestic production and importing. These substances could continue to be used after the deadlines if companies could find sources of supply through recycling or existing inventories. Under the EPA's phaseout program, companies were allocated production and importing allowances for ozone depleters based on prior production. The allowances would be gradually reduced each year until production and importing were eliminated.

The EPA Designates Passive Smoke as a Human Carcinogen

The EPA assessment of secondhand tobacco smoke concluded that environmental tobacco smoke (ETS), also known as secondhand smoke, is a human lung carcinogen responsible for approximately 3,000 lung cancer deaths annually among U.S. nonsmokers. It also concluded that passive smoking resulted in serious respiratory problems for infants and young children.

This risk assessment added new peer-reviewed evidence to the growing scientific consensus that smoking is not just a health danger for smokers, but a significant risk for nonsmokers, particularly children, who are exposed to secondhand smoke. The EPA would work closely with the Department of Health and Human Services and other organizations to ensure that officials around the world were made aware of the findings of this important risk assessment. Tobacco smoke had long been recognized as a major cause of death and disease, especially lung cancer and chronic respiratory disease, in smokers. In recent years there had been concern that nonsmokers might also be at increased risk as a result of their exposure to the smoke exhaled by smokers and given off by burning cigarettes, pipes, or cigars. This smoke contains more than 4,000 substances, at least forty-three of which cause cancer in humans or animals and many of which are strong eye or respiratory irritants.

The lung cancer findings in the EPA's assessment were based on several important analytical findings: (1) the chemical and physical similarity of ETS to smoke inhaled by smokers; (2) the known lung carcinogenicity of tobacco smoke to smokers; (3) the known exposure to ETS and its uptake by the human body; and (4) a thorough and comprehensive review of more than thirty studies in both the United States and abroad that examined the relationship between lung cancer and exposure to secondhand smoke in people who never smoked (usually the spouses of smokers). The EPA concluded from the total "weight of evidence" of all the studies that ETS increased the risk of lung cancer in nonsmokers. The report's conclusions on childhood respiratory health were based on more than 100 studies of children documenting the fact that secondhand smoke is a problem for young children and infants. Some of the effects cited were the following:

- ETS exposure caused additional episodes and increased severity of symptoms in asthmatic children—it was estimated that 200,000 to 1 million asthmatics had their condition worsened by exposure to ETS.

- ETS exposure was a risk factor for new cases of asthma in children who had not previously displayed symptoms.

- ETS exposure caused an increased risk of lower respiratory tract infections, such as bronchitis and pneumonia, in infants and young children—the report estimated that exposure to parents' secondhand smoke would lead to 150,000 to 300,000 cases annually in children up to eighteen months old.

- ETS exposure caused an increased prevalence of fluid in the middle ear, symptoms of upper respiratory tract irritation, and a small yet significant reduction in lung function.

Following a second review in the summer of 1992, the EPA's Science Advisory Board (SAB) fully endorsed the risk assessment, including the conclusion that ETS should be classified as a known human carcinogen (officially called an EPA Group A carcinogen, the Agency's category of greatest scientific certainty for known or suspected carcinogens). The SAB also endorsed the risk estimate that between 2,500 and 3,300 lung cancer deaths per year among U.S. nonsmokers were attributable to ETS exposure, as well as the findings on other respiratory effects. The SAB is the EPA's independent panel of outside scientific advisers that routinely reviews draft EPA reports. (See discussion of SAB in Chapter 5.)

1994

Superfund cleanups were greatly accelerated, resulting in as many cleanups completed in twelve months as had been completed in the program's first decade—an accomplishment that would be repeated in 1995. New grants were launched by the EPA to help fifty U.S. communities revitalize inner-city brownfields—abandoned, contaminated sites that were formerly industrial or commercial properties—and return them to productive use for the community, resulting in both economic and environmental gains. The EPA almost doubled the list of toxic chemicals that must be publicly reported under the community right-to-know laws, giving Americans a dramatic increase in the information about toxic pollution from manufacturing facilities in communities nationwide.

Federal Environmental Justice Order Signed

The EPA announced a competition for new grants to help communities develop innovative ways to overcome obstacles to the cleanup and reuse of potentially contaminated urban properties. The Brownfields Initiative was intended to demonstrate ways to return unproductive abandoned urban sites to productive use and to ensure that future development is done in a sustainable, environmentally sound manner. In order to encourage redevelopment of these brownfields and to prevent the siting of future industrial sites in more pristine rural areas, or "greenfields," the EPA initiated the Brownfields Economic Redevelopment Initiative. Under its projects, communities would strive to find developers to restore abandoned sites and thereby create new jobs and economic growth, increase property values, stimulate tax revenues, and rejuvenate neighborhoods. The EPA would work with the federal, state, and local officials to develop a coordinated federal strategy to help initiate a significant national effort to encourage cleanup and redevelopment of brownfields. All the brownfields pilot projects featured cooperative efforts between community groups, investors, lenders, developers, regulators, and other involved parties. (See discussions of environmental justice in Chapters 1, 3, and 9.)

1995

The Common Sense Initiative Is Formed

The EPA announced the selection of the first six major U.S. industries to participate in an effort to transform the process of environmental regulation into a comprehensive system for strengthened environmental protection. The new program, called the Common Sense Initiative, was designed to achieve greater environmental protection at less cost by creating pollution control and prevention strategies on an industry-by-industry basis, rather than the current pollutant-by-pollutant approach. The initiative would analyze the overall environmental impact of each industry.

"The successes that are available if we continue down the path of traditional regulation are incremental at best," EPA Administrator Browner said. "The current regulatory system is about going from A to B and B to C. The changes we undertake today are about going from A to Z. I don't think anyone in this country, whether environmental leader or corporate CEO, believes incremental steps will achieve the kind of future we all want." Browner said that through the Common Sense Initiative, "Government officials at all levels, environmentalists and industry leaders will come together to create industry-by-industry strategies that will work cleaner, cheaper, and smarter to protect public health and our natural resources." The Common Sense Initiative was expected to result in significant improvements to existing regulations, as well as proposals for Congress to consider in cases where legislative reforms might be required. Consensus proposals generated by the Initiative would be designed to better protect the environment, reduce pollution overall in the United States, and reduce by billions of dollars the costs that industries faced. The six industries selected by Browner to participate in the pilot phase of the initiative were auto manufacturing, computers and electronics, iron and steel, metal finishing and plating, petroleum refining, and printing.

For each of the selected industries, Browner announced formation of a team headed by top EPA officials and including environmental vice presidents from the industries, as well as representatives from national and grassroots environmental groups, state environmental commissioners, local government officials, labor union representatives, environmental justice groups, and, in some cases, officials from other federal agencies. The teams would examine every aspect of environmental regulation as it affected an industry and the environment, and identify opportunities for greater reductions in pollution through flexible, innovative environmental protection strategies.

As a group the industries involved in the initiative spent more than $8.2 billion in 1992 on compliance with environmental laws, according to the U.S. Department of Commerce. Their combined release of toxic pollutants into the environment came to 395 million pounds that year, 12.4 percent of all reported emissions nationally. The six industries were selected as the first participants in the initiative because they are among the nation's largest, employing almost 4 million people and accounting for almost 14 percent of the gross domestic product. Another section of the initiative required municipal incinerators to reduce toxic emissions to 10 percent of 1990 levels.

The EPA announced a final rule to reduce toxic air emissions from the chemical industry, one of the biggest industrial sources of these pollutants, by almost 90 percent. It also announced a separate final rule for electric utility power plants to help reduce acid rain. "This is the most far-reaching effort ever taken to reduce air toxics, and a giant step forward in protecting the health of our citizens," said Administrator Browner. "Today's rule signifies that the gridlock of the past on clean air controls has now been broken."

Browner also emphasized the pollution prevention and environmental justice aspects of the chemical industry rule, noting that more than 10 percent of all emission reductions under the regulation would result from pollution prevention techniques, such as using covers to prevent evaporation from storage tanks. In the chemical industry, evaporation prevention translates into significant product savings. The final rule affected about 370 chemical plants in thirty-eight states, the majority in Texas, Louisiana, and New Jersey. The 1990 amendments to the Clean Air Act listed 189 air toxics, from a variety of industries, that the EPA must regulate by the turn of the century. This rule reduced emissions of 112 of these toxics by 506,000 tons annually, an 88 percent reduction from current levels. Although the rule was aimed at controlling air toxics, as a beneficial by-product it would also significantly decrease levels of volatile organic compounds (VOCs), the prime ingredient in the formation of ground-level ozone (smog)—the nation's most pervasive air pollutant. VOC levels would drop by 1 million tons a year, an 81 percent reduction. These VOC cuts were equivalent to removing 38 million cars from the road, about one-fourth of all U.S. cars.

Under the new rulemaking, chemical industry sources must achieve emission limits reflecting application of maximum achievable control technology, as defined by the Clean Air Act. For new sources, this meant the standards must be as stringent as the emission control achieved in practice by the best-controlled similar source anywhere in the country. For existing sources, the standards must be as stringent as the average emission control achieved by the best-performing 12 percent of existing plants. The rule contained an innovative compliance alternative called "emissions averaging," which chemical manufacturers could use only if approved by the state in which the plant operated. This option let companies avoid excessive costs as long as public health was protected. Emissions averaging meant that if a facility did not wish to control a particular pollution source, emissions from that source could be offset by emission reductions—greater than required by law—at other sources in the same plant.

However, to ensure environmental protection and enforceability, the EPA added strict requirements for the use of emissions averaging that had not existed when the rule was proposed in the George H. W. Bush administration. For instance, emissions averaging could be used by only a small number of emission sources in a facility. Also, any emissions averaging must result in an extra 10 percent reduction in toxic emissions over what would have occurred if this option had not been used. In addition, emission averaging could be utilized only within one facility, not between plants in different locations. An example of emissions averaging in practice would be a chemical plant with substantial pollution control technology already in place but, because of the new rule, would need new control technology. The emission averaging option might allow this plant to avoid ripping out existing controls if it could provide equivalent toxic reductions—plus an extra 10 percent—from elsewhere within the facility.

The EPA estimated that the rule's total nationwide capital costs to the chemical industry would be $450 million and total annual costs would be $230 million. These costs would result in a "worst-case" estimated price increase to customers of less than 3 percent. The EPA predicted no plant closures as a result of this rule. Existing chemical industry sources must comply with this rule within three years; new sources must comply immediately or on startup of operations, whichever occurs later.

Besides the chemical industry toxic rule, the EPA announced a final acid rain rule that would cut annual emissions of nitrogen oxide (Nox) by 1.8 million tons annually from 700 coal-fired electric utility power plants by 2000. Nox and sulfur dioxide (SO_2) are the prime ingredients in the formation of acid rain, and the rule complements the Agency's final acid rain rule for SO_2 issued in January 1993. The EPA also announced four other rules regarding toxins in air to help protect public health. One final rule established generic general provisions for all future standards for air toxins under the Clean Air Act. The general provision rule would eliminate redundancy in general information that would have to be repeated each time a new standard was issued, and it would maintain the consistency of future regulations. It would be the primary vehicle for informing industry of its basic compliance responsibilities under the Clean Air Act. Another proposed rule provided guidance for implementing a provision of the 1990 Clean Air Act Amendments requiring maximum achievable control technology (MACT) for new, reconstructed, and modified major sources of air toxics. (See discussion in Chapter 3.) New sources required stringent controls, while modified sources faced less stringent limits. Another proposed rule would remove 4.6 million pounds of toxic air pollutants yearly from the magnetic tape manufacturing industry (audio cassettes, etc.). Most toxic sources in this industry would face air toxin reductions of 95 percent from uncontrolled levels. The air toxic ethylene oxide would be cut by 2.2 million pounds annually under another proposed EPA rule controlling commercial sterilization operations such as those for medical equipment. The rule would reduce this toxic at major sources by 99 percent from uncontrolled levels. Under the Clean Air Act states have the authority to toughen the federal EPA regulations announced, but they cannot weaken them.

Refinery Air Toxics Rule Passed

The EPA announced the first comprehensive control of toxic air pollution from petroleum refineries. The final rule would protect the health of 4.5 million Americans living near refineries by reducing by almost 60 percent chemicals, such as benzene, that can cause cancer and other serious health effects. The new rule also would greatly reduce air pollutants that contribute to smog. The rule would cut emissions of eleven air toxics by 53,000 tons annually, representing a 59 percent reduction from current levels. The regulation would also reduce smog-causing volatile organic compound (VOC) emissions by 277,000 tons annually, representing a 60 percent reduction from current levels. VOCs are the prime ingredient in the formation of ground-level ozone (smog), the nation's most pervasive air pollutant. The smog reduction benefits alone were valued at more than $150 million annually, and the total cost of the rule was approximately $95 million each year.

Petroleum refineries process crude oil to produce automotive gasoline, diesel fuel, lubricants, and other oil-based products. The rule would affect 192 existing refineries and any new facilities built in the future. Many of these refineries were located in heavily populated areas in California, Texas, Louisiana, New Jersey, and Pennsylvania. Approximately 4.5 million Americans living near these facilities were potentially at risk for health problems including cancer, respiratory illness, and reproductive disorders. The EPA would require these refineries to use maximum achievable control technology, a term generally defined by the Clean Air Act as the best demonstrated pollution control technology or practice in current use by similar sources anywhere in the United States.

The rule contained a commonsense principle, called "emission averaging," that would allow facilities flexibility in deciding which emission sources to control. Plants might find it more cost-effective to overcontrol certain emission sources and undercontrol others, the overall result being greater emission reduction at less cost. Additional flexibility was provided by permitting the use of emissions averaging among petroleum refineries, marine terminal loading operations, and gasoline distribution facilities located at the same site. The rule, however, specified to what extent facilities could use emissions averaging and which emission points could be included. The regulation would require controls for emissions of air toxics for storage tanks, equipment leaks, process vents, and wastewater collection and treatment systems.

The EPA Expands Acid Rain Emissions Trading

As part of its flexible, commonsense approach to smarter environmental and public health protection, the EPA extended to all industrial fossil fuel-burning sources the option of reducing acid rain by trading pollution credits.

Trading pollution credits provided industry the flexibility to produce the very best environmental results for the least cost. Emissions trading already saved industry, and consumers, $2 billion per year. The final rule would allow combustion sources to voluntarily enter the pollution credit trading program. Their participation would expand this program beyond electric power plants to include more facilities that emit sulfur dioxide (SO_2), the prime ingredient in the formation of acid rain. The Clean Air Act Amendments of 1990 required that 1980 SO_2 emission levels from electric power plants be cut in half by 2010—a 10 million-ton yearly reduction. To achieve this reduction, the EPA offered electric utilities the option of using an innovative, market-based "allowance" trading system. An allowance gave a utility unit the right to emit one ton of SO_2 a year. The EPA granted allowances to utilities based on their past fuel usage. The allowance program gives a utility an economic incentive to reduce acid rain pollution: If a plant reduced its SO_2 emissions below its level of allowances, it would have leftover emission credits it could sell to other utilities or anyone that wanted to buy them.

This rule set up an "opt-in" program, allowing combustion sources other than utilities, such as industrial steam boilers, to participate in allowance trading. Just like utilities, opt-in sources would get their own allocation of allowances from the EPA and would also have an economic incentive to reduce pollution. The EPA believed the overall cost of SO_2 control would be lowered as opt-in facilities sold their unused allowances to electric utility units. Utilities could use these allowances to comply with the acid rain rules at less cost than for traditional pollution control equipment. Opt-in sources must comply with monitoring, enforcement, and other Clean Air Act requirements similar to those applicable to utilities. Regardless of the number of allowances held, no opt-in source could exceed standards protecting public health and the environment.

1996

EPA Implements Lead-based Paint Right to Know

Friday, December 6, 1996, marked the first time that all home buyers and tenants had the right to know about known or potential lead-based paint hazards before buying or renting older (pre-1978) housing under a new EPA/ U.S. Department of Housing and Urban Development program.

More than 1.7 million American children under the age of six had unsafe blood-lead levels, making lead poisoning a top environmental health hazard for young children. Most of those children were poisoned by deteriorated lead-based paint and the contaminated soil and dust it generated. Children with too much lead in their bodies can experience lowered IQ, reading and learning disabilities, impaired hearing, and other problems. More than 80 percent of the U.S. housing stock built before 1978 (the year the sale of residential lead-based paint was banned)—some 64 million residences—contained lead paint. The new requirements apply to sales and rentals of residences built before 1978.

The EPA Finalizes Leaded Gas Ban

The EPA took the last steps concluding a twenty-five-year effort to phase out leaded gasoline. Administrator Browner signed a final rulemaking to elim-inate requirements that had become obsolete or unnecessary as a result of the ban, including certain record-keeping and reporting requirements for gasoline refiners and importers. "The elimination of lead from gas is one of the great environmental achievements of all time," Browner said. "Thousands of tons of lead have been removed from the air, and blood levels of lead in our children are down 70 percent. This means that millions of children will be spared the painful consequences of lead poisoning, such as permanent nerve damage, anemia or mental retardation." Fetuses and children are especially susceptible to low doses of lead, often suffering central nervous system damage or slowed growth.

Lead had been blended with gasoline, primarily to boost octane levels, since the early 1920s. The EPA began working to reduce lead emissions soon after its founding, issuing the first reduction standards in 1973; these called for a gradual phasedown of lead to 0.10 gram per gallon by 1986. The average lead content in gasoline in 1973 was two–three grams per gallon, about 200,000 tons of lead a year. In 1975, passenger cars and light trucks began to be manufactured with a more elaborate emission control system that included a catalytic converter which required lead-free fuel. In 1995 leaded fuel accounted for only 0.6 percent of total gasoline sales and less than 2,000 tons of lead per year. Effective January 1, 1996, the Clean Air Act banned the sale of the small amount of leaded fuel that was still available in some parts of the country for use in on-road vehicles.

Safe Drinking Water Act

A new safe drinking water law provided strengthened protections to ensure that American families have clean, safe tap water when the EPA announced key reform proposals for the Safe Drinking Water Act. The new law was based on provisions in the Clinton administration's 1993 reform proposal, including a drinking water treatment loan fund and protections for drinking water sources. The new law would strengthen and expand the nation's drinking water protections in three important ways:

1. It gave the public the right to know about tap water water quality, contaminants, and sources, and whether the water posed a risk to health.

2. The new law strengthened standards that would protect the public from contaminants that pose the greatest health risks. The law set clear schedules for developing standards for deadly microbial contaminants such as cryptosporidia, and called for considering special populations such as the elderly, children, and people with HIV/AIDS when standards were set, in order to ensure stronger health protection. The law also mandated technical assistance to help water systems nationwide do a better job of delivering safe, clean water.

3. The new law authorized up to $9.6 billion in loan funds that would go straight to the states to upgrade community drinking water treatment systems nationwide through the year 2003. In 1993, President

Clinton had proposed establishing a loan fund for safe drinking water. The new law called for identifying and assessing potential pollution threats to local sources of water; it also provided states with a flexible, commonsense framework to develop and fund local projects to protect the rivers, lakes, streams, and groundwater that serve as the sources of tap water.

1997

The EPA Implements Food Quality Protection Act

The EPA issued a comprehensive, detailed plan for implementing the 1996 Food Quality Protection Act (FQPA). The new law included sweeping new food safety protections and required major changes in how pesticides were regulated, with the goal of improving environmental and public health protection, especially for children. The FQPA implementation plan was based on five guiding principles: sound science; a protective, health-based approach to food safety; promotion of safer, effective pest control methods; an open, fair, and consistent process that involves consultation with stakeholders and an informed public; and public accountability for the EPA's actions and resources to achieve the goals of the law.

The major provisions of the new law included the following:

- Establishing a single, health-based standard for all pesticide residues in food, whether raw or processed;
- Providing for a more thorough assessment of potential risks, with special protections for potentially sensitive populations, such as infants and children;
- Requiring the EPA to reassess roughly 9,000 existing tolerances (maximum legally permissible residue levels in food) to ensure they meet the new standard;
- Requiring the EPA to develop consumer information, to be displayed in grocery stores, on the risks and benefits of pesticides used in or on food, as well as recommendations to consumers for reducing exposure to pesticides while maintaining a healthy diet;
- Ensuring that all pesticides will be periodically reevaluated to make sure they meet current testing and safety standards.

Among the major reforms of FQPA were requirements that the EPA routinely address a number of new considerations in establishing tolerances for pesticide residues in food. Many of these new provisions raised complex scientific issues and called for new policies and evaluation methods. The EPA had already

343

brought a number of these issues before expert scientific review panels and would continue to consult with these expert bodies as implementation proceeded. Specifically, FQPA required the EPA to do the following:

- Use an extra safety factor in conducting risk assessments to assure the protection of infants and children;
- Assess total pesticide exposure from all nonoccupational sources, including the diet, drinking water, and household pesticide use;
- Assess effects of exposure to multiple pesticides with a common mechanism of toxicity;
- Assess effects of in utero exposure;
- Assess potential effects on the endocrine system.

1998

The EPA Common Sense Initiative Wins Hammer Award

On Thursday, December 17, 1998, Vice President Gore's Hammer Award was presented to Carol M. Browner, administrator of the EPA, for bringing commonsense reform to environmental regulation. "This Common Sense Initiative is reinventing government at its best," Vice President Gore said. "Together, government, industry, and the private sector are finding new, more effective ways to protect our environment and our children."

CSI—a partnership of more than 300 individuals from industry, state and local governments, environmental and environmental justice groups, and labor—served as a laboratory for testing new environmental management approaches, based on the needs of industry and other interest groups. Six industrial sectors were selected to experiment with new approaches: automobile manufacturing, computers and electronics, iron and steel, metal finishing, petroleum, and printing. These sectors were chosen to represent a broad array of industrial challenges. CSI spawned environmental regulatory reforms and changes in industry and government business practices.

1999

The EPA proposed that by 2007 new emissions standards for cars, sport utility vehicles, minivans, and trucks would require them to be 75 percent to 95 percent cleaner than in 1999.

The EPA proposed new requirements to improve air quality in national parks and wilderness areas.

Superfund reform accelerated hazardous-waste cleanups.

2000–2005: POLLUTION PREVENTION POLICIES IMPLEMENTED

The EPA affirmed a rule to lower the threshold for reporting of lead used by industry. The new standard would require any company that manufactures, processes, or uses 100 pounds of lead or more annually to report such use to the EPA as part of the toxics release inventory. This would significantly increase the information available to the public about the uses of lead in communities. Past practice showed that such information generally led to decreased emissions of reportable toxics by companies, thereby leading to public health and environmental benefits.

2000

The EPA Endorses Cleaner Diesel Fuels Plan

Cleaner diesel fuels would provide greatly improved air quality for all Americans, reducing smog-causing nitrogen oxides from diesel vehicles by 95 percent and harmful particulate matter (soot) by 90 percent. It was the clean air equivalent of removing the pollution generated by 13 million trucks from the air. Soot and smog pollution were scientifically associated with 15,000 deaths, and a million cases of respiratory problems, each year. They were also responsible for some 400,000 asthma attacks every year, including thousands of aggravated cases of asthma, especially in children. This action would reduce the sulfur content in diesel fuel by 97 percent. This meant that for the first time, heavy-duty trucks and buses would be able to use pollution-control devices to meet emission standards, just as passenger cars had been doing since the 1970s. These devices are sensitive to sulfur and will not work unless the amount of sulfur in the fuel is dramatically reduced. Specifically, adopting this proposal would mean that over 100 million Americans living in areas that had difficulty meeting clean-air standards would be able to breathe healthier air in the future.

In the past, engine manufacturers were able to meet permissive emission standards without the aid of control devices. However, the stringent standards in this proposal would result in the first broad use of emission control devices such as three-way catalysts and soot traps on these engines. These devices would allow manufacturers to produce dramatically cleaner engines. This proposal would allows adequate lead time and flexibility for industry to meet the new standards. The current level for sulfur in diesel fuel of 500 parts per million would be reduced to 15 parts per million by June 2006. New trucks and buses would be required to meet standards progressively, beginning in 2007 and with full compliance by 2010. This would assure accomplishment of the transition to cleaner vehicles cost effectively and without any disruptions.

EPA Bans Most Dursban Uses

The banning of Dursban—the result of an agreement with the manufacturers—would significantly minimize potential health risks from exposure to Dursban (chlorpyrifos), especially for children, who are among the most vulnerable to the risks posed by pesticides. Dursban (the common trade name) was one of more than 800 products containing chlorpyrifos. Chlorpyrifos was commonly found in many home-and-garden bug sprays; it was used in some treatments for termites; and it was used on some agricultural crops. It belongs to a family of older, riskier pesticides called organophosphates, some of which date back to the 1950s or earlier.

2001

The EPA Responds to September 11 Terrorist Bombing

Seconds after the first explosion, Kathy Callahan, then acting director of the region's Emergency and Remedial Response Division, telephoned Bruce Sprague, head of the Response and Prevention Branch in Edison, New Jersey, to set in motion the region's emergency response. Many employees witnessed the second plane's impact from their office windows at 290 Broadway, just a few blocks from the World Trade Center. Within minutes, Sprague dispatched the first crew of Agency on-scene coordinators (OSCs) from Edison to New York City to monitor ambient environmental conditions. The OSCs had to scramble just to find where New York City had set up its temporary command center. The city's state-of-the-art Emergency Operations Center had been located in the World Trade Center complex and was destroyed in the collapse, sending the mayor and other top officials scurrying for safety. All radio communications were lost, and the dust was so bad that not even the EPA's satellite phones worked. Overcoming such obstacles, the OSCs took the first dust samples within an hour or two of the collapse; the EPA collected air, dust, water, river sediment, and drinking water samples following the collapse of the WTC towers. The Agency received data from more than thirty fixed air monitors in and around Ground Zero and additional monitors in the Bronx, Brooklyn, Queens, New Jersey, and Staten Island. The outdoor sampling ended June 2002. Additional information about World Trade Center monitoring is available on the Web at http://www.epa.gov/wtc.

2003

The EPA Issues a Strategic Plan for Homeland Security

The bombing of the World Trade Towers in New York City on September 11, 2001, highlighted the importance of homeland security. As the federal government moved to refocus its organization, the EPA examined its own functions and capabilities. In November 2001, it had convened the Homeland Security Working Group to discuss homeland security issues within the Agency. The EPA quickly responded to its new post–9/11 responsibilities in emergency response cleanup, infrastructure and building protection, and advancing science to better prevent and respond to terrorist events by aligning agency personnel and resources to support new responsibilities. This realignment of resources and priorities was reflected in the EPA Homeland Security Strategy, which detailed the results of strategic planning for homeland security within the EPA and outlined EPA's activities and initiatives involving homeland security. This compendium stated the standing responsibilities to homeland security, and further emphasized the need for coordination and collaboration across the Agency.

On February 6, 2003, Administrator Christine Todd Whitman established the EPA's Office of Homeland Security (OHS), fulfilling the need for a similar coordinating body. Since then the OHS has been coordinating the implementation of homeland security tasking and initiatives. It works closely and collaboratively with the program and regional offices to ensure that homeland security policy is carried out in a consistent and efficient manner and that redundancy and gaps are identified and addressed. To help increase security against potential terrorist acts, the 2006 federal budget provides a $79 million increase for the EPA homeland security efforts, including $44 million to launch a pilot program of monitoring and surveillance in select cities to provide early warning of contamination; an increase of $19.4 million for environmental decontamination research and preparedness, with an additional $4 million requested for the Safe Buildings research program; and more than $11.6 million in new resources to support preparedness in environmental laboratories.

2004

The EPA finalized its decision to remove the Love Canal site in Niagara County, New York, from the Superfund National Priorities List. (See discussion of Love Canal in Chapter 3.) All cleanup work at the site had been completed, and follow-up monitoring conducted since 1990 and confirmed that the cleanup goals had been reached. Through a series of plans, the EPA, together with the New York State Department of Environmental Conservation, contained and secured the wastes disposed of in the canal so that they were no longer leaking into surrounding soils and groundwater, and also revitalized properties in the neighborhood surrounding the canal. Forty acres were covered by a synthetic liner and clay cap and surrounded by a barrier drainage system. Contamination from the site was also controlled by a leachate collection and treatment facility. Neighborhoods to the west and north of the canal were revitalized, with more than 200 formerly boarded-up homes renovated and sold to new owners, and ten newly constructed apartment buildings.

2005

The EPA Awards Brownfield Grants to Clean Up Contaminated Properties

To ensure cleaner lands and economic revitalization through waste site cleanups, the EPA budget provided $210 million for the national Brownfields Program, an increase of $46.9 million over enacted 2005 funding. Under this program, the EPA was working with its state, tribal, and local partners to meet its objective of cleaning up contaminated properties and abandoned sites.

With the extension of the brownfields tax credit, the EPA expected to achieve the following in fiscal year 2006:

- Acquire access to 1,000 brownfields properties;
- Clean up sixty properties using brownfields funding;
- Leverage an additional $1 billion in cleanup and redevelopment funding;
- Create 5,000 jobs related to the brownfields efforts.

APPENDIX 1

Executive Order 12898: "Environmental Justice": Federal Actions to Address Environmental Justice in Minority Populations and Low-Income Populations

By the authority vested in me as President by the Constitution and the laws of the United States of America, it is hereby ordered as follows:

SECTION 1-1. IMPLEMENTATION

1-101. Agency Responsibilities

To the greatest extent practicable and permitted by law, and consistent with the principles set forth in the report on the National Performance Review, each Federal agency shall make achieving environmental justice part of its mission by identifying and addressing, as appropriate, disproportionately high and adverse human health or environmental effects of its programs, policies, and activities on minority populations and low-income populations in the United States and its territories and possessions, the District of Columbia, the Commonwealth of Puerto Rico, and the Commonwealth of the Mariana Islands.

1-102. Creation of an Interagency Working Group on Environmental Justice

a. Within 3 months of the date of this order, the Administrator of the Environmental Protection Agency ("Administrator") or the Administrator's designee shall convene an interagency Federal Working Group on Environmental Justice ("Working Group"). The Working Group shall comprise the heads of the following executive agencies and offices, or their designees:

   a. Department of Defense;

   b. Department of Health and Human Services;

   c. Department of Housing and Urban Development;

   d. Department of Labor;

e. Department of Agriculture;

f. Department of Transportation;

g. Department of Justice;

h. Department of the Interior;

i. Department of Commerce;

j. Department of Energy;

k. Environmental Protection Agency;

l. Office of Management and Budget;

m. Office of Science and Technology Policy;

n. Office of the Deputy Assistant to the President for Environmental Policy;

o. Office of the Assistant to the President for Domestic Policy;

p. National Economic Council;

q. Council of Economic Advisers; and

r. other such Government officials as the President may designate.

The Working Group shall report to the President through the Deputy Assistant to the President for Environmental Policy and the Assistant to the President for Domestic Policy.

a. The Working Group shall:

1. provide guidance to Federal agencies on criteria for identifying disproportionately high and adverse human health or environmental effects on minority populations and low-income populations;

2. coordinate with, provide guidance to, and serve as a clearinghouse for, each Federal agency as it develops an environmental justice strategy as required by section 1-103 of this order, in order to ensure that the administration, interpretation and enforcement of programs, activities and policies are undertaken in a consistent manner;

3. assist in coordinating research by, and stimulating cooperation among, the Environmental Protection Agency, the Department of Health and Human Services, the Department of Housing and Urban Development, and other agencies conducting research or other activities in accordance with section 3-3 of this order;

4. assist in coordinating data collection required by this order;

5. examine existing data and studies on environmental justice;

6. hold public meetings as required in section 5-502(d) of this order; and

7. develop interagency model projects on environmental justice that evidence cooperation among Federal agencies.

1-103. Development of Agency Strategies

a. Except as provided in section 6-605 of this order, each Federal agency shall develop an agency-wide environmental justice strategy, as set forth in subsections b–e of this section that identifies and addresses disproportionately high and adverse human health or environmental effects of its programs, policies, or activities on minority populations and low-income populations. The environmental justice strategy shall list programs, policies, planning and public participation practices, enforcement and/or rulemakings related to human health or the environment that should be revised to, at a minimum:

1. promote enforcement of all health and environmental statutes in areas with minority populations and low-income populations;

2. ensure greater public participation;

3. improve research and data collection relating to the health of and environment of minority populations and low-income populations; and

4. identify differential patterns of consumption of natural resources among minority populations and low-income populations. In addition, the environmental justice strategy shall include, where appropriate, a timetable for undertaking identified revisions and consideration of economic and social implications of the revisions.

b. Within 4 months of the date of this order, each Federal agency shall identify an internal administrative process for developing its environmental justice strategy, and shall inform the Working Group of the process.

c. Within 6 months of the date of this order, each Federal agency shall provide the Working Group with an outline of its proposed environmental justice strategy.

d. Within 10 months of the date of this order, each Federal agency shall provide the Working Group with its proposed environmental justice strategy.

e. Within 12 months of the date of this order, each Federal agency shall finalize its environmental justice strategy and provide a copy and written description of its strategy to the Working Group. During the 12-month period from the date of this order, each Federal agency, as part of its environmental justice strategy, shall identify several specific projects that can be promptly undertaken to address particular concerns identified during the development of the proposed environmental justice strategy, and a schedule for implementing those projects.

f. Within 24 months of the date of this order, each Federal agency shall report to the Working Group on its progress in implementing its agency-wide environmental justice strategy.

g. Federal agencies shall provide additional periodic reports to the Working Group.

1-104. Reports to the President

Within 14 months of the date of this order, the Working Group shall submit to the President, through the Office of the Deputy Assistant to the President for Environmental Policy and the Office of the Assistant to the President for Domestic Policy, a report that describes the implementation of this order, and includes the final environmental justice strategies described in section 1-103(e) of this order.

SECTION 2-2. FEDERAL AGENCY RESPONSIBILITIES FOR FEDERAL PROGRAMS

Each Federal agency shall conduct its programs, policies, and activities that substantially effect human health or the environment in a manner that ensures that such programs, policies, and activities do not have the effect of excluding persons (including populations) from participation in, denying persons (including populations) the benefits of, or subjecting persons (including populations) to discrimination under, such programs, policies, and activities, because of their race, color, or national origin.

SECTION 3-3. RESEARCH, DATA COLLECTION, AND ANALYSIS

3-301. Human Health and Environmental Research and Analysis

a. Environmental human health research, whenever practicable and appropriate, shall include diverse segments of the population in epidemiological and clinical studies, including segments at high risk from environmental hazards, such as minority populations, low-income populations and workers who may be exposed to substantial environmental hazards.

b. Environmental human health analyses, whenever practicable and appropriate, shall identify multiple and cumulative exposures.

c. Federal agencies shall provide minority populations and low-income populations the opportunity to comment on the development and design of research strategies undertaken pursuant to this order.

3-302. Human Health and Environmental Data Collection and Analysis

To the extent permitted by existing law, including the Privacy Act, as amended (5 U.S.C. section 552a):

a. Each Federal agency, whenever practicable and appropriate, shall collect, maintain, and analyze information assessing and comparing environmental and human health risks borne by populations identified by race, national origin, or income. To the extent practicable and appropriate, Federal agencies shall use this information to determine whether their programs, policies, and activities have disproportionately high and adverse human health or environmental effects on minority populations and low-income populations.

b. In connection with the development and implementation of agency strategies in section 1-103 of this order, each Federal agency, whenever practicable and appropriate, shall collect, maintain and analyze information on the race, national origin, income level, and other readily accessible and appropriate information for areas surrounding facilities or sites expected to have a substantial environmental, human health, or economic effect on the surrounding populations, when such facilities or sites become the subject of a substantial Federal environmental administrative or judicial action. Such information shall be made available to the public, unless prohibited by law; and

c. Each Federal agency, whenever practicable and appropriate, shall collect, maintain, and analyze information on the race, national origin, income level, and other readily accessible and appropriate information for areas surrounding Federal facilities that are:

   1. subject to the reporting requirements under the Emergency Planning and Community Right-to-Know Act, 42 U.S.C. section 11001–11050 as mandated in Executive Order No. 12856; and

   2. expected to have a substantial environmental, human health, or economic effect on surrounding populations. Such information shall be made available to the public, unless prohibited by law.

d. In carrying out the responsibilities in this section, each Federal agency, whenever practicable and appropriate, shall share information and eliminate unnecessary duplication of efforts through the use of existing data systems and cooperative agreements among Federal agencies and with State, local, and tribal governments.

SECTION. 4-4. SUBSISTENCE CONSUMPTION OF FISH AND WILDLIFE

4-401. Consumption Patterns

In order to assist in identifying the need for ensuring protection of populations with differential patterns of subsistence consumption of fish and wildlife, Federal agencies, whenever practicable and appropriate, shall collect, maintain, and analyze information on the consumption patterns of populations who principally rely on fish and/or wildlife for subsistence. Federal agencies shall communicate to the public the risk of those consumption patterns.

4-402. Guidance

Federal agencies, whenever practicable and appropriate, shall work in a coordinated manner to publish guidance reflecting the latest scientific information available concerning methods for evaluating the human health risks associated with the consumption of pollutant-bearing fish or wildlife. Agencies shall consider such guidance in developing their policies and rules.

SECTION 5-5. PUBLIC PARTICIPATION AND ACCESS TO INFORMATION

a. The public may submit recommendations to Federal agencies relating to the incorporation of environmental justice principles into Federal agency programs or policies. Each Federal agency shall convey such recommendations to the Working Group.

b. Each Federal agency may, whenever practicable and appropriate, translate crucial public documents, notices and hearings relating to human health or the environment for limited English-speaking populations.

c. Each Federal agency shall work to ensure that public documents, notices, and hearings relating to human health or the environment are concise, understandable, and readily accessible to the public.

d. The Working Group shall hold public meetings, as appropriate, for the purpose of fact-finding, receiving public comments, and conducting inquiries concerning environmental justice. The Working Group shall prepare for public review a summary of the contents and recommendations discussed at the public meetings.

SECTION 6-6. GENERAL PROVISIONS

6-601. Responsibility for Agency Implementation

The head of each Federal agency shall be responsible for ensuring compliance with this order. Each Federal agency shall conduct internal reviews and take such other steps as may be necessary to monitor compliance with this order.

6-602. Executive Order No. 12250

This Executive Order is intended to supplement but not supersede Executive Order No. 12250, which requires consistent and effective implementation of various laws prohibiting discriminatory practices in programs receiving Federal financial assistance. Nothing herein shall limit the effect or mandate of Executive Order No. 12250.

6-603. Executive Order No. 12875

This Executive Order is not intended to limit the effect or mandate of Executive Order No. 12875.

6-604. Scope

For the purposes of this order, Federal agency means any agency on the Working Group, and such other agencies as may be designated by the President, that conducts any Federal program or activity that substantially affects human health or the environment. Independent agencies are requested to comply with the provisions of this order.

6-605. Petitions for Exemptions

The head of a Federal agency may petition the President for an exemption from the requirements of this order on the grounds that all or some of the petitioning agency's programs or activities should not be subject to the requirements of this order.

6-606. Native American Programs

Each Federal agency responsibility set forth under this order shall apply equally to Native American programs. In addition, the Department of the Interior, in coordination with the Working Group, and after consultation with tribal leaders, shall coordinate steps to be taken pursuant to this order that address Federally recognized Indian tribes.

6-607. Costs

Unless otherwise provided by law, Federal agencies shall assume the financial costs of complying with this order.

6-608. General

Federal agencies shall implement this order consistent with, and to the extent permitted by, existing law.

6-609. Judicial Review

This order is intended only to improve the internal management of the executive branch and is not intended to, nor does it create any right, benefit, or trust responsibility, substantive or procedural, enforceable at law or equity by a party against the United States, its agencies, its officers, or any person. This order shall not be construed to create any right to judicial review involving the compliance or noncompliance of the United States, its agencies, its officers, or any other person with this order.

WILLIAM J. CLINTON
THE WHITE HOUSE,
February 11, 1994.

APPENDIX 2

Principles of Environmental Justice

PREAMBLE

WE THE PEOPLE OF COLOR, gathered together at this multinational People of Color Environmental Leadership Summit, to begin to build a national and international movement of all peoples of color to fight the destruction and taking of our lands and communities, do hereby re-establish our spiritual interdependence to the sacredness of our Mother Earth; to respect and celebrate each of our cultures, languages and beliefs about the natural world and our roles in healing ourselves; to ensure environmental justice; to promote economic alternatives which would contribute to the development of environmentally safe livelihoods; and, to secure our political, economic and cultural liberation that has been denied for over 500 years of colonization and oppression, resulting in the poisoning of our communities and land and the genocide of our peoples, do affirm and adopt these Principles of Environmental Justice:

1. Environmental justice affirms the sacredness of Mother Earth, ecological unity and the interdependence of all species, and the right to be free from ecological destruction.

2. Environmental justice demands that public policy be based on mutual respect and justice for all peoples, free from any form of discrimination or bias.

3. Environmental justice mandates the right to ethical, balanced and responsible uses of land and renewable resources in the interest of a sustainable planet for humans and other living things.

4. Environmental justice calls for universal protection from nuclear testing, extraction, production and disposal of toxic/hazardous wastes and poisons and nuclear testing that threaten the fundamental right to clean air, land, water, and food.

5. Environmental justice affirms the fundamental right to political, economic, cultural and environmental self-determination of all peoples.

6. Environmental justice demands the cessation of the production of all toxins, hazardous wastes, and radioactive materials, and that all past and current producers be held strictly accountable to the people for detoxification and the containment at the point of production.

7. Environmental justice demands the right to participate as equal partners at every level of decision-making including needs assessment, planning, implementation, enforcement and evaluation.

8. Environmental justice affirms the right of all workers to a safe and healthy work environment, without being forced to choose between an unsafe livelihood and unemployment. It also affirms the right of those who work at home to be free from environmental hazards.

9. Environmental justice protects the right of victims of environmental injustice to receive full compensation and reparations for damages as well as quality health care.

10. Environmental justice considers governmental acts of environmental injustice a violation of international law, the Universal Declaration of Human Rights, and the United Nations Convention on Genocide.

11. Environmental justice must recognize a special legal and natural relationship of Native Peoples to the U.S. government through treaties, agreements, compacts, and covenants affirming sovereignty and self-determination.

12. Environmental justice affirms the need for urban and rural ecological policies to clean up and rebuild our cities and rural areas in balance with nature, honoring the cultural integrity of all our communities, and providing fair access for all to the full range of resources.

13. Environmental justice calls for the strict enforcement of principles of informed consent, and a halt to the testing of experimental reproductive and medical procedures and vaccinations on people of color.

14. Environmental justice opposes the destructive operations of multi-national corporations.

15. Environmental justice opposes military occupation, repression and exploitation of lands, peoples and cultures, and other life forms.

16. Environmental justice calls for the education of present and future generations which emphasizes social and environmental issues, based on our experience and an appreciation of our diverse cultural perspectives.

17. Environmental justice requires that we, as individuals, make personal and consumer choices to consume as little of Mother Earth's resources and to produce as little waste as possible; and make the conscious decision to challenge and reprioritize our lifestyles to ensure the health of the natural world for present and future generations.

Adopted today, October 27, 1991, in Washington, D.C.

Annotated Bibliography

BOOKS

Bullard, Robert D., ed., *The Quest for Environmental Justice: Human Rights and the Politics of Pollution*. San Francisco: Sierra Club Books, 2005.

> Dr. Bullard is a respected scholar in the area of environmental justice. Here he has assembled the latest collection of essays on environmental abuses and human rights violations in the United States and around the world. In many of the U.S. cases, the EPA involvement was substantial.

Colten, Craig E., and Peter N. Skinner. *The Road to Love Canal: Managing Industrial Waste Before EPA*. Austin: University of Texas Press, 1996.

> This book examines industrial waste disposal before the formation of the Environmental Protection Agency in 1970. Colten and Skinner build their study around three key questions: What was known before 1970 about the hazards of certain industrial wastes and their potential for causing public health problems? What were the technical capabilities for treating or containing wastes during that time? What factors other than technical knowledge guided the actions of waste managers before the enactment of explicit federal laws? The authors find that significant information about the hazards of industrial waste existed before 1970.

Mintz, Joel A. *Enforcement at the EPA: High Stakes and Hard Choices*. Austin: University of Texas Press, 1995.

> At the beginning of the 1990s, the United States was spending over $80 billion a year on pollution control and regulation, as thousands of industries and businesses attempted to comply with a complex body of governmental requirements. This book offers the first comprehensive history of an often neglected part of EPA's responsibilities—the enforcement of federal environmental standards. Drawing on extensive interviews with the political appointees, administrators, and staff who have provided the agency's direction, as well

as his own professional experience with the EPA, Joel A. Mintz explores the historical evolution of the agency's enforcement program, its institutional setting within the larger political arena, and its current strengths and shortcomings. He also examines the controversial tenure of Reagan-appointed administrator Anne Gorsuch and the agency's attempts to restart its enforcement programs following her ouster. He concludes with a discussion of how to evaluate regulatory enforcement effectiveness, and offers practical suggestions on how to improve the EPA's long-term enforcement effectiveness.

ARTICLES

Hertwich, Edgar G., Sarah F. Mateles, William S. Pease, and Thomas E. McKone. "Human Toxicity Potentials for Life Cycle Assessment and Toxics Release Inventory Risk Screening." *Environmental Toxicology and Chemistry* 20, no. 4 (2001): 928–939.

The human toxicity potential (HTP), a calculated index that reflects the potential harm of a unit of chemical released into the environment, is based on both the inherent toxicity of a compound and its potential dose. It is used to weight emissions inventoried as part of a life-cycle assessment (LCA) or in the toxics release inventory (TRI) and to aggregate emissions in terms of a reference compound. Total emissions can be evaluated in terms of benzene equivalence (carcinogens) and toluene equivalents (noncarcinogens). The potential dose is calculated using a generic fate and exposure model, CalTOX, which determines the distribution of a chemical in a model environment and accounts for a number of exposure routes, including inhalation; ingestion of produce, fish, and meat; and dermal contact with water and soil. Toxicity is represented by the cancer potency $q1^*$ for carcinogens and the safe dose (RfD, RfC) for noncarcinogens. This article presents cancer and noncancer HTP values for air and surface-water emissions of 330 compounds. This list covers 258 chemicals listed in U.S. Environmental Protection Agency TRI, or 79 by weight percent of the TRI releases to air reported in 1997.

Kellogg, Wendy A. "Community-based Organizations and Neighborhood Environmental Problem Solving: A Framework for Adoption of Information Technologies." *Journal of Environmental Planning and Management* 42, no. 4 (July 1, 1999): 445–469.

Community-based organizations (CBOs) today seek improved capacity to address environmental problems in urban neighborhoods. Many seek access to information technologies such as the Internet and Geographic Information Systems (GIS) to expand information about their neighborhood's environmental quality to support their planning and service efforts. Experience with information technologies in planning at the municipal and state levels reveals a set of technical, organizational, and personal prerequisites that bolster successful and effective adoption of information technologies. This article reviews these prerequisites as they pertain to CBOs and makes recommendations for transactions that could enhance CBO adoption of the Internet and GIS to address environmental problems in urban neighborhoods. One way the EPA supports community-based environmental planning is through technical assistance grants for these activities. The article concludes that a constellation of prerequisite conditions, most predominantly data availability problems, staff skill acquisition, and staff retention problems, offer the greatest challenges for CBOs seeking to adopt information technologies to manage environmental problems more effectively.

Nadeau, L. W. "EPA Effectiveness at Reducing the Duration of Plant-Level Noncompliance." *Journal of Environmental Economics and Management* 34, no. 1 (September 1997): 54–78.

This article looks at the effectiveness of the EPA in reducing the time that manufacturing plants spend in a state of noncompliance. Plants that are found in violation of EPA standards may remain in violation for a period of years. The EPA's policy of making a timely and appropriate response to noncompliance brings returning violators to compliance as quickly as possible. The effectiveness of the timely and appropriate response policy is tested by estimating parametric survival models for the pulp and paper industry. The results indicate that the EPA is effective at reducing the time plants spend violating standards.

Veleva, V., J. Bailey, and N. Jurczyk. "Using Sustainable Production Indicators to Measure Progress in ISO 14001, EHS System and EPA Achievement Track." *Corporate Environmental Strategy* 8, no. 4 (December 2001): 326–338(13).

This article is written for industries trying to measure their progress toward sustainability using current measurement methods from the International Standards Organization and the EPA. Many ISO 14001 standards are incorporated in international treaties and agreements.

REPORTS

Beierle, Thomas C. *Public Participation in Environmental Decisions: An Evaluation Framework Using Social Goals* Discussion Paper 99-06. Washington, DC: Resources for the Future, November 1998.

This paper presents a framework for evaluating mechanisms that involve the public in environmental decision-making. These include traditional participatory mechanisms (e.g., such as public hearings, notice and comment procedures, and advisory committees), as well as those considered more innovative (e.g., such as regulatory negotiations, mediations, and citizen juries). The framework is based on a set of "social goals," defined as those goals that are valued outcomes of a participatory process, but that transcend the immediate interests of any party in that process. The goals are: educating the public, incorporating public values and knowledge into decision-making, building trust, reducing conflict, and assuring cost-effective decision-making.

Environmental Protection: Assessing the Impacts of EPA's Regulations Through Retrospective Studies: A Report to Congressional Sequesters. Washington, DC: U.S. General Accounting Office, 1999.

This report examines the use of retrospective regulatory impact assessment on EPA regulations. Many policymakers, in this case Congress, use this approach to evaluate current proposals to increase or decrease budgetary allocations.

A Look at EPA Accomplishments: 25 Years of Protecting Public Health and the Environment. Washington, DC: EPA Office of Communications, Education and Public Affairs, November 1995.

This report from the EPA provides a chronology of its efforts and policy approaches to protecting the public health from its inception to 1995.

Remember the Past, Protect the Future: 30 Years of Environmental Progress: 1970–2000. Seattle, WA: U.S. Environmental Protection Agency, Region 10, The Pacific Northwest and Alaska, 2000.

This report provides a chronology of the development of EPA Region 10 from its inception to 2000. The regions of the EPA often offer different policy approaches and emphases.

WEB SITES

Agency for Toxic Substances and Disease Registry (ATSDR), http://atsdr1.atsdr.cdc .gov/atsdrhome.html.

The mission of the Agency for Toxic Substances and Disease Registry (ATSDR), an agency of the U.S. Department of Health and Human Services, is to serve the public by using the best science, taking responsive public health actions, and providing trusted health information to prevent harmful exposures and disease related to toxic substances. ATSDR is directed by congressional mandate to perform specific functions concerning the effect on public health of hazardous substances in the environment. These functions include public health assessments of waste sites, health consultations concerning specific hazardous substances, health surveillance and registries, response to emergency releases of hazardous substances, applied research in support of public health assessments, information development and dissemination, and education and training concerning hazardous substances.

"Ecological Monitoring," U.S. Environmental Protection Agency, http://www.epa .gov/ebtpages/ecosecologicalmonitoring.html.

The EPA undertakes regular monitoring and assessment of the status and trends of the nation's ecological resources. Monitoring is conducted through surveys, sampling, and other direct measurements, as well as models. The EPA strives to gather both small- and large-scale data in a holistic approach that studies the interrelation of all media and the transport of pollutants from region to region. The data gathered through monitoring is used to determine the overall health of the nation's environment, to gauge the effects of pollution releases, and to help set new environmental guidelines and standards.

"History," U.S. Environmental Protection Agency, http://www.epa.gov/history/top ics/index.htm.

This is the EPA's history of important environmental issues over the last thirty-five years.

"Human Health & Ecological Risk," U.S. Environmental Protection Agency, http:// www.epa.gov/superfund/health/index.html.

Human Health & Ecological Risk includes information about health, safety, and risk assessment issues related to Superfund sites. Here you will find links to information regarding the hazards related to exposure to contaminants, risk assessment information, tips for reporting or responding to Superfund-related emergencies, and safety guides for cleaning up and preventing environmental hazards.

Library Network, U.S. Environmental Protection Agency, http://www.epa.gov/nat libra/libraries.html.

The EPA Library Network, established in 1971, is composed of libraries in the Agency's headquarters, regional and field offices, research centers, and specialized laboratories located throughout the country. The combined network collection contains a wide range of general information on environmental protection and management; basic sciences such as biology and chemistry; applied sciences such as engineering and toxicology; and extensive coverage of topics featured in legislative mandates such as hazardous waste, drinking water, pollution prevention, and toxic substances. Several of the libraries maintain collections focused on special topics to support specific regional or program office projects. The library network provides access to its collections through the Online Library System (OLS), a Web-based database of library holdings. The OLS offers author, title, and keyword access to documents and makes it possible to retrieve information relevant to almost every request.

National Environmental Justice Advisory Council, http://www.epa.gov/Compliance/environmentaljustice/nejac/index.html.

The National Environmental Justice Advisory Council (NEJAC) is a federal advisory committee established to provide independent advice, consultation, and recommendations to the EPA administrator on matters related to environmental justice.

The following NEJAC reports are the result of its most recent meetings:

Advancing Environmental Justice Through Pollution Prevention: A Report Developed from the National Environmental Justice Advisory Council Meeting of December 9–13, 2002

Ensuring Risk Reduction in Communities with Multiple Stressors: Environmental Justice and Cumulative Risks/Impacts

Environmental Justice and Community-Based Health Model Discussion: A Report on the Public Meeting Convened on May 23–26, 2000

Environmental Justice in the Permitting Process: A Report on the Public Meeting Convened by the NEJAC November 30–December 2, 1999

Fish Consumption and Environmental Justice: A Report on the Public Meeting Convened on December 3–6, 2001

Meaningful Involvement and Fair Treatment by Tribal Environmental Regulatory Programs

NEJAC Report on Integration of Environmental Justice in Federal Programs: A Report on the Public Meeting Convened on December 11, 12, and 14, 2000

NEPAnet, http://www.whitehouse.gov/ceq/, select the link for NEPAnet.

This Web site describes the work of the task force established by Council on Environmental Quality to address modernizing the implementation of the National Environmental Policy Act (NEPA) to make the environmental assessment process more effective, efficient, and timely. Other organizations and groups are also examining the National Environmental Policy Act, and some have provided Web sites with information about their separate but related efforts.

Office of the Administrator, U.S. Environmental Protection Agency, http://www.epa .gov/adminweb/html.

The Office of the Administrator provides executive and logistical support for the EPA administrator and the staff offices that directly support the administrator. The administrator is responsible to the president, and is assisted by the deputy administrator and staff offices. The Office of the Administrator supports the leadership of the EPA's programs and activities to protect human health and safeguard the air, water, and land on which life depends.

Office of the Inspector General, U.S. Environmental Protection Agency, http:// www.epa.gov/oig/index.html.

The Office of Inspector General is an independent office within EPA that helps the EPA protect the environment in a more efficient and cost-effective manner. It consists of auditors, program analysts, investigators, and others with extensive expertise. Although it is a part of the EPA, Congress provides it with funding separate from the EPA to ensure its independence. It performs audits, evaluations, and investigations of the EPA and its contractors to promote economy and efficiency and to prevent and detect fraud, waste, and abuse. It also provides ombudsman and hotline services to review public complaints about EPA programs and activities. It discusses issues with EPA management and others, including Congress, and provides detailed reports. Twice a year, it provides a semiannual report to Congress that identifies significant EPA deficiencies and proposed corrective actions and profiles its accomplishments.

Permitting Innovations Database, http://www.epa.gov/permits/database.html.

The Permitting Innovations Database is a repository of information about innovative permits and permitting initiatives from a variety of national, state, and local agencies. The database is one of EPA's tools to disseminate information about pilot efforts and improve the knowledge base for entities looking to pilot future innovative permits undertakings. Information contained within this database has been gleaned from published documents, reports, and/or information available on public Web sites. This database may be useful to permit writers, governmental officials, facility owners, or community groups looking for concrete examples of new and innovative approaches to permitting.

Science Advisory Board, U.S. Environmental Protection Agency, http://www.epa .gov/sab/html.

Congress established the EPA Science Advisory Board in 1978 and gave it a broad mandate to advise the EPA on technical matters. The board's principal mission includes reviewing the quality and relevance of the scientific and technical information being used or proposed as the basis for Agency regulations; reviewing research programs and the technical basis of applied programs; reviewing generic approaches to regulatory science, including guidelines governing the use of scientific and technical information in regulatory decisions, and critiquing such analytic methods as mathematical modeling; advising the EPA on broad scientific matters in science, technology, social and economic issues; and advising the EPA on emergency and other short-notice programs.

Science Policy Council, http://www.epa.gov/osa/spc/htm/2cumrisk.html.

The processes that EPA and others follow to assess environmental risk are of great interest to both environmental professionals and the public, and increasing attention is being given to the combined effects of multiple environmental stressors. Consistent with this, the EPA and others are asking more questions about the wider and more complex issues that define a cumulative approach to risk assessment. EPA guidance directs each office to take into account cumulative risk issues in scoping and planning major risk assessments and to consider a broader scope that integrates multiple sources, effects, pathways, stressors, and populations for cumulative risk analyses in all cases for which relevant data are available.

"Sustainability," U.S. Environmental Protection Agency, http://www.epa.gov/sustainability/html.

Sustainability is the ability to achieve economic prosperity while protecting the natural systems of the planet and providing a higher quality of life for its people. Individuals, communities, and institutions are developing and implementing sustainability practices with the help of dozens of EPA programs, partnerships, and policy tools. This site provides links to many EPA programs and tools that contribute to sustainability.

Toxics Release Inventory, U.S. Environmental Protection Agency, http://www.epa.gov/tri/html.

The Toxics Release Inventory (TRI) is a publicly available EPA database that contains information on toxic chemical releases and other waste management activities reported annually by certain covered industry groups and federal facilities. This inventory was established under the Emergency Planning and Community Right-to-Know Act of 1986 (EPCRA) and expanded by the Pollution Prevention Act of 1990.

Index

grayfields, 115–16

Great Lakes, 25; Great Lakes Program, 28, 233, 244, 276; Great Lakes Water Quality Agreement, 28–29, 120, 306–7

Greenpeace: *Playing with Fire*, 235

Green Power Partnership, 261

Guidance for Performing Preliminary Assessments Under CERCLA, 125

Guidance for Performing Site Inspections Under CERCLA: Interim Final, 125

Guidelines for Carcinogen Risk Assessment, 143, 144–46

Guidelines for Preparing Economic Analyses, 136

Gulf of Mexico, 244

Gwichin'in Indians, 88

Hampshire Research Institute, Assessing Aggregate and Cumulative Risk Using Life-Line, 268

Hanford, Wa., 98, 99

Hazardous and Solid Waste Amendments, xxxvi, 12, 203

hazardous chemical inventory, 48, 211. *See also* toxics release inventory (TRI)

Hazardous Chemical Reporting Rule, xxxvi

Hazardous Materials Transportation Act (HMTA), 12

hazardous waste, xxxv, 1, 152, 166, 245, 279; classifications of, 62; defined, 62; Emergency Planning and Community Right-to-Know Act (EPCRA), 12, 47–49, 174, 183, 211, 218, 228, 318, 320–21, 326, 327–28, 333, 353; under Gorsuch, 281–83; Hazardous and Solid Waste Amendments, xxxvi, 12, 203; Hazardous Waste Enforcement and Emergency Response System, 309; land disposal of, xxxvii, 13, 63, 223, 266; Love Canal, xxxiii, 73–79, 82, 83, 106, 123, 143, 236, 309, 312–13, 347–48; medical waste, 35, 325; from mining activities, 327; mixture rule vs. derived from rule, 62; Orphaned Sources Program, 261–62; Resource Conservation and Recovery Act (RCRA), xxxvi, 10, 12, 59, 63–64, 77, 120, 174, 197, 218, 304, 306, 311, 313, 315, 327, 328–29; state-EPA interaction regarding, 310–13, 318; Times Beach, Mo., xxxvi, 282–83, 312, 313; in urban areas, xxxvi, 112–18, 254, 256, 260,

267, 272, 284–85, 295, 336; in Warren County, N.C., 79, 106–8, 234, 308, 312; Yucca Mountain repository, xxxiv, 70, 97–102, 106. *See also* Superfund

hazard ranking system (HRS), 47, 124, 125–27; Quickscore, 126–27; Superscreen, 126

Hendrie, Joseph, 94

Hill, Barry, 112

Hoechst Celanese Corporation, 327

Homeland Security Council, 183

Homeland Security Working Group, 347

Hooker Chemicals and Plastic, 74, 75, 76, 309, 312–13

Hubbs Marine Institute, 84

Hudson River, 290

Hunt, James B., 107

hydrocarbons, 74, 86, 138, 300, 320

hydrochloric acid, 227

hydrochlorofluorocarbons (HCFCs), 218

incentives for compliance, 169–70, 171, 172–74, 176, 192, 193

independent quality assurance team (IQAT), 129, 130–31

Indiana: Stream Pollution Control Board, 301

Indian tribe-EPA interaction, 169, 190, 232, 247; regarding air quality, 186; American Indian Environmental Office, 188; regarding enforcement, 192, 193; regarding environmental cleanup, 348; Native American Task Force, 238, 239; regarding permits, 186, 203; and Tribal Emergency Response Commission (TERC), 48, 212; regarding water quality, 45, 197, 198, 320; regarding Yucca Mountain, 100–101

INFORM, Inc., 40

innovation, 26, 189–90, 192–93, 194, 204–5, 250–51, 252–53

Inspector General Act, 193

Institute of Nuclear Power Operations, 96

Interagency Working Group on Environmental Justice (IWG), xxxv, 237, 238–42, 349–50; demonstration projects, 239, 240–42, 243; Environmental Justice Directory, 243; Health Disparities Task Force, 238–39; Integrated Federal Interagency Environmental Justice Action Agenda, 240–41; Native American

About the Author

ROBERT W. COLLIN is Senior Research Scholar at Willamette University, a member of two Federal Advisory Committees to the EPA, Advisor to Oregon's Governor on Environmental Justice, and has written many book chapters and published in law reviews.